Annual Series: 1995

ART AND CULTURE

ENDEAVOURS IN INTERPRETATION

In Memory of
Professor Mohammad Habib

ART AND CULTURE

ENDEAVOURS IN INTERPRETATION

EDITORS

AHSAN JAN QAISAR
SOM PRAKASH VERMA

ABHINAV PUBLICATIONS

abhinav publications

First published in India 1996

Published by
Shakti Malik
Abhinav Publications
E-37 Hauz Khas
New Delhi-110016

ISBN 81-7017-315-9

Text Typeset by
Tara Chand Sons
Naraina, New Delhi

Printers
D.K. Fine Arts Press P. LTD
Ashok Vihar, Delhi

TABLE OF CONTENTS

FOREWORD

For long we have been contemplating to bring out a series of volumes on Art and Culture. When consulted, our well-wishers in the academic circle welcomed our idea, and encouraged us in this venture.

The *raison d'etre* for this undertaking is the absence of any *regular* publication in India encompassing matters related to specific aspects of society in one volume.

We are interested in everything which is of human concern, such as philosophy, education, literary criticism, aesthetics, sexology, social medicine, gender studies, environment/ecology, art and architecture, etiquette and manners, etc. Even articles on political and economic aspects come in our orbit. But we wish to underscore that mere narration of events or ideas, etc. is not enough. To put it clearly, *interpretation* is the key-word. But as cautioned by Umberto Eco, 'overinterpretation' should be shunned. In fact the problem of interpretation is intensely fragile. Who is interpreting what? In a situation when there is a possibility of a set of multiple interpretations, which is the 'best' one? What should be the criteria to determine the 'best' one? Eco agrees with the Popperian principle according to which "if there are no rules to help to ascertain which interpretations are the 'best' ones, there is at least a rule for ascertaining which ones are 'bad'." Perhaps this opinion might not solve the problem in its entirety. Therefore, the least that the writers should do is to restrain the urge to violate the boundaries of the evidence/text. Perhaps the assessment of the readers/audience might act as a deterrent in case imagination is left unfettered. At any rate, our point is to emphasize the act of interpretation without which an academic product would be dry and barren.

Another objective of our endeavour is to gradually lure the scholars to cultivate the habit of brooding and writing within the syndrome of social mores and values. Actually, the value-system itself is a result of some societal forces, and, at the same time, it is an integral part of these forces. Values, in turn, reinforce the existing structure. This applies more to political history. For example, one could examine the problem of hierarchy of political loyalty in any society—past or present—instead of plain description. Again, the struggle for power among the ruling elite, or the political aspirations of the less privileged groups could be interpreted in the perspective of value-system. Here we suggest that greater attention should be paid to the role of the ego of the individuals in society. Similarly, the mercantile groups' mode of thinking and attitude should be explored in depth.

Thus, our purpose is to produce volumes carrying articles drawn from diverse disciplines and set in some conceptual framework to make them really meaningful and relevant. To concretize the themes for the present, the following categories may serve as a sort of guideline: (a) Cultural Set-up and Values; (b) Art and Architecture, and (c) Science and Technology. Finally, the contents of the proposed volumes under our scheme will not be restricted to any particular period of history or geographical area. The present volume is just a humble beginning.

We look forward to an increasing cooperation from young responsive writers more than the veterans for some of whom it might be difficult to adjust their intellectual antennae to what we aspire for.

We are greatly thankful to our publisher Mr. Shakti Malik (Abhinav Publications, New Delhi) for accepting the onerous task to bring out the intended volumes regularly.

This first volume of the annual series of *Art and Culture* is dedicated to Professor Mohammad Habib (b. 1895; d. 1971).

March 6, 1994
Centre of Advanced Study
Department of History
Aligarh Muslim University

Ahsan Jan Qaisar
Professor of Social and Cultural History
Som Prakash Verma
Professor of History

LIST OF PLATES

15. Siberian crane (*c.* 1600 [?]). Unascribed. Indian Museum Calcutta (Published in Havell, op. cit., pl. 61).

16. Venus and Cupid (*c.* 1676-77). Painted by Muhammad Zaman. Institute of the Peoples of Asia, Moscow (Reproduced in A.A. Ivanov, et al, *Album of Indian and Persian Miniatures, XVI-XVIII Centuries,* Moscow, 1962, pl. 83).

17. Abraham's sacrifice (*c.* 1684-5). Painted by Muhammad Zaman. Institute of the Peoples of Asia, Moscow (Reproduced in Ivanov, op. cit., pl. 85).

18. Holy Trinity/Family (*c.* 1682-3). Painted by Muhammad Zaman. Institute of the Peoples of Asia, Moscow (Reproduced in Ivanov, op. cit., p. 84).

19. Mary and Elizabeth (*c.* 1678). Painted by Muhammad Zaman. F.R. Martin Collection (Reproduced in Martin, op. cit., pl. 173 (a)).

20. The Flight into Egypt (*c.* 1675). Painted by Muhammad Zaman. F.R. Martin Collection (Reproduced in Martin, op. cit., pl. 173 (b)).

21. Venus and Cupid, undated. Painted by Paris Bordone. Ca 'd' Oro, Venice (Reproduced in I.E. Relouge (ed.), *The Nude in Art,* London, 1959, p. 121).

22. Abraham's sacrifice (*c.* 1635). Painted by Rembrandt. The Hermitage, Leningrad (Reproduced in *Masterpieces of Western European Art from the Hermitage, Leningrad* (Exhibition Catalogue), Leningrad, 1987, pl. 35).

23. Abraham's sacrifice (*c.* 1635). Painted by Rembrandt. Hermitage, Leningrad (Reproduced in Horst Gerson, *Rembrandt,* New York, 1968, pl. 74).

24. Abraham's sacrifice (*c.* 1599). Unascribed. *Yusuf o Zulaykha,* India Office Library, London, No. 737, fol. 9b (Reproduced in T.W. Arnold, *Painting in Islam: Study of the Place of Pictorial Art in Muslim Culture,* London, 1928, pl. 31).

25. Bookbinding (*c.* 1600-10). Unascribed. Freer Gallery of Art, Washington (Reproduced in Esin Atil, *The Brush of the Masters: Drawings from Iran and India,* Washington, 1978, pl. 63).

26. Bookbinders at work (*c.* 1585-90). Painted by Nanha. The Keir Collection of Edmond de Unger (Reproduced in B.W. Robinson, et al, *Islamic Painting and the Arts of the Books,* Faber, 1978, pl. 63).

27. Bookbinder (*c.* early 18th century). Unascribed. India Office Library and Records, London, Add. Or. 111 (Reproduced in Albertine Gaur, *Writing Material of the East,* London, 1979).

28. *Mohrah kash* (detail of plate 25).

29. Scribe (detail of plate 25).

30. Bookbinder (detail of plate 25).

31. Bookbinder with *shikanja* (detail of plate 25).

32. Goldsmith (detail of plate 25).

33. Carpenter making bookrest (detail of plate 25).

60. *Raga Vasant.* Carved at the base of the pillar (28 x 35 cms.).

61. Princess and a musician. Carved at the base of a pillar.

62. Dance and music. Carved at the base of a pillar.

63. Domestic scene. Carved at the base of a pillar.

64. Dance and music. Carved at the base of a pillar.

65. Dance and music. Carved at the base of a pillar.

66. Part of the panel of Bodhisattva Padmapani, Ajanta Cave 1 (*c.* 500-600). Published in Ajit Ghosh, *Ajanta Murals,* New Delhi, 1967, pl. 24.

67. Part of the story of *Vidhurapandita-Jataka,* Ajanta Cave 2 (*c.* 500). Published in Ghosh, op. cit., pl. 54.

68. Dance scene (*c.* 700). Bagh Cave. Published in S. Rawson Phillip, *Indian Painting,* London, 1961, pl. on p. 50.

69. Bodhisattva Vajrapani (*c.* 1700). *Astasahasrika-Parjnaparamita,* Bodleian Library, Oxford, MS Sansk., a. 7 f. 92b (Published in Saryu Doshi (ed.), *Pageant of Indian Art,* Bombay, 1983, pl. on p. 69).

70. Siege of Lanka (*c.* 1700). Unascribed. A.K. Coomaraswamy Collection (Published in A.K. Coomaraswamy, *Rajput Painting,* Vol. II, 2nd edition, New Delhi, 1976, pl. 25).

71. Folio from the *Hamzanama* (*c.* 1570-5). Unascribed. Published in Erster Band, *Hamzanama,* Graz, 1974, p. 9, pl. 35.

72-3. List of the rulers to whom *tabarruk* was sent by Syed Muhammad Masud, the son of Syed Muhammad Murad (1737). From the Collection of Syed Muhammad Murad and Syed Muhammad Masud, Ajmer.

74. *Vikalatnama* of Bajirao Peshwa in the name of Syed Muhammad Murad (1736). From the above collection.

75. *Vikalatnama* of Maharaja Daulat Rao Sindhia of Gwaliar in the name of Syed Muhammad Masud (1797). From the above collection.

76. Letter of Thakur Gopal Singh Shekhawat, *Zamindar* of *qasba* Udaipur, *sarkar* Narnaul, Shahjahanabad in the name of Syed Muhammad Masud (1737). From the above collection.

77-8. Record of the commission paid to the *fotadars* from the salaries of officials and *rozinadars* of the *Dargah.* From the Collection of the *Dargah* File, Rajasthan State Archives, Bikaner.

79-81. Documents related to the grant of daily allowance from the *Dargah Waqf* for feeding the poor at the Hanuman temple near the Dodhia well in Ajmer City. From the Collection of the *Dargah* File, Rajasthan State Archives, Bikaner.

CONTRIBUTORS

Iqtidar Husain Siddiqui
Professor of History
Centre of Advanced Study
Department of History
Aligarh Muslim University

Satya Prakash Singh
Professor
Department of Sanskrit
Aligarh Muslim University

Madhu Trivedi
Senior Lecturer in History
School of Correspondence Courses
University of Delhi

Som Prakash Verma
Professor of History
Centre of Advanced Study
Department of History
Aligarh Muslim University

Mridula Ramanna
Lecturer in History
South Indian Education Society's College
University of Bombay

Ahsan Jan Qaisar
Professor of Social and Cultural History
Centre of Advanced Study
Department of History
Aligarh Muslim University

Mahesh Sharma
Fellow
Indian Institute of Advanced Study, Shimla

J.V. Naik
Professor of History
Department of History
University of Bombay

Rana Firdaus
Former Research Scholar
Centre of Advanced Study
Department of History
Aligarh Muslim University

Neelima Vashishtha
Reader
Faculty of Fine Arts
University of Rajasthan

Hassan Imam
Senior Research Assistant
Centre of Advanced Study
Department of History
Aligarh Muslim University

A. Padma
Research Scholar
Department of History
University of Hyderabad

Kamlesh Mohan
Lecturer in History
Department of History
Panjab University

Abdul Matin
Lecturer
Department of Sociology
Aligarh Muslim University

S. Liyaqat H. Moini
Lecturer in History
Centre of Advanced Study
Department of History
Aligarh Muslim University

ART AND CULTURE

ENDEAVOURS IN INTERPRETATION

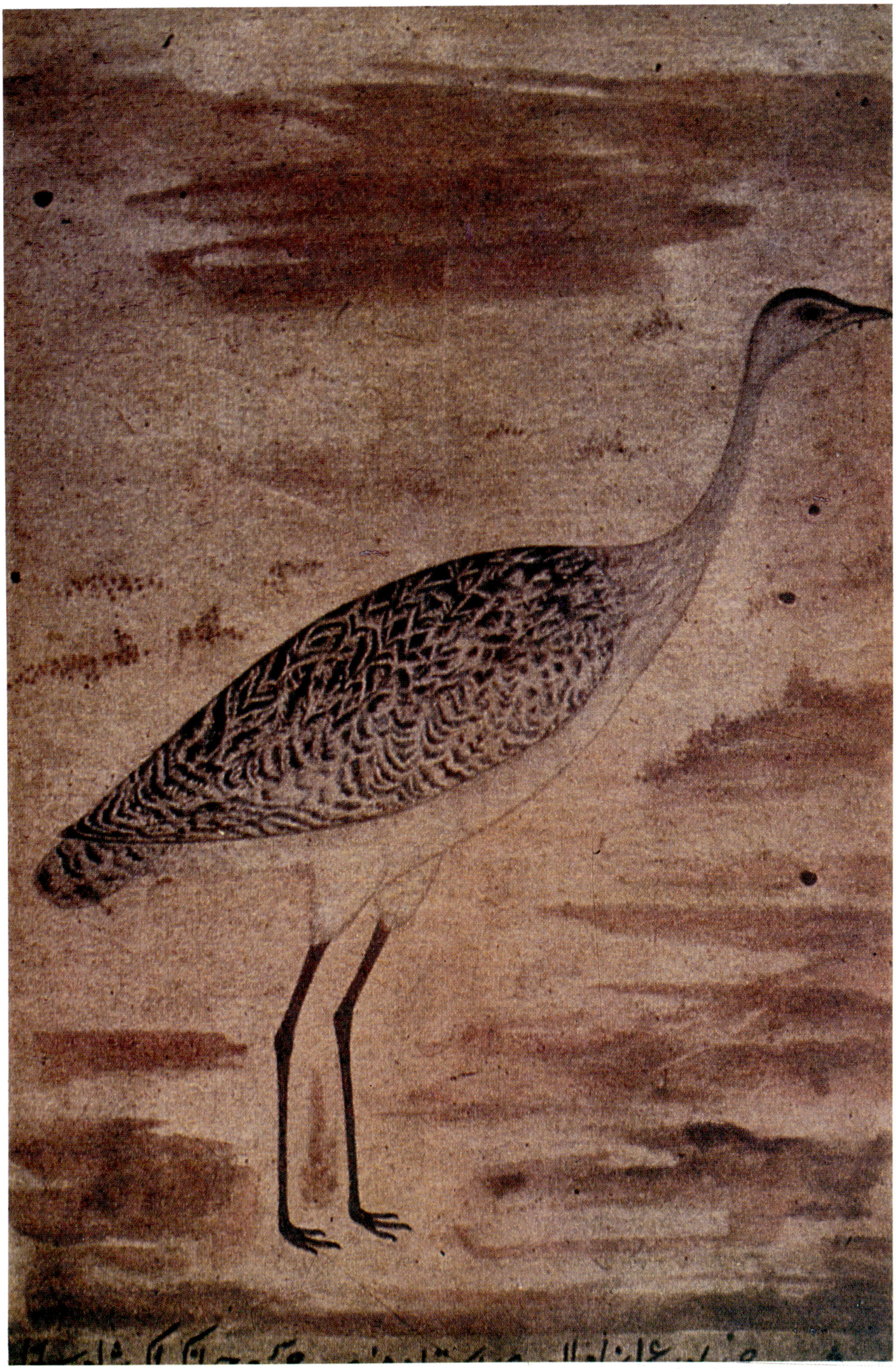

5. *Jurz bar* (Indian bustard), dated 1619. Painted by *Nadir ul Asr Ustad* Mansur. Indian Museum, Calcutta.

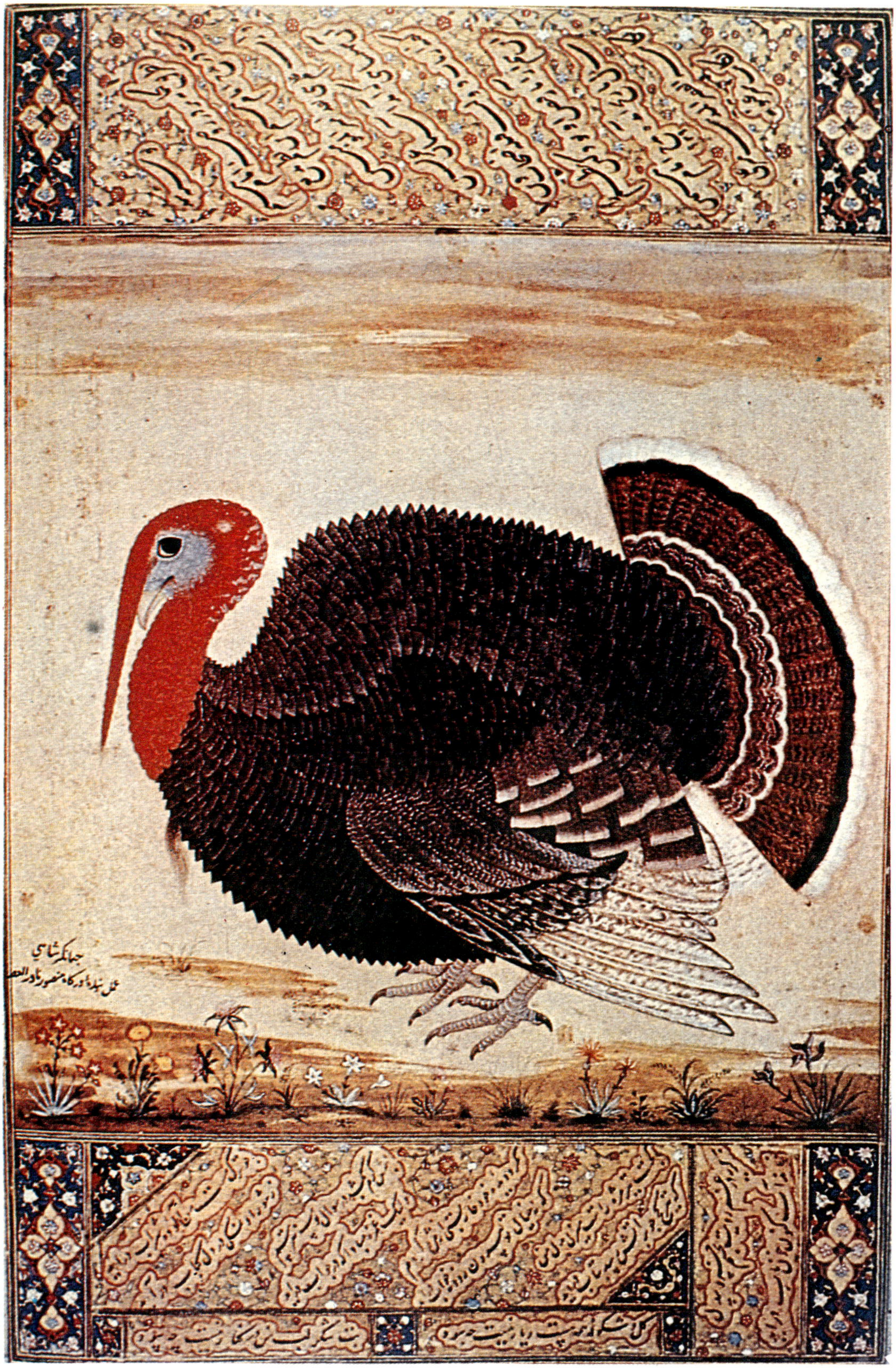

8. Turkey cock (*c.* 1612). Painted by *Nadir ul Asr* Mansur.
Wantage Collection, Victoria and Albert Museum, London.

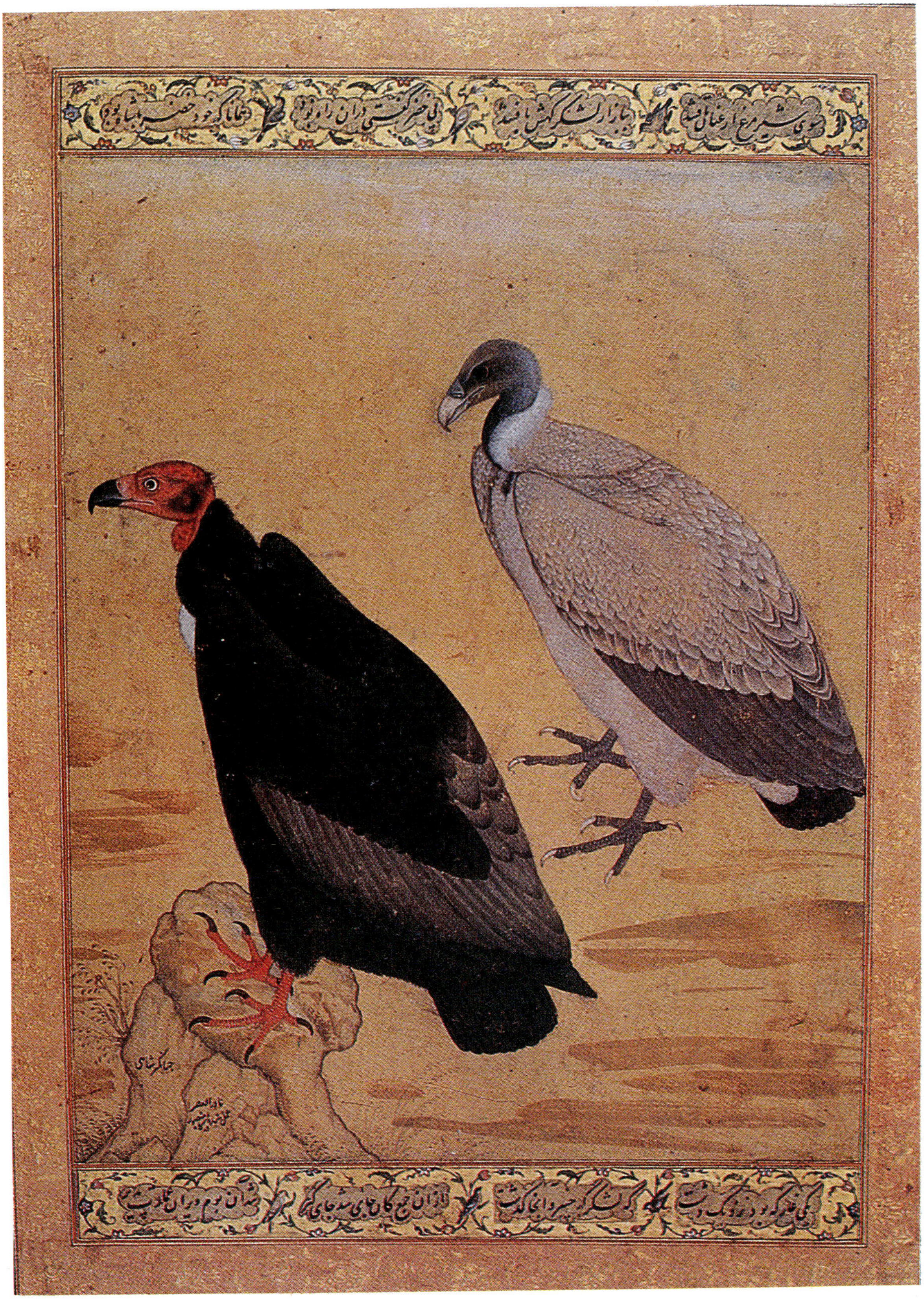

11. King vulture and Himalayan griffon (*c.* 1615-20). Painted by *Nadir ul Asr* Mansur. The Metropolitan Museum of Art, New York.

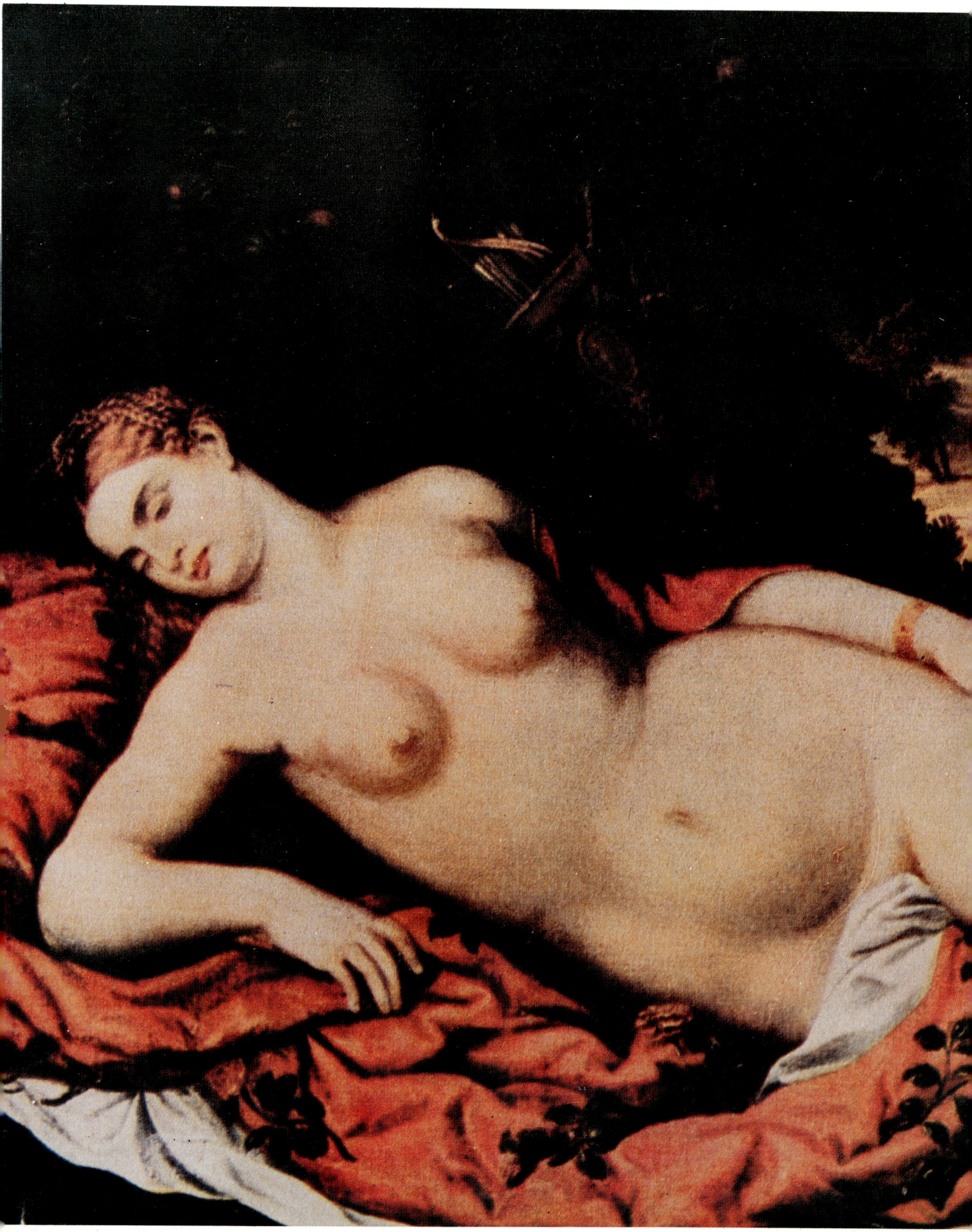

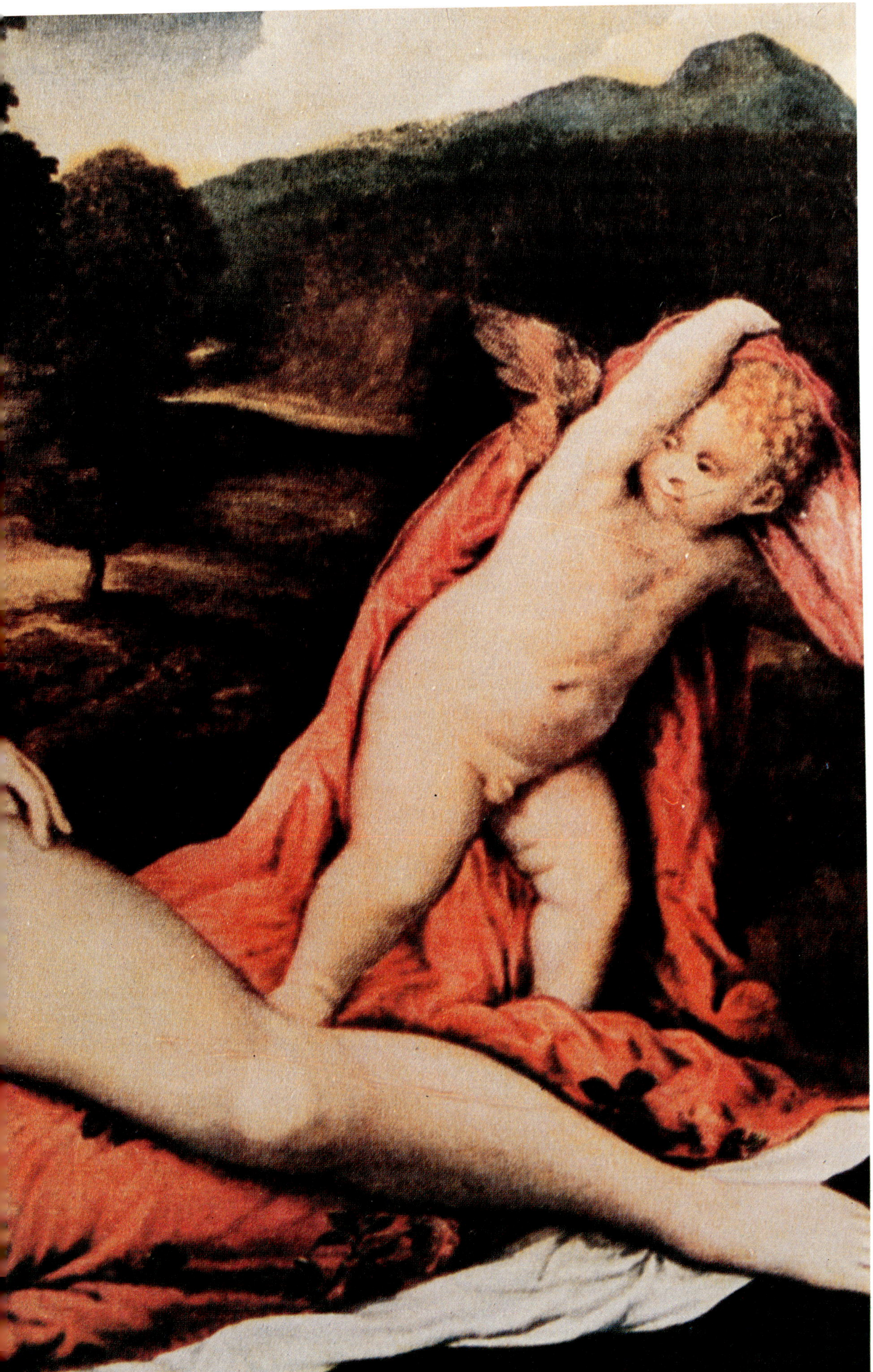

21. Venus and Cupid, undated. Painted by Paris Bordone. Ca 'd' Oro, Venice.

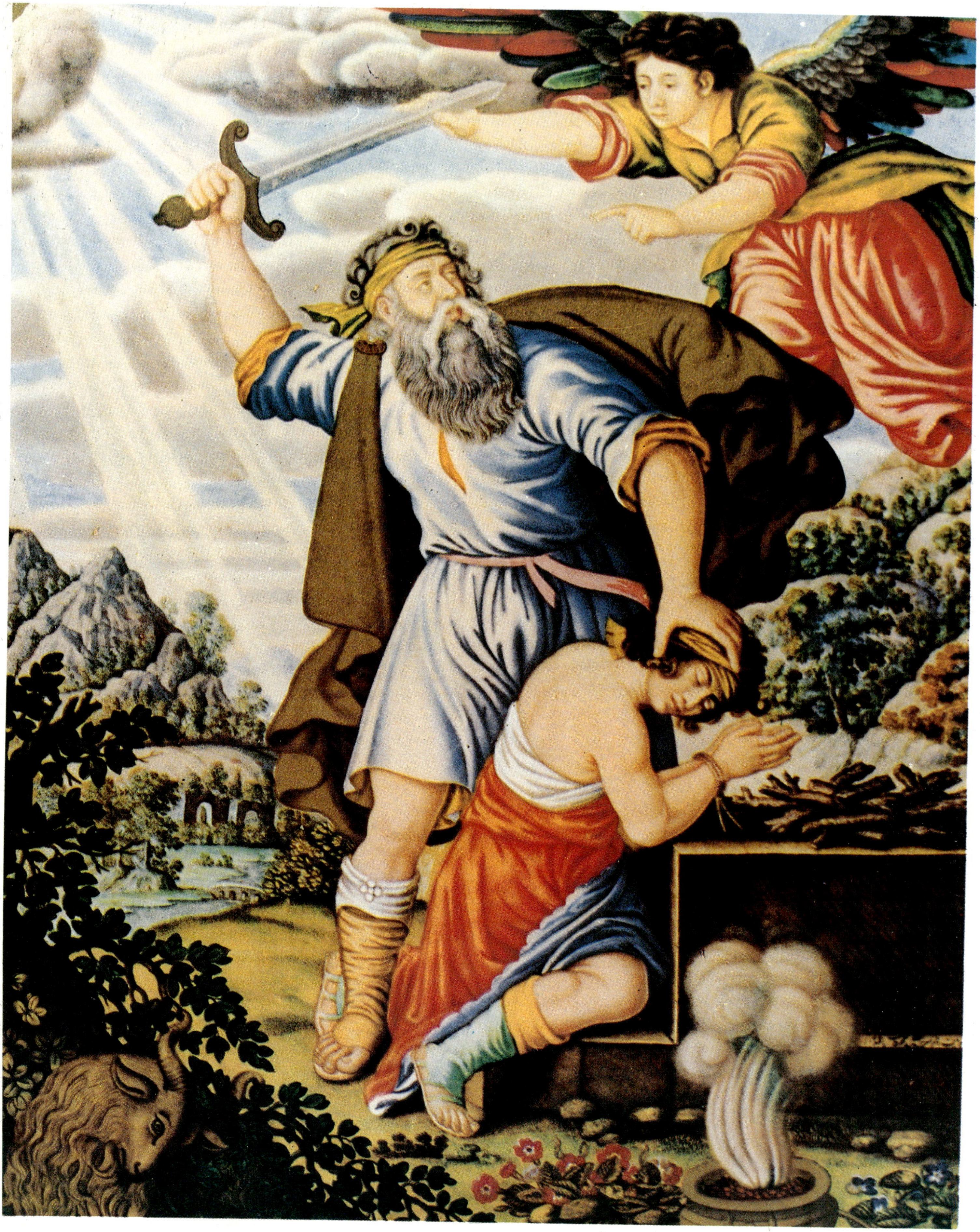

17. Abraham's sacrifice (*c.* 1684-5). Painted by Muhammad Zaman. Institute of the Peoples of Asia, Moscow.

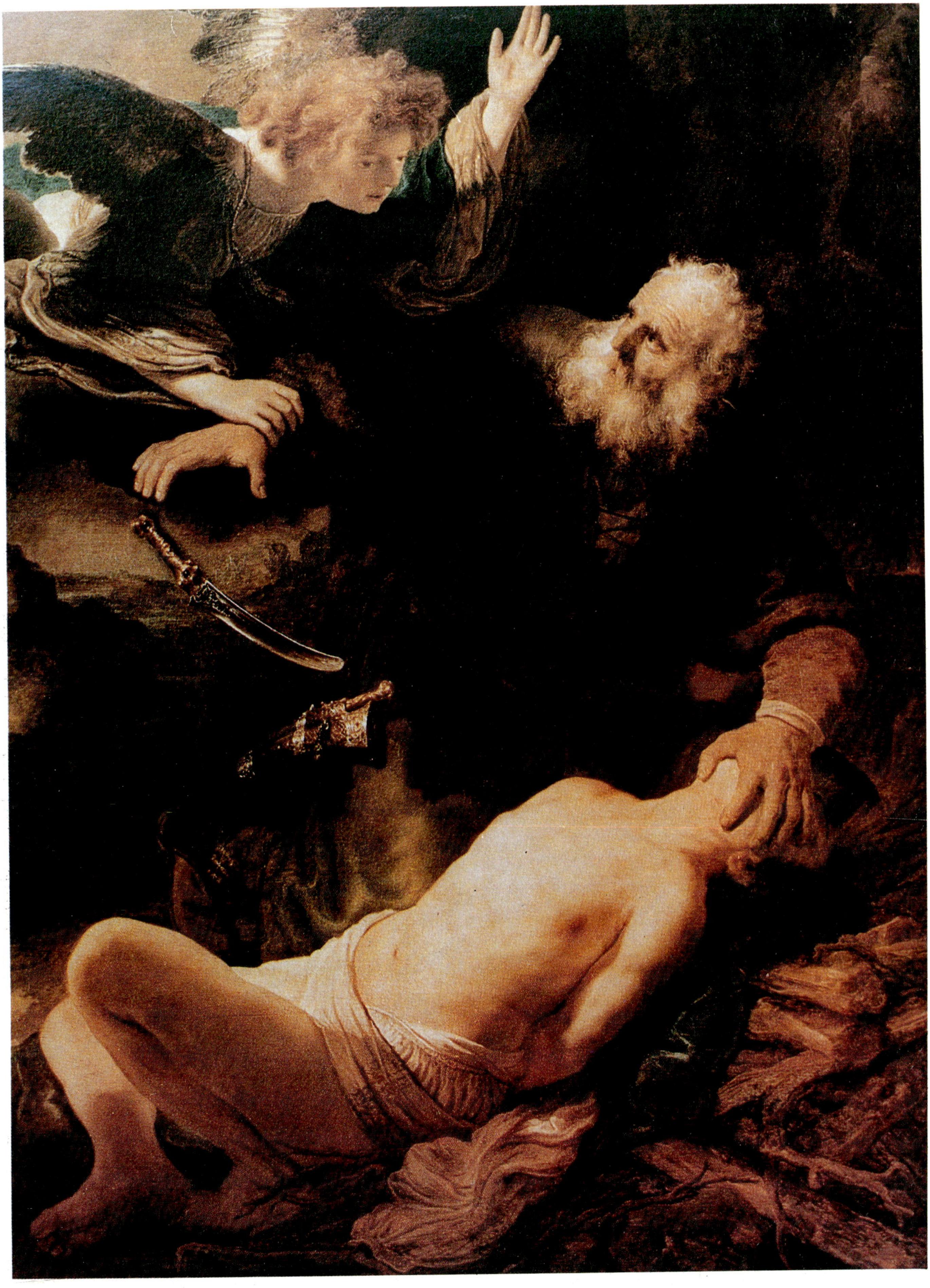

22. Abraham's sacrifice (*c.* 1635). Painted by Rembrandt. The Hermitage, Leningrad.

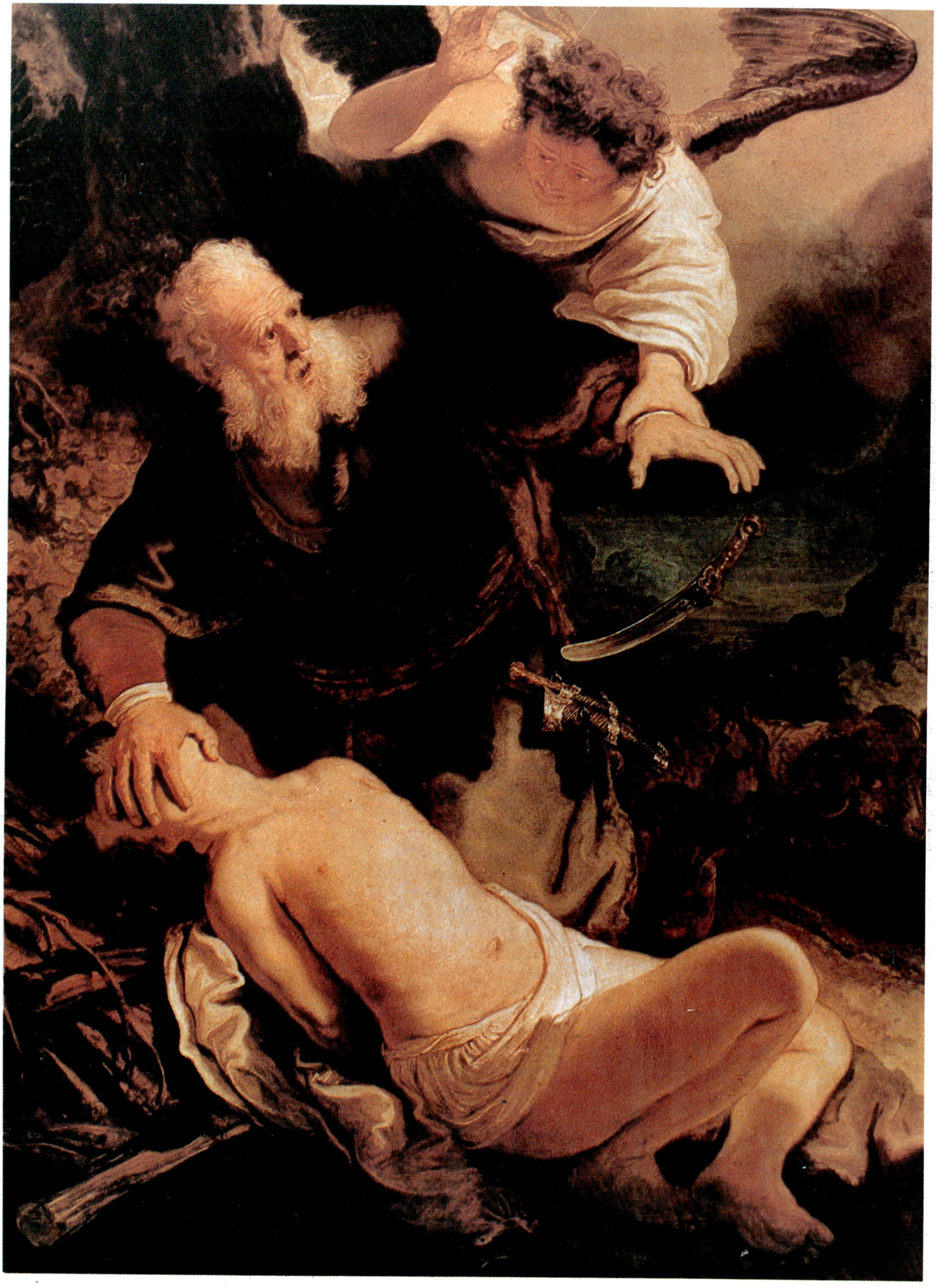

23. Abraham's sacrifice (*c.* 1635). Painted by Rembrandt. Hermitage, Leningrad.

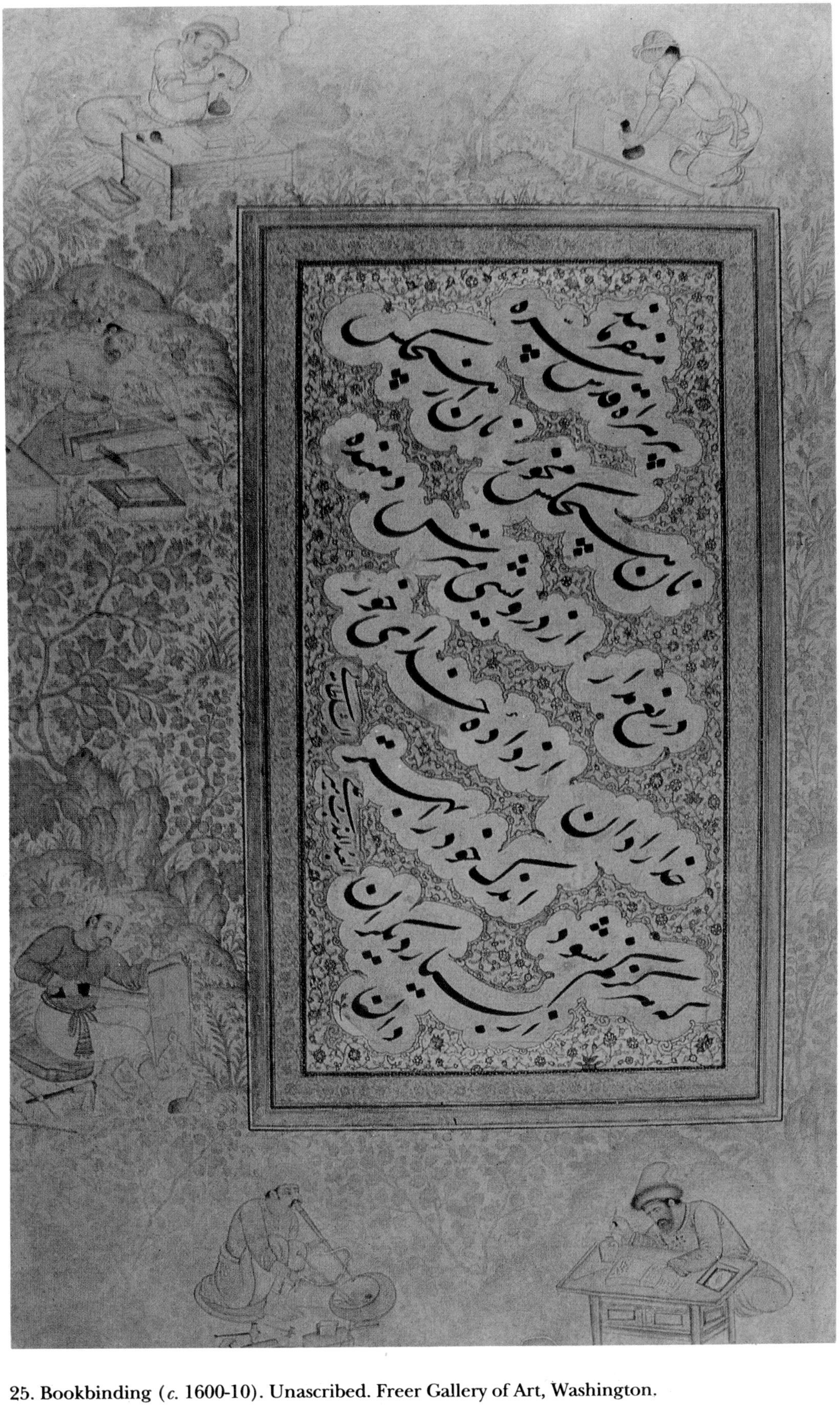

25. Bookbinding (*c.* 1600-10). Unascribed. Freer Gallery of Art, Washington.

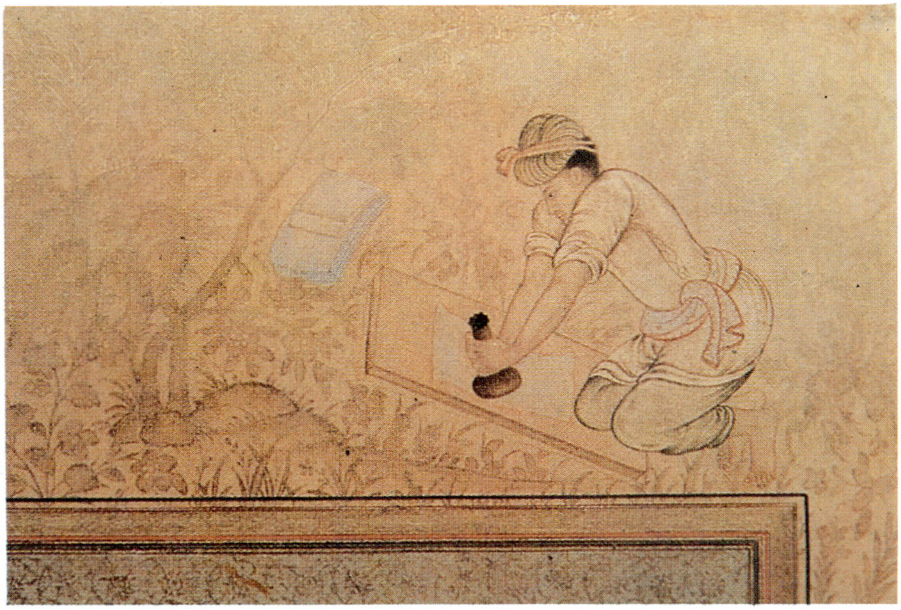

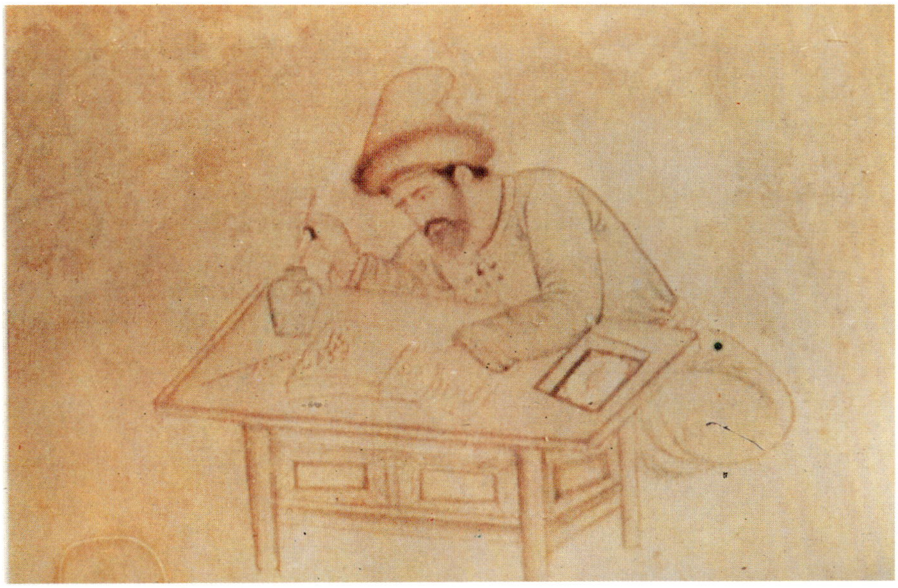

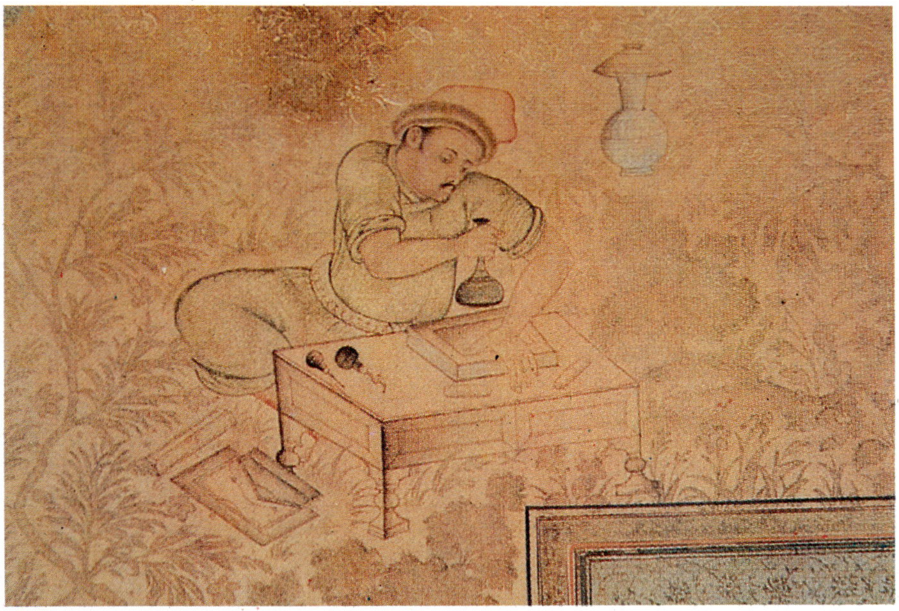

28. *Mohrah kash* (detail of plate 25).

29. Scribe (detail of plate 25).

30. Bookbinder (detail of plate 25).

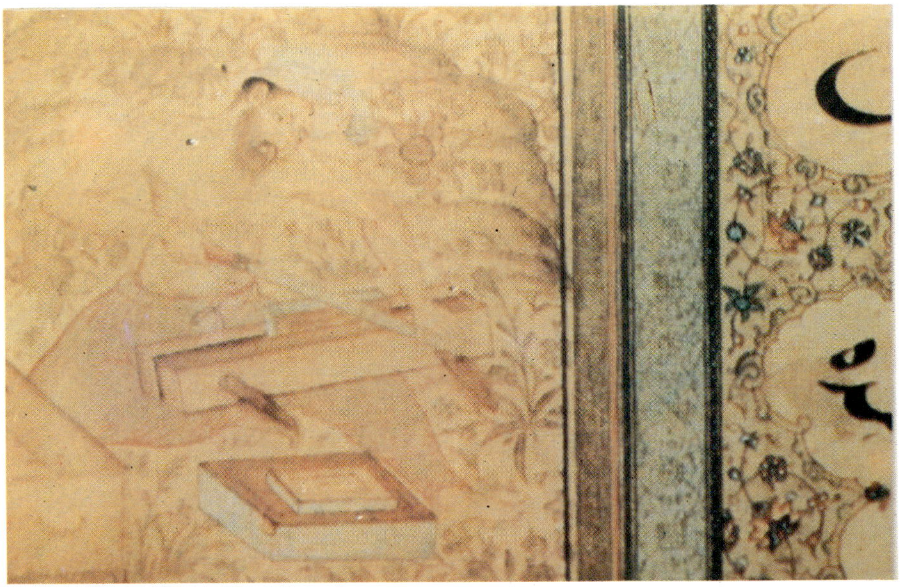

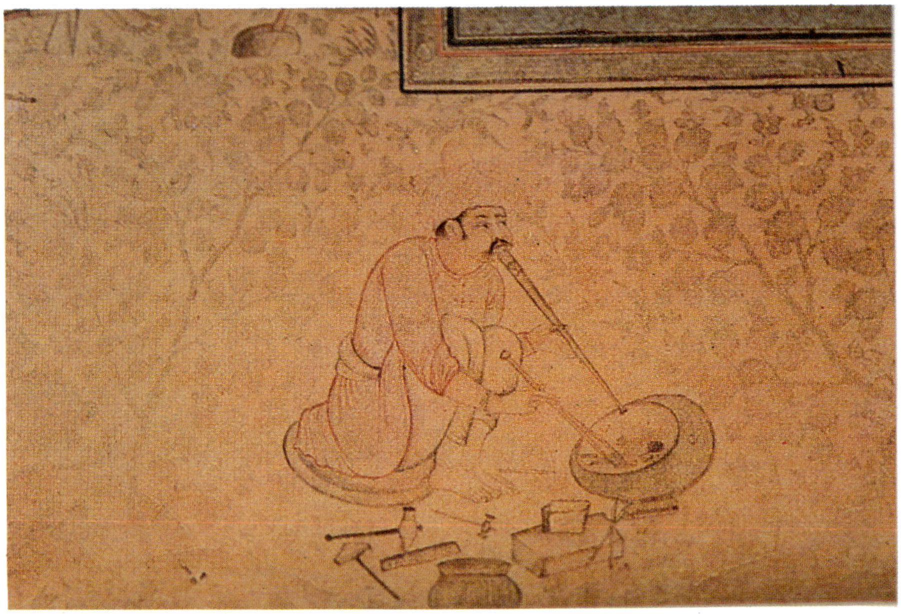

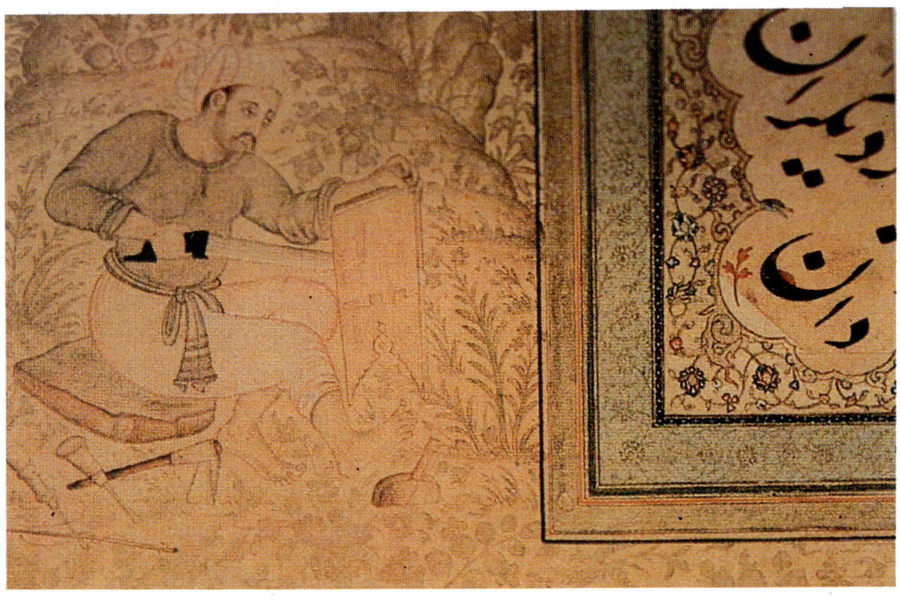

31. Bookbinder with *shikanja* (detail of plate 25).

32. Goldsmith (detail of plate 25).

33. Carpenter making bookrest (detail of plate 25).

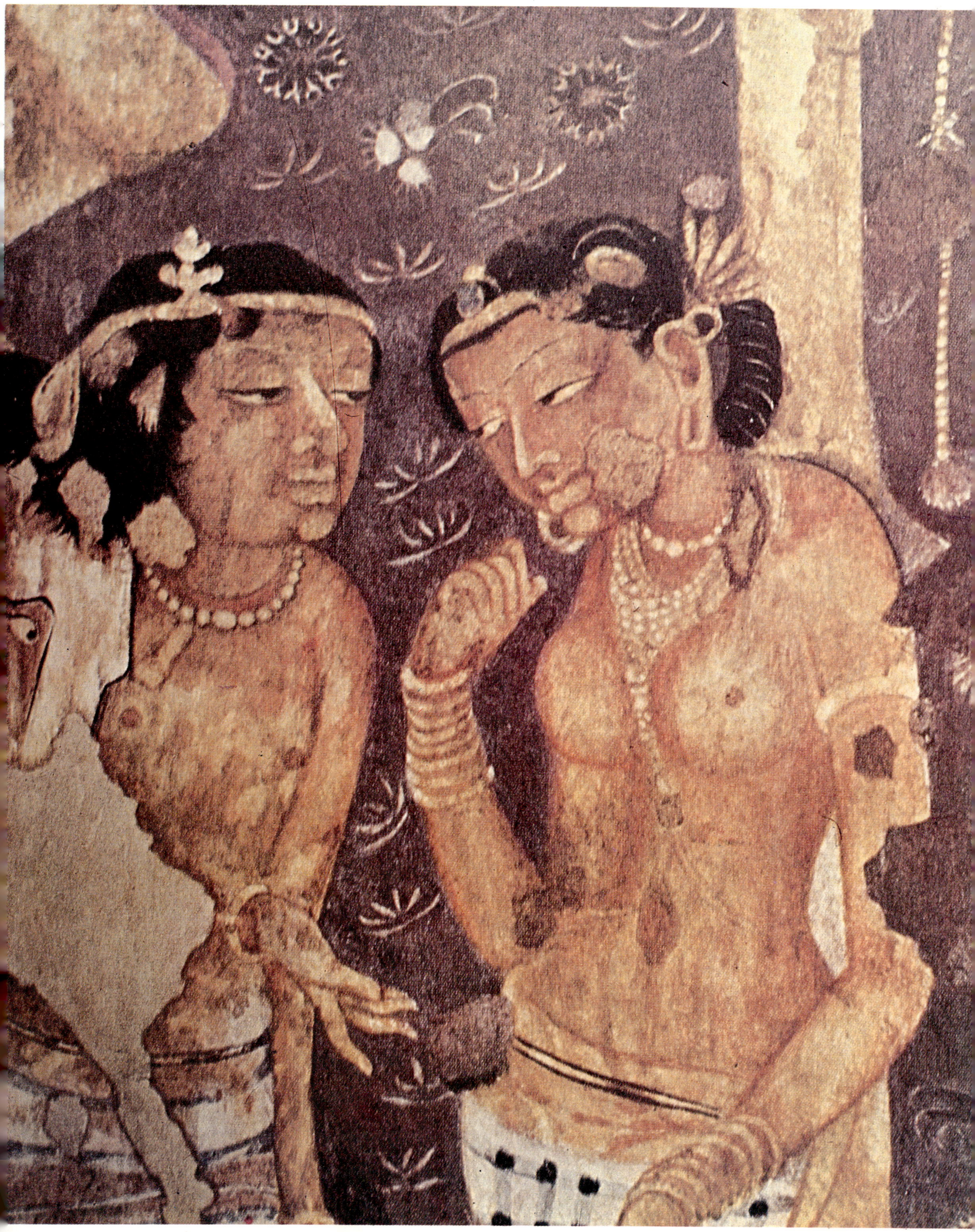

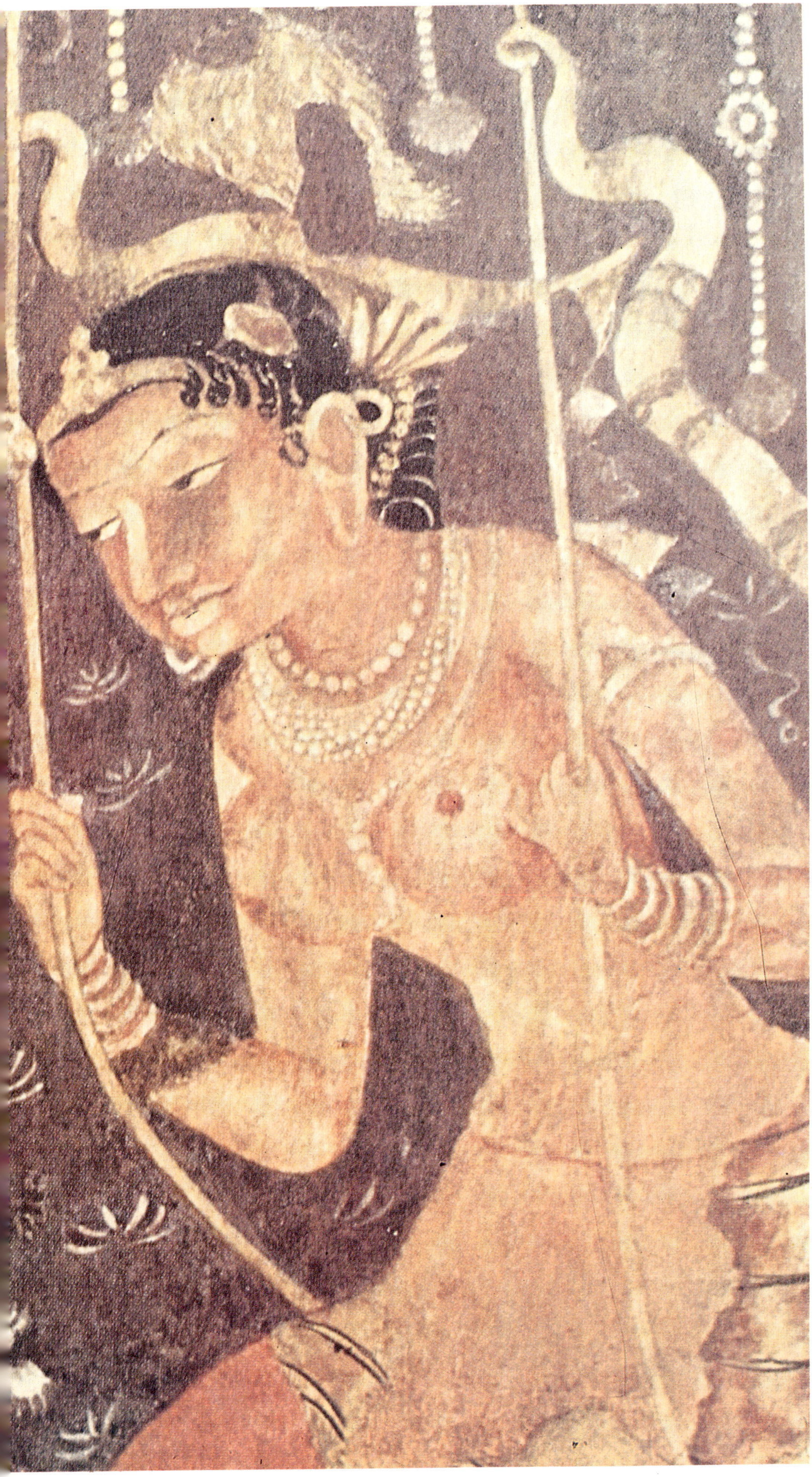

67. Part of the story of *Vidhurapandita-Jataka,* Ajanta Cave 2 (*c.* 500).

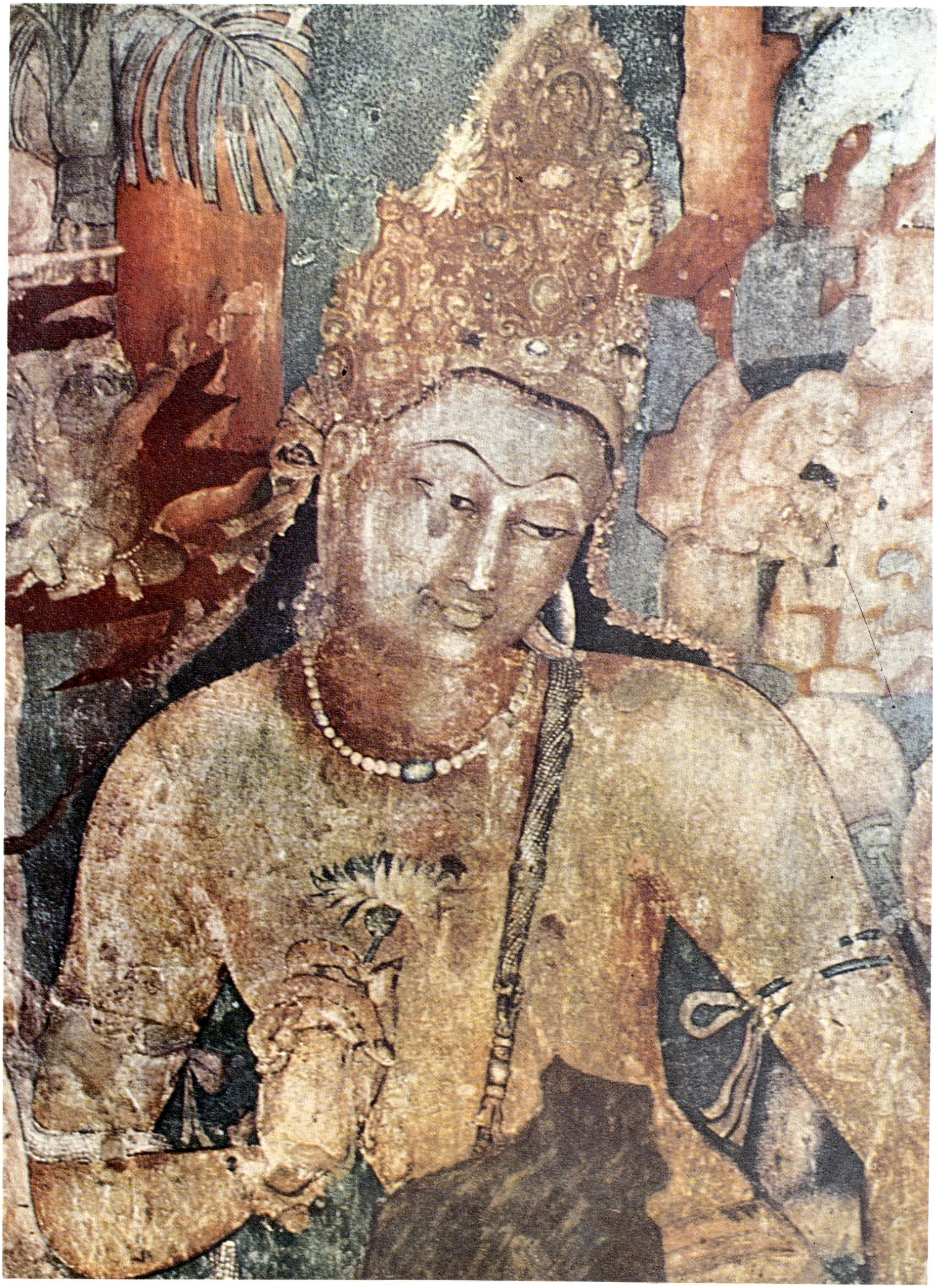

66. Part of the panel of Bodhisattva Padmapani, Ajanta Cave 1 (*c.* 500-600).

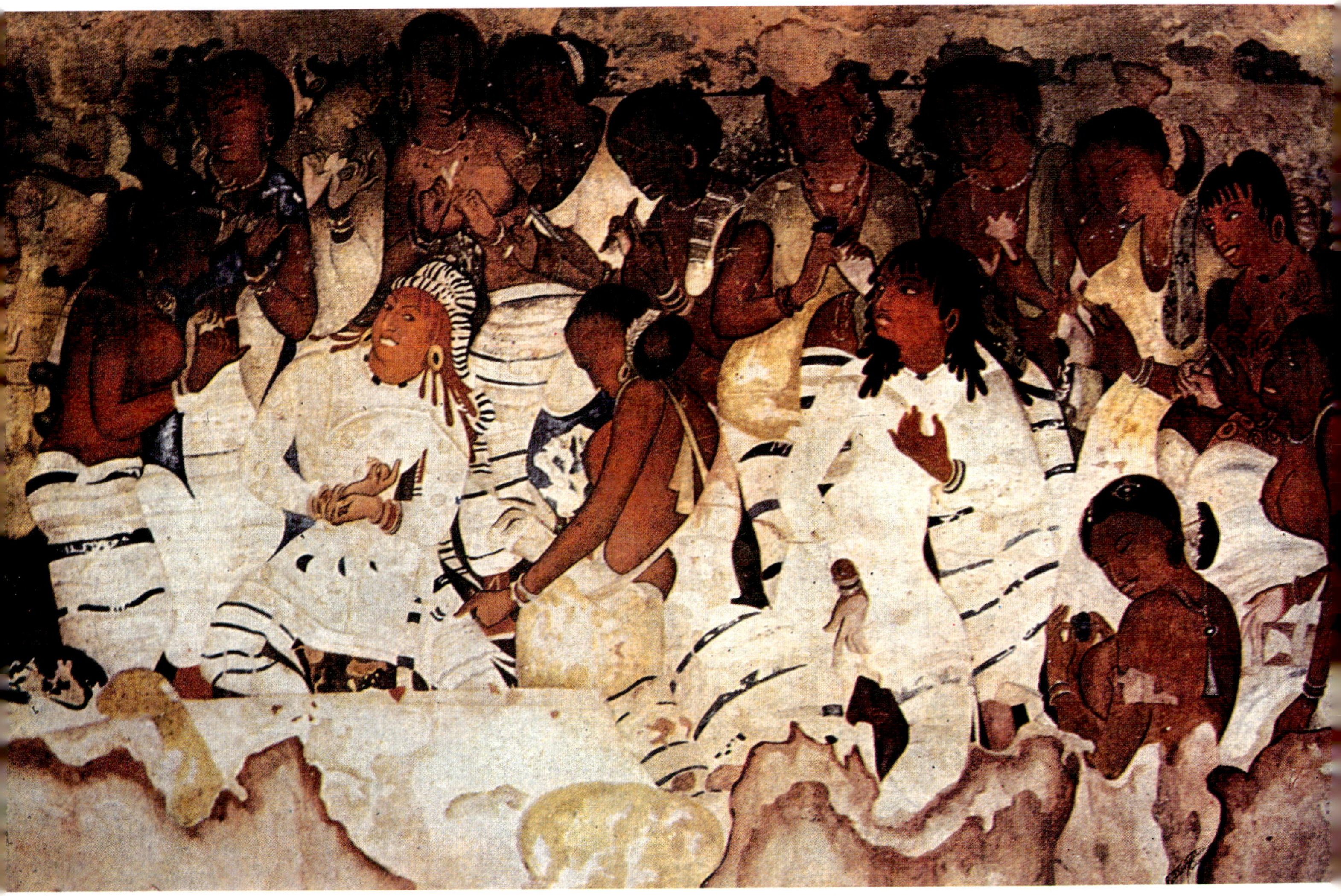

68. Dance scene (*c.* 700). Bagh Cave.

69. Bodhisattva Vajrapani (*c.* 1700). *Astasahasrika-Parjnaparamita,* Bodleian Library, Oxford.

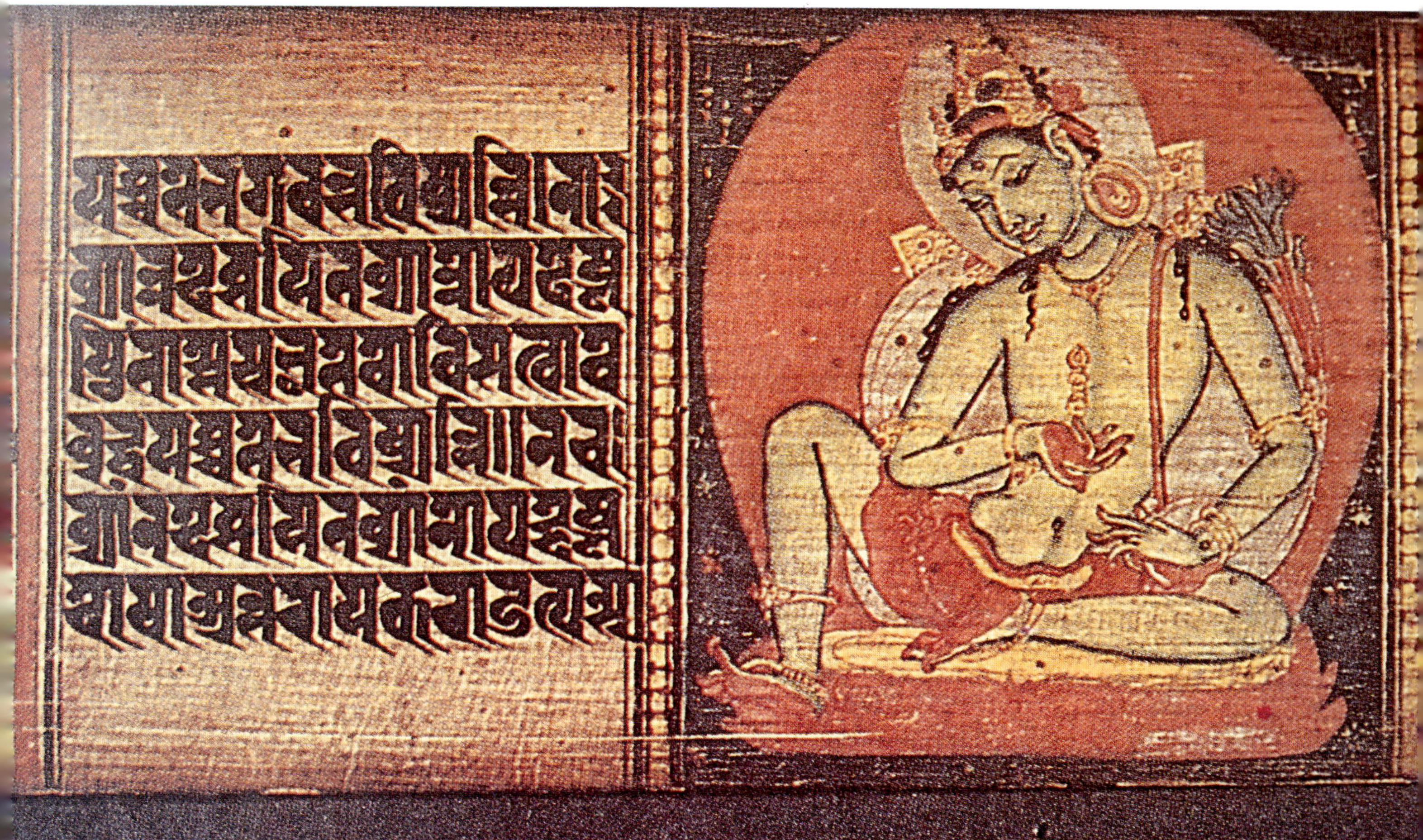

1. Himalayan cheer pheasant (*c.* 1612 [?]). Painted by *Ustad* Mansur [?]. Sawai Man Singh II Museum, Jaipur.

2. Himalayan cheer pheasant (*c.* early 19th century). Unascribed. Baron Maurice Rothschild Collection, Paris.

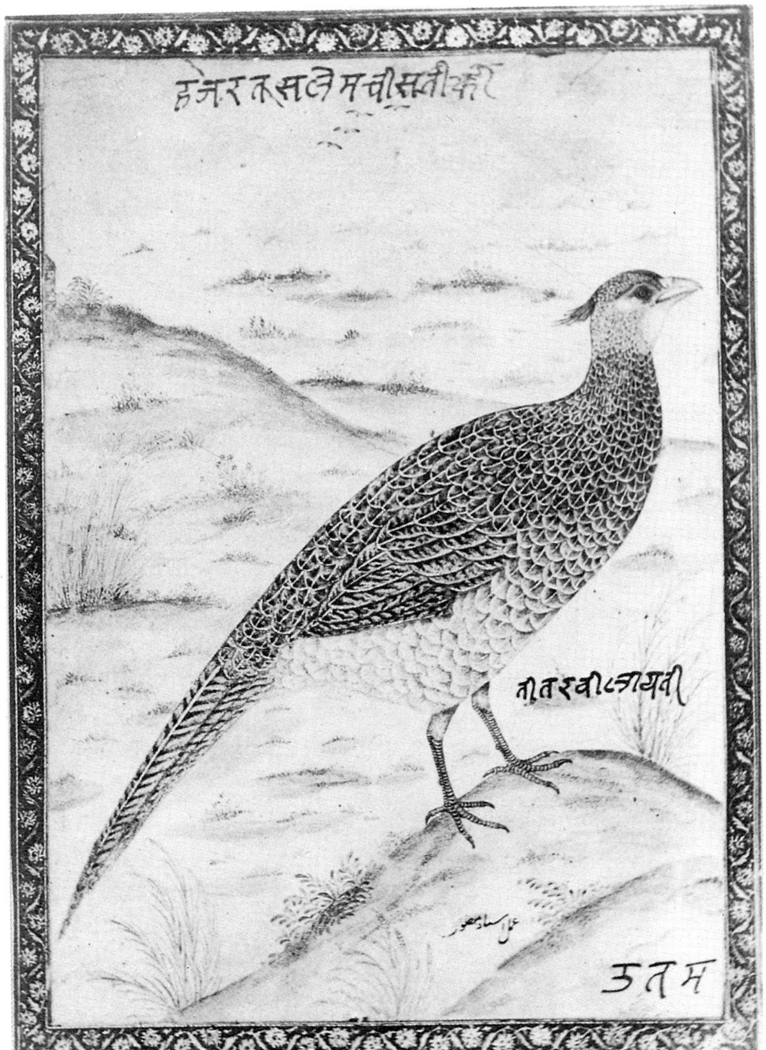

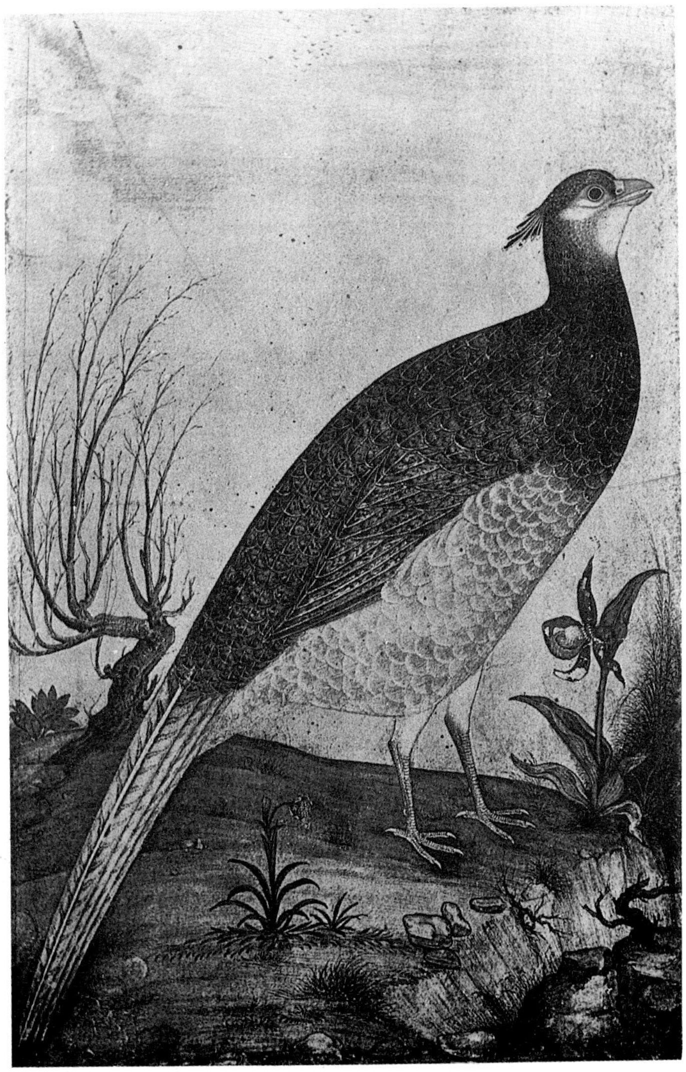

3. Himalayan cheer pheasant (*c.* early 19th century).
Unascribed. Bernard Quartich Collection, Paris.

4. Falcon (*c.* 1619 [?]). Painted by *Nadir ul Asr* [?]. Sawai Man Singh II Museum, Jaipur.

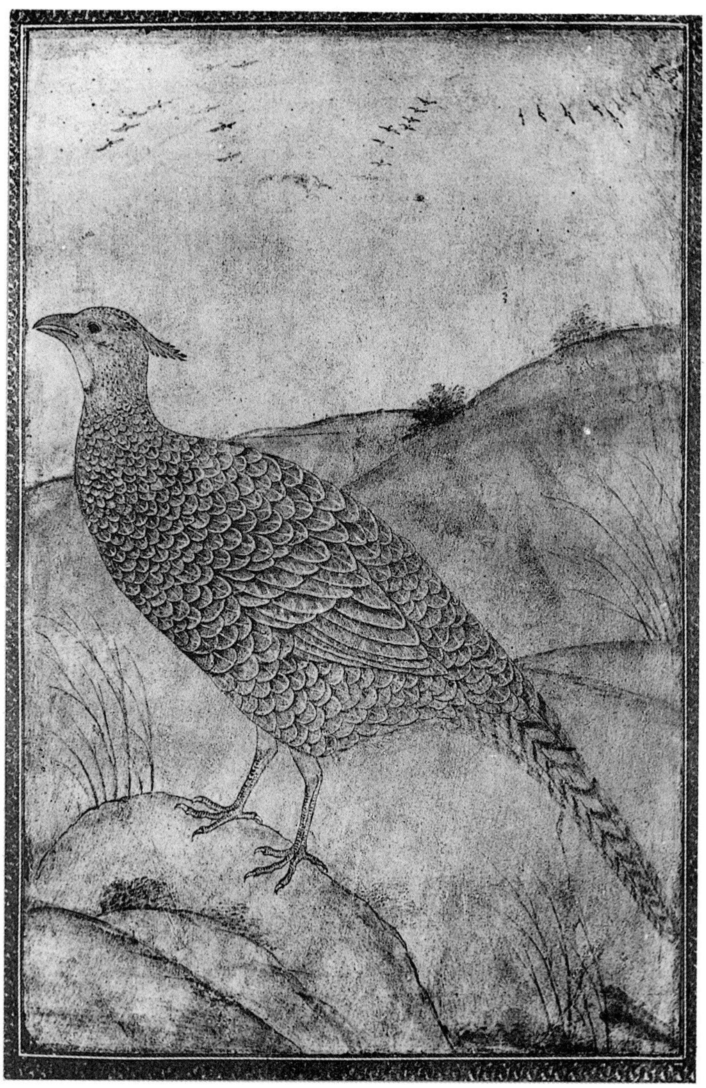

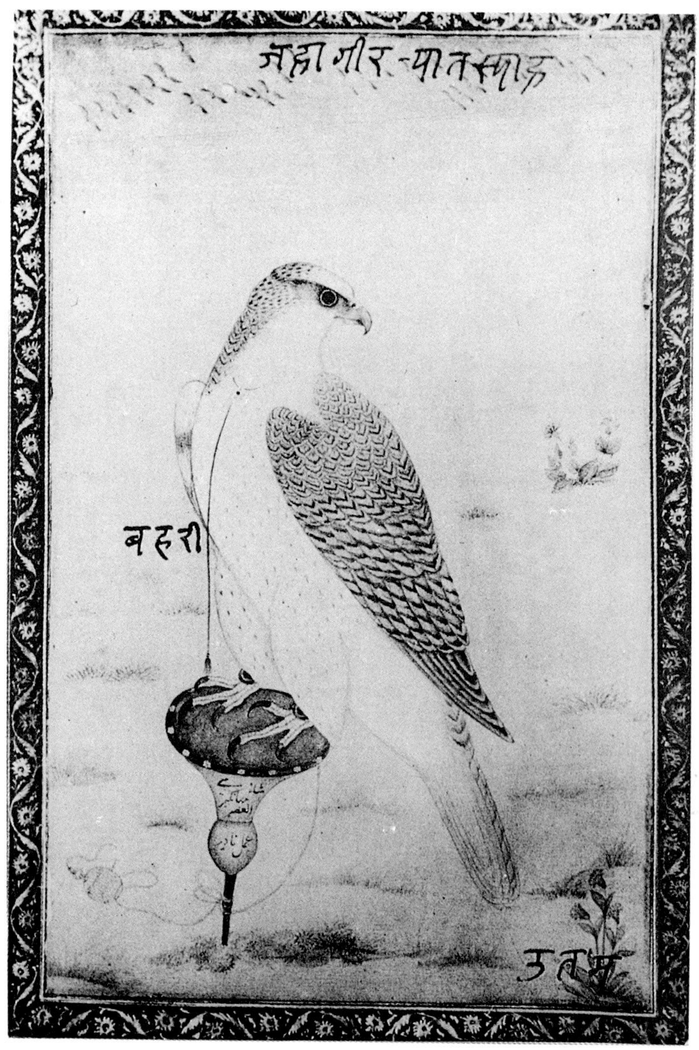

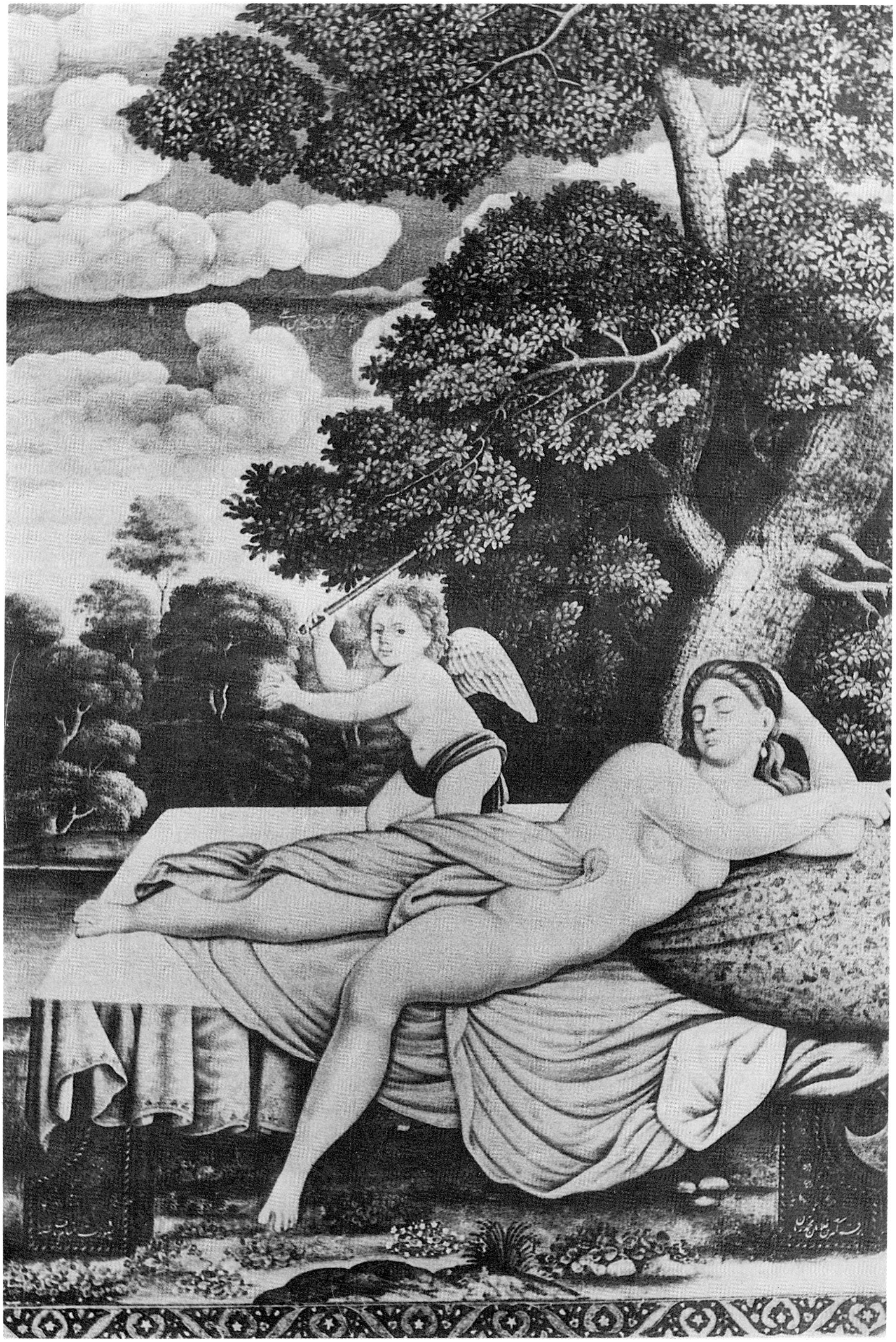

16. Venus and Cupid (*c.* 1676-77). Painted by Muhammad Zaman. Institute of the Peoples of Asia, Moscow.

14. Prince on the back of an elephant (dated 1607-8 [?]). Painted by Bichitr [?]. Indian Museum, Calcutta.

15. Siberian crane (*c.* 1600 [?]). Unascribed. Indian Museum, Calcutta.

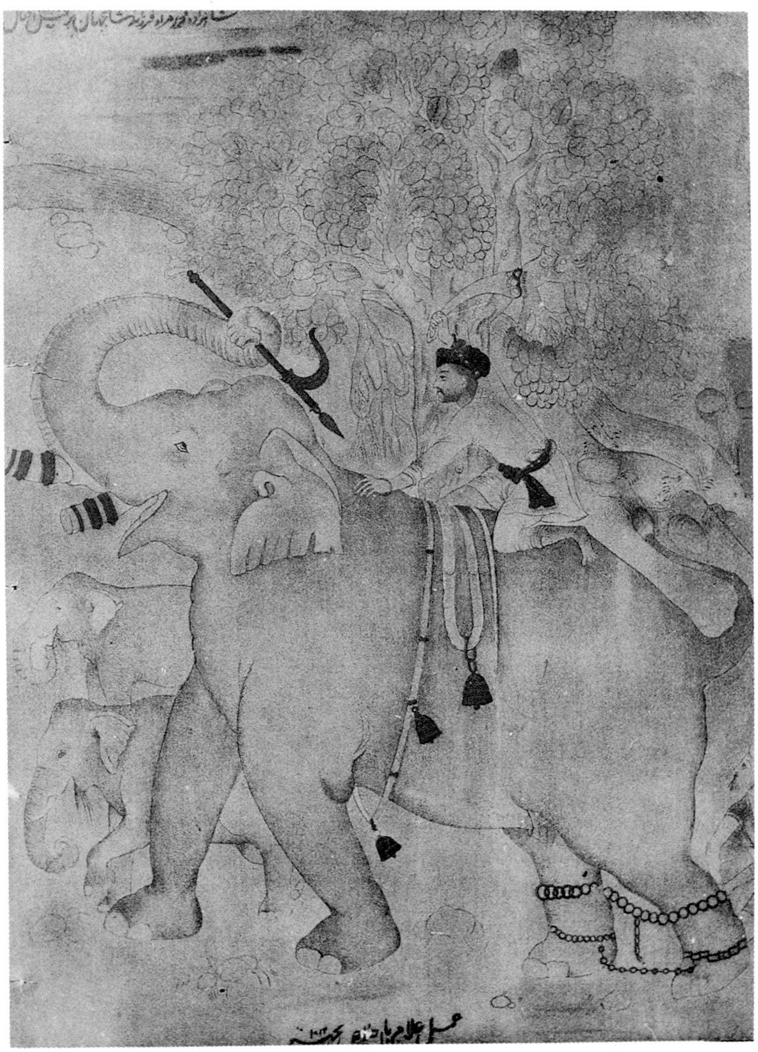

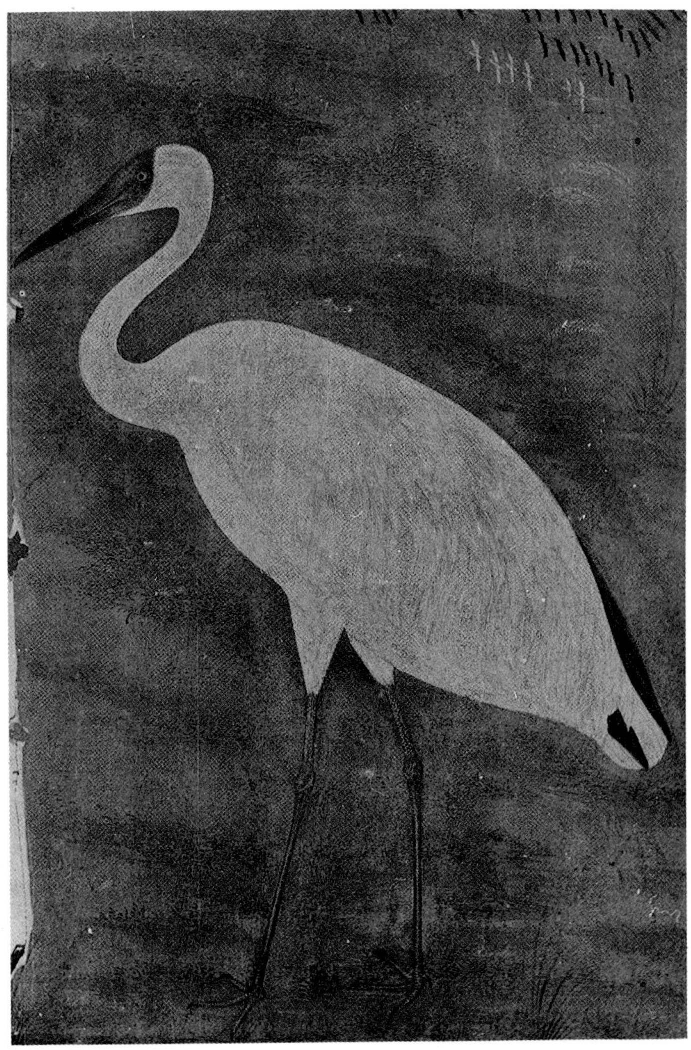

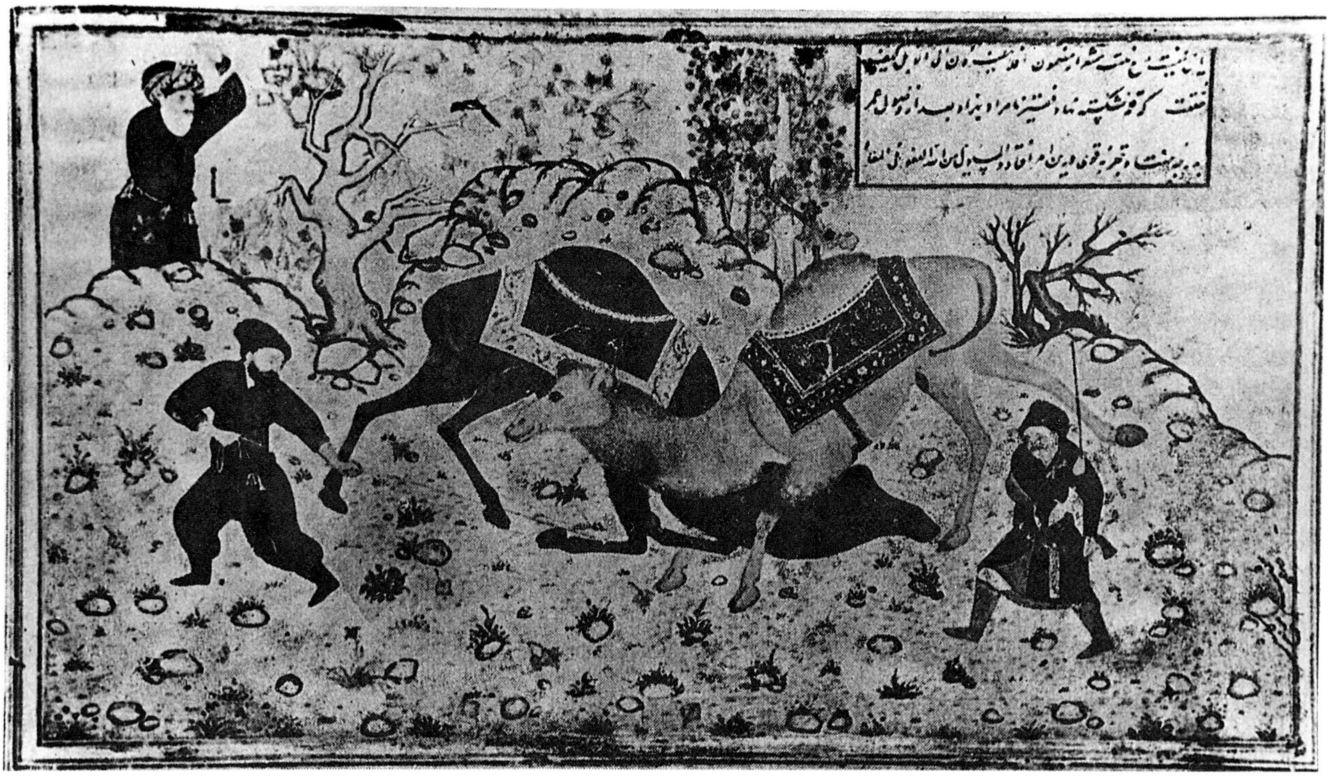

12. Camel fight (*c.* 1525). Painted by Bihzad. *Muraqqa-i Gulshan*, Gulistan Palace Library, Teheran.

13. Camel fight, dated 1608-9. Painted by Nanha. Gulistan Palace Library, Teheran.

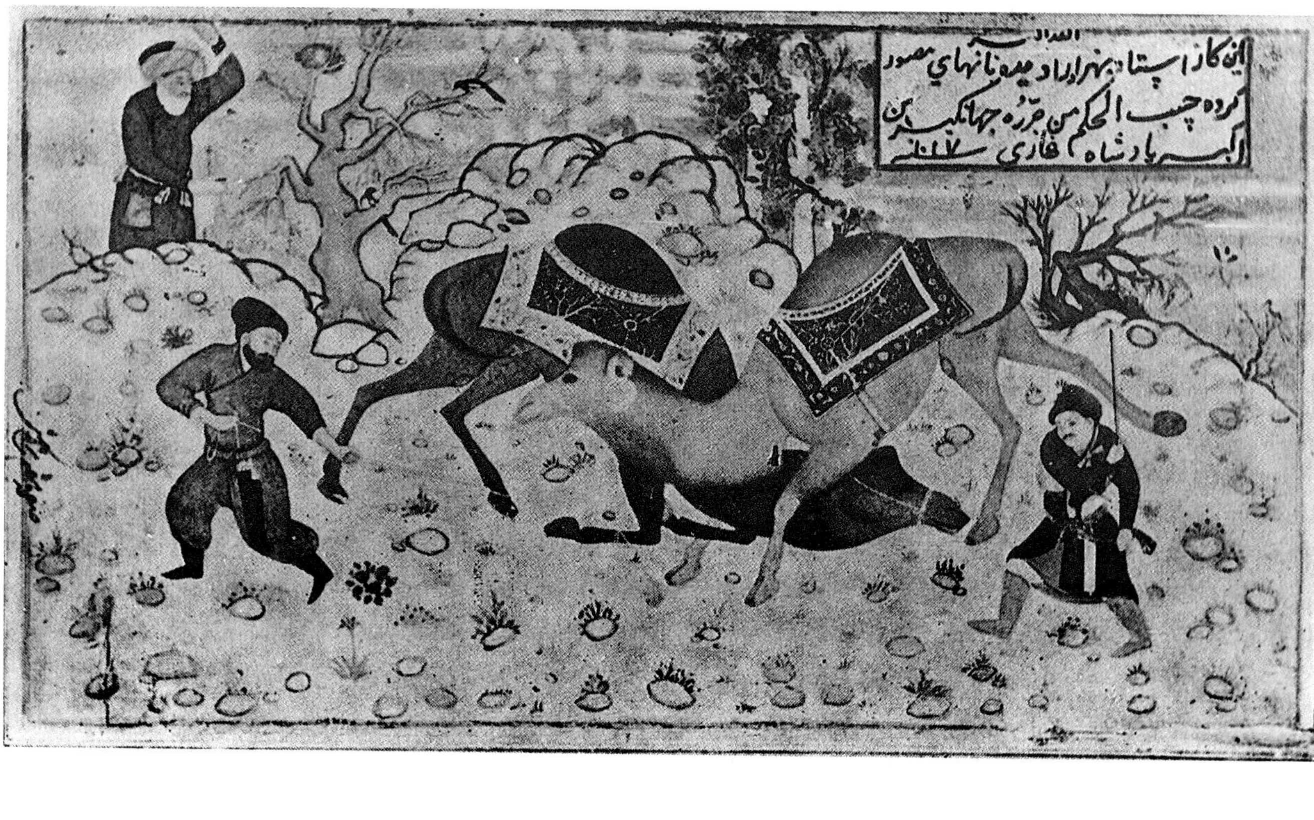

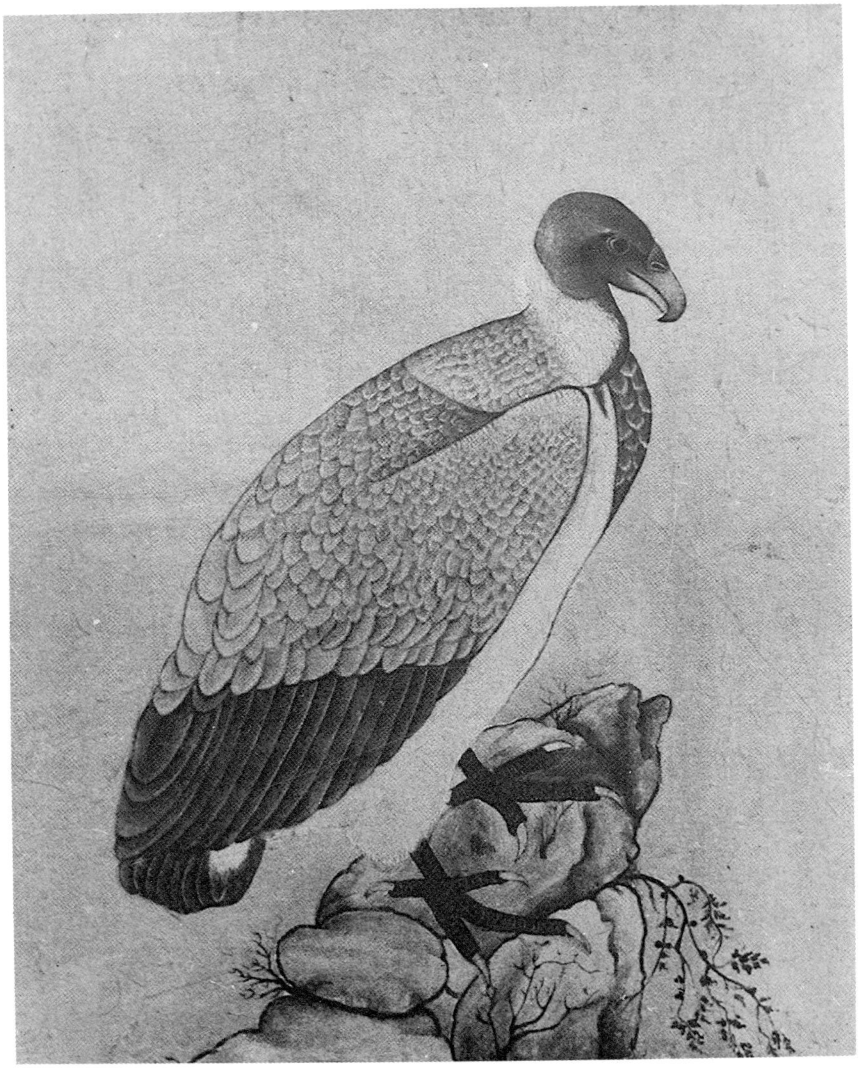

10. Himalayan griffon (*c.* early 19th century). Unascribed. Chester Beatty Library, Dublin.

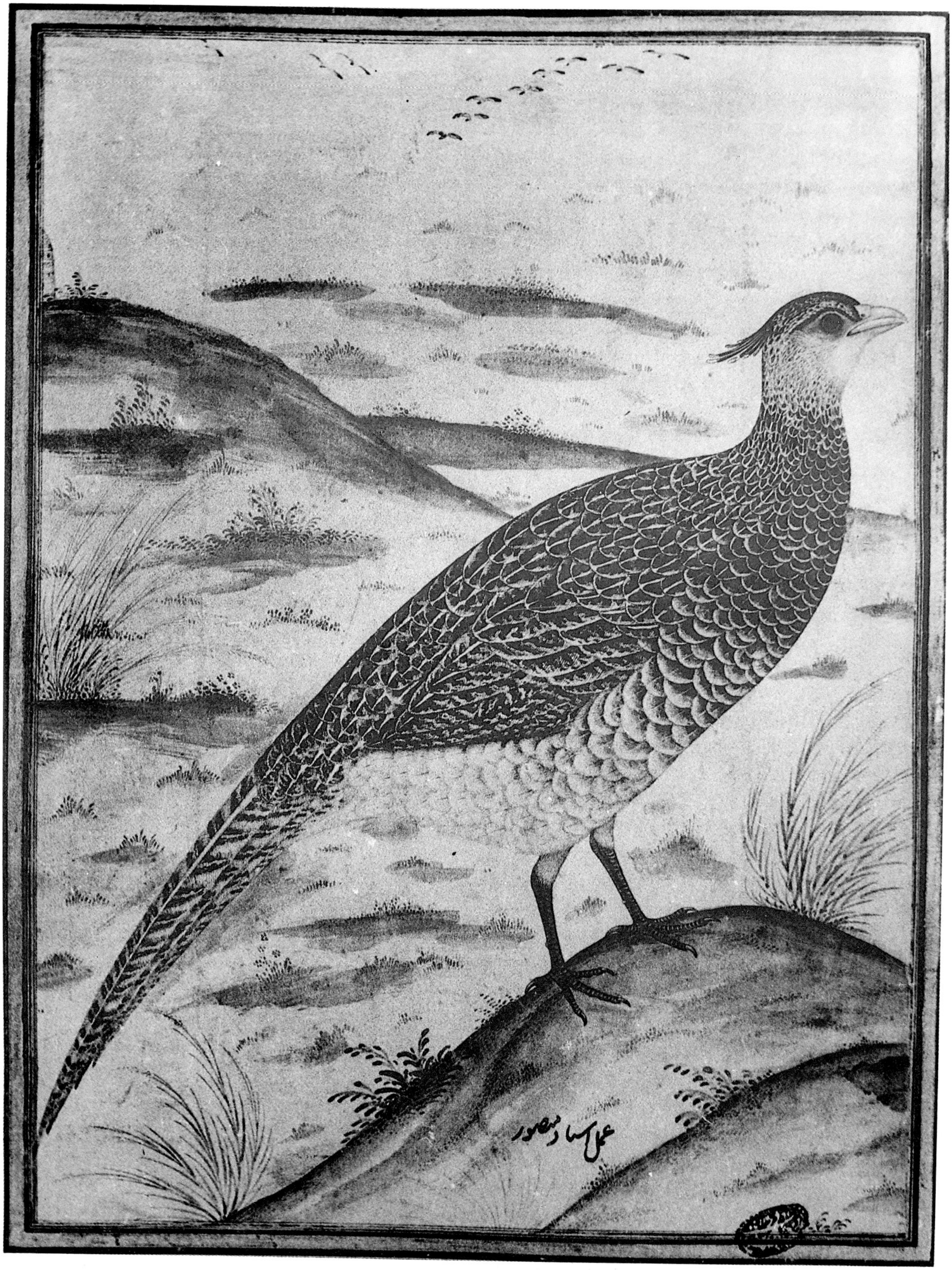

6. Himalayan cheer pheasant (*c.* 1612). Painted by *Ustad* Mansur. Wantage Collection, Victoria and Albert Museum, London.

7. Turkey cock (*c.* 1612 [?]). Unascribed. Indian Museum, Calcutta.

9. Himalayan griffon (*c.* early 19th century). Painted by Mansur [?]. Freer Gallery of Art, Washington.

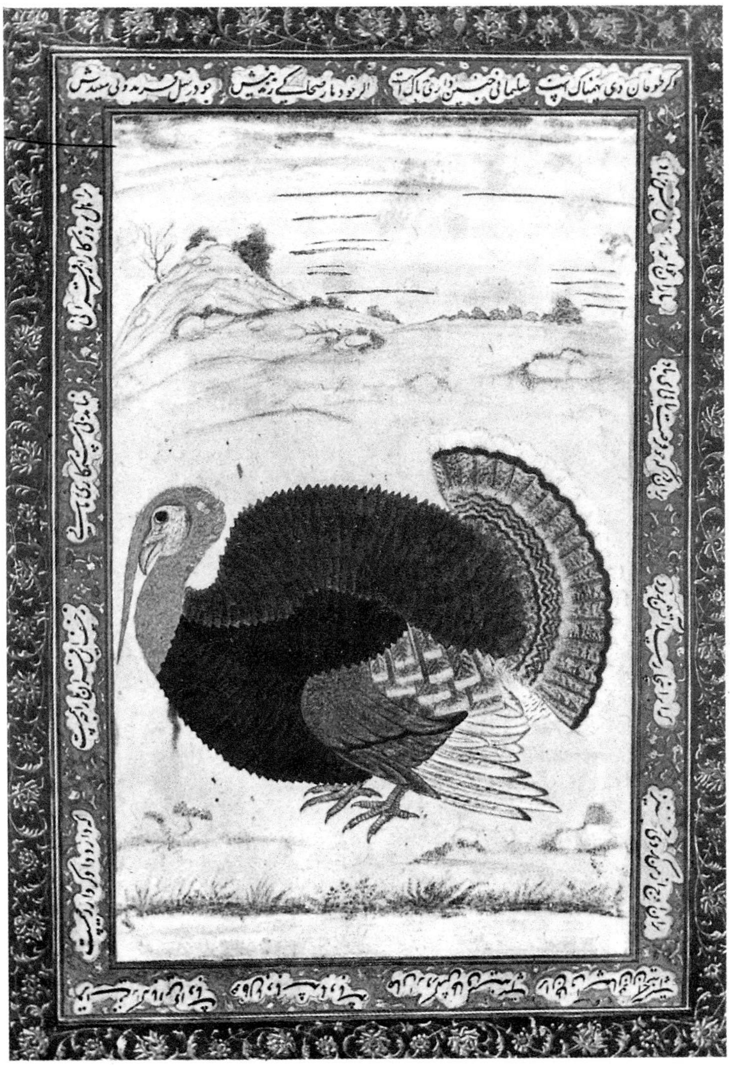

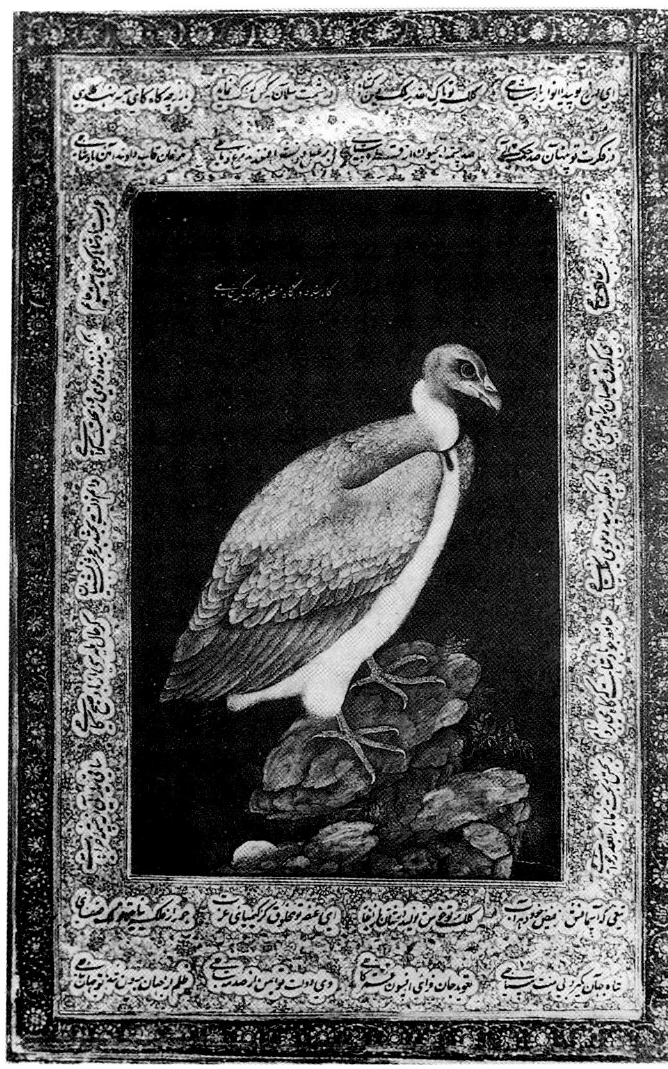

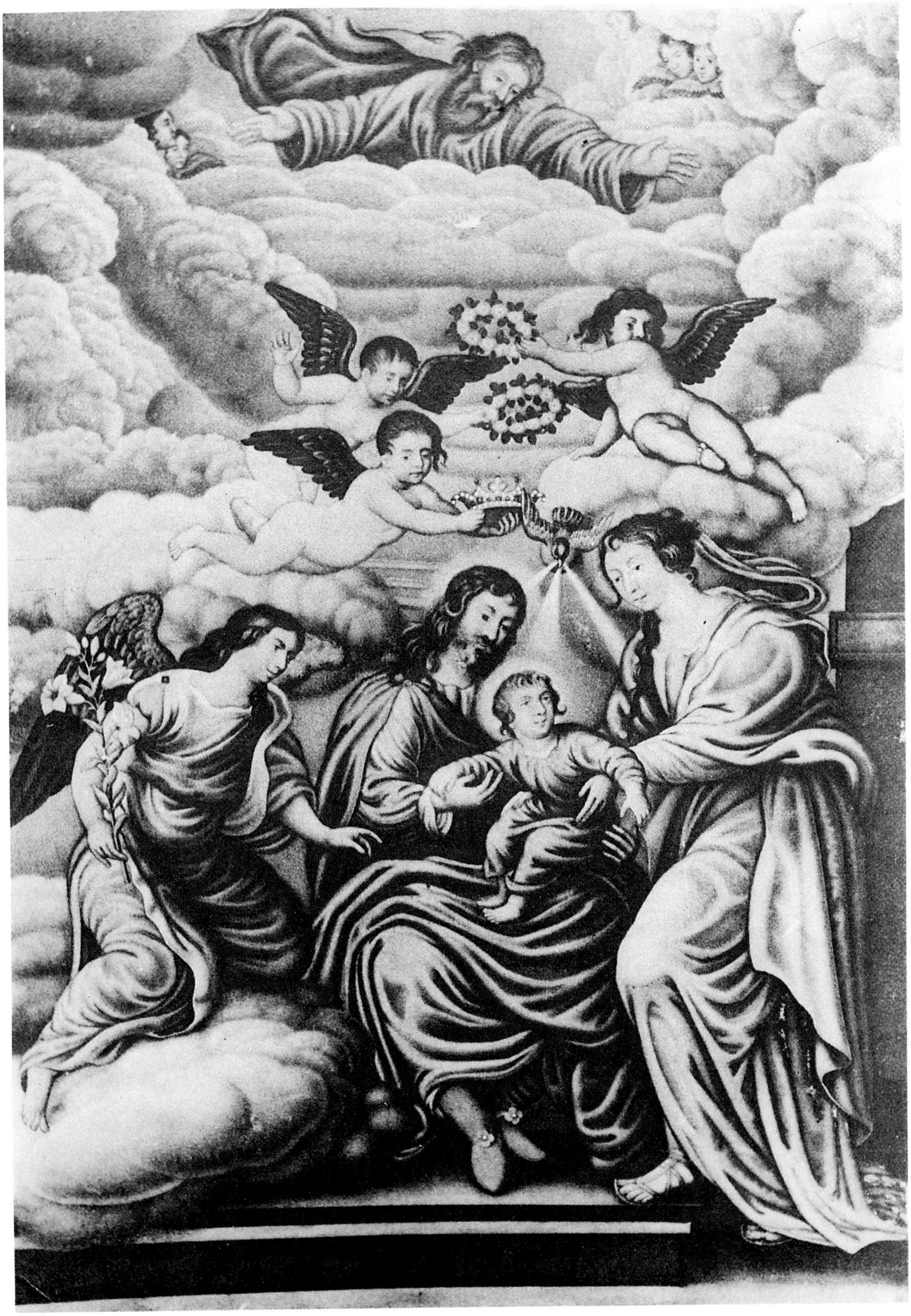

18. Holy Trinity/Family (*c.* 1682-3). Painted by Muhammad Zaman.
Institute of the Peoples of Asia, Moscow.

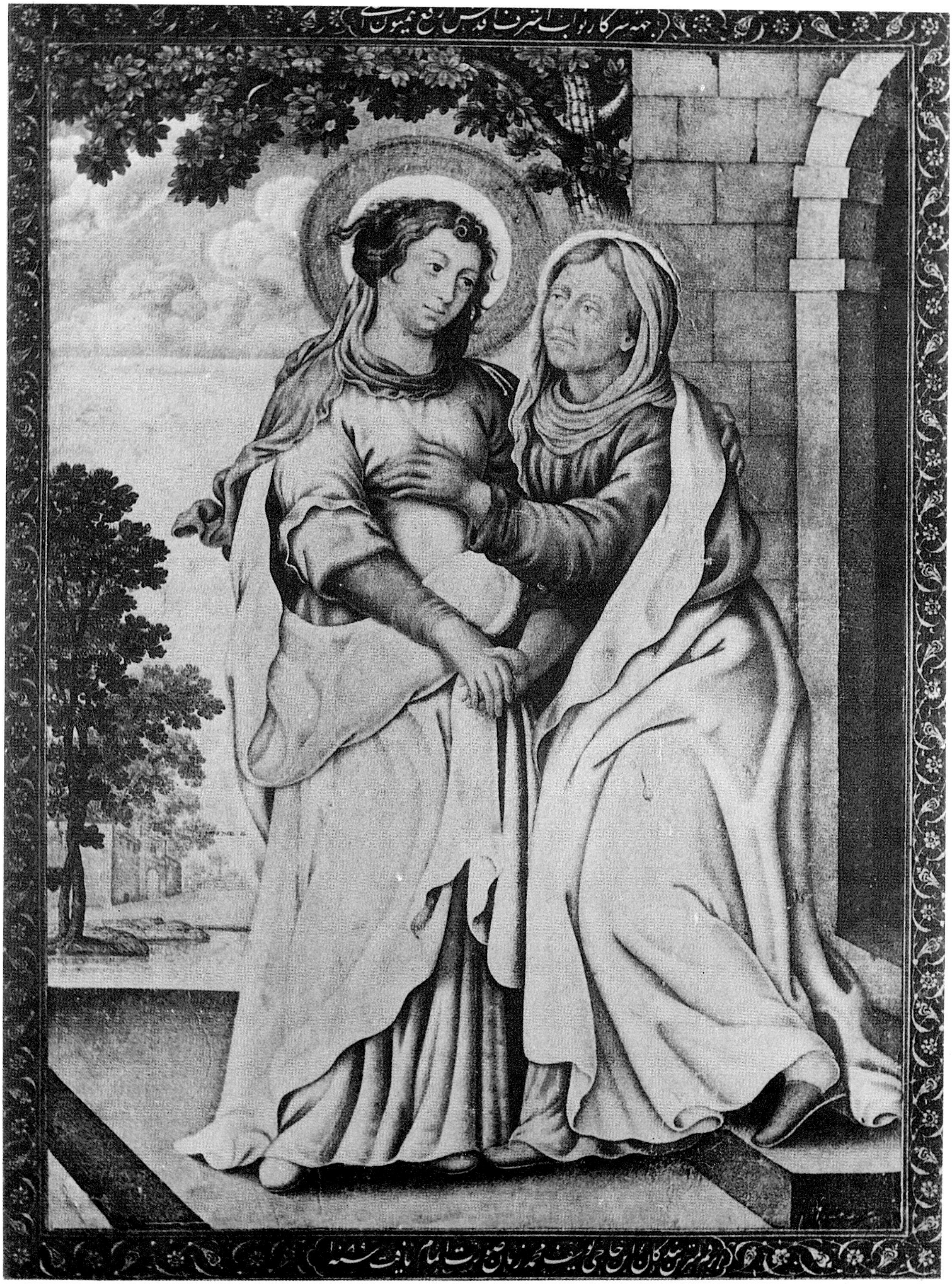

19. Mary and Elizabeth (*c.* 1678). Painted by Muhammad Zaman. F.R. Martin Collection.

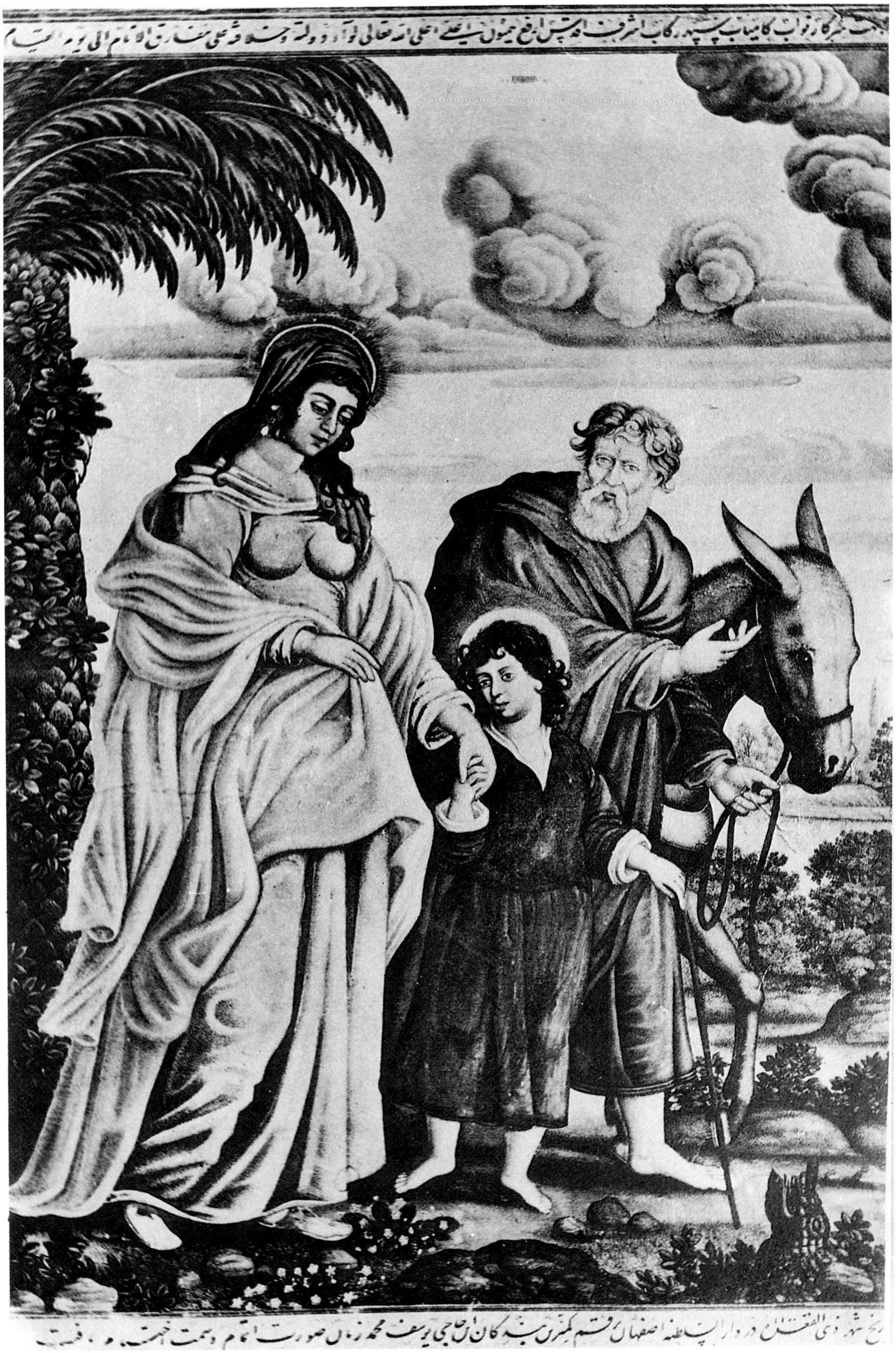

20. The Flight into Egypt (*c.* 1675). Painted by Muhammad Zaman. F.R. Martin Collection.

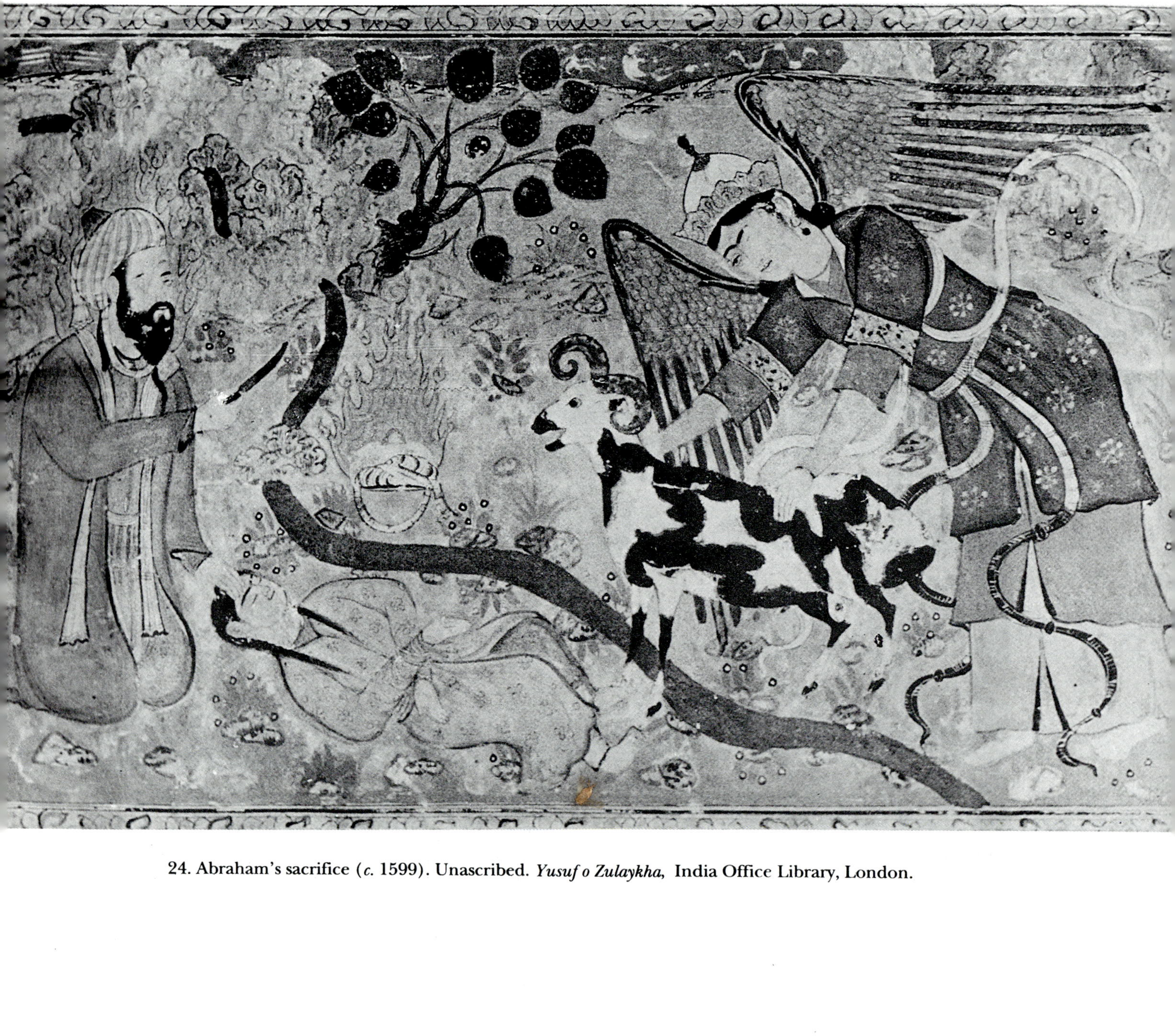

24. Abraham's sacrifice (*c.* 1599). Unascribed. *Yusuf o Zulaykha,* India Office Library, London.

26. Bookbinders at work (*c.* 1585-90). Painted by Nanha.
The Keir Collection of Edmond de Unger.

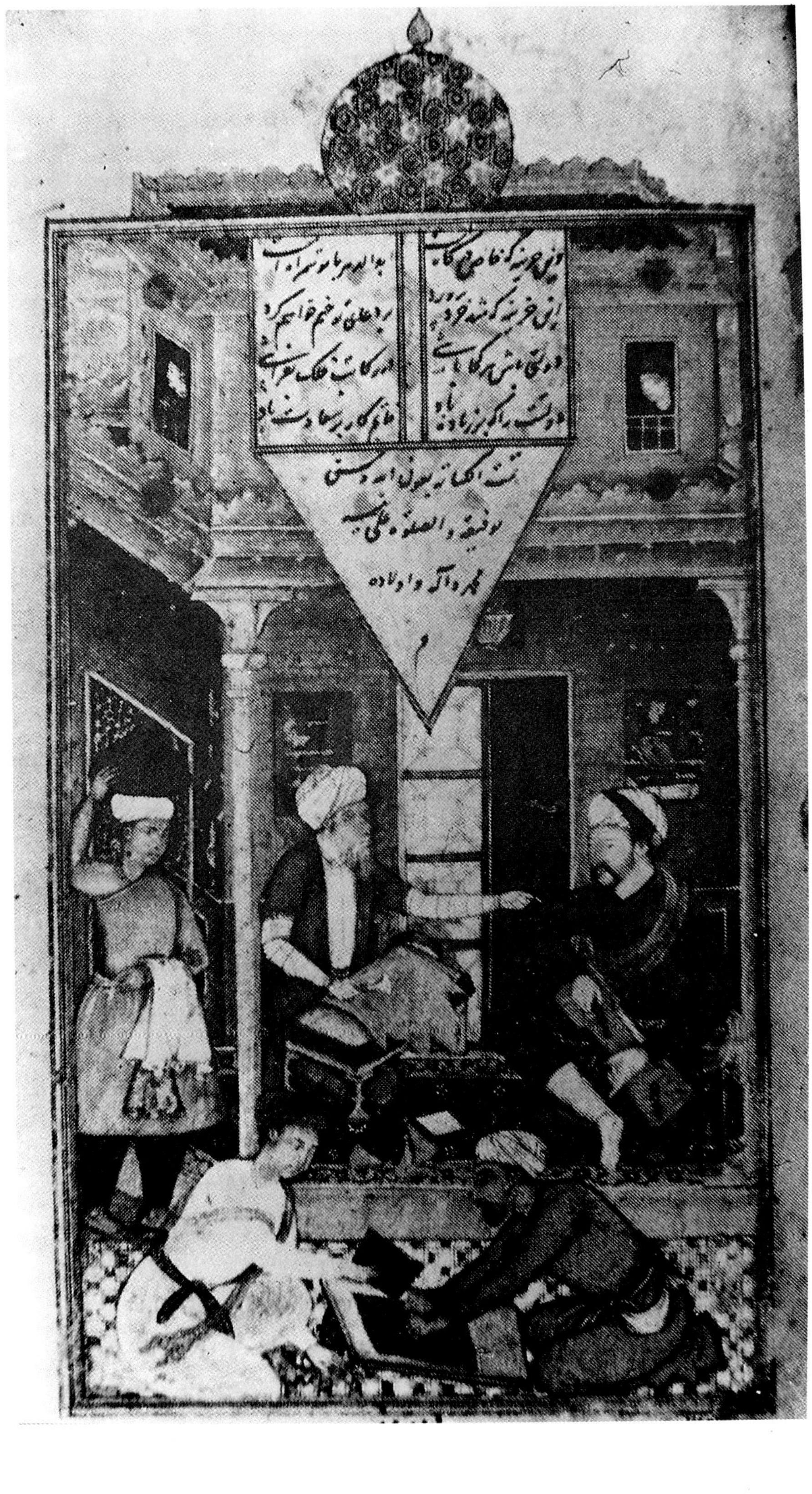

27. Bookbinder (*c.* early 18th century). Unascribed. India Office Library and Records, London.

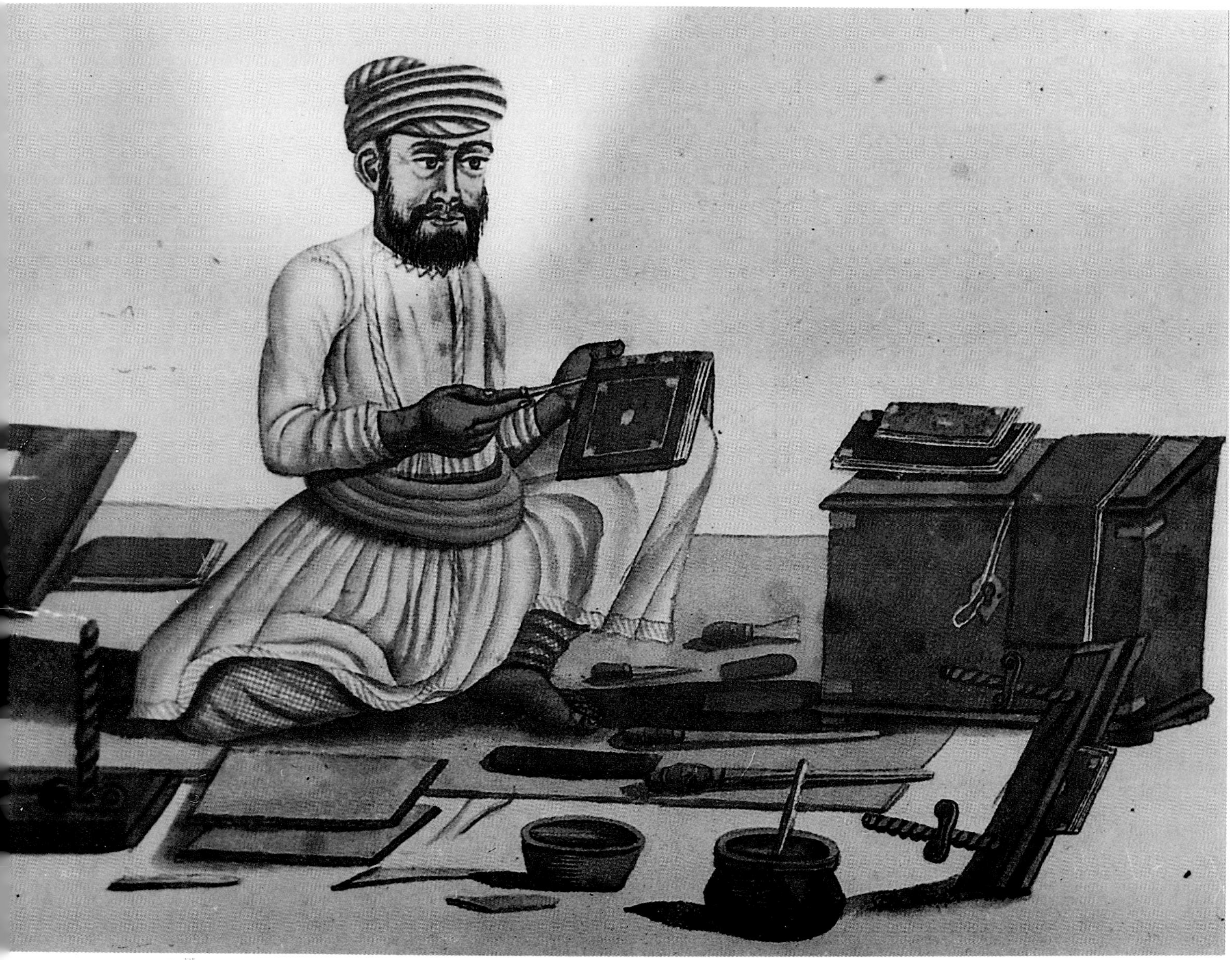

34. Cenotaph of Sawai Jai Singh II.

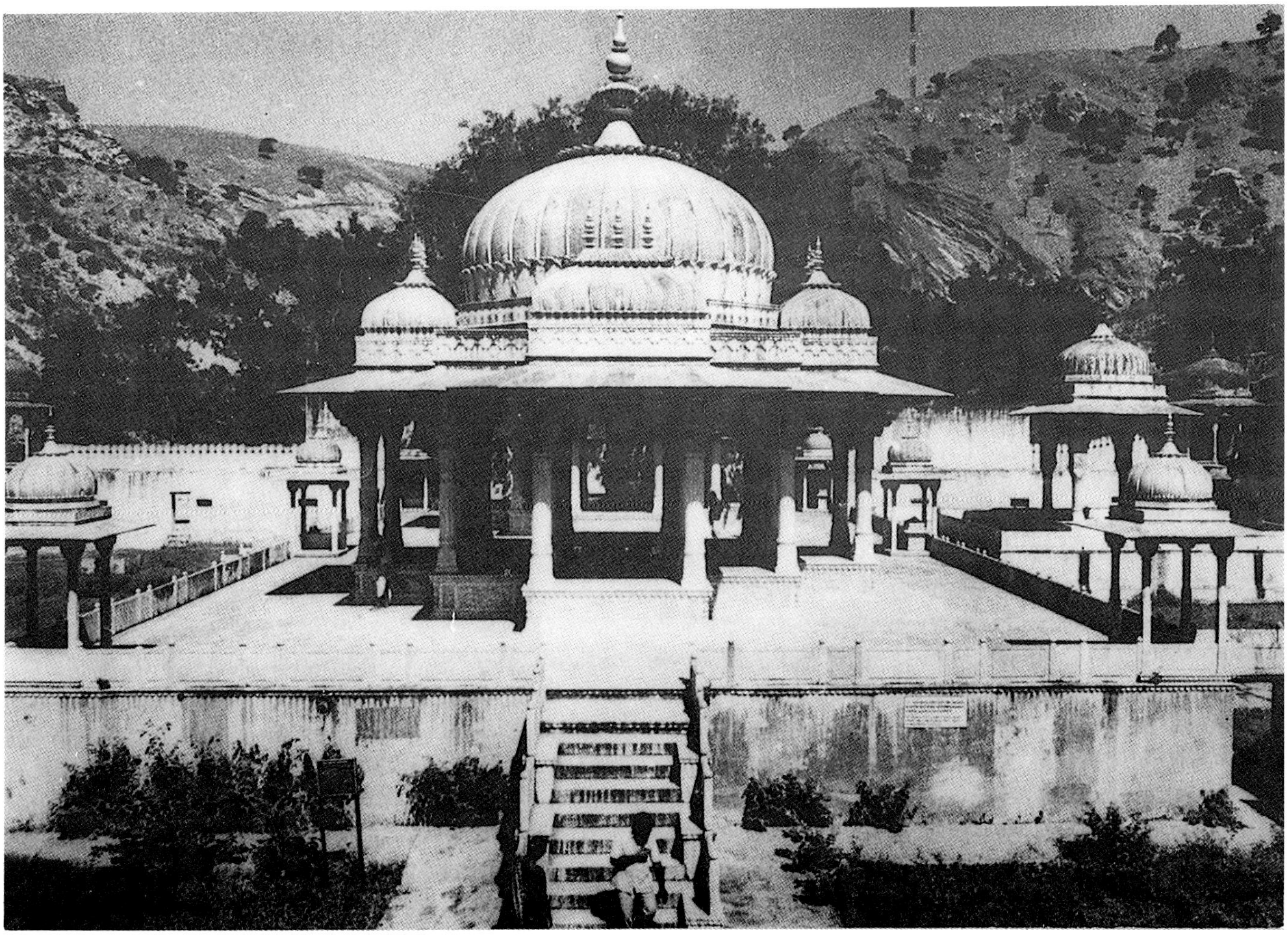

37. Plan of *Chhatri* of Sawai Jai Singh II reproduced from the *Jaipur Portfolio of Architectural Details, Vol.12.*

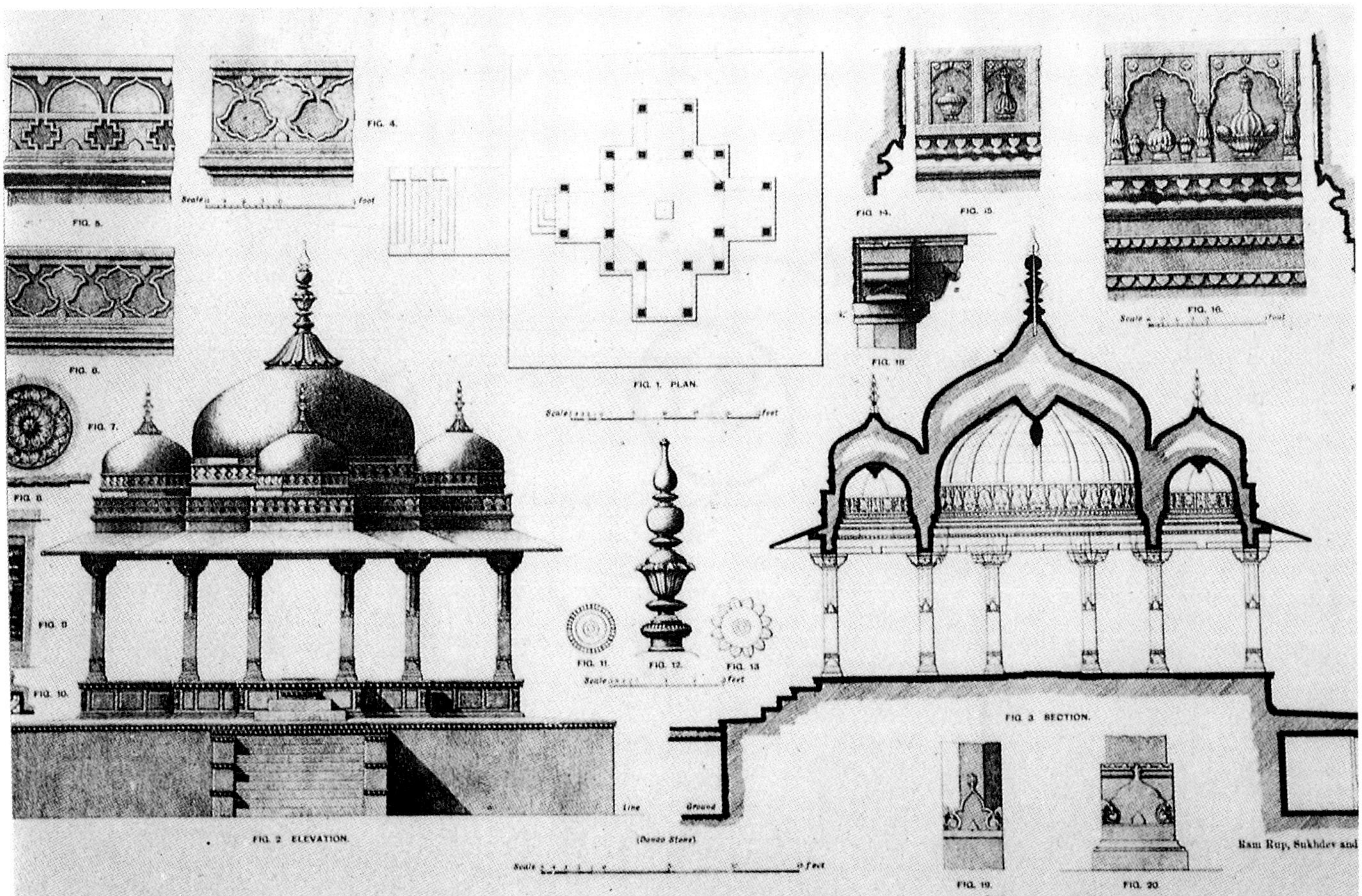

35. Copy of the order dated 1881 (courtesy State Archives, Jaipur Branch).

36. Copy of the estimate of Rambilas Usta (courtesy State Archives, Jaipur Branch).

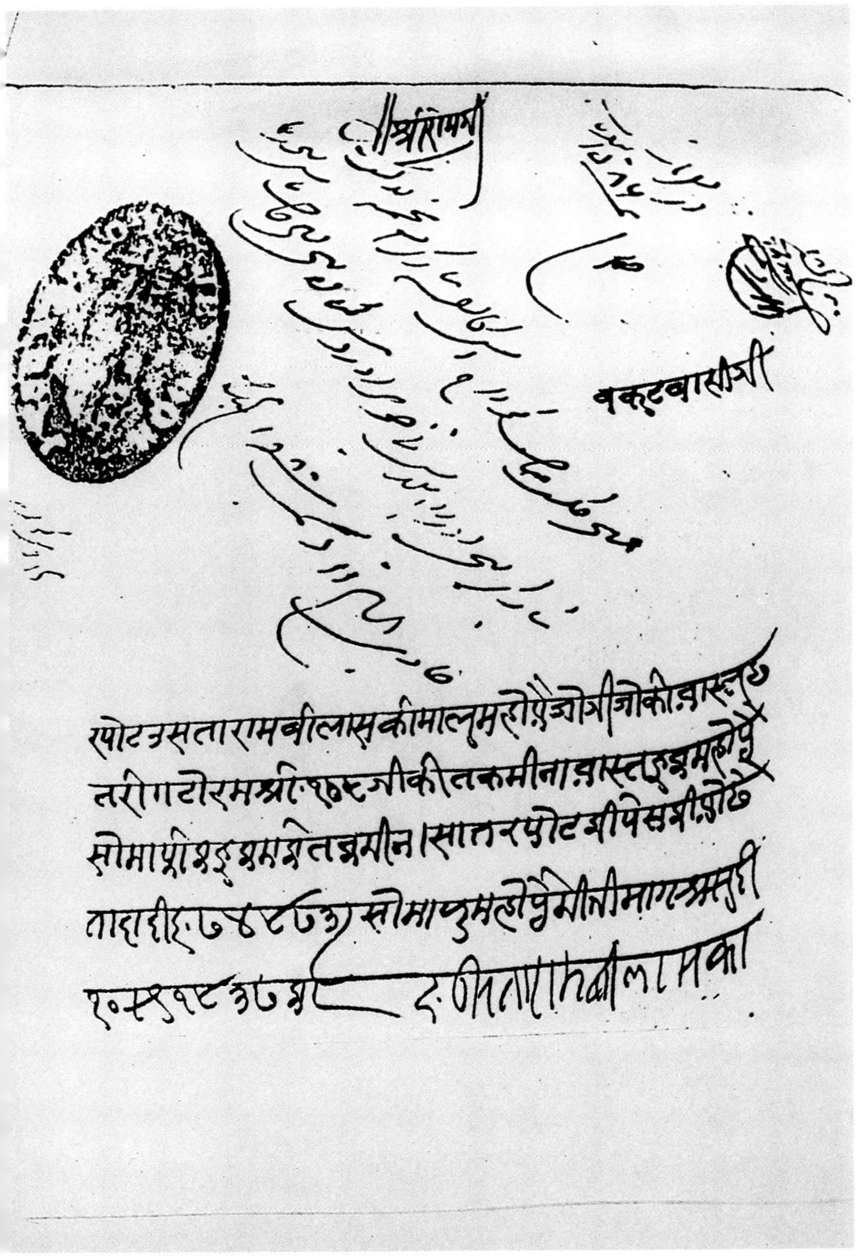

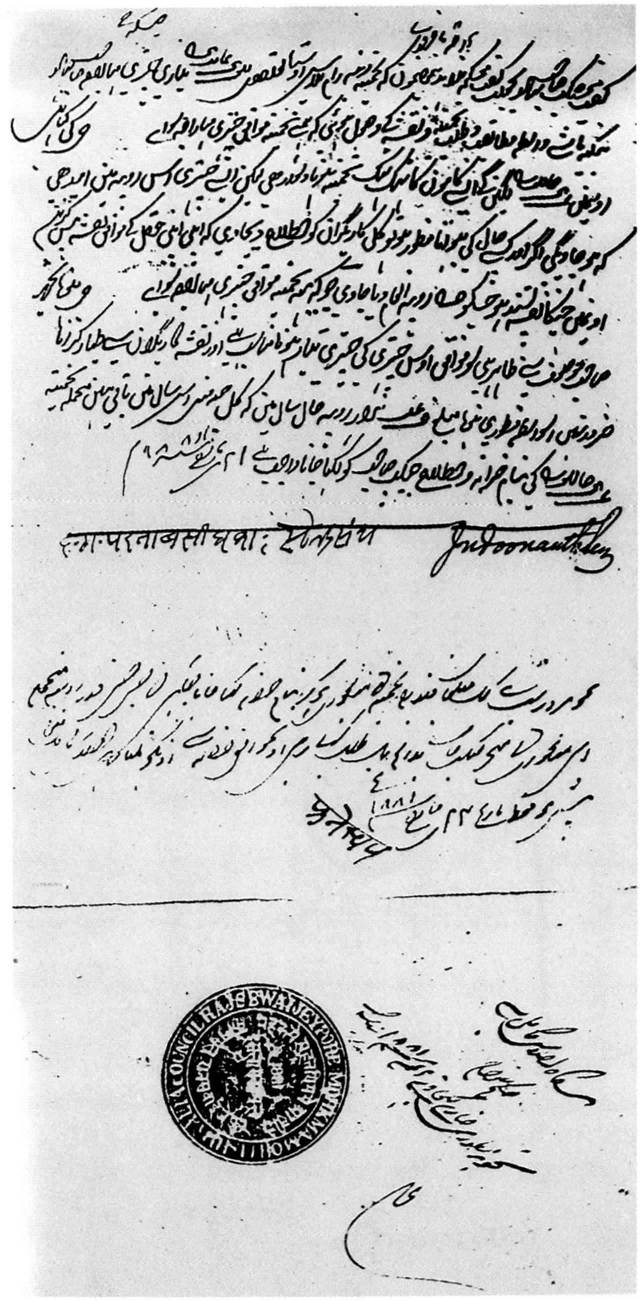

38. Detail of plate 37.

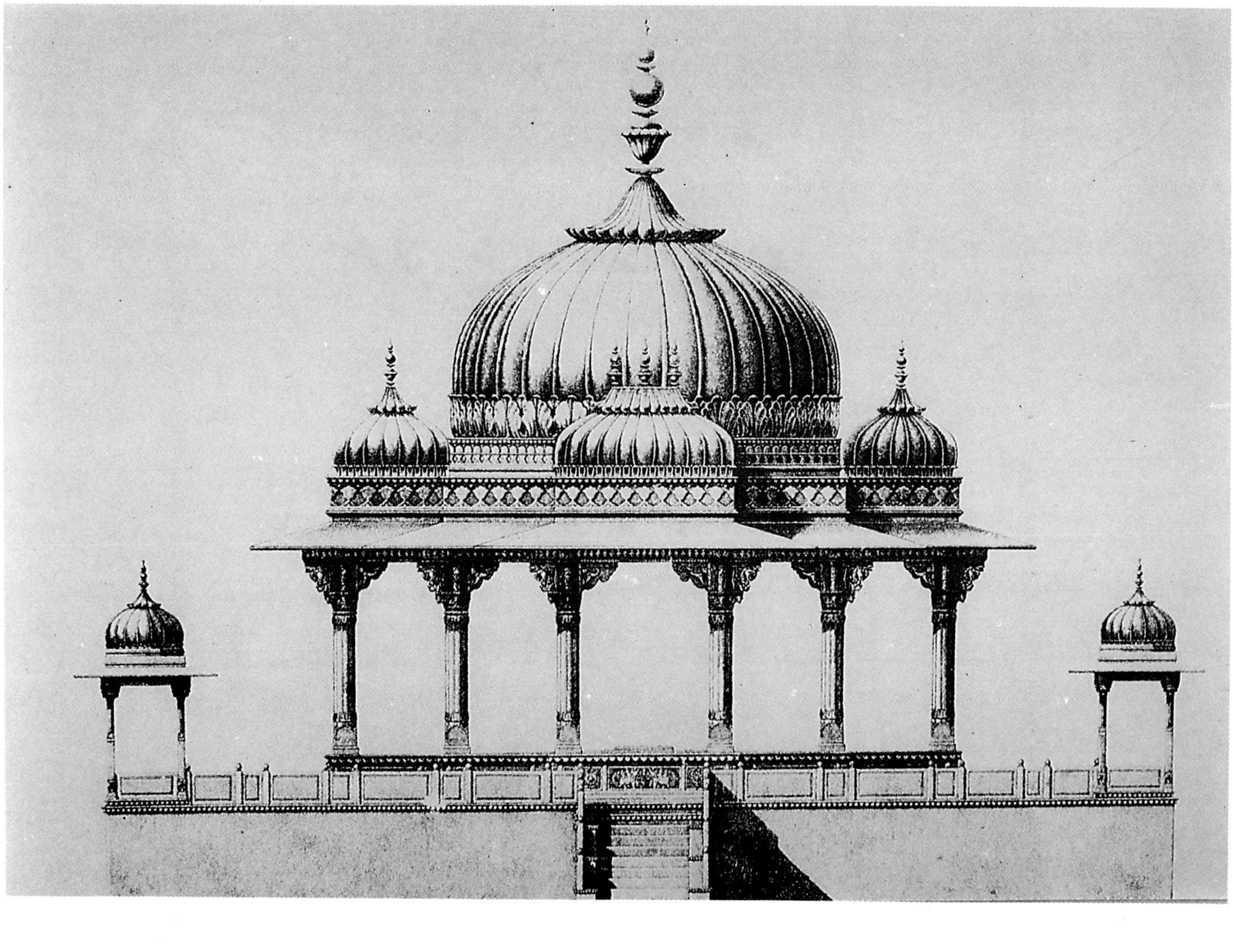

39. Panel on the eastern side of the plinth (41 x 116 cms.).

40. Panel on the southern wall of the plinth (41 x 116 cms.).

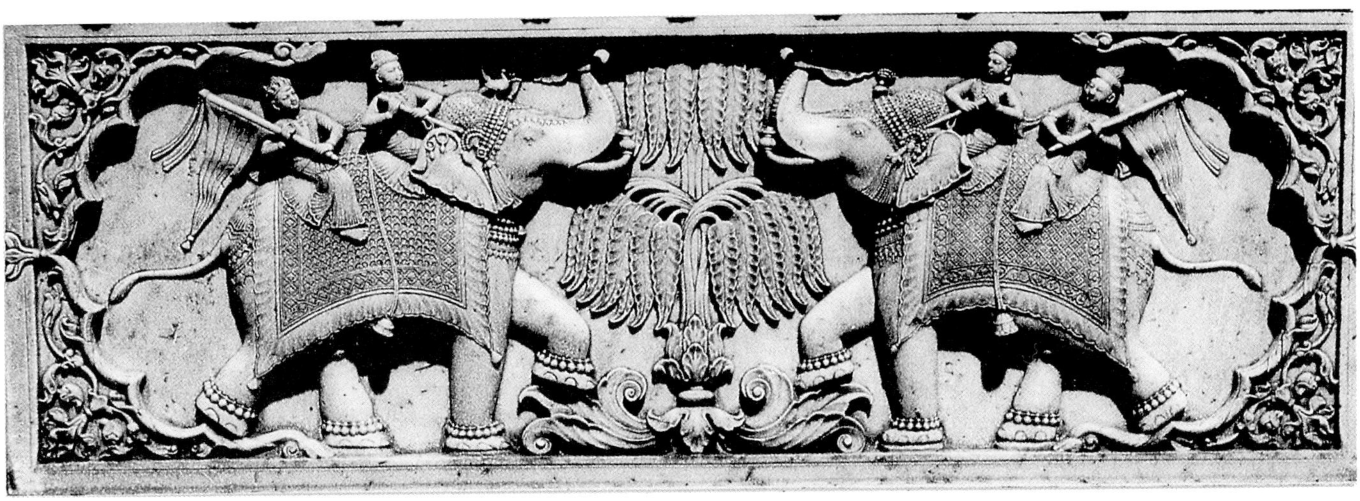

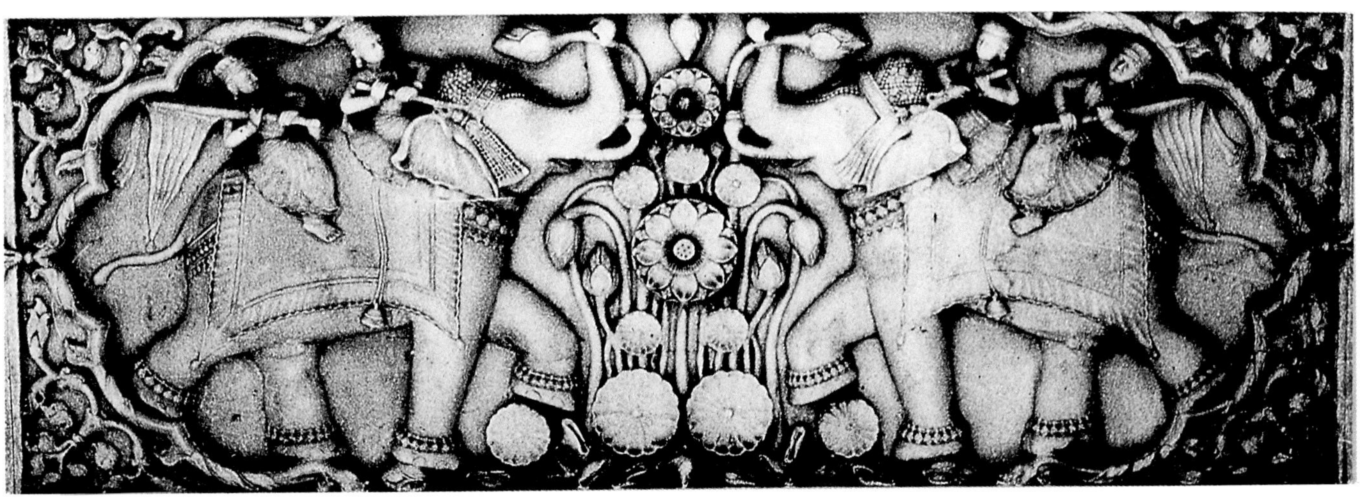

41. Tiger hunt. Another panel on the southern wall of the plinth (41 x 116 cms.).

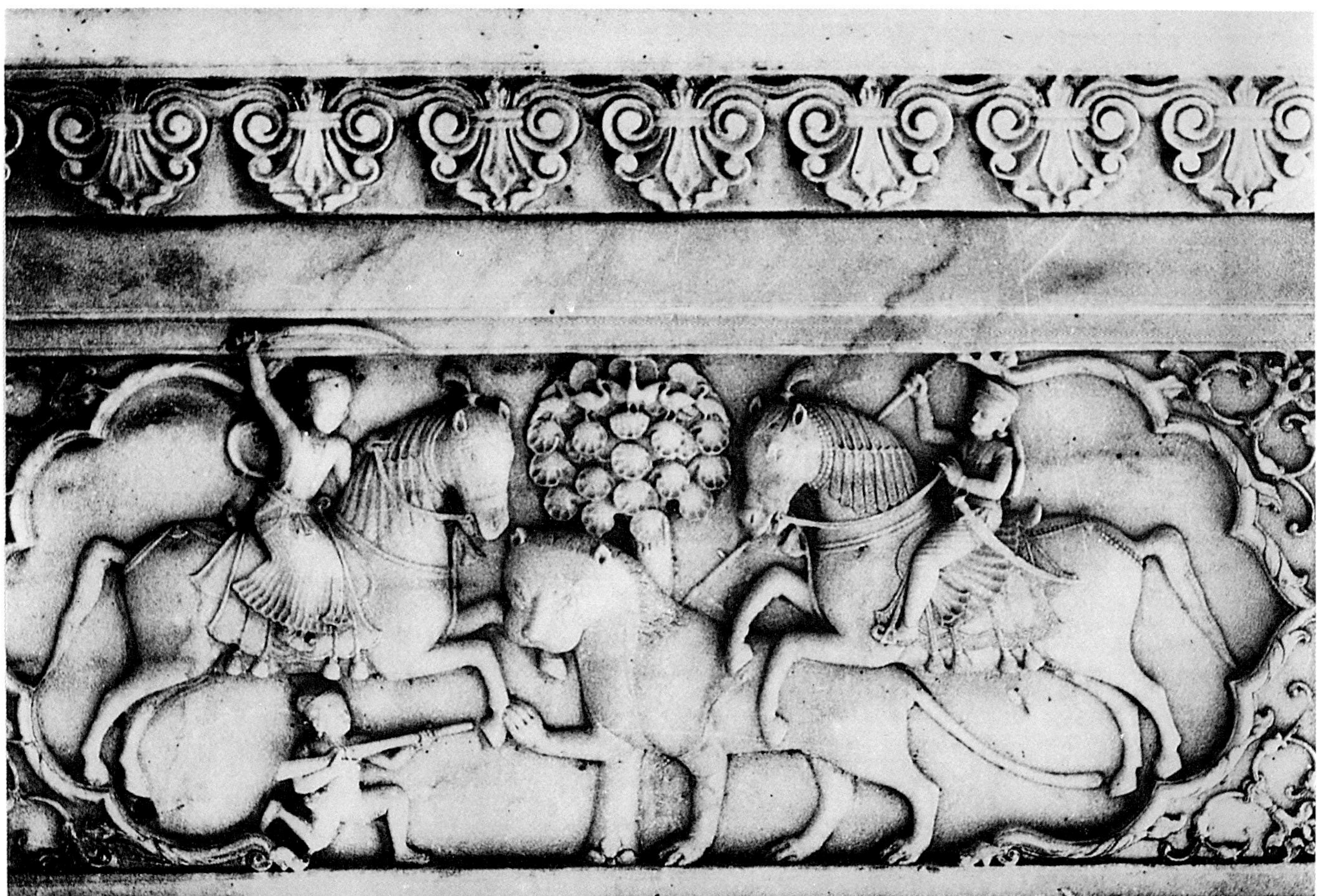

42. Game of *satmari*. Panel on the northern wall of the plinth (41 x 116 cms.).

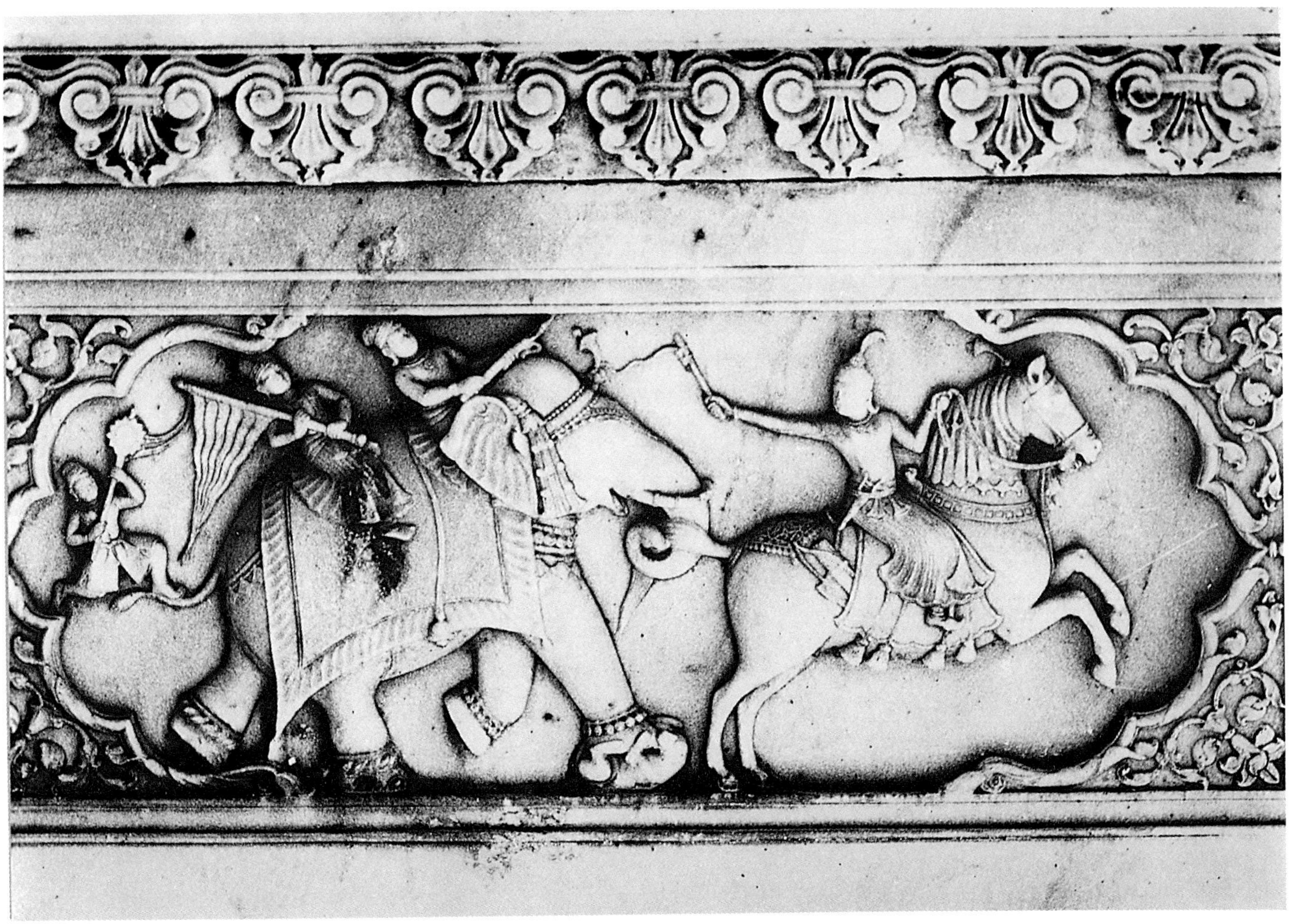

43. Ravana engaged in battle. Panel carved on the inner side of the dome.

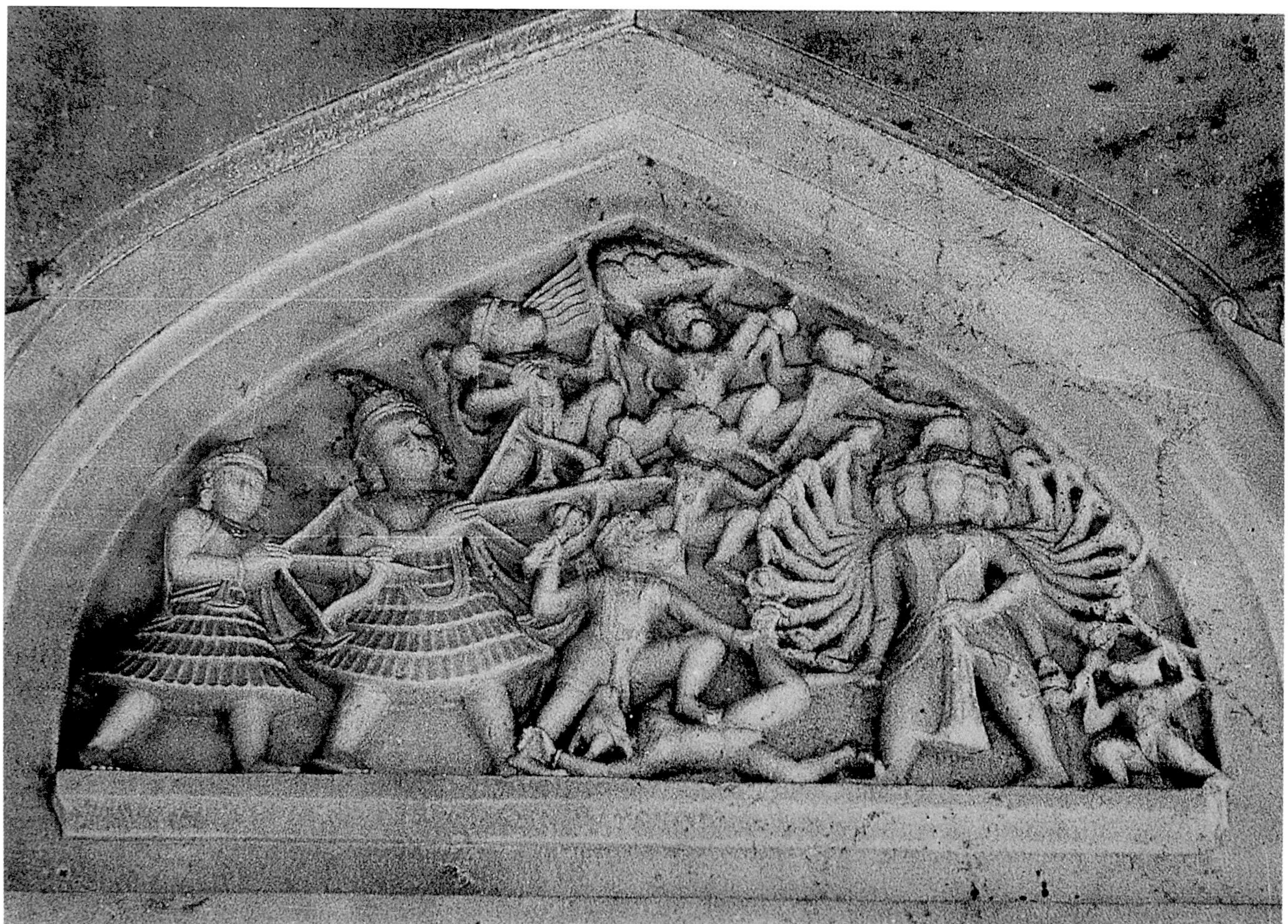

44. Family of Shiva. Panel carved on the inner side of the dome.

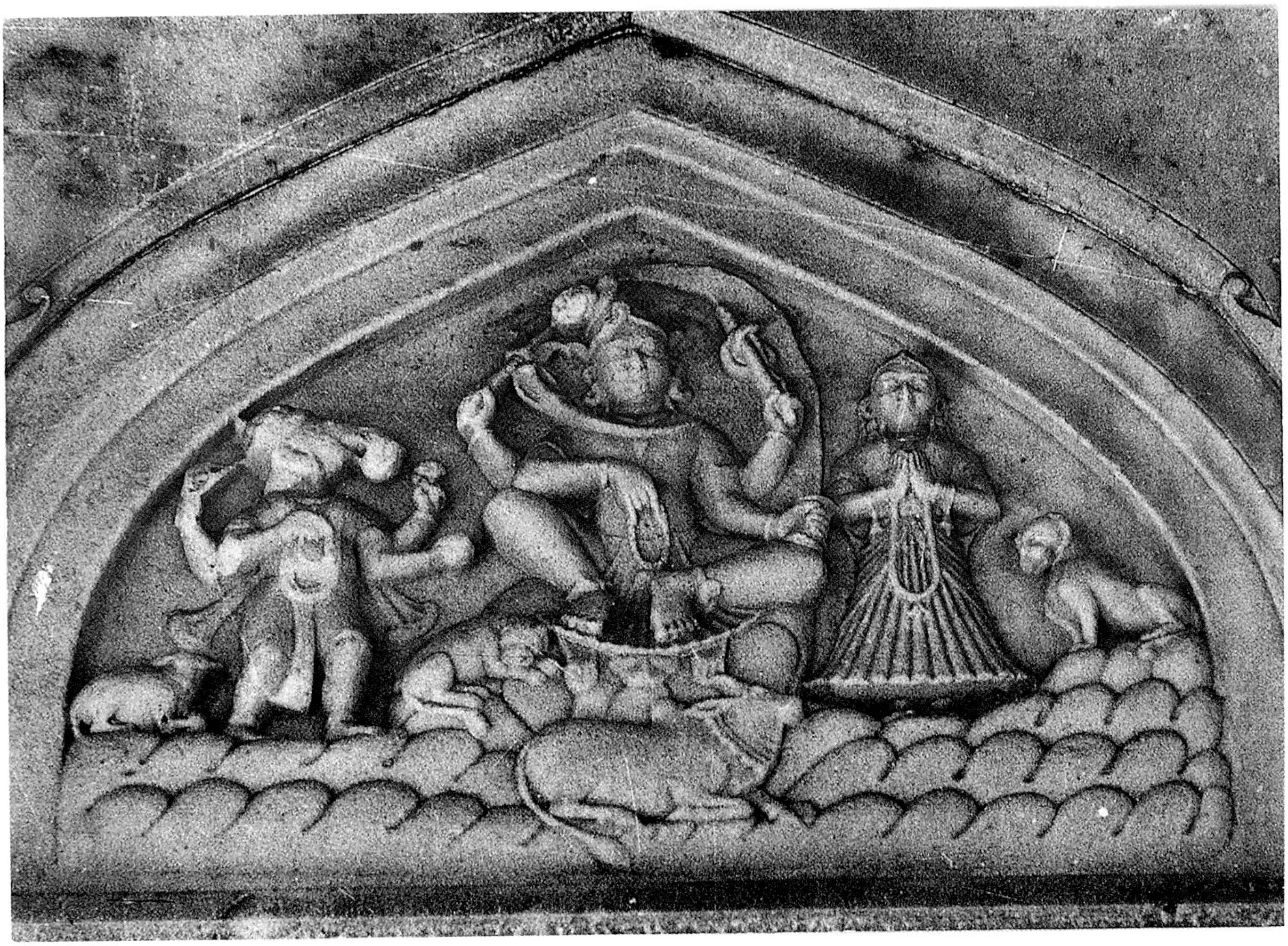

45. *Chiraharan.* Panel carved on the inner side of the dome.

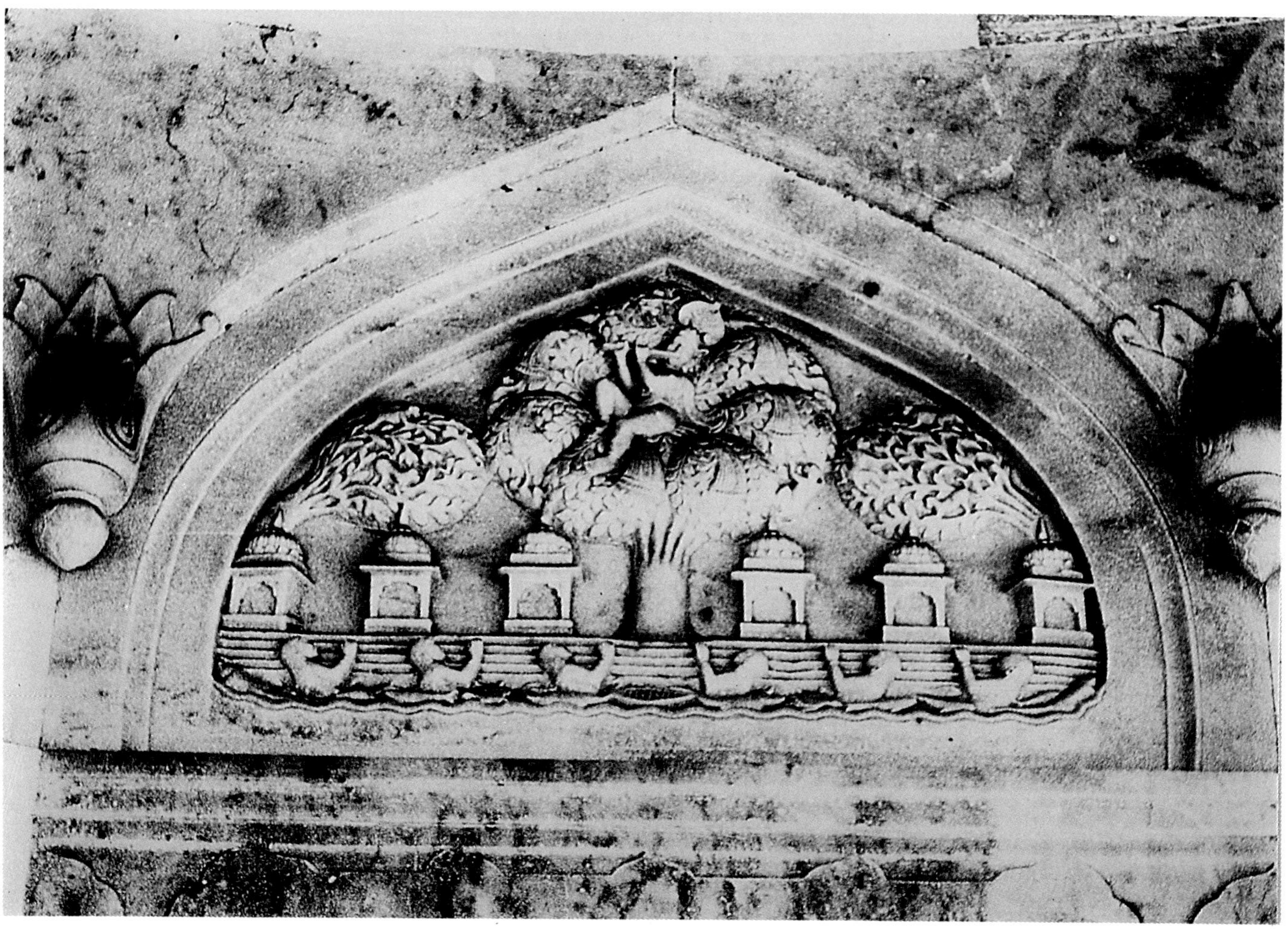

46. Krishna playing flute. Panel carved on the inner side of the dome.

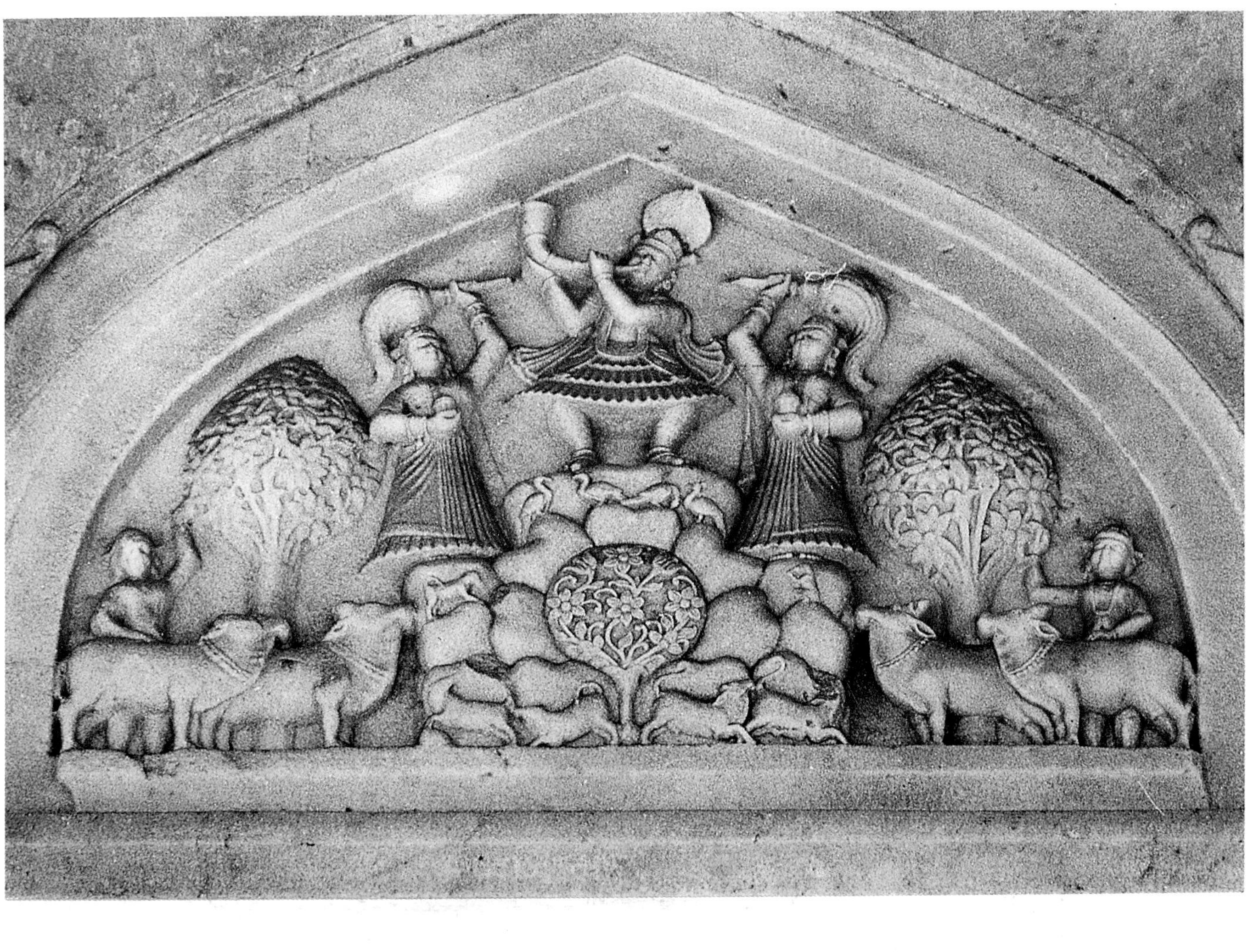

47. Krishna and Balrama entering the palace. Panel carved on the inner side of the dome.

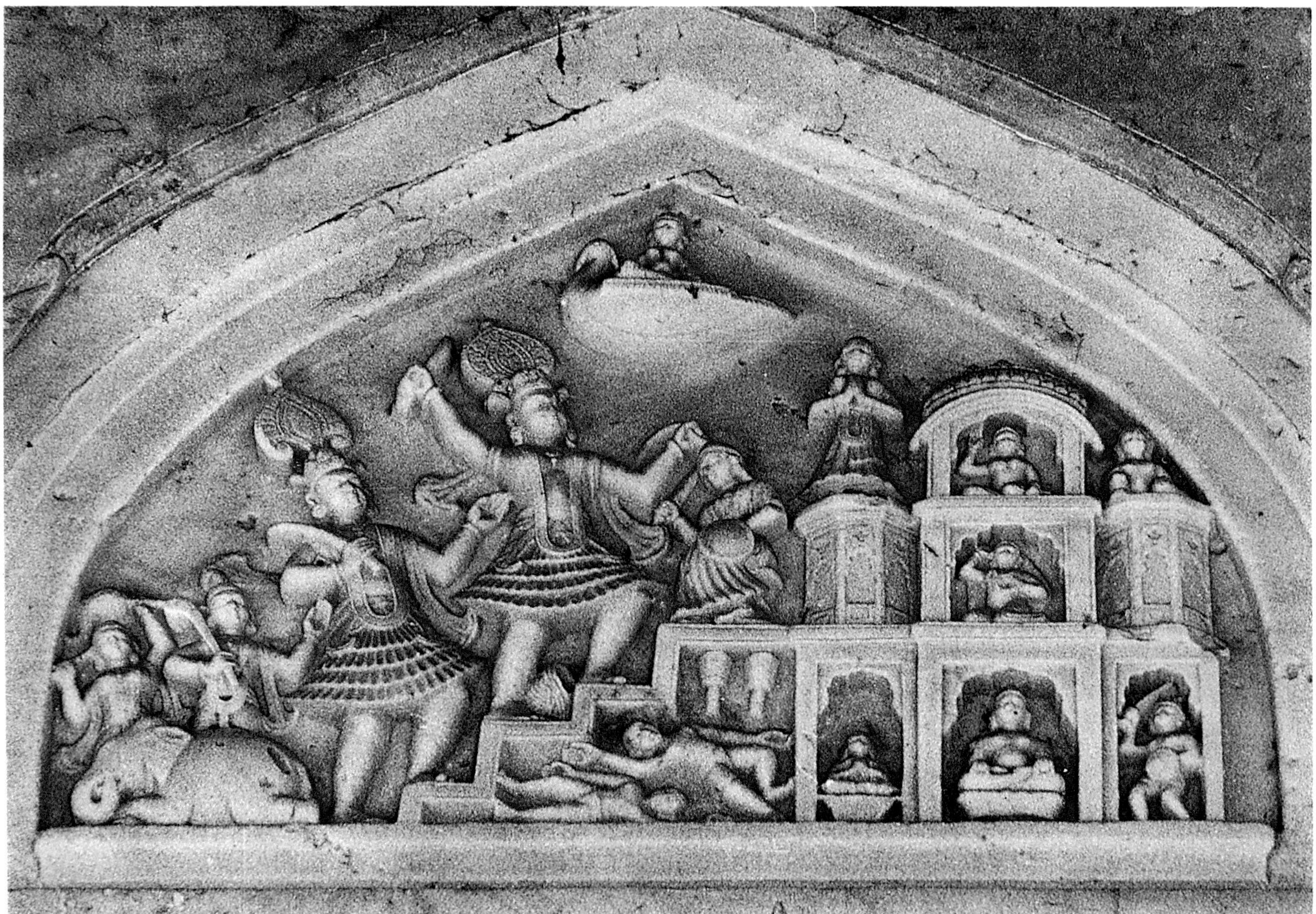

48. *Mahisasurmardini.* Panel carved on the inner side of the dome.

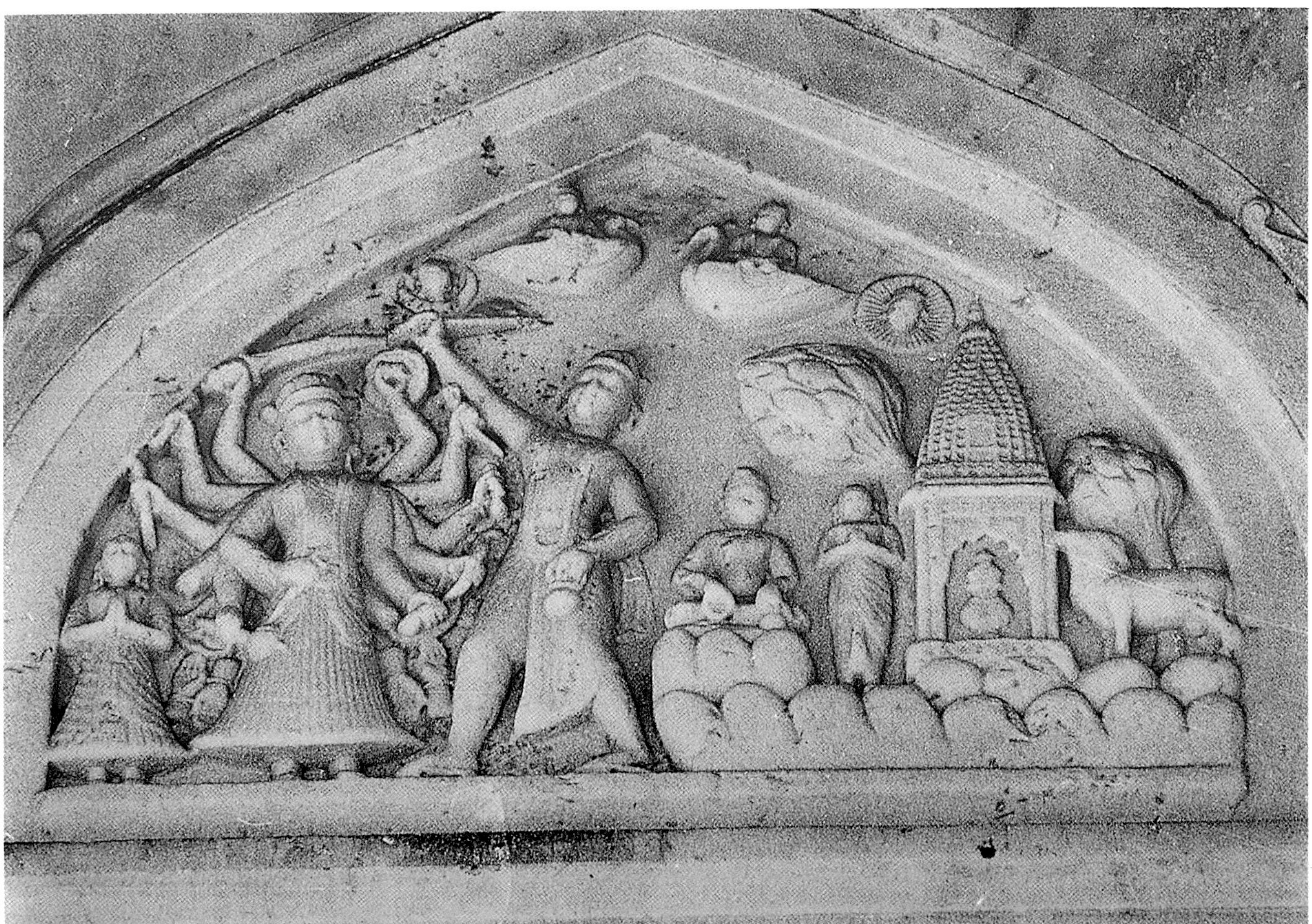

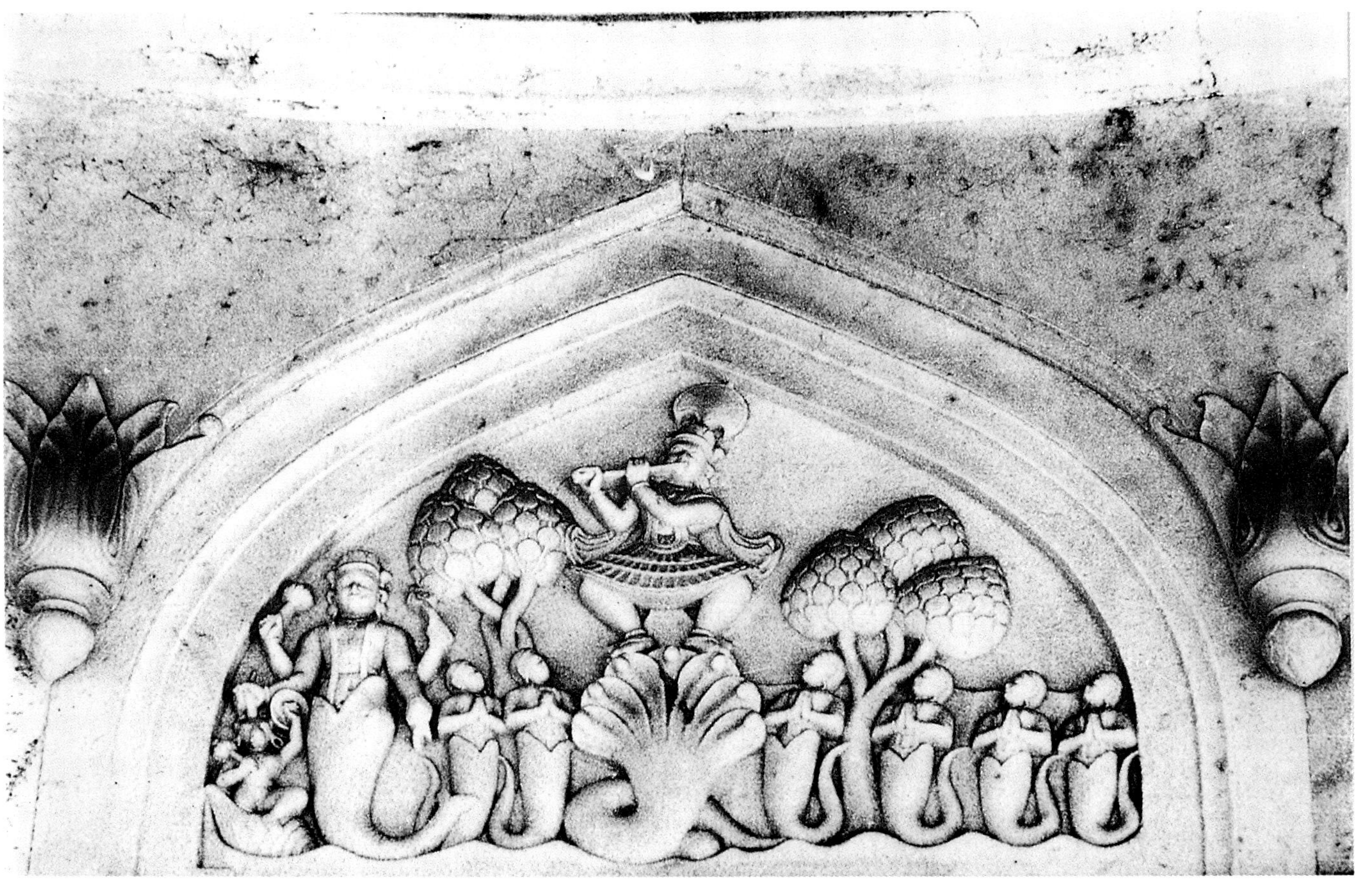

49. *Kaliyadaman*. Panel carved on the inner side of the dome.

50. Return of the army. Panel carved on the inner side of the dome.

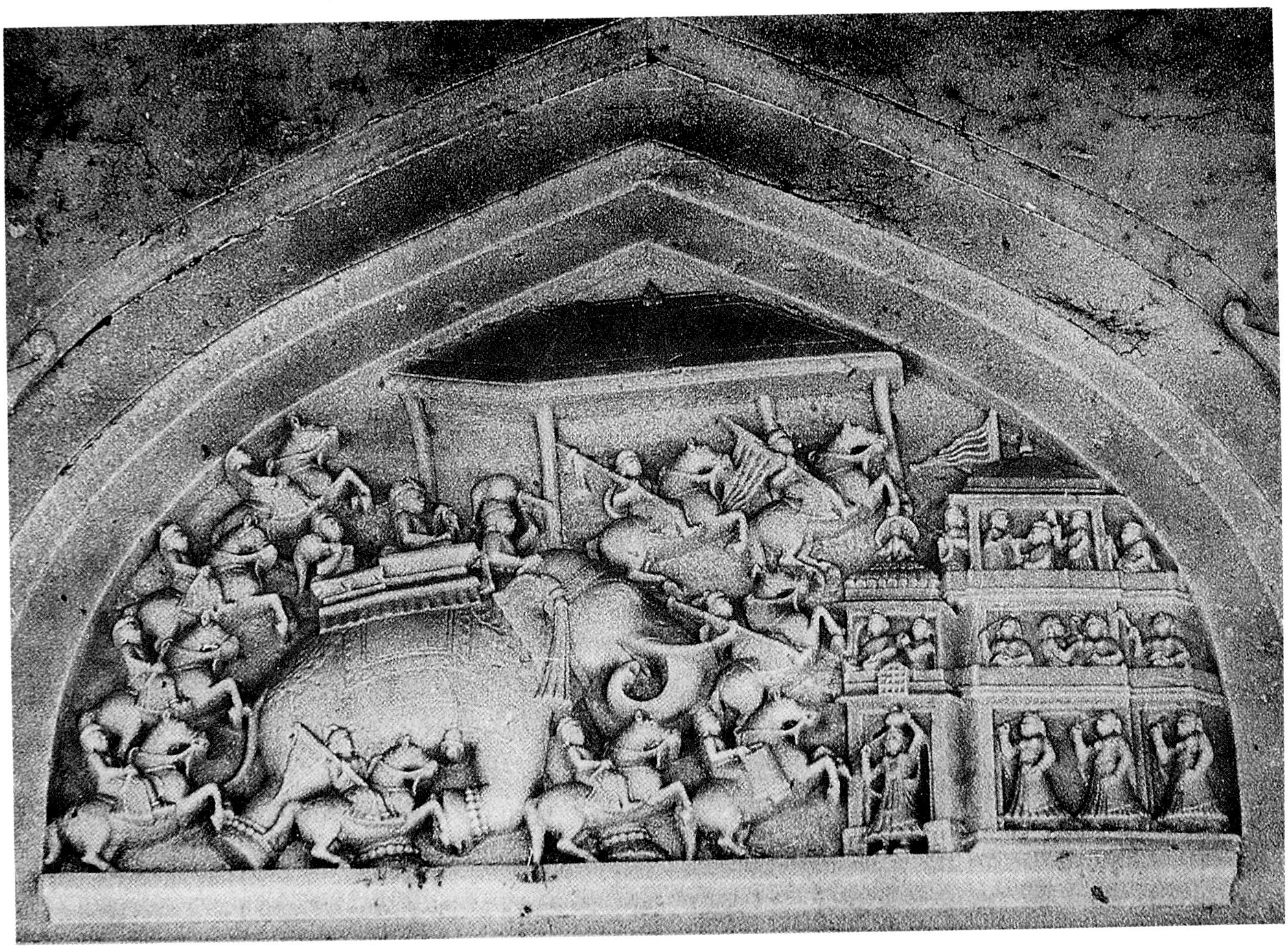

51. *Samudramanthan.* Panel carved on the inner side of the dome.

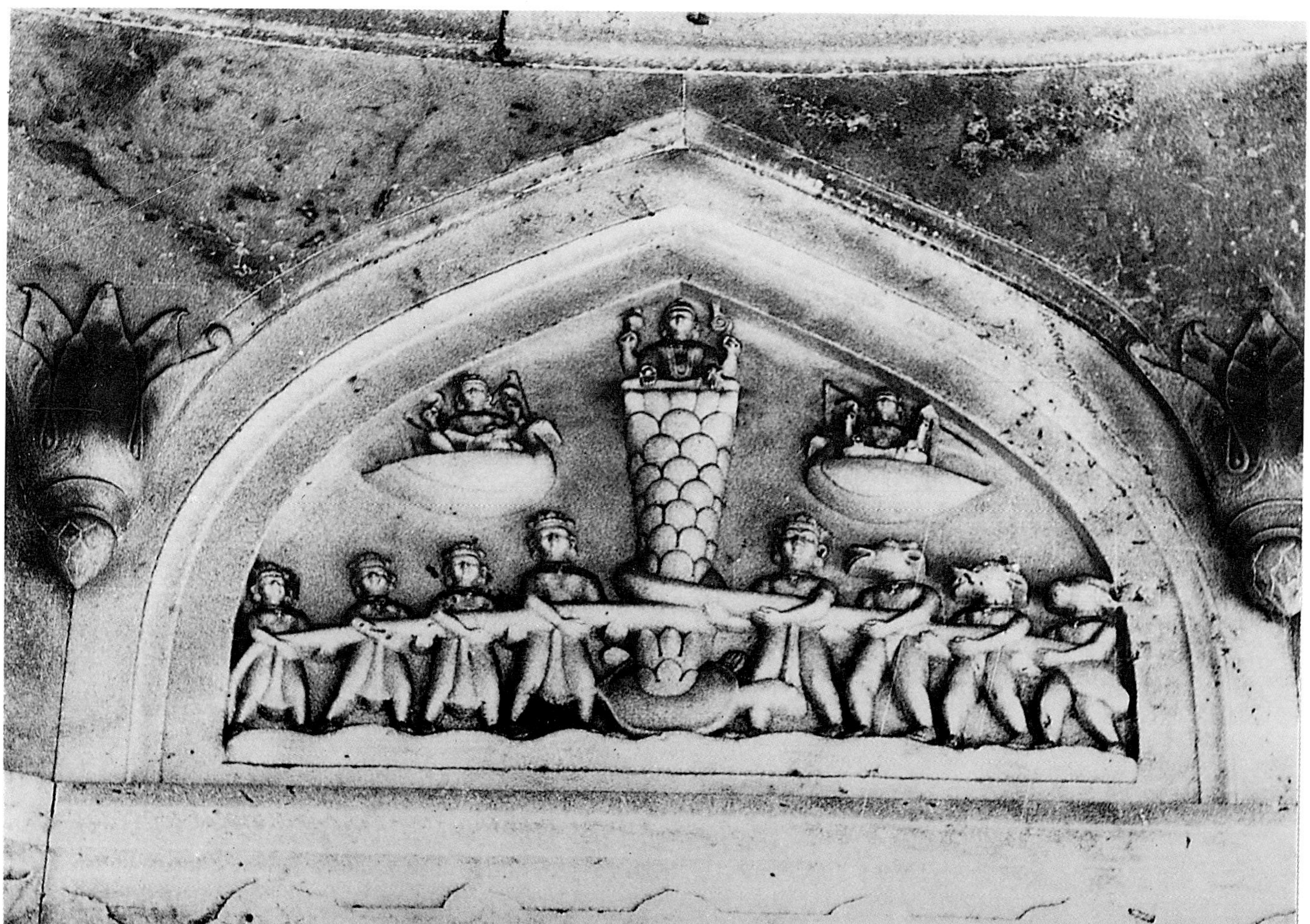

52. Female dancer. Carved on the pillar of the main *chhatri* (56 cms. in height).

53. Female musician. Carved on the pillar of the main *chhatri* (56 cms.).

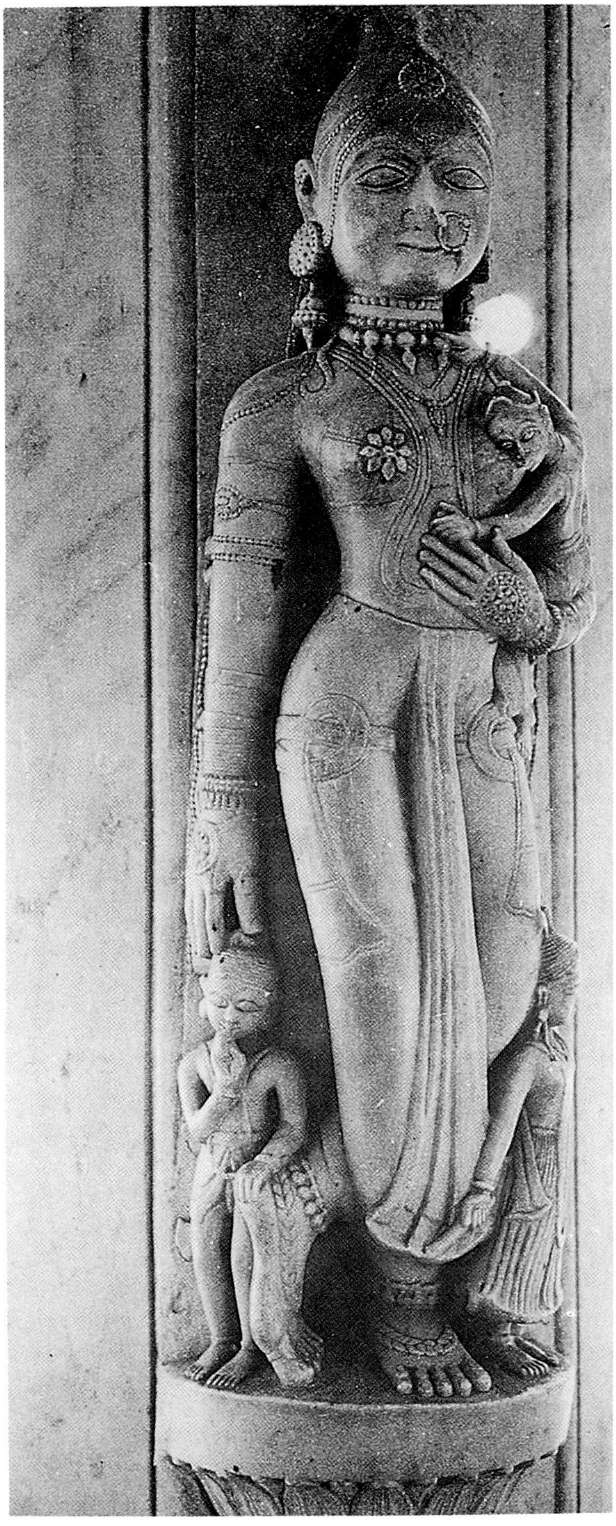

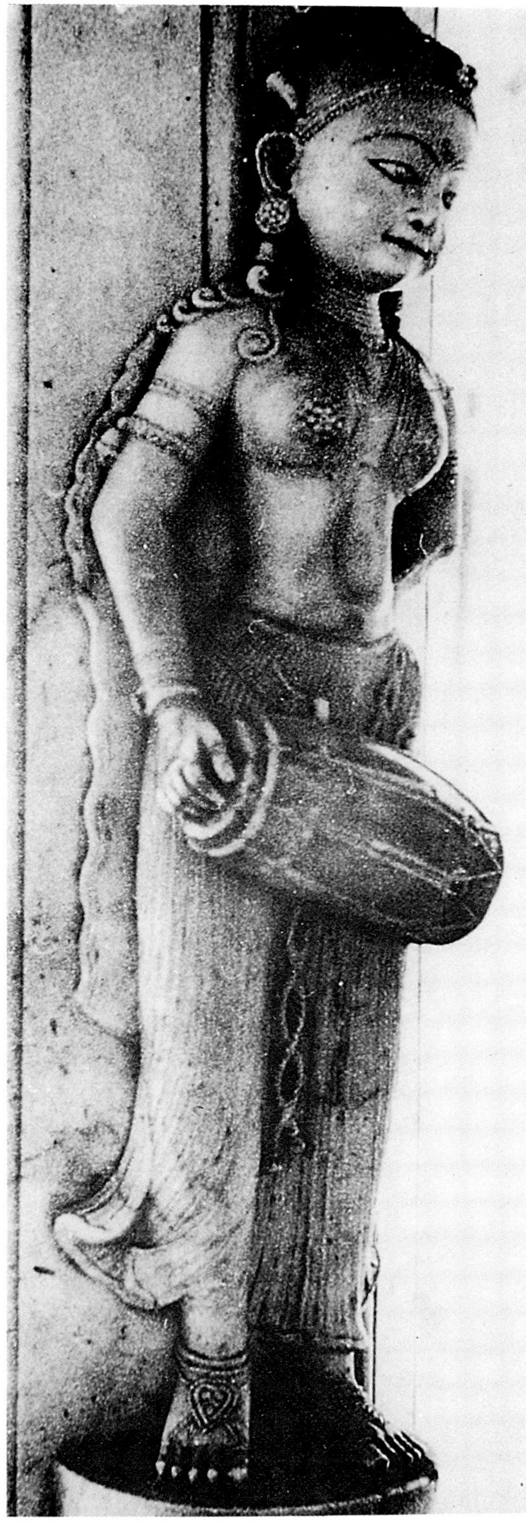

54. Female musician. Carved on the pillar of the main *chhatri* (56 cms.).

55. Female dancer. Carved on the pillar of the main *chhatri* (56 cms.).

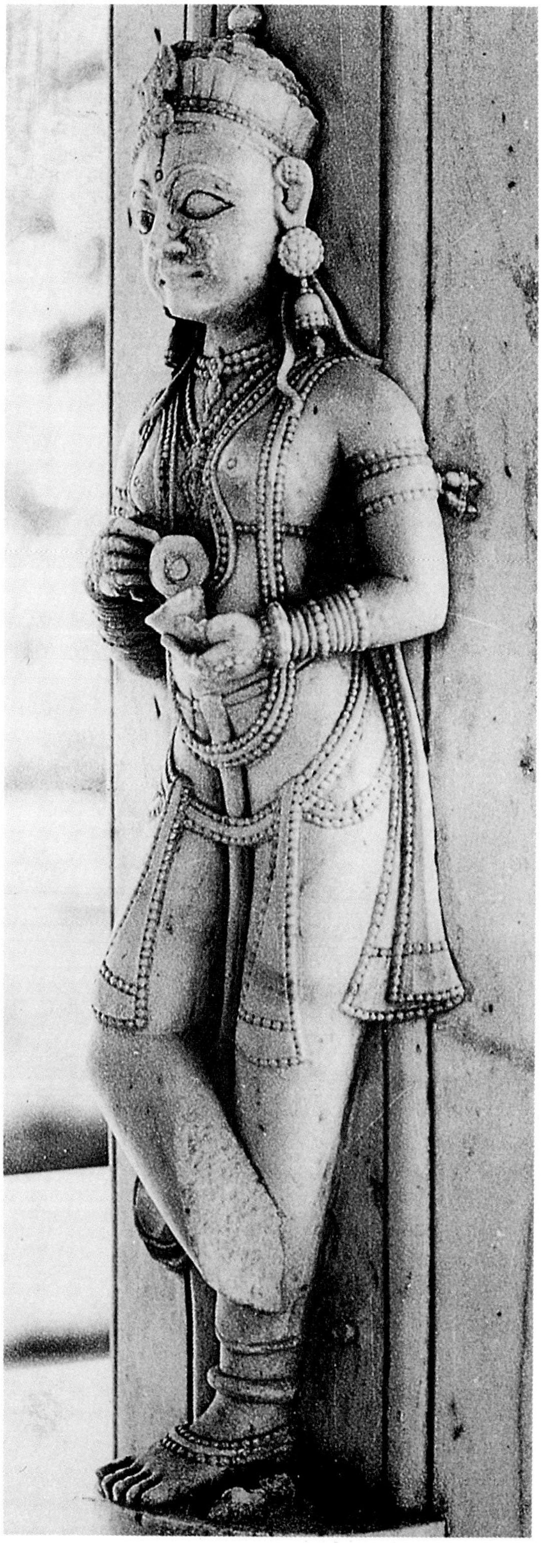

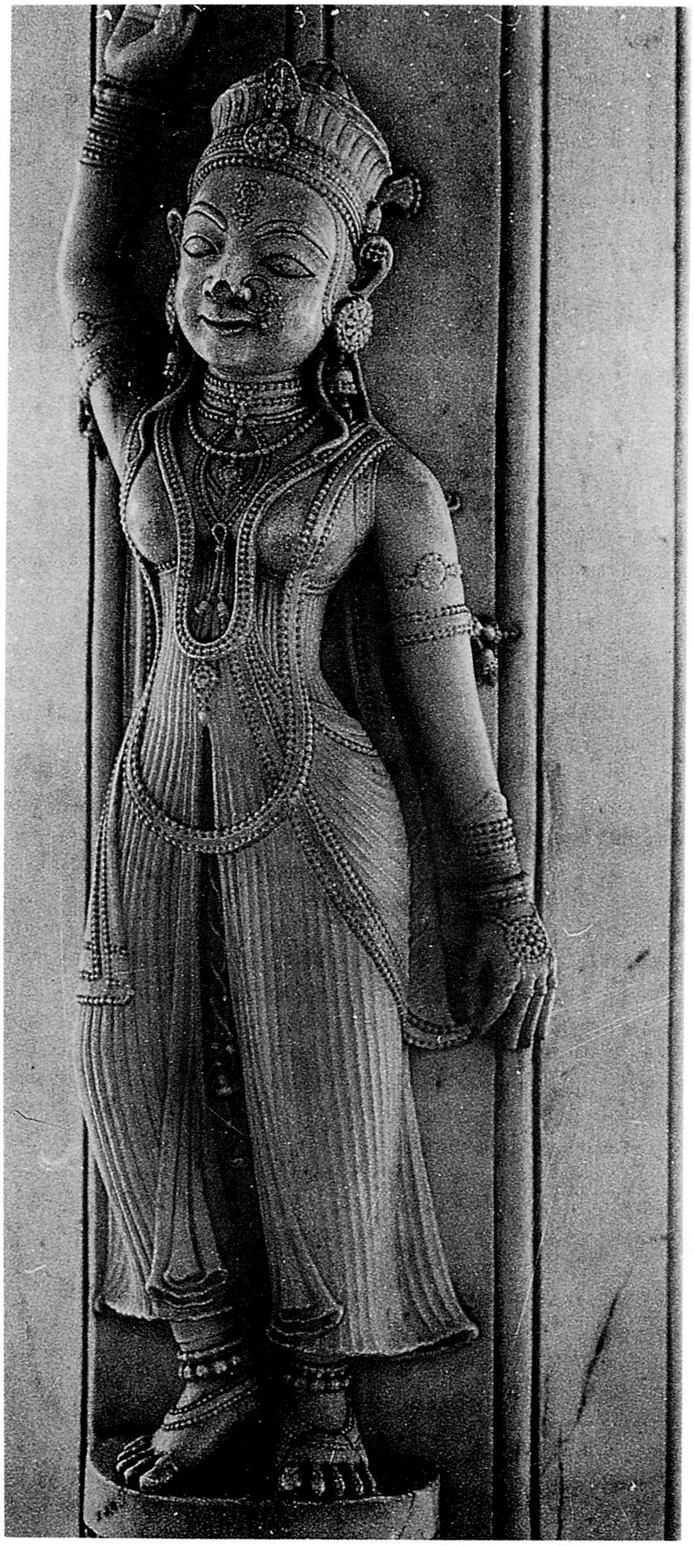

56. Female musician. Carved on the pillar of the main *chhatri* (56 cms.).

57. Female musician. Carved on the pillar of the main *chhatri* (56 cms.).

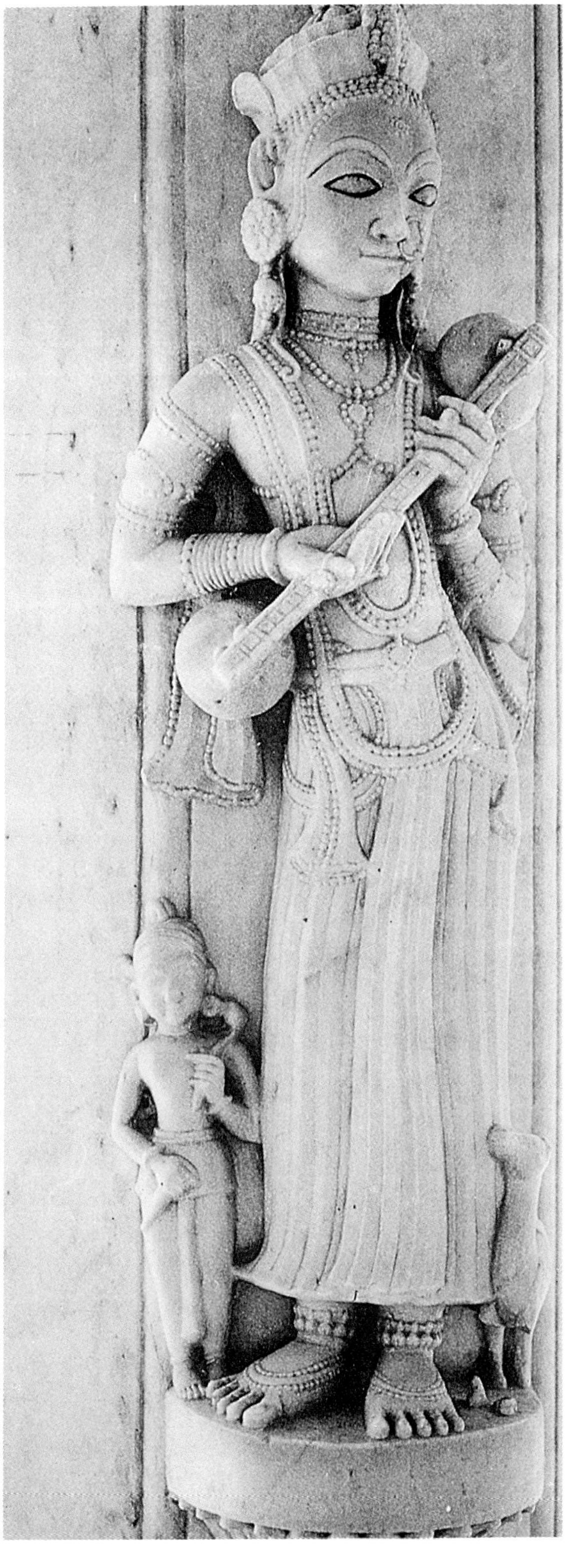

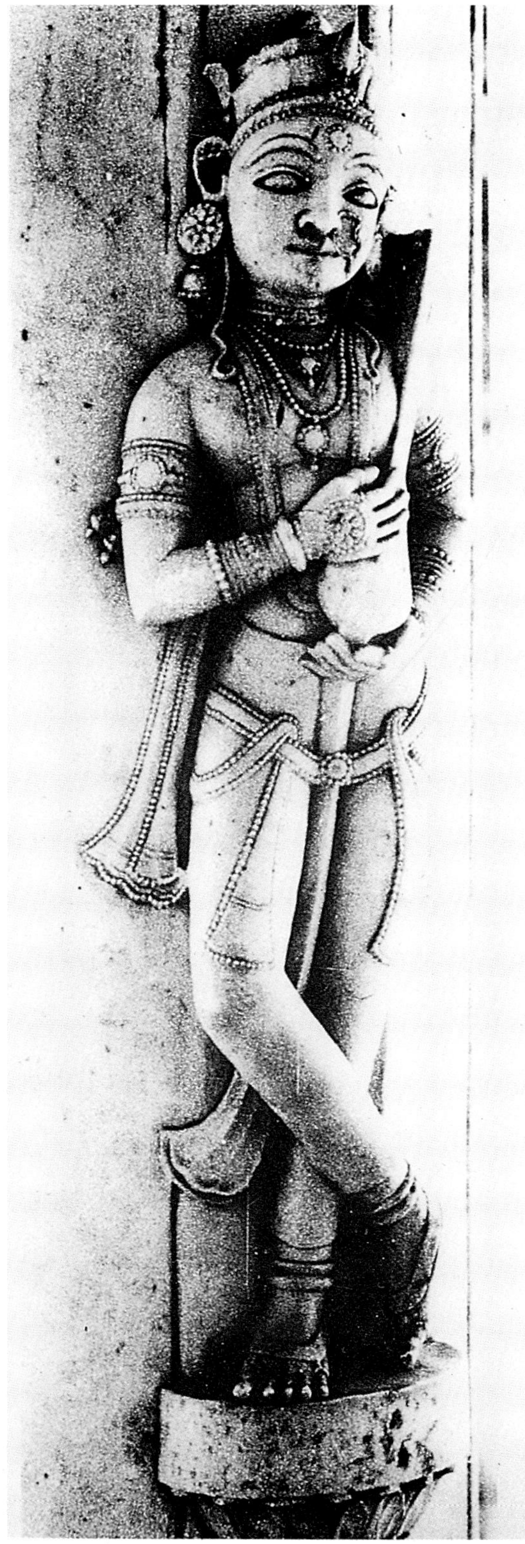

58. *Ragini Kakubha.* Carved at the base of the pillar (28 x 35 cms.).

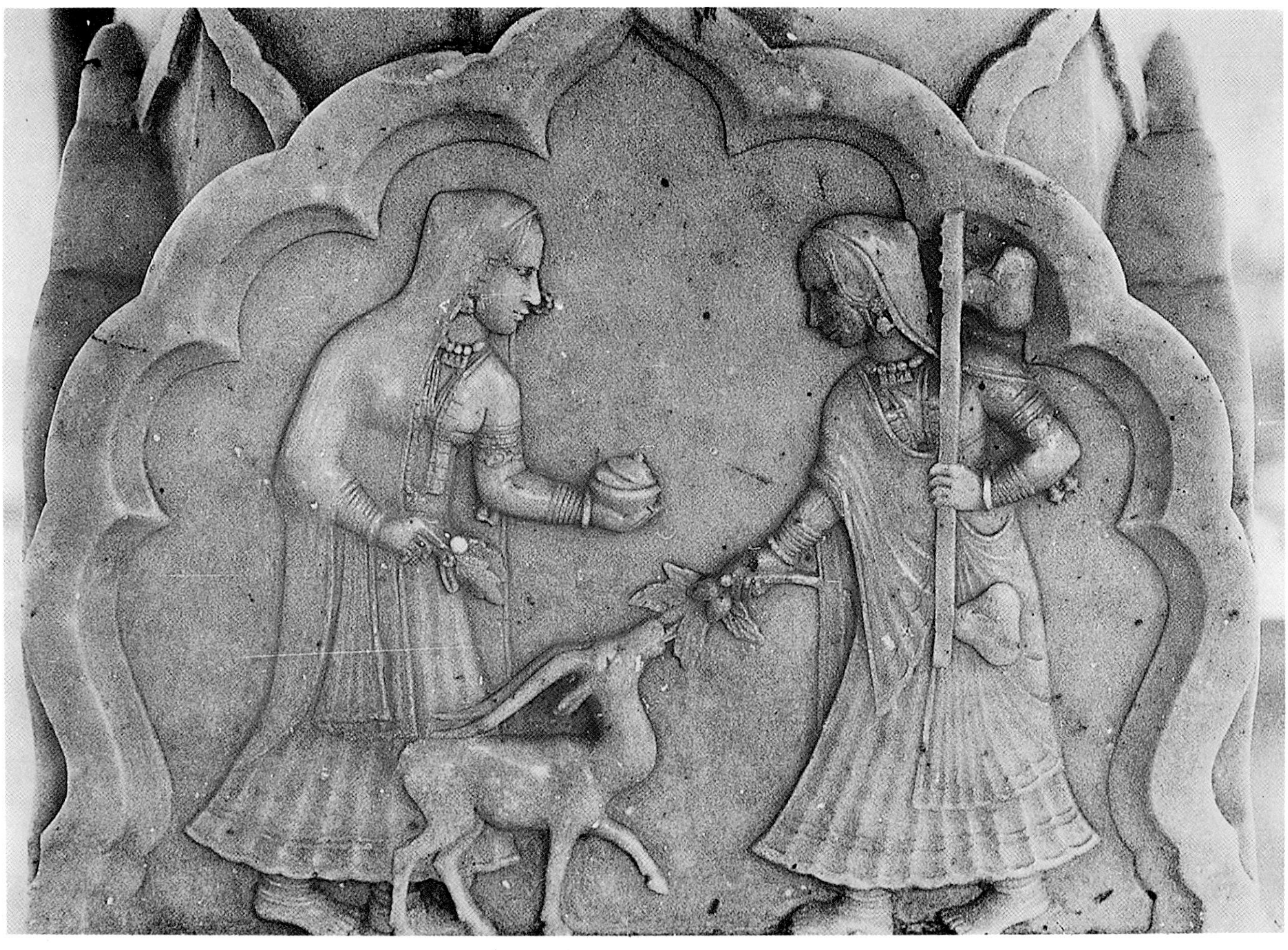

59. *Ragini Todi.* Carved at the base of the pillar (28 x 35 cms.).

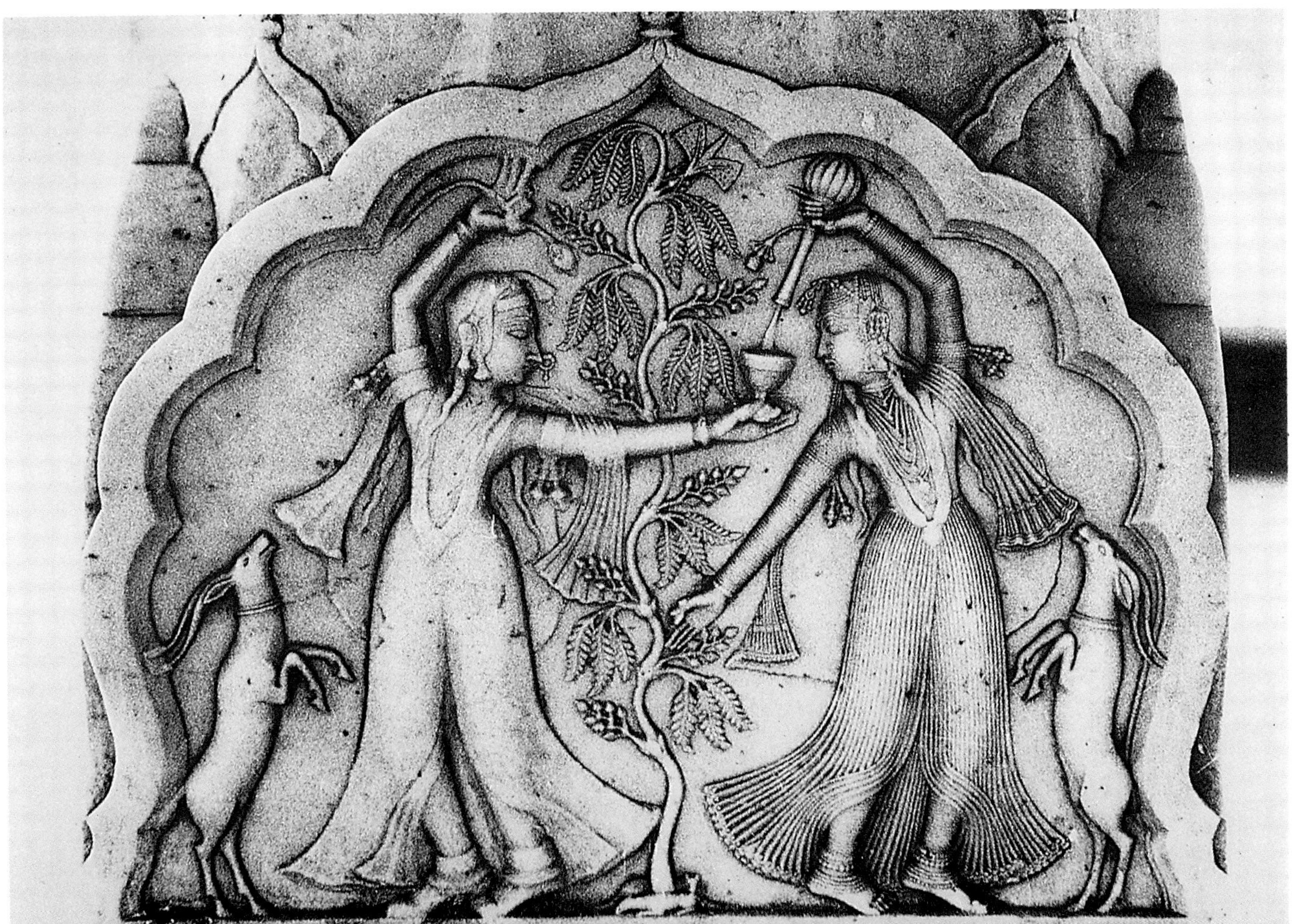

60. *Raga Vasant.* Carved at the base of the pillar (28 x 35 cms.).

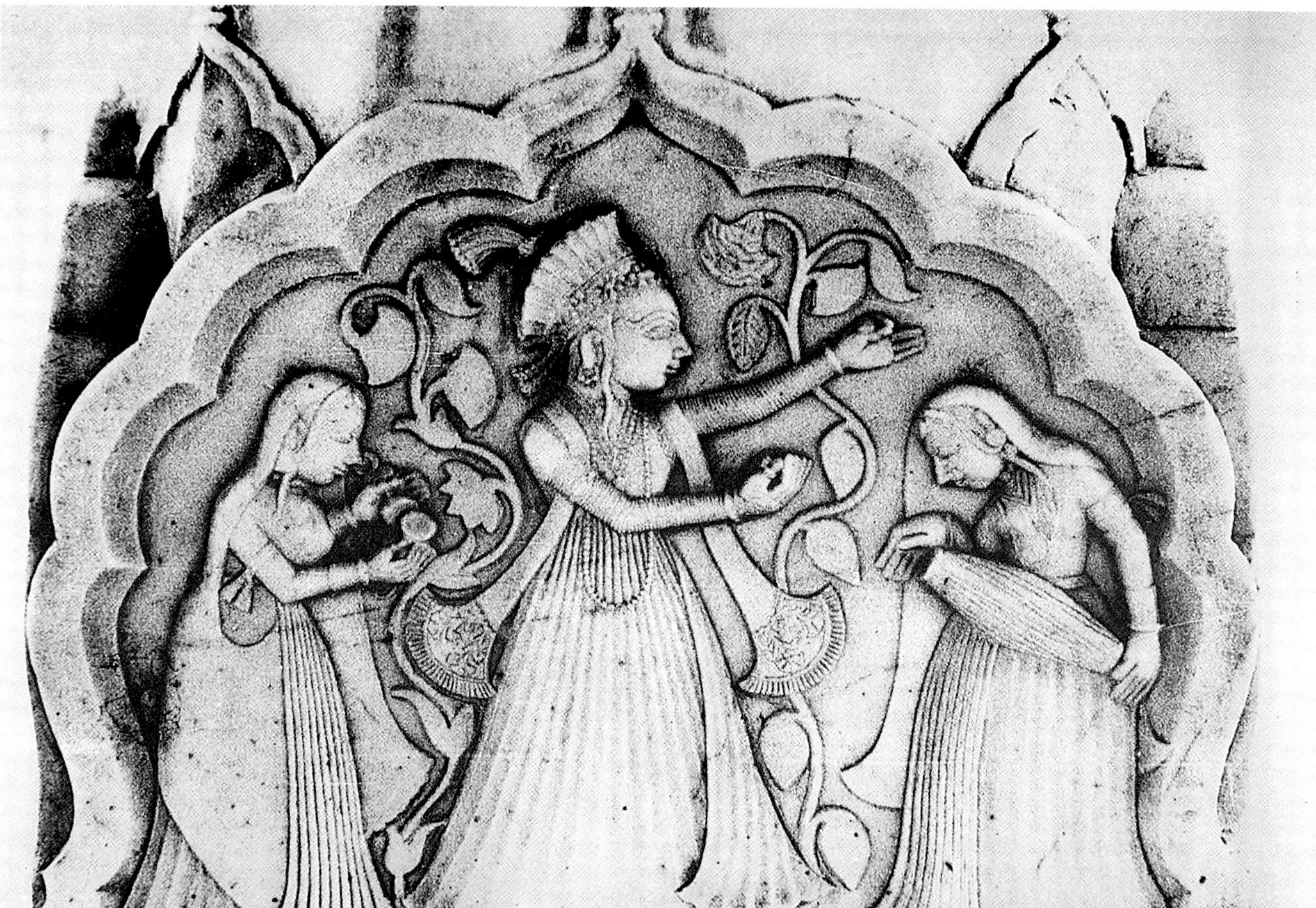

61. Princess and a musician. Carved at the base of a pillar.

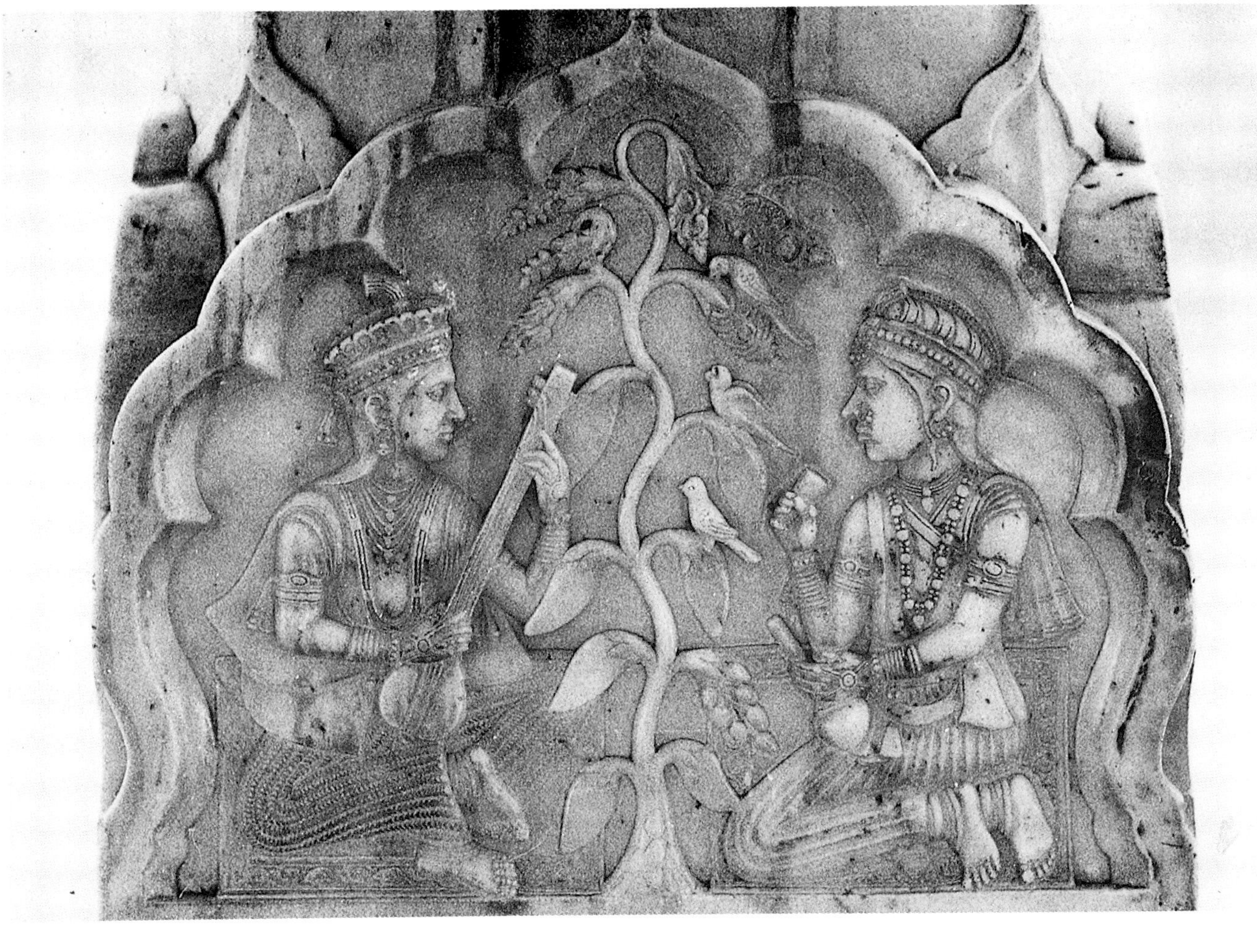

62. Dance and music. Carved at the base of a pillar.

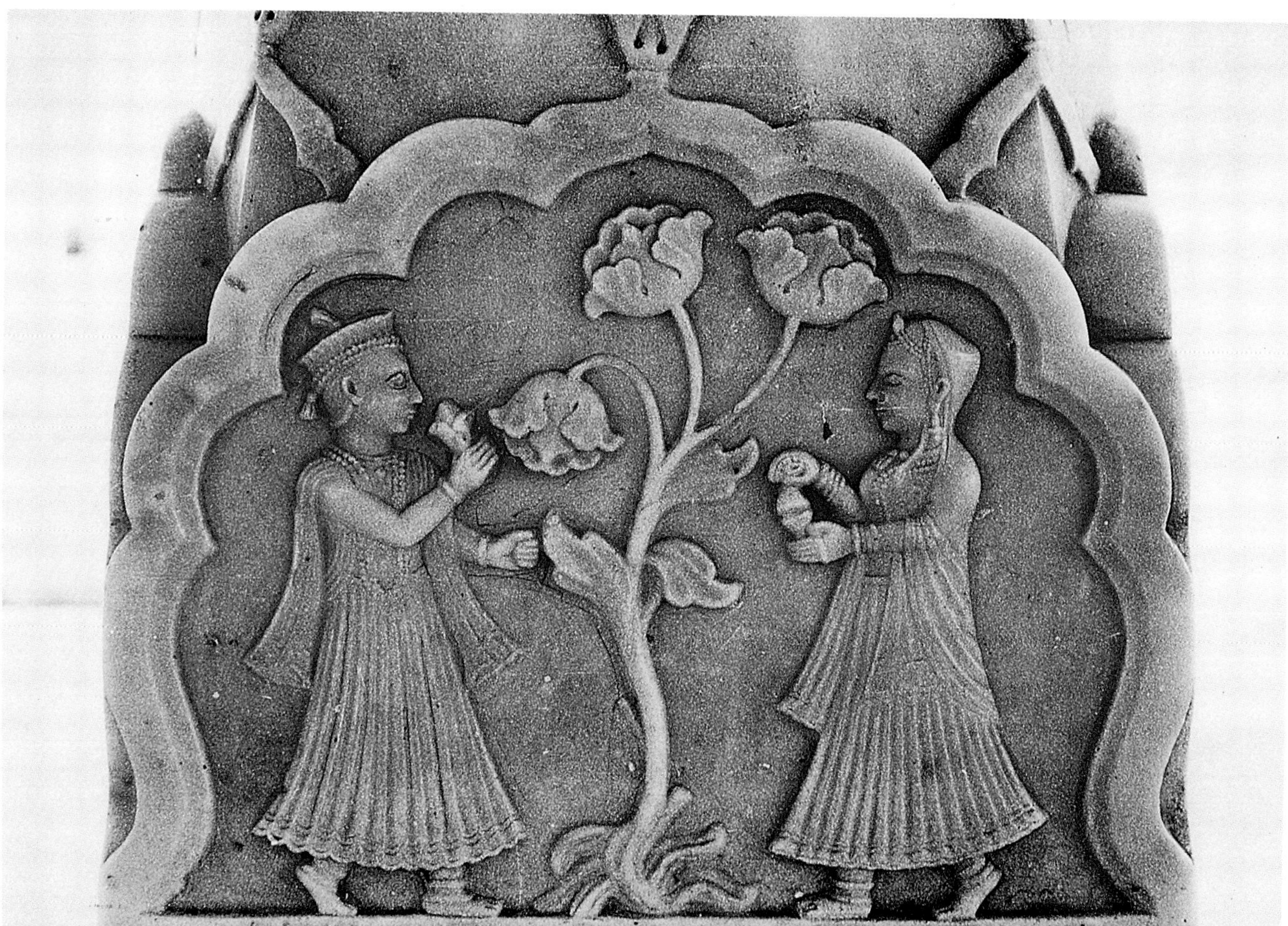

63. Domestic scene. Carved at the base of a pillar.

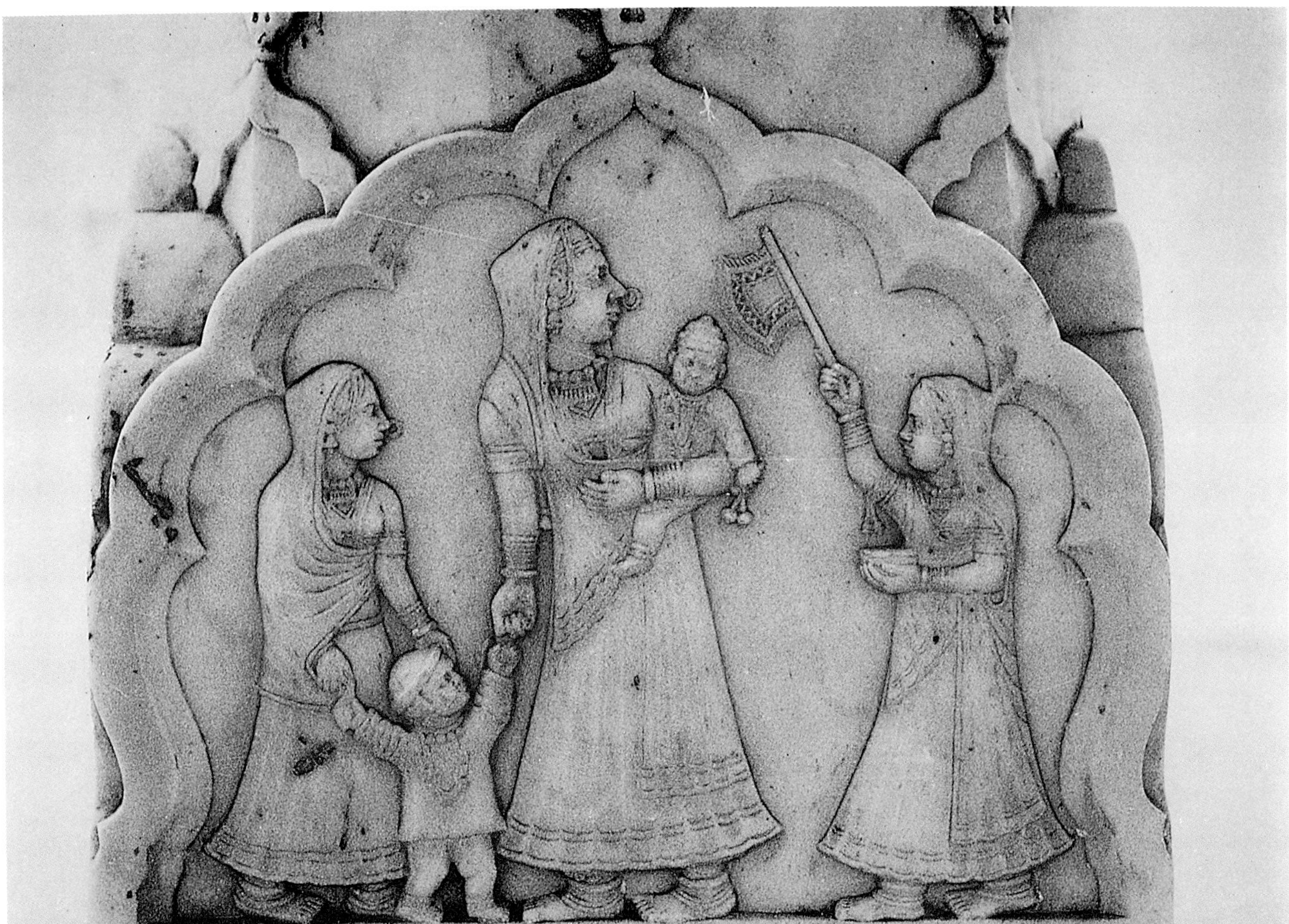

64. Dance and music. Carved at the base of a pillar.

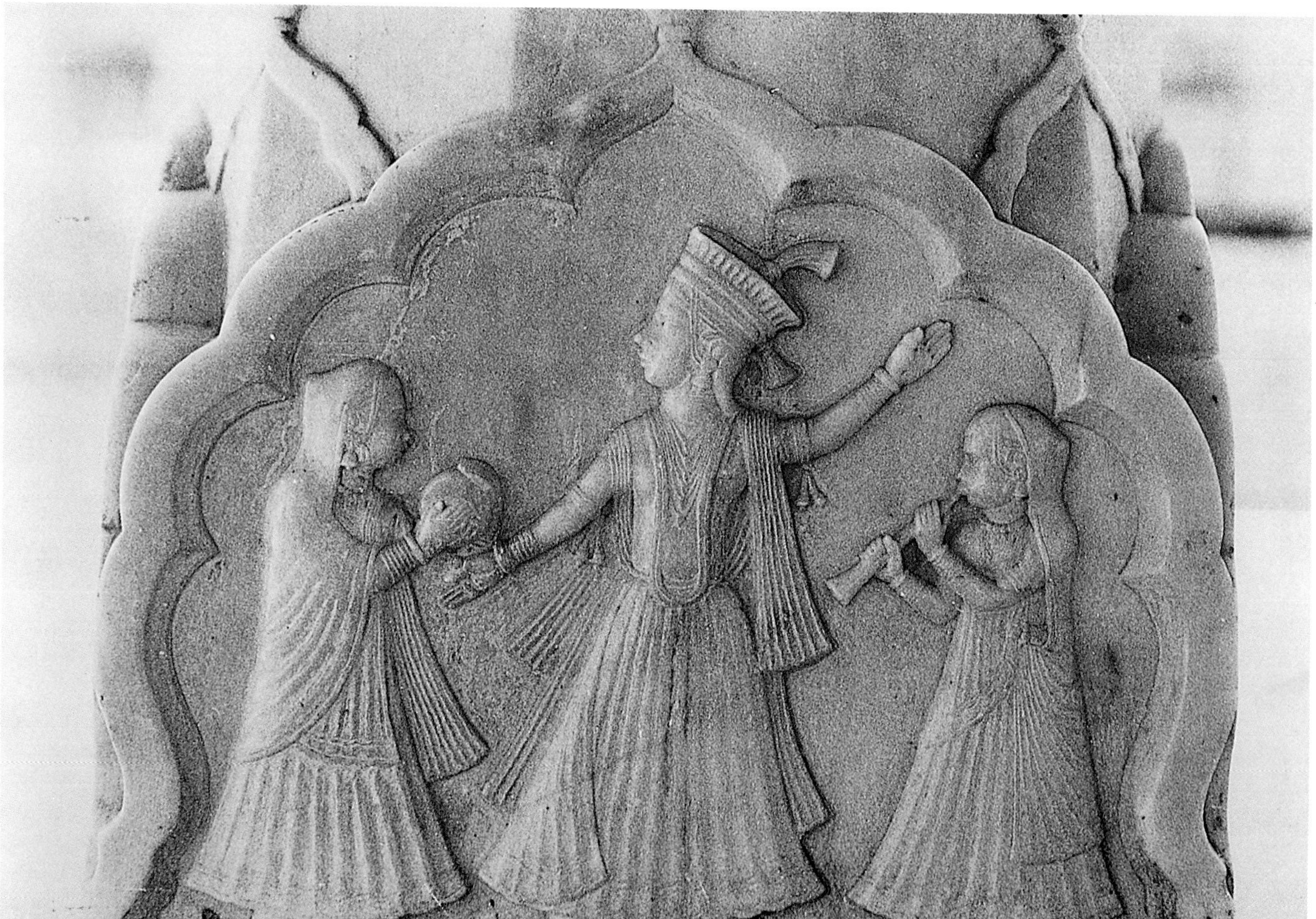

65. Dance and music. Carved at the base of a pillar.

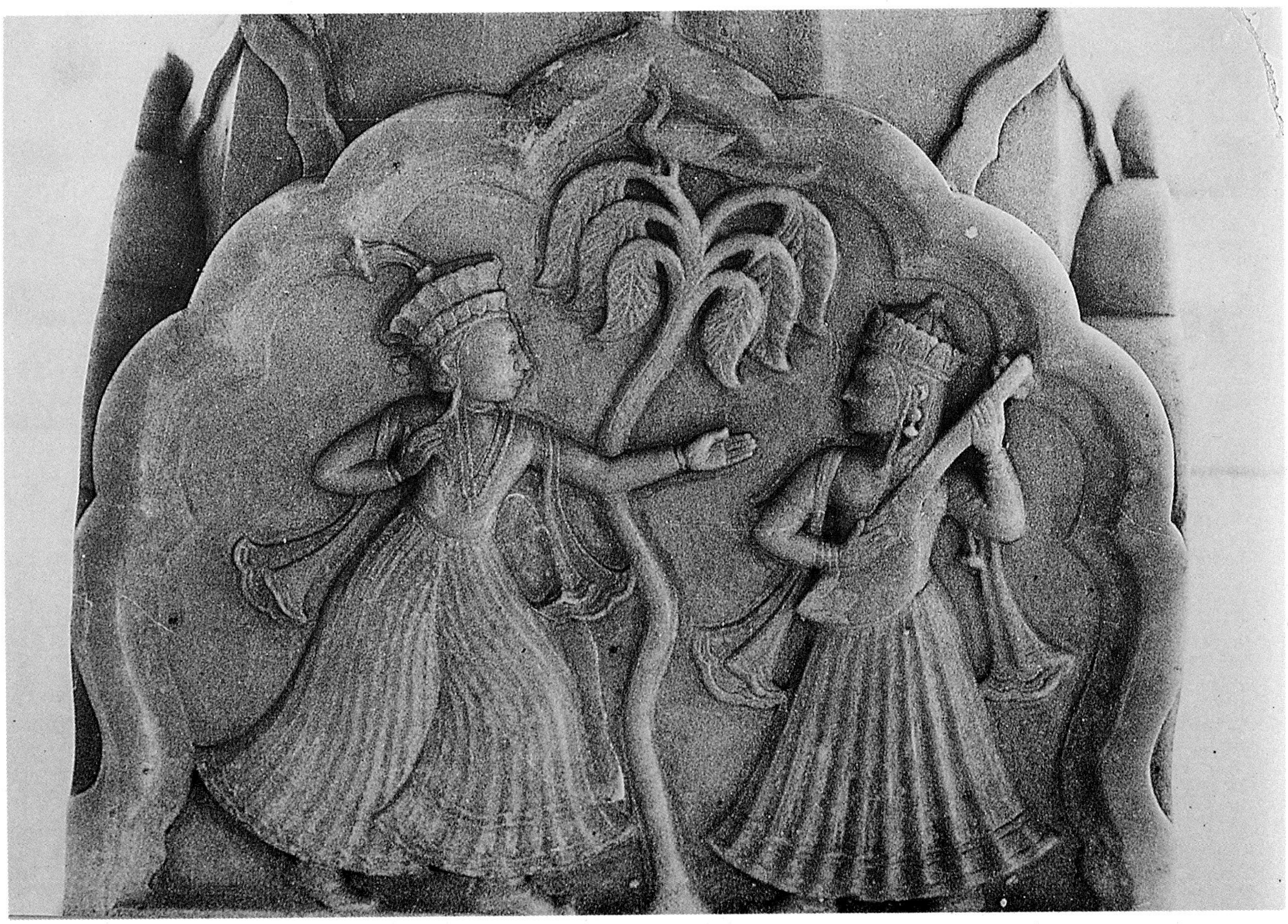

70. Siege of Lanka (*c.* 1700). Unascribed. A.K. Coomaraswamy Collection.

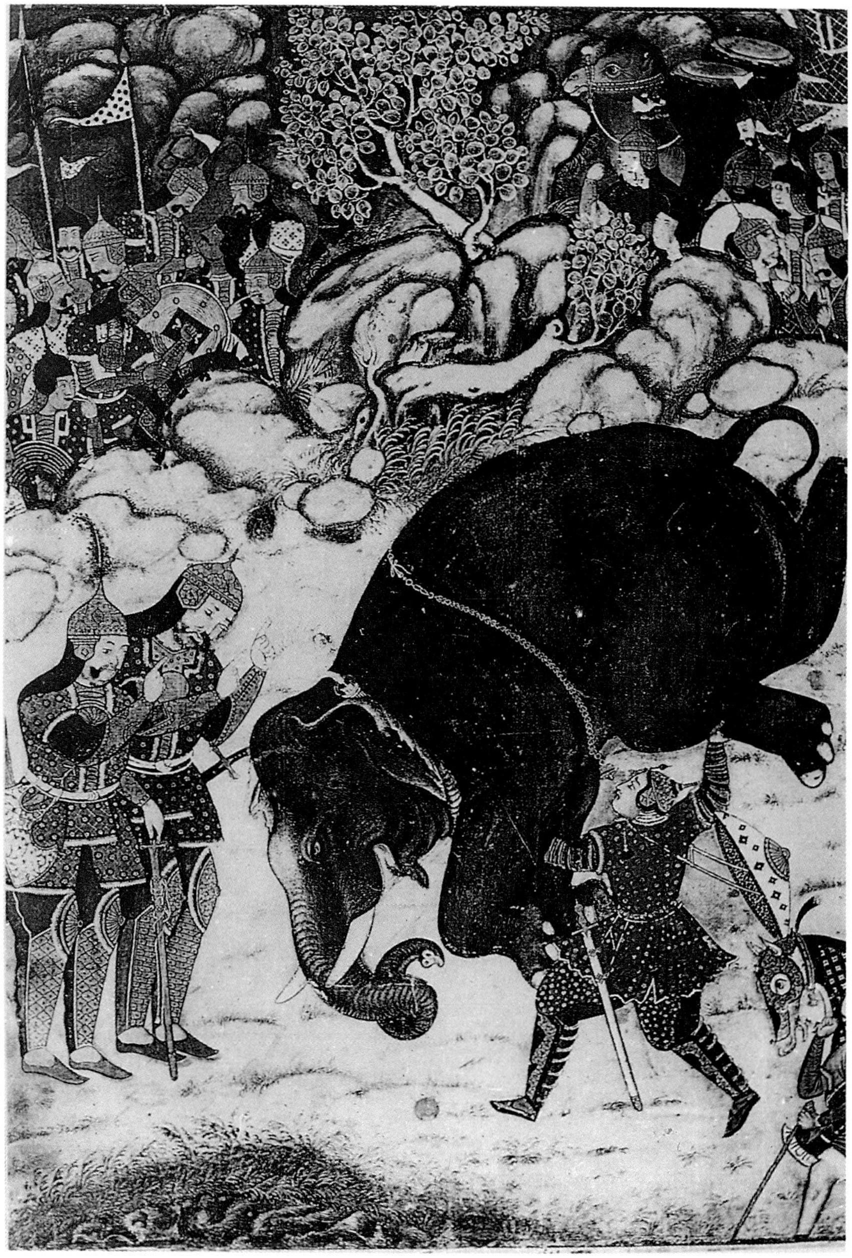

71. Folio from the *Hamzanama* (*c.* 1570-5). Unascribed.

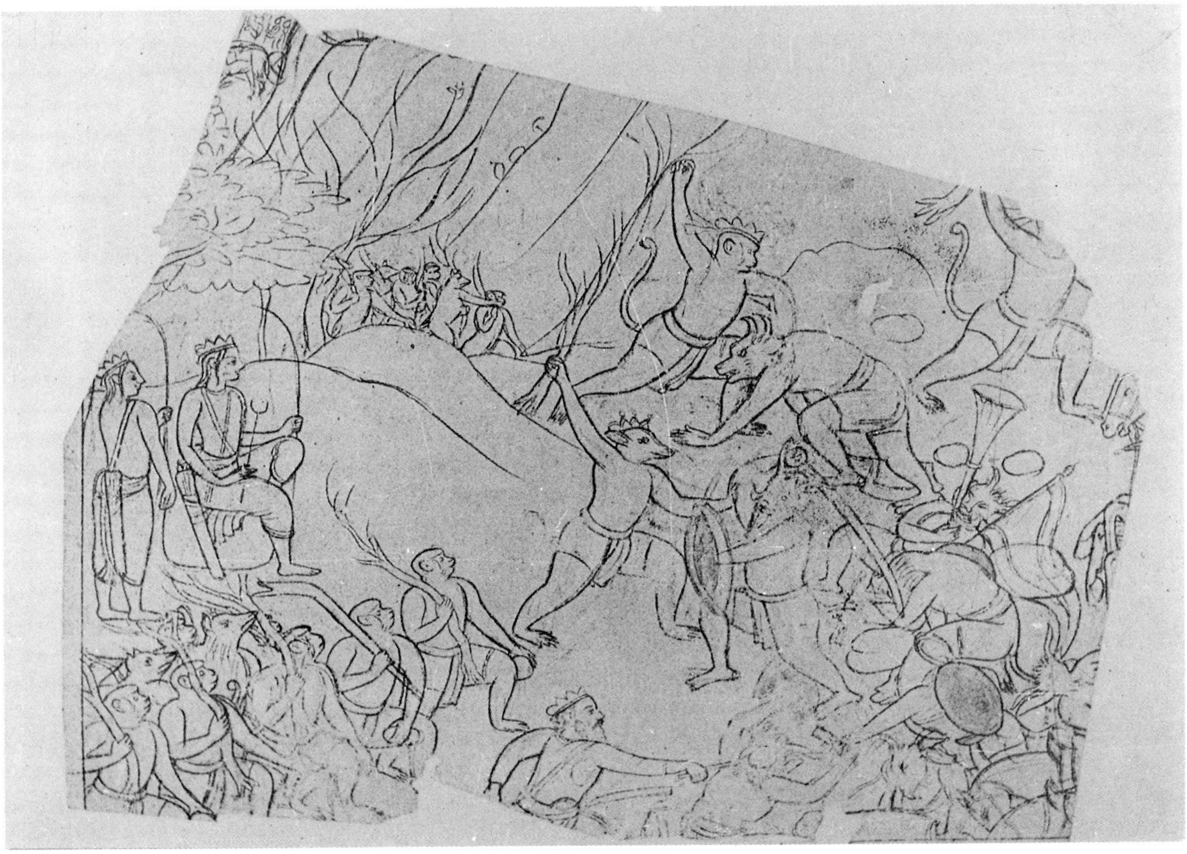

72-3. List of the rulers to whom *tabarruk* was sent by Syed Muhammad Masud, the son of Syed Muhammad Murad (1737).

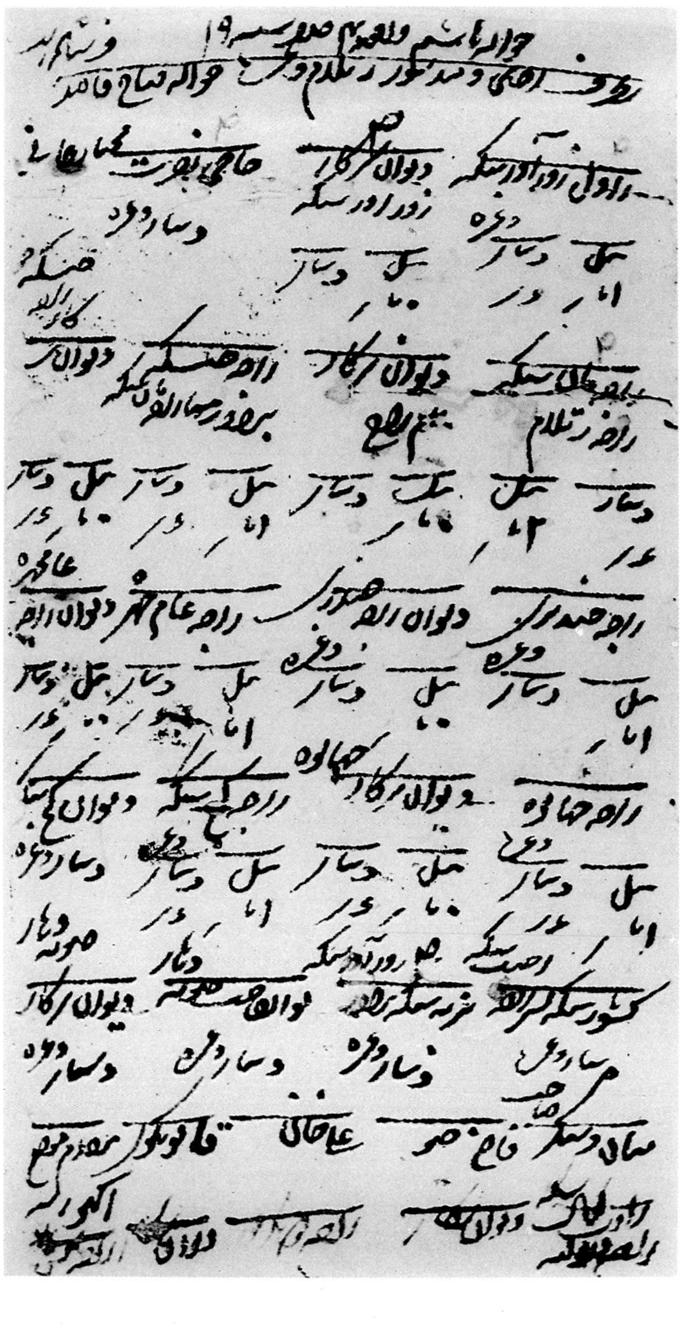

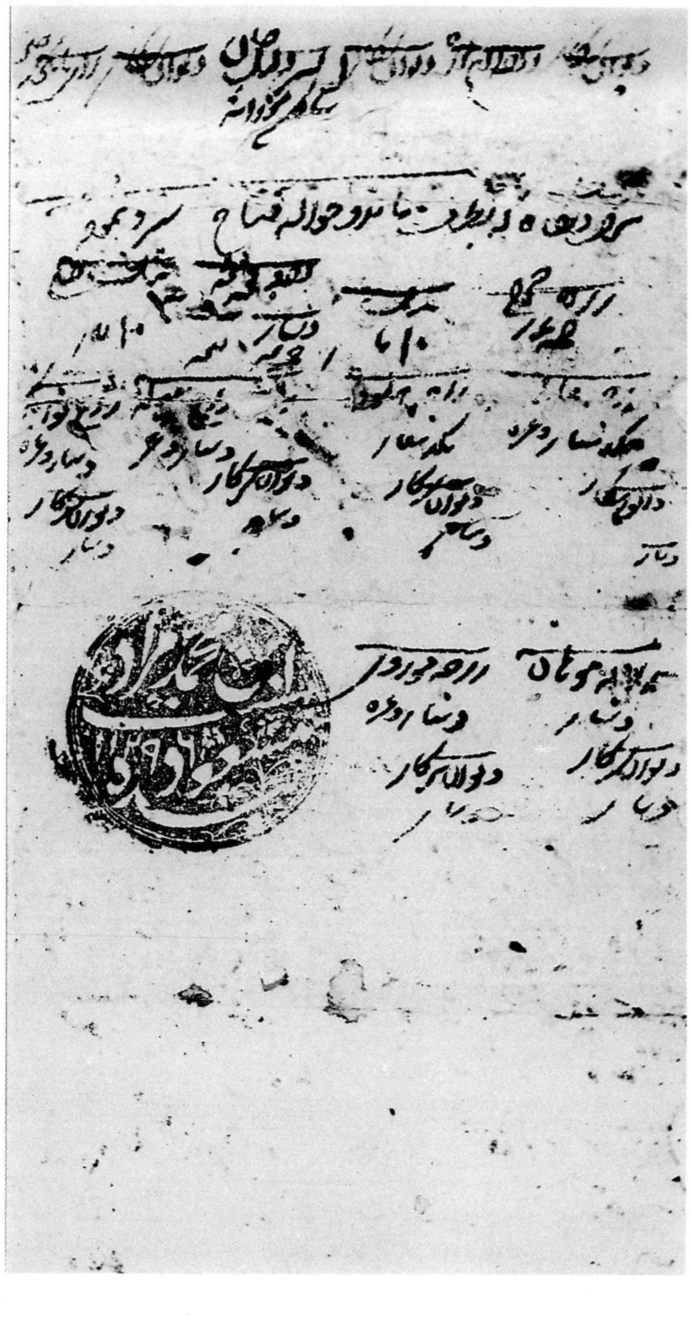

74. *Vikalatnama* of Bajirao Peshwa in the name of Syed Muhammad Murad (1736).

75. *Vikalatnama* of Maharaja Daulat Rao Sindhia of Gwaliar in the name of Syed Muhammad Masud (1797).

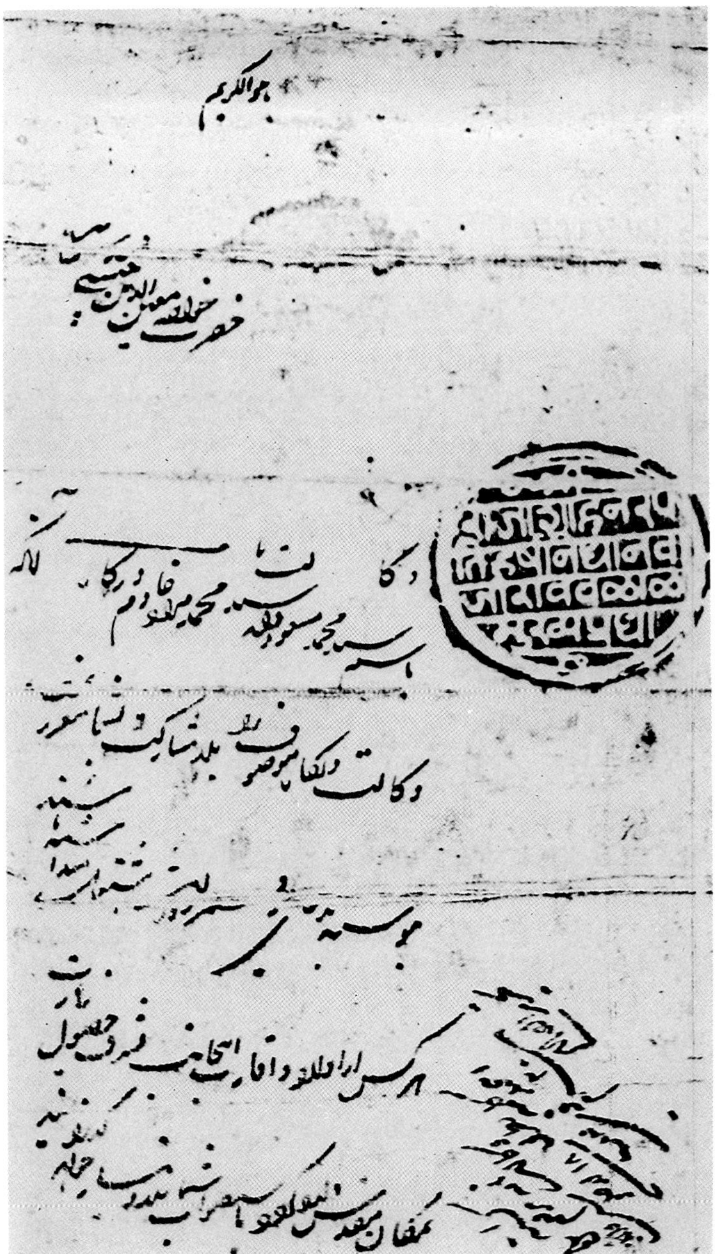

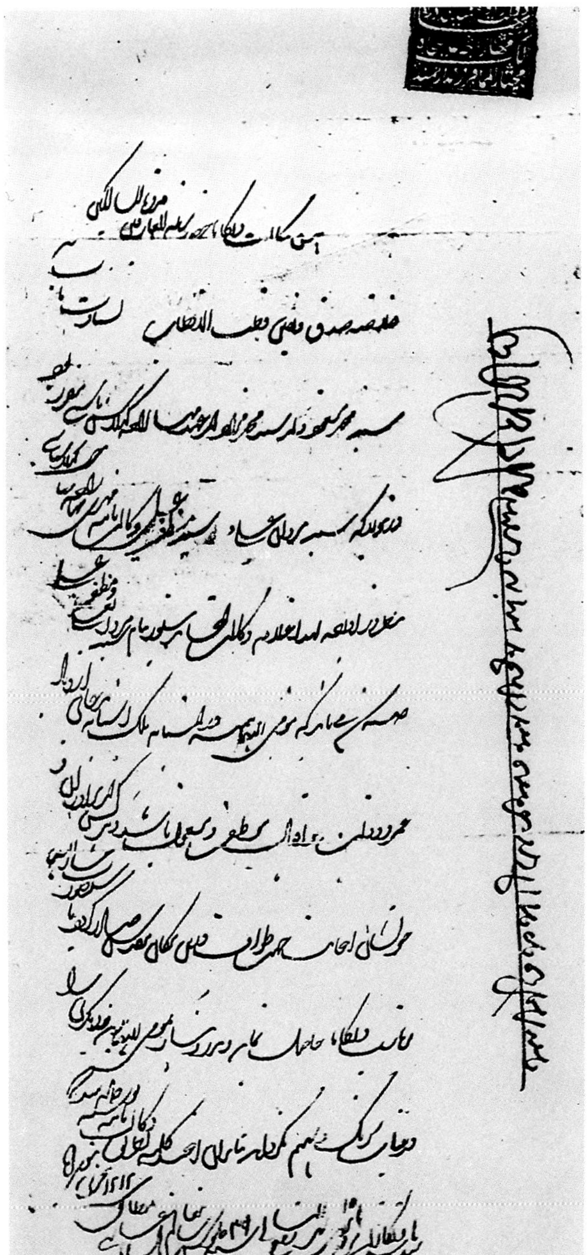

76. Letter of Thakur Gopal Singh Shekhawat,
Zamindar of *qasba* Udaipur, *sarkar* Narnaul,
Shahjahanabad in the name of Syed Muhammad Masud (1737).

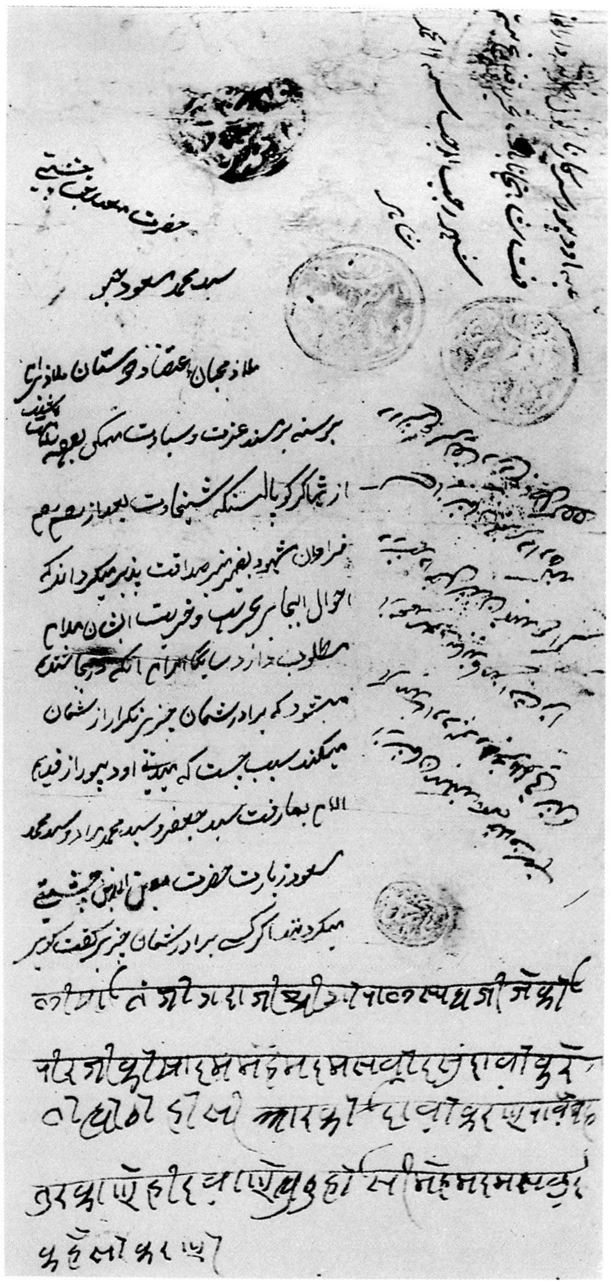

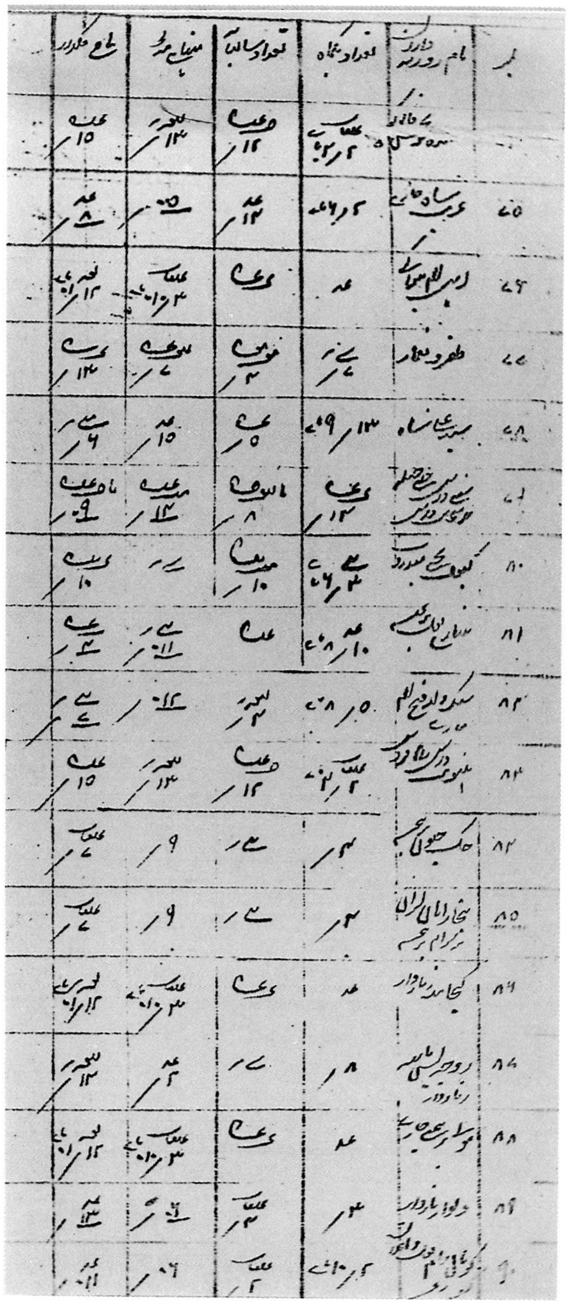

77-8. Record of the commission paid to the *fotadars* from the salaries of officials and *rozinadars* of the *Dargah*.

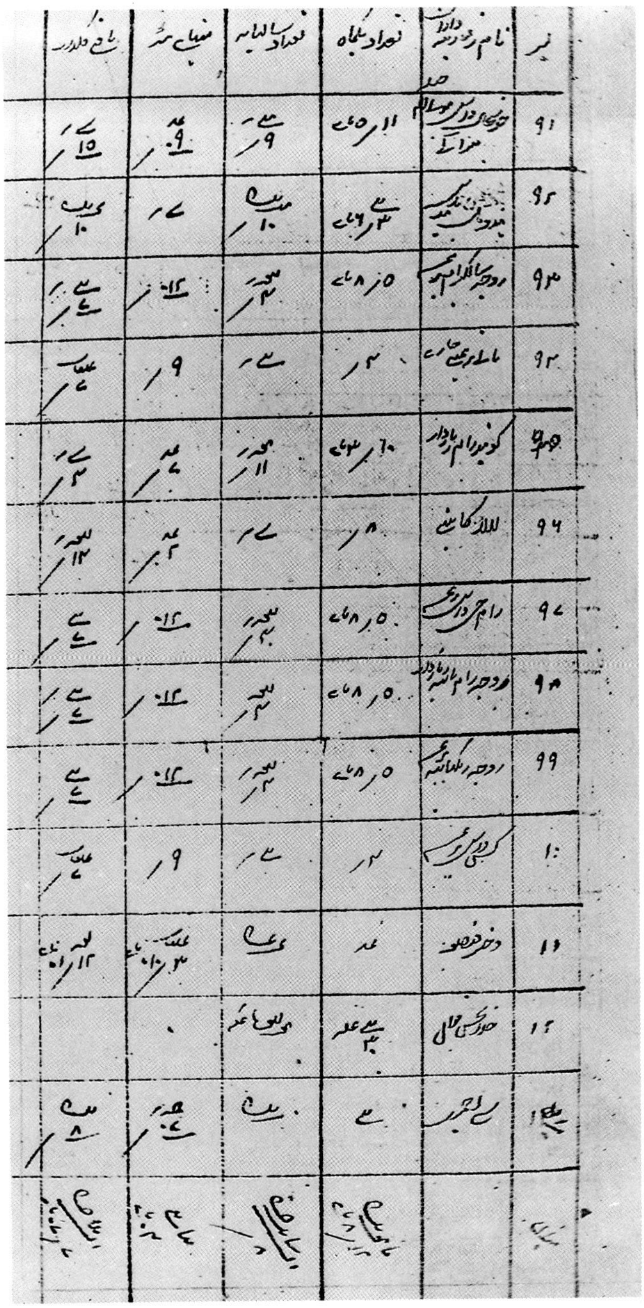

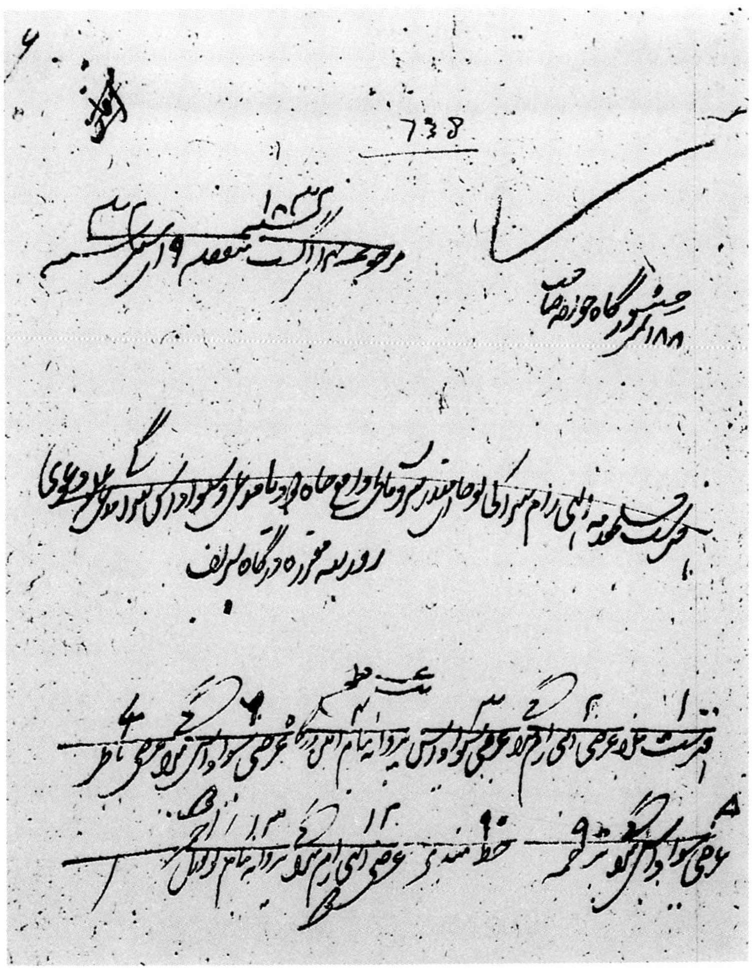

79-81. Documents related to the grant of daily allowance from the *Dargah Waqf* for feeding the poor at the Hanuman temple near the Dodhia well in Ajmer City.

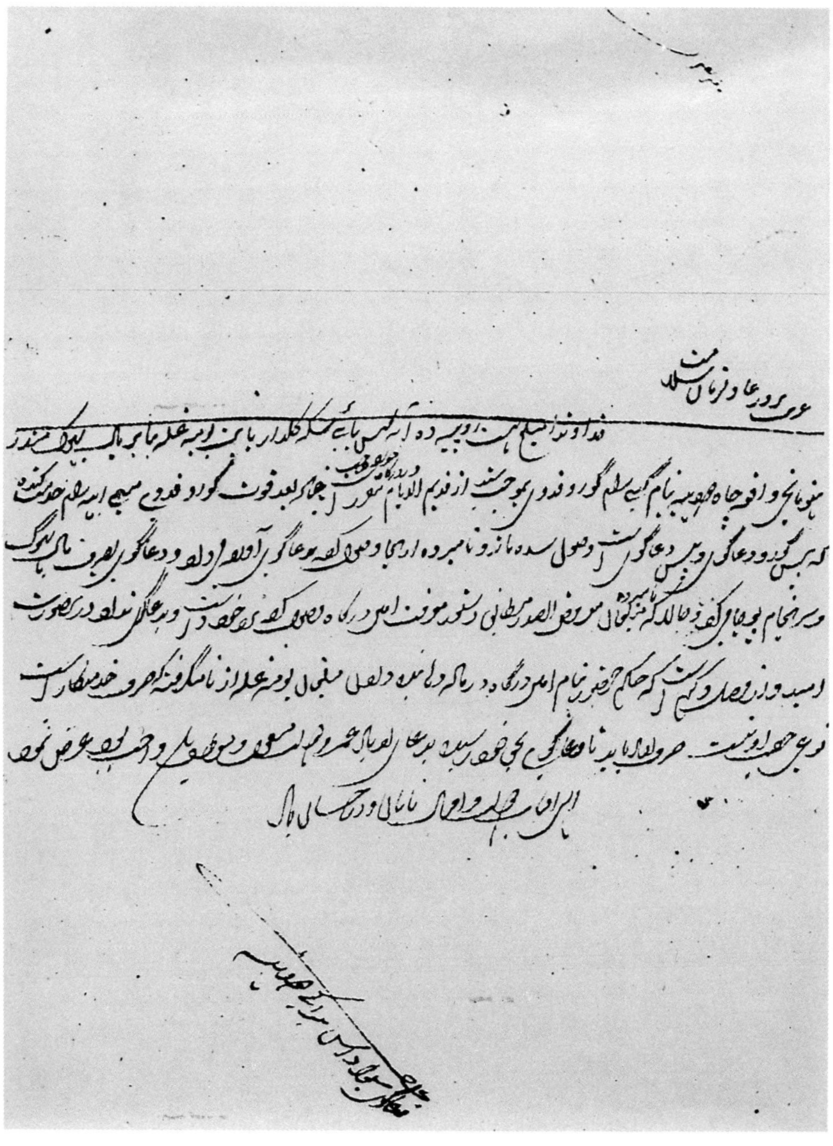

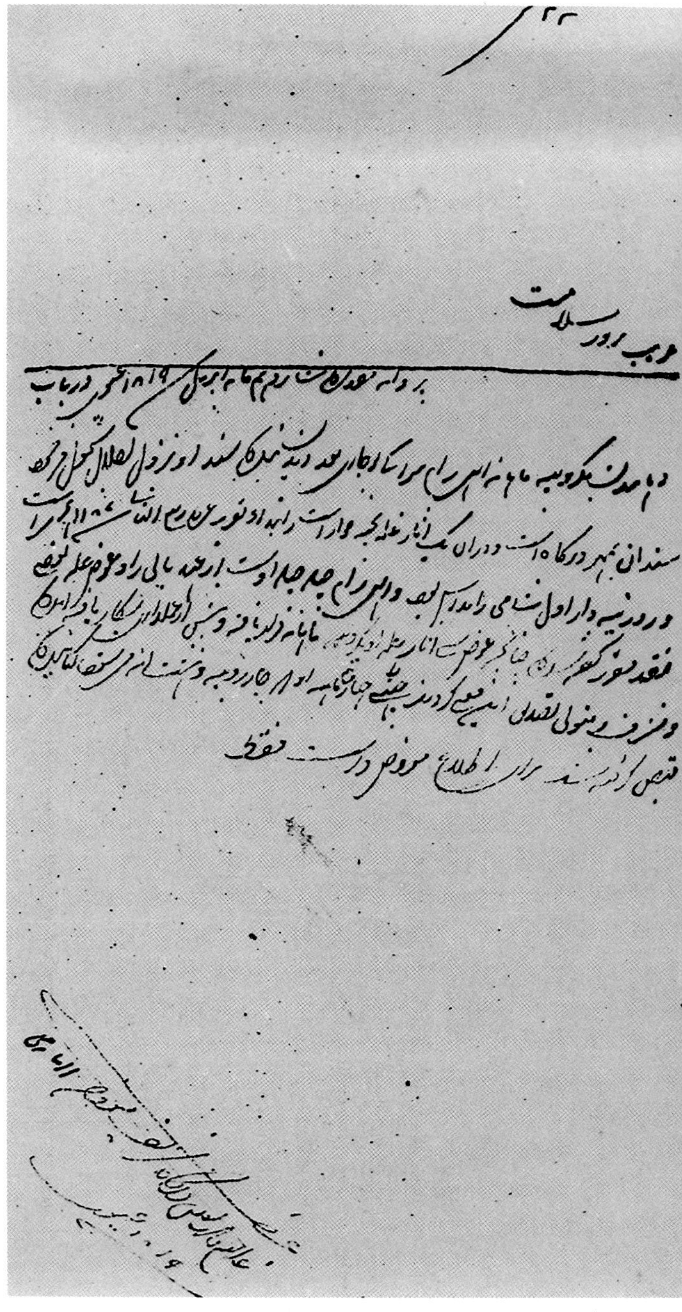

1

The Process of Acculturation in Regional Historiography: The Case of Delhi Sultanate

IQTIDAR HUSAIN SIDDIQUI

In recent years western scholars have drawn attention to the need of applying geographical methods to the study of cultural patterns in different regions in terms of 'Shatter' zones, and 'Core' areas or 'nuclear' zones. In their studies, certain areas in the South Asian subcontinent have been designated as "Core" ones because, according to them, they generally exhibit stable cultural patterns, including fairly persistent political tradition, social stratification, linguistic unity, etc. Their studies also imply that unlike the 'Core' areas, the 'Shatter' zones, exposed to foreign invaders as well as peaceful immigrants from foreign lands, became melting pots of various cultures, with the result that they had neither stable cultural patterns nor any persistent political tradition, or linguistic unity.[1]

It is, however, worth recalling that even an area which remained traditionally a 'march land' for the foreign invaders could not necessarily become the confluence of different cultures if it lacked the resources for sustaining new settlers in any large number. But it influenced the 'Core' areas with which it was geographically connected; thereby the 'Core' areas turned into melting pots of various cultures that went a long way to provide variety and richness to life there. The aim of this article is to have an argument on the adequacy or inadequacy of the application of geographical methods and also suggest if other methods, such as sociological and anthropological, could also be helpful in delineating the process of acculturation in the history of a particular region. We have selected for our study four regions, namely, the north-western frontier region, Panjab, Haryana and the Delhi *doab*, during the pre-Mughal times. The former region, linked with Panjab, Haryana and the Delhi *doab*, remained traditionally a 'march land'. It did not undergo any major change insofar as the life and culture are concerned between the 11th and 13th centuries; yet the 'Core' areas in Panjab and Haryana up to Delhi had turned into 'Shatter' zones, and then became 'nuclear' zones for a new cultural pattern that came to be known as composite or Indo-Muslim culture in course of time.

The waves of foreign invaders and the exodus of people from the neighbouring countries in the wake of conquest by the foreigners coming through the north-western frontier region to the plains changed both the culture and demography of the urban centres there. Unlike the plains, the hilly region in north-western India, inhabited by the Afghan tribes from ancient times, did not undergo any major social or political change during medieval times even after total conversion of its people to Islam. The brief references to the Afghans available in the early medieval sources tend to reveal that the Afghan population in that region was nomadic as well as sedentary.[2] As regards the social-political organization, it always remained rudimentary even during the political hegemony of the Ghaznavi rulers who belonged to the area of higher culture. Since the *qabila* (tribe) or clan (*khail*) was the unit of social organization in this region, people were divided into tribes and sub-tribes which lived independent of one another under their respective tribal chiefs, the latter being first among the equals. According to Akhund Durweza who worked among the Afghans as a religious missionary during the sixteenth century, 'The Afghans have followed since ancient times a system in which they, out of ignorance and robustness of heart, never considered it proper to have a king over them. Their pride and vanity would not let them bow and prostrate before one of their own kith and kin. Further, if they agreed to call one a king, they feared that they would thereby reduce themselves to the level of servants. They would rather like all of them to be treated as equals. Therefore, all Afghans whether small or great were addressed as *maliks*.'[3] The only unifying factor among the Afghans was the Pushto language.

Since the entire region was hilly and suffered from the scarcity of water, agriculture was possible only where water was available from the streams of small rivers. In fact, the lack of natural resources, including enough fertile agricultural land, compelled the Afghans to depend for livelihood on small cultivation, rearing flocks and herds of cattle and sheep, horse-trading, riding and plundering the neighbouring settled countries, and collecting toll from merchant caravans passing through their territories.[4] In short, the poverty of the region prevented the invaders from the lands of high culture during medieval times from settling down there. On the foundation of the Sultanate in northern India in the beginning of the thirteenth century, the Afghan territories to the north of the Indus supplied soldiers to the Sultanate army which benefited the former in economic terms. The Afghans manufactured swords called *surman* and *turman*, which found a good market in India because their demand increased after the foundation of the Sultanate.[5] Moreover, the Afghan land was found good for horse breeding. On the Mongol conquest of Central Asia and Iran, the supply of war horse to India ceased temporarily. This gave an opportunity to the Afghans in certain areas of their region to establish horse-breeding centres for supplying horses to Delhi.[6] A fourteenth century document suggests that some Afghan traders had acquired considerable influence at the Delhi court because horse trade carried on by them had great importance for the Sultan.[7] The accumulation of wealth through horse trade led to economic inequalities within the same Afghan tribe or clan in their homeland.[8] Yet the economic differences among the members of a tribe did not lead to any social change in the society; the individuals continued to enjoy equality at the social plane.[9] In fact, their tribal customs eliminated the chances of the creation of an Afghan state and thus reduced the possibility of settled economic development. Their poverty gave a fillip to migrations in groups and families into India since the thirteenth century. As they migrated, they brought with them their customs and traditions, though in the new environment neither the tribal organization could remain intact, nor could the condition of living remain the same. That is the reason why the descendants of the first Afghan immigrants in the Delhi Sultanate seem to have started imitating the Muslim aristocratic life as they rose slowly in status in the official hierarchy.[10]

As for the impact of Islam on the Afghans, they were superficially Islamised. The Islamic law and faith do not seem to have influenced them much in their homeland: the old pagan customs and practices continued to be in vogue. The only thing that distinguished them from non-Muslims was their outward love for the *saiyids* and *sufis* and their graves after their death. The absence of schools and colleges in their land deprived them of the advantages of learning and education.[11] No influence from the neighbouring countries of higher culture seems to have ever left its mark on the life and conditions in the Afghan lands.

It follows from the above discussion that the social environment and the cultural background of the inhabitants do play an important role in the process of acculturation. For the sake of illustration, we may cite the example of Makran that was mostly a barren desert with little water from the streams, but it attracted the Arab traders who settled down in its towns and turned them into trading centres. These merchants formed an important link in the overseas and overland trade between India, Asia and Middle East.[12] Makran also had a local ruling dynasty till the beginning of the thirteenth century. Its ruler Tajuddin Abul Makarim is mentioned by the contemporary poet Siraj Khurasani as a patron of poets, scholars and men of arts.[13]

As for Panjab, it had not only been a 'Core' area of Hindu culture and religion but also played an important role in 'Hinduising' the invaders of India from across the border. It was first in Panjab that interaction between Hindu and foreign culture took place and then the cultural synthesis resulting from it influenced the life in the Gangetic plain. It is also worth recalling that the vitality of Hindu tradition was such that it soon became preponderant in the life of the foreign conquerors such as the Greeks, the Kushanas and the white Huns during ancient times. The defence of Hindu culture had been one of Panjab's historical role. It, however, changed its role after its conquest by Sultan Mahmud of Ghazni.

Annexation by Sultan Mahmud of the north-western Panjab up to Lahore in 1021-22 was followed by the process of urbanization in the region. The Sultan is reported to have brought with him from Ghazni a large number of blacksmiths and carpenters for the construction of forts at strategic points in Panjab. Lahore, that was only a village, was selected as the headquarter of the *sipahsalar* (governor) and the army, and thus it began to serve as a military base for the Sultan to invade distant places in northern India. The scanty authentic evidence contained in the contemporary sources reveals that in Panjab Sultan Mahmud followed a policy of reconciliation towards the Hindu chiefs with a view to stabilising his authority with the local support. Consequently, certain Hindu chiefs in the Salt Range embraced Islam, and the Sultan is said to have posted *'ulama* there to educate the new converts about the tenets and philosophy of Islamic faith. In the same year (1022), Nandanath town (now in Jhelum district of Pakistan) was garrisoned by a strong Muslim force, and adorned with mosques and *madrasas.*[14]

It may also be recalled that Lahore began to develop into an important city that eventually emerged as the centre of Islamic learning and culture. A number of villages emerged around Lahore where leading scholars and poets were settled with land grants. All this led to important changes in demographic and cultural patterns in Panjab. A large number of Hindus were recruited in the Ghaznavi army and settled in a separate quarter at Ghazni. The commanders of the Hindu soldiers were also Hindu such as Tilak, a barber by caste, and Suvendhray, probably a *thakur.* Both of them rendered important services in Central Asia.[15]

In short, the establishment of the Ghaznavi rule over north-western Panjab created an atmosphere in which interaction between the Hindu and Islamic cultural traditions could take place. The descendants of the early Muslim immigrants adopted Hindvi[16] for social intercourse with the local population and through them many Hindi words strayed into their Persian writings; on the other hand, many Persian words were adopted in Hindvi. As a result, a new cultural pattern emerged that ultimately helped the fusion of the two cultures. In fact, Panjab had become the nucleus of composite culture even before the foundation of the Sultanate in the beginning of the thirteenth century.

With the Ghuri conquest of northern India at the close of the twelfth century, the other 'Core' areas of Hindu culture (such as Haryana and Delhi *doab*) underwent changes. The multi-state system created by the Rajputs gave way to a centralized political organization, enabling the country to acquire political individuality in course of time. The 'caste cities' were changed into cosmopolitan urban centres as their gates were thrown open to all irrespective of birth or creed. The low caste artisans seem to have built their huts even in the vicinity of the royal palace.[17] The city of Delhi which had been a *pargana* town emerged as the most important centre of culture and learning in the

Eastern Islamic world; indeed, it had become the repository of all the best that had developed in Iran and Central Asia after the Mongol conquest of these countries pushed their elite to India.[18]

The construction of new forts, palaces and mosques with graceful domes and minarets in different cities transformed the skyline.[19] Further, the outlying territories were linked with Delhi through highways with *thanas* (police posts) established for ensuring security to the travellers. Thereafter, the foreign merchants moving in caravan between foreign countries and India could travel without any fear up to Lakhnauti (in Bengal).[20] Consequently, Lahore and Multan in Panjab, situated along the historic trade routes connecting India with Iran, Ghazni (or modern Afghanistan) and Central Asian lands, benefited from the expansion of overland trade, resulting from the 'internationalist' attitude of the Sultans. Hansi in Haryana, which lay along the caravan route running between Multan and Delhi (the supreme centre of consumption), also benefited from the transit trade.[21] It soon changed from a town into an important city. Many scholars, *sufis* and traders settled down there.[22] As a matter of fact, the urban and mercantile ethos of foreign Muslim immigrants went a long way to create conditions favourable for economic prosperity in different regions. Talking about the extravagance and luxurious life of the nobles of Sultan Balban's reign, Barani mentions that the Hindu moneylenders and bankers had acquired great wealth. The nobles took loan from the Multanis and *Shahs*, and repaid it with interest by drafts on their *iqta's*.[23] Amid Sunami, the thirteenth century poet, tells us that the moneylender got twelve for every ten (*tankas*) per month.[24] The luxury and other fancy goods brought by merchants for the use of the ruling elite led to the introduction of crafts and modification of the indigenous ones. Anything that impressed the Sultan or an important noble, was given to the skilled artisans to make its like in the *karkhana* (workshop).[25] No doubt, all this encouraged diversity in Indian culture. It is also worthy of note that the merchants transmitted information about conditions of life of different regions and countries as well as contemporary intellectual trends.[26]

Of the important immigrants to India, mention may also be made of the *sufis* who entered India in the beginning of the thirteenth century and settled down in different cities and towns in northern India. They performed important social roles. Their teachings gave rise to theistic trends in the Indian society and their devotion to the service of man, irrespective of birth and creed, attracted the non-Muslims to their *khanqahs*. A critical study of the authentic hagiographical literature as well as historical sources reveals that for most of them service to humanity was a life-long mission, and spirituality their genuine concern.[27] As people belonging to different strata of the society were included among their *murids* (disciples), interaction between the 'great tradition' and 'little tradition' of culture also took place.

Equally important was the introduction of Persian language in northern India. It gave linguistic uniformity because, according to Amir Khusrau, in India the language and dialect of people changed after every hundred miles. Now Persian became the *lingua franca* in the Sultanate. Lahore and Multan in Panjab, and Hansi and Sunam in Delhi *doab*, emerged as centres of Persian language. Along with Persian, Haryanvi that was spoken in Delhi as well began to develop into a literary language. It now came to be known as Hindvi (i.e. Persianised Hindi). The Muslim elite learnt it for social intercourse with the local people with the result that Arabic and Persian words got their way into Haryanvi. The second generation of the Muslims seems to have spoken it among themselves and composed poems in it. Sultan Muhammad Tughlaq (1324-1351) is reported to have patronised Hindvi poets along with Arabic and Persian poets.[28]

The sixteenth century Mughal historians would have us believe that the Hindus in northern India started learning Persian during the reign of Sultan Sikandar Lodi (1488-1517) when the use of any language other than Persian was banned in the state departments which led the Hindus to acquire proficiency in Persian.[29] But the presence of Hindu scholars of Persian and Islamic disciplines during Sikandar Lodi's reign suggests that interaction between the Hindu-Muslim elite had aroused interest among them to learn Persian and Sanskrit for having an understanding of each other's religious philosophy long before him. Mulla Abdul Qadir Badauni refers to Dhunkar Brahman who had gained fame as a gifted poet of Persian and scholar of Islamic disciplines. He gave the Muslim students instruction in books of popular sciences.[30]

Besides, the Indian languages in different regions were enriched by taking words and terms from Persian. Even the south Indian languages of Dravidian stock contain a number of Persian and Arabic words.

The introduction of new technological devices also acted as catalysts. Mention may be made here of the application of one device, that is, *saqiya* or Persian wheel that went a long way in changing the landscape both in Panjab and Haryana. The relevant evidence casts interesting light on the engineering skill that went into the construction of water works and the changes that irrigation system underwent during the Delhi Sultanate period.[31] In fact, the diffusion of advanced irrigation technology in a region brought about prosperity and helped the growth of material culture.

To conclude, it may be stressed that for a deep study of the life or the process of acculturation in a particular region, different factors — social, religious, economic and geographical—play a vital role. Therefore, the use of any one particular methodology in such a study is not adequate. The growth and progress of culture owes much to the psychology, social customs and political system of the region as well.

NOTES

1. O.H.K. Spate is the pioneer in pointing out the areas that acted in Indian history as 'Core' areas and 'Shatter' zones (cf. *India and Pakistan: A General and Regional Geography*, 3rd edition, London, 1967, pp. 175-179).
   In 1976, Bernard Cohn highlighted the fact that the 'Shatter' zones that connect the 'nuclear' areas, socially and culturally tend to be more of a mosaic than a relative unitary kind of social structure (cf. Bernard Cohn, 'Regions Subjective and Objective: Their Relation to the Modern Indian History and Society', in *Region and Regionalism in South Asian Studies*, ed. Robert I. Crans, Durham, N.C., 1967, p. 12).
2. The eleventh century work, *Tarikh al-Yamini* of al-'Utbi mentions the Afghans as pagans given to rapine and rapacity. They were defeated by Subuktigin and converted to Islam (cf. *Tarikh al-Yamini*, early 13th century Persian translation by Abu-Ush-Sharaf al-Jarbaza Khani, British Museum, London, Add. 24,950, ff. 24b, 25a; also Fakhr Mudabbir, *Adab-al Harb Wa'l-Shuja'a*, ed. E.S. Khavansari, Tehran, 1346 Shamsi, p. 314).
3. Akhund Durweza, *Tazkirat al-Abrar wa'l-Ashrar*, British Museum, London, Or. 222, ff. 23 a-b.
4. Amir Khusrau, *Miftah al-Futuh*, ed. Shaikh Abdur Rashid, Aligarh, 1954, p. 8; Ibn Battuta, *Travels of Ibn Battuta*, Vol. 3, tr. H. Gibb, Cambridge, 1971, p. 592; *Tazkirat al-Abrar wa'l Ashrar*, op. cit., ff. 132a-133a; Mulla Qati'i Harevi, *Majma'al-Shu'ra-i Jahangir Shahi*, ed. Salim Akhtar, Karachi, 1979, pp. 51-52.
5. Simon Digby, *War Horse and Elephants in the Sultanate of Delhi*, Karachi, 1971, p. 19.
6. Ziauddin Barani, *Tarikh-i Firozshahi*, Bib. Ind., Calcutta, 1862, p. 53.
7. Cf. Ain al-Mulk Mahru, *Insha-i Mahru*, ed. Shaikh Abdur Rashid, Lahore, 1965, pp. 212-213 (Letter no. 120).
8. Ni'matullah Harevi, *Tarikh-i Khan Jahani*, ed. Imam al-Din, Dacca, 1962, Vol. 2, p. 772.
9. Ibid., pp. 552-53.
10. I.H. Siddiqui, 'The Afghans and their Emergence in India as a Ruling Elite during the Delhi Sultanate Period', *Central Asiatic Journal*, Vol. 26, Nos. 3-4, 1982, pp. 250-57.
11. *Tazkirat al-Abrar wa'l-Ashrar*, ff. 27b, 30a.
12. Andre Wink has discussed in detail the emergence of Makran as a crossroad in international trade between the Islamic World and the Far Eastern countries. With the settlement of Arab traders, a number of new towns were founded as centres of trade and commerce (cf. *Al-Hind: The Making of the Indo-Islamic World*, Vol. 1, New Delhi, 1990, pp. 51-53).
13. Sirajuddin Siraji Khurasani, *Diwan-i Siraji*, ed. Nazir Ahmad, Aligarh, 1972, pp. 15-18, 24-28, passim.
14. Cf. Abu Sa'id Gardezi, *Zain al-Akhbar*, ed. Abdul Hai Habibi, Iran, 1374 Shamsi, pp. 179, 181.
15. C.E. Bosworth, *The Ghaznavids: Their Empire in Afghanistan and Eastern Iran (994-1040 A.D.)*, Edinburgh, 1963, pp. 110, 127.
16. During early medieval times, the Muslim immigrants in India called every Indian dialect Hindvi. The Hindvi spoken in Panjab was the Panjabi dialect whereas Gujri was the dialect in Gujarati, but the Muslim writers mention these dialects by the same term Hindvi (cf. Sadiduddin Awfi, *Jawami'ul Hikayat wa'l-Livami' al rivayat*, Hyderabad, Vol. 1, Part 2, 1966, p. 255.
17. Isami, *Futuh-us Salatin*, ed. Usha, Madras, 1948, pp. 105-106.
18. Ibn Battuta, op. cit., pp. 618-26; Shihabuddin al-Umari, *Masalik al-Absar fi Mamalik al-Amsar*, Eng. tr. I.H. Siddiqui, *A Fourteenth Century Arab Account of India under Sultan Muhammad bin Tughlaq*, Aligarh, 1971, pp. 36-37.

19. Barani, op. cit., p. 65.

20. Ibid., pp. 34, 57, 59.

21. Hasan Sijzi, *Fawaid al-Fuad*, p. 67; Mir Khurd, *Siyar al-Auliya*, Delhi, 1302 A.H., pp. 62, 163, 180-81, 187, 252; Ibn Battuta's description is more graphic (op. cit., p. 617).

22. Ibid.

23. Barani, p. 120.

24. Amid Lowiki Sunami, *Diwan*, ed. Nazir Ahmad, Lahore, 1984, p. 100; I.H. Siddiqui, *Perso-Arabic Sources of Information on the Life and Conditions in the Sultanate of Delhi*, New Delhi, 1992, p. 69.

25. Ibn Battuta, p. 775.

26. Amir Khusrau, *Ijaz-i Khusravi*, Lucknow, Vol. 4, 1876, pp. 137-141; Barani, p. 188.

27. Cf. I.H. Siddiqui, *Islam and Muslims in South Asia: Historical Perspective*, Delhi, 1987, pp. 5-6.

28. Cf. I.H. Siddiqui, *A Fourteenth Century Arab Account & C*, op. cit., p. 41.

29. Nizamuddin Ahmad, *Tabaqat-i Akbari*, Vol. I, Bib. Ind., Calcutta, 1913, p. 171; Firishta, *Gulshan-i Ibrahimi* (known as *Tarikh-i Firishta*), Lucknow, 1281 A.H., p. 188.

30. See Mulla Abdul Qadir Badauni, *Muntakhab-ut Tawarikh*, text, Vol. I, Bib. Ind., Calcutta, 1864, p. 323.

31. I.H. Siddiqui, 'Water Works and Irrigation System in India during Pre-Mughal Period', *Journal of the Economic and Social History of the Orient*, Vol. XXIX, Part I, 1986, p. 70.

2

Erotic Elements in Temple Art

SATYA PRAKASH SINGH

Numerous Indian temples carry erotic scenes on their walls. This is a pan-Indian phenomenon prevailing from Gujarat to Assam and from Kashmir to deep in the peninsula. In the historical perspective also it makes itself tangible in the oldest extant temple belonging to the post-Gupta era.[1] And this trend goes on reaching its climax in the 13th-century Konarak temple.

Naturally, the question arises as to what such a sacred structure has to do with erotic scenes. This paradox, however, did not strike the Indians until it was brought to the latter's notice by foreign visitors and writers. This resulted in a number of theories seeking to explain this strange juxtaposition. Kanwar Lal has brought all these theories together in one of his works.[2] For instance, one opinion is that the erotic sculptures 'ward off evil and render the building immune to destruction'.[3] Another treats the erotic scenes as inducement to the potential visitors to the temple.[4] The third theory seeks to explain the depiction in terms of gratification of man's inclination to sex by way of fulfilling the demand of *kama*, the third *purusartha.*[5] *Dharma, artha, kama, moksa* are the four *purusarthas*, the objectives of life. Out of these, while *kama* and *moksa* relate purely to this world, *dharma* is the bridge between this world and the other. *Moksa* is the *summum bonum* of life. While entering into a temple which is supposed to be the place of *dharma* and *moksa* one should not ignore *kama* and *artha.* Erotic scenes on the walls of temple offer the devotee an opportunity to get his *purusartha* of *kama* fulfilled. The next theory explains that the erotic sculptures were meant to educate the public in sex acts. 'What the written texts of those days...attempted in words, these sculptures presented in plastic form.'[6] In view of the sensual depictions of certain *yogins* and *tantrikas,* it is held by some that these might be some sort of sexo-yogic exercises projected on behalf of *tantrikas, saktas, kaulas* and *kapalikas.*[7] Finally, some relate these scenes to the Upanisadic doctrine of delight as experienced through reunification of the Atman and Brahman. The deity inside the temple represented Brahman, and the devotee embodies the Atman. A visit to the temple by the devotee amounts to the return of the Atman to Brahman along with all the beatitudes in stock for it. The carvings on the walls of temples are symbolic of those beatitudes.[8]

Thus, explanations for resolving the above mentioned paradox range from commonplace to sublime. Each seeks to annul completely or at least to subordinate the other viewpoint. An instance of annulment can be had in Devangana Desai's view, characterizing all such theories as purely speculative and projecting her own explanation in terms of socio-cultural phenomenon dictated mainly by magical beliefs.[9] This process of formulation, reformulation and rejection of views leaves the problem unresolved.

The basic drawback with almost all these theories is that they try to understand the erotic carvings without paying due attention to the nature of structure *per se*. Usually the institution of temple is taken to be a Puranic phenomenon emerging in complete departure from the Vedic mode of worship. The departure is supposed to have taken place due to the reassertion of the non-Aryan elements which obviously had their concentration in the South. But, contrary to this supposition, the oldest extant temple in India is found in the North itself.[10] There is no denying that the temple is the proper substitute of the Vedic institution of sacrifice. The *Rig Veda* speaks of two modes of offering to the Divine, namely, *havana* and *bali*. The first was made in the fire, while the second in water and on solid ground. According to the instructions of Aruni imparted to his son Svetaketu, the ultimate Reality called *Sat* (Existence) manifests itself first in the form of *tejas*, light or fire, which in its turn gives rise to water, and the latter to *anna* or earth.[11] In the Vedic sacrifice the sacred pit was dug, the fire was kindled, the deities were invited to sit around the sacred pit, offerings were made and were consumed by fire leaving behind only a heap of ashes after the ceremonial sending off of the deities. Need for perpetualization of all this must, therefore, have been felt gradually as a psychological necessity. The institution of temple is a result of the fulfilment of this need. If the Divine could be reached through *tejas*, its initial manifestation, as the Upanisad holds, it could as well be reached through subsequent manifestations such as *apah* (water) and *anna* (solid matter). This philosophical position provided authenticity to the shift in the mode of worship. The most likely result was that the subtle presence of deities at the place of Vedic sacrifice was made tangible in the form of clay models, wooden and stone carvings and statues. When the divinities were thus conceived in material forms and were made to dwell in the physical world, they had to be provided with suitable dwelling place which obviously had to be heavenly as well as physical in nature and cosmic in dimension, if not actually, at least symbolically. Concretization of this idea resulted in the temple along with the rites and cults associated with it. While *Agni* as the manifest form of *Sat* assumed the form of Vishnu and Shiva, the lesser gods and goddesses got concretized in the form of subordinate divinities around them, and the *yajnasala* was given the status of the *garbhagrha*. The same Agni was shaped into the solar deity in Konarak eventually. Presence of sacrificial pits and pillars in temples, sacrifices of all varieties made in them, besides the attachment of ponds, all are obviously reminiscent of their origin in sacrifice.

As regards sacrifice, it is erroneous to take it as some sort of fertility rite based on certain magical principles such as imitation and contagion.[12] The Vedic sacrifice was a universal principle controlling the process of cosmic creation. The celebrated hymn to Purusa in the *Rig Veda* is just a summary of the Vedic position in this regard.[13] According to it, the world is a product of the primeval sacrifice performed by the Supreme Being by giving Himself over as oblation. It implies objectification, concretization and thus manifestation of the Self in the form of the world. As the world is an act of self-creation undergone by the Supreme Being, each individual here, being created as His replica, has to perform the same act and be creative likewise so as to conform to His basic nature.

This fundamental Vedic vision gets reflected and deliberated upon in the *Brahmanas* in elaborations of sacrificial acts, rites and performances. As sex is the most intimate and tangible form of self-creation, it has often been used in the *Brahmanas* as a symbol of creation of all varieties both on individual and universal scale. In the *Satapatha Brahmana,* for instance, it is observed that '*Vedi* (the sacrificial pit) is the woman attended to from all around by gods and learned Brahmanas. As such, she was not to be kept naked. That is why *barhi,* the sacred grass, is strewn all over it.'[14] Accordingly, the shape of the *vedi* is also sometimes made to conform to the body of a young lady. 'Just as the body of a young beautiful lady is admired when it is heavy on the hips, slender in the middle and again heavy on the breast even so', observes the *Brahmana,* 'the *vedi* is liked by gods when it is heavy on the hips and the breast and easy to hold in the middle.'[15] Further, the *garhapatya agni* put in the sacrificial pit is conceived as the semen ejaculated into the private part of a woman.[16] At another place, the *Brahmana* states that the sun is the fire which serves as semen in the sacrificial pit, and, when the oblation is dropped into it, it is equivalent to fertilization of the womb.[17] Elsewhere, in the same *Brahmana,* participation of the wives in the sacrifice is explained like this: 'Progeny is eventually born of sacrifice. Having been born of sacrifice initially it gets born of the couple. Thus, though supposed to be born of the couple, it eventually is born of the sacrifice. Role of the couple in procreation is just a means. The clarified butter is indeed the semen. This is why it is dropped into the sacrificial pit by keeping mute. *Soma* is also the semen. Offering of the oblation of *Soma* is really the offering of the semen.'[18] It again explains the participation of the wives, both human and divine, in the sacrifice in the following manner:

> Oblation is made by couples. Procreation is made possible through copulation. One who procreates, becomes the *rashtra.* One who does not procreate, ceases to be a *rashtra.* Thus couples sustain the *rashtra.* Gods sustain the *rashtra* on account of being in couples.[19]

Equation of the *vedi* with the private part of a woman and that of the fire and the oblation, including *ghrta* and *Soma,* with the semen is symbolic of the creative process taking place in all planes of being. As is evident from the texts quoted above, it symbolizes primarily the creativity of gods. In order to be creative, they have to live in couples, as the text says. By virtue of this, they create the world. *Agni* and *Soma* as products of the creativity operating on the divine plane act as semen in the creation of the world. If the sacrifice performed by the mortals is a replica of the primeval sacrifice taking place on the divine plane, the act of sex is an extension of the same sacrifice to the vital plane of our being. Symbolization of this act in terms of sacrifice is intended to associate it with the creativity operating on the divine plane. Thus, though appearing obscene, the association of sexual functions with the act of sacrifice is meant for integrating the individual with the design of the Creator and the Cosmos. The symbol of sex was so prominent to the authors of the *Brahmana* that even the relationship between the earth and the horizon was conceived on that line. The earth has been envisaged as the female and the horizon the male. Once, however, alternatively, both are conceived as males, one discharging its semen from the earth in the form of vapour, and the other from above in the form of rain, thereby giving birth to creatures.[20] The same idea has alternatively been presented in terms of sacrifice also.

Sacrifice as the act of sex appeared so integrated to the Vedic seer that they have become alternative ways of explaining the creation of the world. If the celebrated hymn to Purusa in the *Rig Veda* explains the creation of the world in terms of sacrifice, the equally celebrated hymn of creation in the same Samhita views it in *kama* the primeval creativity. If the former maintains that the Supreme Purusa offered himself as oblation in the primeval sacrifice resulting in the creation of the world, the latter observes that it was *kama* which arose first in the process of creation as the semen of the Creator giving rise eventually to the two sorts of entities, one bearing the semen while the other endowed with greatness.[21]

Obviously, the primeval principles of masculinity and femininity, as born of the ultimate Being, came to assume, in course of time, the form of the *Shivalinga* and the *yoni* in literature. These images got concretized subsequently in the form of icons and were placed in the innermost apartment of the temple called *garbhagrha*, symbolizing the core of Being. As Man and Woman, however, the same principles were translated into sculptures of Shiva and Parvati by the Shaivites and Vishnu and Lakshmi by the Vaishnavites. The Shaivite concept of *ardhanarishvara*, in which one half of the icon represents Shiva while the other Parvati, is symbolic of that state of the Being in which the latter was still androgynous and was as yet to be bifurcated into two. The subsequent image of Radha and Krishna carved in close embrace of each other is a Vaishnavite version of the same idea.

When the *ekam sat* of the *Rig Veda* out of its *kama* or creative joy bifurcated itself as the Upanisadic Purusa into the male and the female and thus began to be transfigured as the *Shivalinga* and *yoni*, Shiva and Parvati, Daksa and Aditi. Vishnu and Lakshmi, Krishna and Radha, the *vedi* came to be developed into the *garbhagrha* and the *yajnasala* into the temple along with the divine sacrifice assuming the form of the creativity of the organic type, the whole of the temple as the Cosmos or the body of God began to vibrate with the creativity of the Divine. The consequence was that the walls of temples began to pulsate with the same creative joy with which the Himalayan resort of Shiva, as recounted by Kalidasa, began to the thrilled at the approach of Kamadeva to Shiva. As the great poet has visualized it, the spring season started putting the mark of its nail as *palasa* flowers on the cheeks of the forests conceived as young ladies, bees became unusually loving to their females, black deer began to rub the eye of its female counterpart with its horn, the Kinnara started kissing the cheek of its beloved and the creepers took in their embrace the trees standing nearby.[22] If this fundamental epic imagery could come to the mind of such a devout poet as Kalidasa, particularly in regard to his most revered divinity like Shiva, there was nothing surprising if the architects and sculptors of the day adorned the abode of their deities with sculptures of the same nature.[23]

The tradition of such carvings is deep rooted in the Indian history. In his *Natyasastra*, Bharata, for instance, mentions that after constructing the *natyamandapa* and plastering its walls, drawings and paintings should be done on them meticulously.[24] The motifs of these drawings, as suggested by Bharata, are men and women indulging in pleasures and creepers intertwining with trees. Creepers are suggestive of enjoyment of men and women. They also suggest the motif of *mithuna,* amorous couple. Amorous couples on the walls of the *natyamandapa* in the early centuries of the Christian era might very well have been extended to temples also since the latter could equally well have required to represent in its structure the divine drama being played on all planes of Being. This possibility gets support from the subsequent attachment of the actual *natyamandapa* to temples like Konarak, for instance. This may be traced in some form or the other centuries earlier. The basic purpose of drama, as spelled out by Bharata, is artistic representation of all possible feelings and emotions evoked by the scenario of the world, including the modes of behaviour displayed by the people.[25] The aspects of behaviour specifically mentioned by Bharata in this regard are *dharma, artha,* and *kama* getting manifested in the form of religious observances, peace of mind, carrying out trades, waging wars, restraints exercised on the wicked, instructions imparted to the ignorant, consolation given to the sufferer, pleasures of life enjoyed through games, amusements and indulgences of all possible varieties.[26] Scenes bearing out these ideas were not only presented on the stage but were also drawn, painted and probably carved on the walls of *natyamandapa.* The latter attached to the temple of Konarak is an extant example. Now if the *natyamandapa* could be sought to be made a perfect replica of the world particularly related to the human life, the temple could as well be conceived as a miniature of the totality of the Reality including the human as well as the divine. This concept of the temple would naturally have got assimilated into it whatever was there on the walls of *natyamandapa.* It would have been sought to be reproduced realistically on the temple since *natyamandapa* presents the drama of life, the temple aims at revealing the Reality as such. Thus, while the carvings on *natyamandapa* revolve around the libido aesthetically to make it enjoyable, those on the walls of the temple make the same libido reveal itself in its stark nakedness so as to generate the will to transcend it either through a comparison of the quantum of felicity involved in the satisfaction of the libido on the one hand, and the vision of the Divine on the other, or through the generation of repulsion towards all libidinous enjoyments whatsoever.

This explains very well the different sorts of erotic images on the walls. As regards the comparison, it has been observed that the erotic images carved on the walls of temples are generally in joyful and rapturous mood. This is quite understandable. Agastya, Vishvamitra, Dirghatamas and Narada are glaring examples of the irresistibility of the impulse to sex. The image of Vishvamitra and Menka placed on the left side of the Konarak temple, particularly in a deep corner, albeit impressively, is one amongst many bearing out the vulnerability of man to the desire for sex. But the pleasure from sex is just elementary. The same, if supported by wealth and power, gains durability. The three combined together, therefore, are taken to form one complete unit of happiness in this world. It is worth noting that the erotic figures in temples, be it Khajuraho, Lingaraja, Konarak, etc., cater usually to the elite of the society. This most possibly reflected the life of indulgence of the rich and ruling classes of the time. This interpretation has no doubt some truth in it in as much as any artist or literary figure would draw his images from the contemporary life. But the walls of a temple can in no case be taken as an art gallery where anything can be drawn or carved just because it reflects the contemporary life. Being the symbol of perpetuity, a temple in its every detail is supposed to symbolize the same perpetuity. Looked from this angle, the cheerful figures on the temples, however contemporary, must stand for a certain permanent value pointing out some higher possibilities. No matter whether such figures are carved on the outer or inner wall or even in the proximity of the Deity, their cheerfulness does by no means match the delight visible on the face of the Divine figure. It is just a semblance of the latter born of accomplishment of the common task of creativity and fulfilment of the respective *purusartha, kama* in the case of the human figure as against *moksa* represented by the Deity. All the semblance notwithstanding, how far behind is this human joy compared to the Divine delight, may be understood from a gradation of joy as given by the *Taittiriya Upanisad.* According to it, if there be a person young, handsome, optimistic, strong in build, energetic and well-settled in mind and at the same time having got to rule over the whole of this earth full of riches, the joy available to him thus would form one full unit of the delight to be experienced at the maximum on the human level. In contrast, the ultimate Divine delight is reckoned as trillions and trillions of times more in quantum.[27]

It is this gradation and the possibility of comparison and quantification which has made it possible to bring erotic scenes in the proximity of the Deity in the temple. The pleasure of unfettered sex depicted on the outer and inner walls and even in the proximity of the Deity is intended to bring home to the devout visitor the idea how infinitely much more blissful would be the understanding of the Reality symbolized by the main figure inside. The scenario of comparison is presented not for creating disdain for sex, but for stimulating the visitor to try to reach the state of Divine beatitude by having an idea of it through the most alluring of all worldly pleasures.

An upshot of the comparison, however, is the danger of getting engrossed in the worldly pleasures and lose sight of the beatitude ahead. One of the earliest literary instances of this in the Indian tradition is the case of Naciketas as recounted in the *Katha Upanisad.* In order to test the intensity of the eagerness of Naciketas for understanding the mystery of the Atman, Yama offers him the pleasure of divine damsels along with all possible wealth. Naciketas weighs the relative worth of the two and declines the latter in favour of the former.[28] The *Yoga Sutra* warns the aspirant that while rising to higher planes of spirituality, one should not get entangled in nor feel boastful when getting alluring invitations since it would involve a deviation from the real pursuit.[29] This is illustrated in the case of Buddha who was approached by Mara along with his three daughters for dissuading him from his path.[30] This motif forms the central theme of erotic paintings and carvings in Buddhist temples.[31] In accordance with this tendency of the Indian psyche, it is just possible that the erotic figures in temples are designed to test the worthiness of the devout visitor to come face to face with the Divine. But, as observed above, this inclination is just a by-product of the basic intention of giving an idea of the final beatitude.

NOTES

1. See Kanwar Lal, *Immortal Khajuraho*, Delhi, 1965, p. 61; Devangana Desai, *Erotic Sculptures of India: A Socio-Cultural Study*, New Delhi, 1975, p. 18.
2. Kanwar Lal, op. cit., pp. 176-84.
3. Ibid., p. 176.
4. Ibid., 177.
5. Ibid., pp. 178-79.
6. Ibid., p. 179.
7. Ibid., pp. 179-81.
8. Ibid., pp. 183-84.
9. Devangana Desai, op. cit., p. 87.
10. Kanwar Lal, p. 61.
11. *Chandogya Upanisad*, VI.1.
12. Devangana Desai, pp. 88-9.
13. *Rig Veda*, X.90.
14. *Satapatha Brahmana*, 1.3.3.9.
15. Ibid., 1.2.5.16.
16. Ibid., VIII.6.3.8-11.
17. Ibid., VI.3.1.7.
18. Ibid., I.9.2.5-12.
19. Ibid., IX.4.1.5.
20. Ibid., VII.4.2.22.
21. *Rig Veda*, X.90 and 129.
22. Kalidasa, *Kumarasambhavam*, III, verses 7, 29,

33, 36, 38, 39.

23. Bharata, *Natyasastra*, II.91.

24. Ibid., I.112.

25. Ibid.

26. Ibid., i.108-111.

27. *Taittiriya Upanisad*, 8.2-4.

28. *Katha Upanisad*, I.1.

29. Patanjali, *Yoga Sutra*, III, 51.

30. Kanwar Lal, pp. 121-2.

31. Hajima Nakamura, *Ways of Thinking of Eastern Peoples*, pp. 314-15.

3

Encounter and Transition — European Impact in Awadh (1765-1856)

MADHU TRIVEDI

Awadh was the largest in extent, richest in resource generation and administratively well governed of all the successor states which emerged during the crisis of the Mughal empire.[1]

The Awadh court, initially located at Faizabad, and then at Lucknow, very soon became refuge of the old culture in northern India. The contemporaries refer to it as the most magnificent, the most cultivated and also the most cosmopolitan. The rulers of Awadh, better known as Nawab Wazir as they had not declared their independence, extended lavish patronage to fine arts, crafts and literature.[2] Professionals flocked to Faizabad in great numbers from different directions, particularly from the Mughal capital Shahjahanabad whose splendour was fading.[3] The Awadh capital was shifted to Lucknow in 1775 which emerged as a centre of art and culture and also became renowned for its luxury products and flourishing trade.[4] In no time the rulers of Awadh became the very symbols of artistic virtuosity to the extent that 'even in their final decadence...they achieved an awful distinction which rivalled the less tarnished splendour of earlier reigns.'[5]

The Awadh culture was Persian oriented as its rulers owed their origin to Nishapur in Persia.[6] Added to this was the fact that their ancestors had migrated to the Mughal court during the early years of the eighteenth century and had, thus, inherited the rich traditions of the Mughals who had a strong bias for Persian culture. Persian manners and customs were followed at the Awadh court, and Persian was the court language. Henry H. Spray commented in 1837: 'Lucknow, it should be observed, is now the only remaining Asiatic Court in Hindoostan in which the things like observance of Asiatic pomp and splendour were preserved.'[7]

However, from the very beginning European influence became visible in Awadh which appeared through two channels: the penetration of the British political influence and, second, through the Frenchmen who were employed by Nawab Shujauddaulah in large numbers.

The Awadh state experienced increasing influence of the British following the defeat of Nawab Shujauddaulah at the Battle of Buxar in 1764. The territory was restored to him by the Treaty of Allahabad (1765). However, the fortunes of Awadh were tied with that of the East India Company. Shujauddaulah had to agree to provide quarters for the British troops in his domain and meet their expenses, too.[8] In 1773, a Resident was appointed who began to intervene in the affairs of the state on the pretext of ensuring regular payment of subsidies. By the Treaty of Benaras (1801), about half the domain was annexed to the British territory and it was also decided that Awadh could not maintain relations with any other power except the British. The state became subsidiary to the Company and the ruler of Awadh was reduced to the position of a puppet.[9]

The conferment of the title of king on Ghaziuddin Haider in 1819 by the East India Company had a deep political purpose. The Company succeeded in severing all formal relations that Awadh had with the Mughals by this measure.[10] The remarks of Captain Mundy, who visited the court of Awadh in 1827, convey the correct meaning of the new arrangement: 'Ostensibly His Nawabship has been promoted with the rank of the servant to that of the Lord. Virtually he has only changed masters. For like other native potentates who have admitted British Residents at their courts, he is so strictly supervised that he can scarcely...enact any important state measure, without the interference of his super attentive allies.'[11]

The situation was not so grim, however, at the time of Shujauddaulah, who enjoyed a fair amount of autonomy in the management of the affairs of his state. His relations with the British remained cordial till the end, and he showed several gestures of friendliness by 'absorbing some of their cultures'. He invited British portraitist Tilly Kettle to Faizabad. At the same time his initiative to augment his military and civil works indicates his awareness of European superiority in these areas which he planned to achieve.[12] It also indicates that he did not trust them. One instance of which was the construction of Calcutta-*khwurd* by the bank of river Ghaghra.[13] The Nawab engaged the services of Antoine Louis Polier, Company's chief engineer at Fort William, Calcutta, to look after some civil works, especially to improve the defences of the city.[14] He also decided to organise his army on European models.[15] He established workshops for the preparation of war materials and, for this, he enlisted the services of the French artillery engineers and officers. This appears to be the first instance of the introduction of European technology in the military spheres by an Indian state.[16]

In 1775, about 200 French and other Europeans were in the service of Nawab Shujauddaulah:[17] these included people like Gentil, Rene Madec, Comte de Modave

Colonel Pedron, Dr. Visage, Aumont, Jean Baptiste de La Fontaine, Michael Filose, besides many other artillery officers and engineers.[18]

Among these, Gentil was the most prominent figure. He was an adviser and an intimate friend of Shujauddaulah, and remained attached to the Awadh court for about 12 years till the Nawab's death.[19] Gentil introduced many Frenchmen to the Awadh court:[20] Rene Madec, for instance, was a renowned adventurer of the eighteenth century. He was the chief of a big private army. Others were also well noted for their military talents and organisational abilities.[21]

The concentration of French military adventurers at the Awadh court alarmed the British who were apprehensive about their potential in north India and the possibility of a union with the Nawab who was trying to organise his military resources under French supervision. The British feared that these two might act together to oust the British from Bengal or, at least, the Nawab could reestablish himself in Karra and Allahabad with the French help. The apprehensions had some ground in view of the fact that Jean Baptiste Chevalier (1776-78), the governor of Chundernagar, had intimate knowledge of north Indian politics: he was in regular touch with the local power centres. Also he was apt in weaving intrigues.[22] Now onwards the British made it a point to remove the French influence at the Awadh court. This opportunity they got after the death of Shujauddaulah. The next ruler Asafuddaulah, soon after his accession, was asked to dismiss all his French employees.[23] In case of refusal, he was threatened with the withdrawal of Company's troops. Reluctantly the Nawab had to comply with their wishes.[24] This signalled the end of French influence at the Awadh court. The Awadh rulers could not employ any foreigner without the recommendations of the British Resident or the Governor General. This also signified the end of the large scale military preparations and production of better quality war materials by using European technology. In no time, whatever progress and expertise was gained in this field, was put to an end. Now onwards, the influence of the English began to increase in the court circle. The only exception was Claude Martin, who was a French but a close associate of the British. It is interesting to note that he became the most celebrated figure of Lucknow during the last quarter of the eighteenth century and exercised immense influence in the court circle. Claude Martin and Colonel John Mordaunt, the commander of the bodyguards of the Nawab, were the favourites of Asafuddaulah.

Asafuddaulah showed unprecedented interest in the collection of European curiosities and he is said to have spent about one million pounds sterling on European artifacts between 1787 and 1797,[25] which included automata, clocks and watches, chronometers, pistols and guns, ornate mirrors, furniture and glassware, especially chandeliers and candelabra, etc.[26] The artifacts were managed through various agencies of Calcutta. Individuals were also commissioned to buy goods for him.[27] The Nawab's

European associates and even the Residents exploited his love for curiosities. Daniel Johnson informs that Claude Martin made every possible effort to procure 'any piece of mechanical, or other curiosity' for the Nawab which he was certain of selling at an immense profit. Such items were procured from Europe and sold to the Nawab at a profit of 200 to 300 per cent. Martin even lent him money to buy these artifacts.[28]

These mechanical pieces and curiosities were kept by the Nawab in the *Ai'nakhana.*[29] According to Twining, a contemporary observer, the *Ai'nakhana* was full of 'European articles of every kind' from paper lantern, knives, snuff-boxes and similar items; for some of them the Nawab had spent two to three thousand pounds sterling. He also notices that the Nawab made no distinction between a valuable chronometer and a watch of most ordinary description, which was because both cost him the same amount. In Twining's opinion, the *Ai'nakhana* was both a museum and a lumber room.[30]

These European artifacts were simply used as toys and there is no evidence which might suggest that any attempt was made to use them, or the technology employed therein for any practical purpose. The same was the case with the later rulers as well as aristocratic circle.[31] Now a scorn for the aesthetic sense of the rulers of Awadh is discernible: Asafuddaulah was criticised for his 'stupendous propensities'[32] and not remembered as a serious collector.

It is to be noted that the process of Europeanisation of the building art began during the reign of Asafuddaulah. He had great admiration for Farhat Bakhsh and Constantia which were constructed by Claude Martin at Lucknow. A number of European styled buildings were designed for the Nawab by Claude Martin and some British engineers in the Company's service. The European influence became more visible and permanent in architecture during the nineteenth century.

Sa'adat Ali Khan, the next ruler, had maximum exposure to European culture. His initial education was supervised by Madam Gailliez, a French lady from Chundernagar.[33] Besides, his exile to Calcutta and Allahabad provided him frequent opportunities to interact with the British so much so that according to a European traveller, Ann Deane, he 'unconsciously imbibed many English ideas'.[34] She further informs that 'he understood the English language perfectly and wrote it correctly, but he could not pronounce the words.'[35] He was also fond of European dresses.[36] However, he adhered to the traditional Indian attire in the court and preferred a *jama* and a *shamla* (a knotted silken turban).[37]

Sa'adat Ali Khan was also well versed in English social etiquettes. He entertained his European guests to banquet in rooms decorated with English furniture, looking glasses, and cut-glass vases. The French cuisine used to be served in English manner.[38]

In fact, it was difficult for the people who attended these dinners to believe that they were seated in the court of an Indian ruler.[39]

In spite of his close relationship and orientation in English culture, Sa'adat Ali Khan showed no inclination for the Europeanisation of the court culture. Also, he did not allow the introduction of European goods except some luxury items and curiosities. Thus, the court culture, arts and crafts retained their oriental character; the only exception was the building art which assumed considerable European taste during the period.

Under the later rulers, however, the vogue for European culture, art and artifacts increased enormously. Ghaziuddin Haider was fond of collecting European, especially English, commodities of all sorts and descriptions.[40] He was the first to adopt the symbols of kingship: throne-chair, crown, and courtly dresses (which had a blending of European art traditions).[41] He had even acquired an English coach, like the Lord Mayor's, 'in the livery of the latest London fashion'.[42] It cannot be denied, however, that Ghaziuddin Haider was the first to adopt European courtly dress and crown for formal occasions. (Reverse response could be noticed among the Europeans. Gentil, Polier, and many other French adventurers adopted semi-oriental life-style in India; they maintained *harem* and indulged in Indian pastimes, smoked *huqqah* and enjoyed the *mehfil* of the nautch-girls. Polier was fond of Indian costumes.) While Europeans are appreciated for their adoption of anything Indian, which is termed as their love for oriental culture, the rulers of Awadh have been branded as Anglo-maniac for their propensity for European fashions and manufactures, and dismissed with scorn. One should always remember that no major change occurred in the life-style or outlook of the Awadh rulers which remained thoroughly Indian.

Among the rulers of Awadh, Nasiruddin Haider is the most ridiculed one: like his father, he was called an Anglo-maniac. He was accused of associating with the low-born, and that he was under the influence of an English barber and was surrounded by European sycophants of the worst type.[43] These charges are made in a contemporary work *The Private Life of an Eastern King* written by William Knighton.[44] He criticises the Nawab for his fondness for English culture, language and costume. This ruler has been described by Shore as a 'profligate who squanders his money like a child'. However, one should not forget the fact that those low-born favourites were recommended by the British Residents and other important officials and, as Shore himself admits, even the Resident used to induce the Nawab to buy trinkets at exorbitant prices.[45] One should also remember that Nasiruddin Haider was an open minded person who established an observatory with the latest equipments for the training of young courtiers in the Western astronomical sciences. He wanted to establish a college in Lucknow on English model. He had established a hospital on European pattern with English doctors and other staff. It may be noted that the King George Medical College of Lucknow owes its origin to the

King's Hospital which was established by Nasiruddin Haider. Many of the above projects remained unfinished due to his untimely death.[46]

One might clearly notice that a pattern of new court culture was emerging since the time of Ghaziuddin Haider and that the court culture was Indian, and to be very precise, Mughal, as far as the court customs, etiquettes and language are concerned; but the symbols of royalty were neither distinctly European nor Indian: they may be characterized as Indo-European, except that the crown and the ceremonial dresses were in the English style as may be gathered from the life-size portraits in oil at display at the Husainabad (Lucknow) Art Gallery. The rulers lived in houses which were constructed and furnished in the European style curtains, looking-glasses, Italian sculptures, etc. These trends were absorbed even by the last three rulers who were no keen admirers of European culture. However, it should also be remembered that the ethos of Indian culture remained unchanged in their private life.[47]

PAINTING

Indian art has always shown great adaptability to foreign techniques and there was 'no reluctance on the part of artists or their patrons to accept innovations'.[48] While the painting of the sixteenth century is dominated by Persian influence, in the seventeenth century it appears to be influenced by European art traditions. According to some scholars, the European influence was actually greater and more permanent than that of Persia.[49] Hajek is of the opinion that European style 'almost certainly attained its greatest influence in the Mughal miniature, where some of its techniques were completely absorbed.'[50]

In spite of the fact that Indian painting absorbed some of the Western techniques, it remained essentially a two-dimensional art. It did not employ the principles of perspective which were strictly followed by the European artists in different manners — perspective of colour, perspective of disappearance, linear perspective, etc. In fact, Indian artists were familiar with perspective. Basawan, a court painter of Akbar, became 'an expert at finding a perspective that would combine the Iranian and Indian traditions with the illusionistic tendencies of the West.'[51] However, these are rare instances of perspective in Indian painting and they do not correspond to visual impressions. The Mughal miniatures did not display sufficient knowledge of shading. They were also not familiar with the principle of the object casting shadows. Such instances may be seen in the paintings of Faizullah, an eminent Delhi artist who worked for Nawab Safdar Jung. Similarly, the three-quarters technique may also be noted. The frontal delineation of the human face was, however, completely lacking in them.[52]

All these techniques were incorporated when Indian artists got ample opportunities for intimate contacts with the European art traditions under European supervision in Awadh during the third-quarter of the eighteenth century. European impact on Awadh painting, in respect of subject, style and technique, was so distinct that virtually two styles flourished on parallel lines: the court style which represented the continuation of the later Mughal tradition (the Delhi *qalam*),[53] and the European style which originated under the French and Swiss patrons, especially Gentil. While the court style declined after the death of Shujauddaulah, the European style continued to flourish in and outside the Awadh court up to the mid-nineteenth century.

There are three distinct phases in the development of the European style. The first phase was that of imitation. These early products belong to the 'pseudo-European School'.[54] The second phase is of adaptation and incorporation of some of the principles of European art. This may be called the period of experimentation. In the third phase there is total acceptance of the European techniques and style. The superiority of European art was acknowledged by all. The comment of Bahadur Singh Nami is worth mentioning: he says that painting had attained its climax of development under the European influence.[55]

The first phase, which corresponds to the reign of Shujauddaulah, is dominated by the French influence. Gentil's fascination with the 'manners and custom of Hindustan' resulted in preparation of several albums of Indian paintings. He employed three local artists at Faizabad for ten years to illustrate his works *Abrege historique des Souverains de L'Indoustan ou Empire Mogol* (published in 1772) and *Divinites de L'Indoustan* (published in 1774).[56] It is on record in an inscribed miniature in the Musee Guimet Collection (Paris) that one of the artists was Nivasi Lal who was well known for his exceptional skill.[57] The details of other artists are not known. Significantly, all inscriptions given in the original manuscripts are in the Devanagiri script.

The themes of these miniatures are depiction of indigenous gods and goddesses, small scenes of royal life, trophies of arms, etc.; yet the artists employed European techniques as may be observed in the frontal depiction of human faces, proper study of human body, correct representation of perspective and the employment of the principle of light and shade. This was an early instance of the introduction of these European characteristics in accordance with precise European standards and not as they appeared to the artist. These paintings are in delicate water colours. The fascination for Indian culture was shared by others, especially Henry Polier who also got several *muraqqas* prepared by the local artists, of whom Meher Chand was of great renown.

The arrival of Tilli Kettle in 1771 at Faizabad belongs to this phase. He was a portraitist and perhaps the first professional artist from Europe to come to India.[58] It is interesting to note that Shujauddaulah invited him to execute portraits of himself and his family members. Kettle executed six large oil paintings for the Nawab: (1) a large size study of the Nawab in gold attire and fur cap; (2) a group portrait of Shujauddaulah and four of his sons receiving an English general, Robert Barker, with his suite of two A.D.Cs., an officer and a Persian interpreter; (3) the painting of the Nawab receiving an English general at Faizabad with his elephant and suite in the background; (4) portrait of the Nawab and his eldest son Asafuddaulah; (5) a portrait showing the Nawab in the Maratha attire; and (6) portrait of the Nawab and his ten sons.[59]

Tilli Kettle, who stayed at Faizabad for about two years, could not much influence the court. This was probably due to the reason that his medium was oil which was not agreeable to the taste of his patron, nor was it compatible with the traditional painting technique of the indigenous artists who took time to appreciate and learn it. However, he influenced the local artists in other ways. Some of his paintings began to be copied in miniatures: it happened at the initiative of Gentil.

Gentil borrowed four paintings of Kettle from the Nawab in order to prepare their miniaturised copies by his own artists. When the first copy of the Nawab and his son was ready, he showed it to the Nawab who insisted on keeping it. Gentil exchanged it with Kettle's original which he later presented to Louis XVI.[60] This event is very significant as it shows that oil painting did not find favour with the Nawab. On the contrary, he liked miniature of it in tempera and exchanged it for oil painting. Of the remaining three, only one picture of the Nawab and his ten sons was copied, which were also presented to Louis XVI.[61] This painting could still be seen at Versailles (No. M.U.3888). It bears an inscription that it was made by Nivasi Lal who appears to be an excellent copyist. His skill may be observed in the balanced composition, delineation of linear perspective, convergence of angles, appropriate shading and variety of modes and postures.

Other local artists, it appears, were fascinated by Kettle's paintings and they began freely to imitate it in tempera. Besides, Kettle's influence appeared in the delineation of facial idioms to the extent that later on it became a characteristic feature of Awadh paintings. Kettle's study of Shujauddaulah became the 'stock figure in trade'. Meher Chand imitated Shuja's figure from Kettle's study of the Nawab and Sir Robert Barker, 'at least in three fresh compositions'. At one place he portrayed the Nawab holding a bow, at another he presented him changing the position of his hand and also the background, in yet another he borrowed the hand and face of the figure. He also copied the painting of the Nawab and his ten sons.[62]

Although Meher Chand used to paint in the traditional Mughal style and made several miniatures in this style for Polier,[63] yet his paintings show an aptitude for European technique. In some of his paintings, which are available to us in the form of reproductions, depth is delineated by diminishing the scale in the objects and distant landscape. This he grasped on his own as there is no evidence to suggest his proper schooling in the European technique in the manner of Nivasi Lal.

Thus, during this phase the local artists were trying to follow European techniques while they still adhered to their traditional medium—tempera. At the court level, no further interest was shown in European paintings or painters.

The second phase corresponds to the last quarter of the eighteenth century. Asafuddaulah appears to be greatly interested in European paintings and he had a vast collection of European prints,[64] though some European observers opine that 'two penny deal board paintings of ducks and drakes and excellent works of Lorraine held the same attraction for him.'[65] Asafuddaulah extended patronage to British painters on a very large scale, such as John Zoffany (an oil painter), William Hodges (landscape painter), Ozias Humphrey (miniature painter), William and Thomas Daniell (landscape painters). Zoffany established himself as an artist very quickly and made numerous paintings for the Nawab and his courtiers. One of his best known paintings is 'Colonel Mordaunt's Cock-fight'. Fanny Parkes regards it an excellent specimen of group portraiture, painted on a copper plate in oil medium in 1785.[66] This painting was extensively copied by the bazar artists in the nineteenth century.[67] Another notable group portraiture by him was Haider Beg's 'Embassy to Calcutta', which was an imaginary representation. Zoffany also made portraits, mostly life-size. Two half-length size portraits by him of charming young women are referred to by Knighton.[68]

Ozias Humphrey visited Lucknow in 1786 and executed five miniatures of the Nawab and his son Vazir Ali. He also got several other commissions but left Lucknow in a state of disappointment. William Hodges arrived with Zoffany but he also could not make much headway at the court.[69] Similarly, Daniells did not stay for long. This suggests that landscape painting as a separate genre failed to appeal the Nawab and this form remained unimitated in Awadh paintings. Zoffany was the only artist who stayed at Lucknow for a longer period, but he exclusively worked for the court circle and for European patrons, especially Martin.[70] His influence on the local artists was confined only to the copying of one of his paintings by them in tempera. Oil medium was still not popular. Instead, the impact of Gentil persisted.

Towards the end of the eighteenth century, many *muraqqas* of miniature paintings of 'native rulers' and 'native characters' were produced. One such is in the India Office Library which has the miniatures of the rulers of Awadh and other princely states.[71] A study of some of the specimens from these *muraqqas* brings out the following characteristics: the colour scheme is sombre in accordance with the contemporary French tradition, and one might assume that these miniatures were done by same artists who were previously working for and trained by Gentil; the faces are drawn in front postures and the exposed part of the faces is shown in light pigment in order to produce a three-dimensional effect; the facial idioms are, however, stereotyped. A face with cross eyes and limp mustache appears again and again with the main figure reminding us of Kettle's study of Shujauddaulah. The hazy effect is given for denoting the mist in the characteristic style of Gentil. These have some new features also — delineation of shadow in dark patches which is extended across the barren soil to suggest direction of light. Actions in the figure are suggested by a variety of poses and changed position of legs.[72] However, a set of deities was executed in a different style with the figures against the pale blue and sandy soil. The paintings were done in delicate water colours.[73]

In fact, this was a period of experimentation. No distinct style was emerging. Aspects of Indian culture and religion were painted in a style which incorporated European techniques for the most part. The local artists adopted water colour medium but they did not paint in oil at this stage. Oil paintings were executed by European artists only: they worked mostly for Claude Martin who had left about 150 oil paintings by Zoffany, Renaldi and others.[74]

The third phase is extended over the first half of the nineteenth century. It appears that a custom grew up at the Awadh court of employing European painters as court artists. George Place, Robert Home, Thomas Longcraft and Charles Smith were patronized by Sa'adat Ali Khan,[75] though he was not much interested in paintings.

George Place and Robert Home continued to paint for Ghaziuddin Haider. Robert Home was a talented artist and was greatly praised by Bishop Heber that he would have been a distinguished painter had he remained in Europe.[76] He executed numerous paintings of the king, his family and state guests.[77] He also prepared artistic designs on paper in water colour for furniture and state carriages, etc. for the king in which he blended the indigenous and European motifs in an exceptional manner.

Nasiruddin Haider patronized George Becchy, Cassanova and Charles Mantz. George Becchy was a competent artist and had distinguished himself in Europe before he left for India. He secured great royal favours and was allowed to enter the royal *harem* for drawing likenesses of the favourite wife of the king.[78] Like Home, he executed life-size paintings also.[79]

Charles Mantz produced many good portraits of the king in Indian and Persian costumes. He also executed the portraits of the queens.[80] He was given a salary of Rupees 1,000 per month.[81] It should be noted that though he was a landscape painter, he was mainly doing portraits which shows that landscape painting never became popular in Awadh.

According to Mildred and Archer, the characteristic style of Awadh painting during the third and the final phase arrived under the 'bazar artists' and it remained in vogue till the annexation of the kingdom. They refer to three important albums in their monographs which are in the Wellesley Collection in the India Office Library, in the Queen's Collection at Windsor and in the Victoria and Albert Museum. The albums, which belong to the early nineteenth century and have three sets of paintings, comprise the portraits of craftsmen like tailor, silversmith, painter, etc.[82] A study of some of the specimens from one of these albums makes it clear that the technique is highly Europeanised, which is reflected in the manner of shading and soft tones of the colour. The paintings are in water colour yet they are not free from the effect of tempera. The treatment of colours still remains hard. The artists still have propensity for bright colour: orange, peacock green, warm browns and yellow are used in abundance. Thick shaded lines are drawn in the objects to suggest the direction of light and shadow. Shadows are given at the bottom of each figure. However, the rest of the scene remains unaffected by the direction of light and, therefore, the foreground and background remain flat. Perspective, as a rule, has been followed by the artists. It seems that by this time the Indian painters had come to terms with scale perspective and geometrical perspective, especially in the representation of buildings. To produce three-dimensional effect in human faces, thick shadowing is done around the neck line. Faces are delineated in all varieties, three-quarters, frontal and also profile with cross-eyed glance.[83]

Of the remaining two sets, which are also in water colour, one represents a pale and insipid colour scheme, while the other is marked by hard knife-edged outlines. Same characteristics are represented in the second collection which is an album of Indian characters painted in 1812 (the Queen's Collection at Windsor).[84] A study of some of the specimens from another volume entitled *Oriental Paintings*[85] at the Victoria and Albert Museum which was painted around 1815, reveals that the painter is trying to depict objects in their natural form. He emphasizes the central theme and the rest of the composition is filled in light pigments. The picture is divided in two parts: vertical and horizontal by introducing the ground line or horizon. Strokes are bold and lines are shaded. Trees shown in the background are treated with details of branches and patches of leaves. The technique is, thus, Europeanised though the colour scheme is very much indigenous. About another volume entitled *Customs of the Court of Awadh*[86] at Windsor, which was painted for Ghaziuddin Haider by Indian artists at the court in 1826, Archer opines that these paintings also depict Europeanised techniques and native colour scheme. The brush work is, however, hurried and the delineation of figures is not up to the mark as they are 'lumpy and ill defined'. The facial idioms are also stereotyped. One finds several paintings of the time of Wajid Ali Shah in support of this view. These paintings are located in the Raza Library at Rampur, the State Museum at Lucknow and the Bharat Kala Bhawan at Varanasi.

A number of new features are discernible at the beginning of the nineteenth century. The court painters adopted the European technique of painting though their subjects and colour scheme were traditional. The local artists began to paint in water colour.

During the period, several painters were engaged in preparing sets of *muraqqas* of native rulers and characters. The production of these became a lucrative trade as these were in great demand among the foreigners and locals. The comments of Bahadur Singh Nami are worth giving here.[87] According to him, the portraits of princes and royal personages were executed for several purposes. These were carried to other countries by the visitors. The kings and nobles were also in the habit of collecting such *muraqqas*. It grew as a fashion among the elite and populace to collect the portraits of the past rulers. It shows that albums of portraits were in great demand in local and foreign markets.

Towards the middle of the nineteenth century, the popularity of oil paintings increased. Bahadur Singh Nami refers to *Tasawir Roghani*, a term which appears for the first time. He also informs us that life-size paintings, called *qadi adam taswir*, began to be painted frequently during this period.[88] Many life-size oil paintings of the rulers of Awadh in their courtly dress can still be seen in the Husainabad Art Gallery. These were exclusively painted by the European artists. However, it is on record that the technique of painting in oil medium was also learnt by the local artists towards the middle of the nineteenth century. Lala Thakur Das Dariyabadi, Fazl Ali Behzad Raqam, Lala Khushlal Singh Luckhnawi and his pupil Ghulam Reza Khan were good exponents of the technique.[89] We have references to full length portraits in oil by the artists of Lucknow.[90] However, it was practised on a limited scale due to the expensiveness of the work.

Bahadur Singh Nami refers to *taswir* as *chhapa* as a curious innovation of the Europeans.[91] Probably he is referring to the art of engraving which came into existence during the fifteenth century with the printing press and was used for multiplication of pictures. There are no instances available of Indian artists adopting this technique which was done on wood and copper, though according to Thevenot, there were some skilled engravers at Delhi in the seventeenth century.[92] However, no specimen is available to confirm this statement for the seventeenth century. Bahadur Singh Nami's comment suggests that this technique was introduced by the Europeans in Lucknow. Probably it became popular with the establishment of litho printing press at Lucknow during the reign of Ghaziuddin Haider.

ARCHITECTURE

Age is sometimes most faithfully reflected in its buildings. This appears to be true in the context of Awadh architecture which displays well the existing aesthetic aspirations and requirements.

The building art originated in the tradition of Mughal architecture. In the early phase, that is, till the third quarter of the eighteenth century, Shahjahanabad remained an ideal to emulate. The tomb of Safdar Jung at Shahjahanabad was a symbol of the growing power of the Nawab Wazir at the centre. The buildings of Faizabad, where Shujauddaulah settled permanently after the Battle of Buxar,[93] were also modelled after the later Mughal architectural style. It becomes interesting in view of the fact that Shujauddaulah showed keenness to employ Polier as an architect and engineer.[94] However, the buildings of Faizabad had no bearing of European architecture. Polier was placed in charge of superintending and directing only the fortification work which the Nawab planned himself.[95] However, in the last quarter of the eighteenth century, European influence began to show itself in the building art and a number of European style buildings were constructed during this period, such as Farhat Bakhsh, Asafi Kothi, Constantia and the Bibiapur Kothi. From now onwards European elements continued to infiltrate increasingly into local architecture.

Nawab Asafuddaulah had great admiration for European style buildings, and soon after his accession he is said to have requested the Resident, John Bristow, to 'produce him the plan of a house after the European taste'. It is on record that one such house was designed and erected for him by an engineer, Captain Charles Marsack.[96] Further details about this house are not available.

Claude Martin designed for Asafuddaulah a town mansion, the Asafi Kothi and Bibiapur Kothi, which was a country house. Asafi Kothi was located in the Daulat Khana palace complex. Another building in European style in this complex was the house of Raja Mehra,[97] which had a semblance with Louvre. This house is a sure proof of the fascination of the local aristocracy for houses in European style. Further details are not available about these two houses or other such buildings, or the architectural style of Daulat Khana itself which was demolished during the reign of Ghaziuddin Haider.[98] However, its view from the riverside is preserved in an engraving by William Hodges which shows a building with a distinct European impact.[99]

European style buildings were constructed in great numbers during the reign of Sa'adat Ali Khan. He took keen interest in designing his own houses in a style which resembled 'Grecian'. A change is noticeable after the death of Martin. Now the rulers started designing on their own in a manner which looked European. The comment of Valentia about Sa'adat Ali Khan is very significant in this respect that he was 'his own architect', and, because he never employed an architect, 'the faults were numerous' in the execution of details.[100] What Valentia characterizes as faults were, in fact, employment of indigenous techniques and materials by local craftsmen for the fashioning of European details. Early nineteenth century was the phase of transition and the beginning of the hybridization of the building art at Lucknow.

The city of Lucknow was greatly improved by Sa'adat Ali Khan.[101] He virtually changed the facade of the old city and imparted it a European look. This was specially true of the southern parts of the city 'from Residency all way downwards the two principal streets and afterwards through the park of Dilkusha.'[102] Hamilton supplies interesting details for the southern part of Lucknow which 'consisted of very handsome street in European fashion like that of Oxford though wider than it...and about a mile in length.'[103] The houses located in it looked 'as if they have been transplanted from Regent Street.'[104] However, the lofty gateways at each extremity of the *chowk* had a peculiar blending of indigenous and European styles. These had a 'Grecian front on one side and Moorish on other.'[105] Even the houses, which were in Hamilton's opinion 'for the most part English in style', had 'a strange occasional admixture of Eastern architecture'. The royal palaces and gardens located in this locality also displayed the same characteristics.[106]

In fact, these buildings were the typical product of the phase of transition. Their style was European but they were created for Indian patrons by native craftsmen; that is why they are not free from oriental touch. The European influence did not penetrate beyond the outward appearance of the buildings. The foreign elements whether Italian, Gothic, French, Palladian or English were never assimilated in the conceptual framework of the Awadh architecture: it remains basically Indian in character. Thus, the foreign elements are used only in their decorative capacity but in oriental settings: triangular pediments, oriels, Roman round arches, Corinthian and composite pillars and pilasters feature amidst the *shahjahani mehrab* (arch with seven cusps), fluted domes, turrets, kiosks and ogee arcades. This characteristic was observed by Fancy Parkes who remarks: 'It is a curious circumstance that many of the palaces of Lucknow have fronts in the imitation of the palaces of Naples and Rome and the native palace is beyond, in an enclosed place.'[107] The exterior of these royal mansions looked European to the extent that the capital of Awadh, in the opinion of Bishop Heber, 'had more the appearance of a smaller Kingdom, Dresden for instance.'[108]

Ghaziuddin Haider also took interest in buildings and, to quote Bahadur Singh Nami, he designed the tomb of his mother Murshidzadi, which is one of the best specimens of Awadh architecture.[109] He also prepared plans for Moti Mahal and Najaf Ashraf.[110] In 1818 he employed an engineer James Lock for effecting certain improvements in the neighbourhood of Farhat Bakhsh, especially the Lal Baradari.[111] Another architect, William Trickett, also served under him. Besides, he retained Captain McLea, who was entrusted the superintendence of several buildings. Yet another civil engineer was J. Munro Sinclair, who performed the duties of a 'general mechanic' and was associated with the making of steam engines and pleasure boats, etc.[112]

The reign of Nasiruddin Haider is noted for the erection of the Bara Chatar Manzil,

Chatar Manzil *Khwurd* and Darshan Bilas (also called Chaumukhi Kothi). In these buildings the employment of Mughal architectural details is minimum.

With the death of Nasiruddin Haider, the tradition of employing British civil engineers came to an end. Instead, local master builders and architects were preferred. Among these, the names of Husain Ali Khan and Chhote Miyan are worth mentioning who designed and erected Sikandar Bagh and Qaisar Bagh respectively. By this time the masons became well versed in the mode of construction and decoration, to which they were exposed, in Martin's buildings. Some of the European details became part of the vocabulary of the local art and began to be employed even in religious structures, especially towards the middle of the nineteenth century. The phase of imitation was over and the local builders were trying to effect a synthesis of the best of the European and indigenous traditions. Sometimes the builders failed completely as may be seen in the buildings of Muhammad Shah; while sometimes the effect is marred because of the tendency of excessive ornamentation and too many details of heterogeneous nature as in the Qaisar Bagh. However, a pleasing synthesis emerges in the Sikandar Bagh. Misappropriation of classical details was also minimised as in the Begum Kothi. The fact is that the process of Europeanisation was still in its early stages when the dynasty came to an end.

European style buildings in Lucknow were subjected to severe criticism by contemporary observers who described them as 'grotesque', 'debased', 'vulgar' and 'bizarre'. Even the Constantia was not spared and declared as a proof of 'builder's eccentricity'. This opinion is shared by modern scholars like Fergusson, Percy Brown, Fuhrer and Sten Nilsson.

Fergusson's main criticism is that in these buildings the details of classical 'order' are misappropriated and they reveal the ignorance of the Indian mason about the European principles of art: 'In the vain attempt to imitate his superiors he has abandoned his own beautiful art to produce the strange jumble of vulgarity and bad taste at Lucknow and elsewhere.'[113] In the opinion of Percy Brown, the classical motifs employed here are of 'inappropriate type', the arabesque foliations are also of a 'corrupt kind'.[114] Nilsson opines that in Constantia 'the series of order is extremely unconventional; three composites above a Tuscan. And in the central tower single pilasters support half columns in pairs with heavy cornices; this arrangement is contrary to all classical functional theories.'[115] The buildings of Nasiruddin Haider and Wajid Ali Shah are declared by Fuhrer as 'the most debased examples of the architecture to be found in India.'[116] He further comments: 'Nowhere can we see more markedly the influence of depraved oriental court and its politics upon art and architecture than in Lucknow.'[117]

One should not forget that the major source of Awadh architecture in the nineteenth century was England, and, at this time the English architecture was at a low ebb. Architects of the eighteenth century had whole-heartedly adopted 'Palladianism'.[118] However, it was degraded after it was tied to the taste of landed aristocracy who claimed a right on the design, and suggested alterations according to their tastes and requirements. Secondly, it was not easy to understand the intricate rules of Palladian art which was based on extremely circumscribed doctrines. Besides, the development of orders in classic or Renaissance architecture was the work of centuries. The native builder was not in a position to produce them according to precise rules and specifications not because he lacked skill, rather he needed time to become conversant with the grammar of their composition. This accounts for the misappropriation of details.

Besides Palladianism, the European style buildings in Awadh display traces of Neo-Classic and Neo-Gothic styles. Towards the mid-eighteenth century, Palladianism slid in France and Italy into Baroque style. In England also its popularity came down towards the third quarter of the eighteenth century, and Neo-Classics gained currency. The new style, popularised by Robert and James Adam,[119] emphasized on beautiful variety of light mouldings. The massive entablatures became outdated.[120] Some characteristics of this style can be seen in the buildings of Claude Martin which persisted in the later period also, such as arabesques and swags were created at Lucknow in stucco. This medium provided ample opportunities to the masons of the eighteenth century for the elaboration of details and mouldings. Adam-style fanlight appeared in almost every important residential and public building of Lucknow. Gothic spires and towers were also not an uncommon sight.

It should be noted that the era of pretentious palatial buildings by Europeans was confined only to the eighteenth century. One reason could be that the European adventurers had immense wealth which they lavished on fine architecture. In the nineteenth century, a marked change may be noticed. The Europeans now preferred to live in bungalows, a practice which was followed till late by the Britishers. Pictorial evidence depicts bungalows which were thatched, tiled or flat-roofed structures. The style of the bungalow was too prosaic to make an impact on Indians who were accustomed to a highly ornate style of building art. In the absence of any fresh source, Constantia always inspired the builders. Its details appeared in one or the other way throughout our period of study. The style of the bungalow was, however, copied in one or two buildings of Sa'adat Ali Khan; for instance, the Kothi Dil Aram.

It would not be correct to say that 'the European features suggest the Nawab's superficial display of regards for the British, yet at the same time an uneasiness with both British dominance and British artistic style.'[121] On the contrary, European decorative features were well assimilated in many of the buildings of the mid-nineteenth century.

Architecture is the result of a definite demand. It meets practical needs, too, besides aesthetic values. While the luxury of the rulers of Awadh and its aristocracy was Europeanised, no change occurred in their mode of day to day life. As a result, their houses were designed in a manner that they had a European look in accordance with the contemporary fashion, but devised so that the local style of living remained unaffected. Claude Martin in his buildings tried to effectively synthesize the European and indigenous styles with the above object in mind. He, thus, designed buildings which had the provision of *zenana* apartments that was attached to the main portion with very high walls either at the back or on the side. These also had the provision of a courtyard surrounded by rooms on either side. This plan, at its best, is synthesized in the Moosa Bagh or the House of Berone which represented a 'well judged union of the comforts of English with the splendour and magnificence of the Asiatic style.'[122]

The European style buildings provide sufficient proof of the adaptability of indigenous masons to European techniques and mode of working. The perfect workmanship which these craftsmen exhibited in the execution of 'relief panels of a wedgewood character',[123] above the pilasters of the walls and arched ceilings of Constantia, made many travellers believe that the work was accomplished by Italian craftsmen. These were produced in stucco.

It is evident from the will of Claude Martin that he particularly trained his two servants 'Mutchoo' and 'Chutta Khaddir' in European techniques. They were well acquainted with his designs, plans of buildings and his mode of working.[124] There were several others who were employed in the Constantia work and thus attained practical knowledge under the expert guidance of Martin.

One can clearly notice three phases of transition in the European style edifices of Lucknow. In the first, the artist was merely imitating; the second one is characteristic of adaptation of European decorative details, and in the final phase there is an effort on the part of the builders to produce a synthesis of the best of the two traditions. These three phases, however, can be chronologically separated in the buildings constructed during the early nineteenth century.

The European edifices were constructed by the royalty and the upper layers of the society who preferred to live in *kothis,* not in *havelis.* This denoted a change in the outlook of the people about residential buildings.

The two capital cities in Awadh evinced an unprecedented building activity. The old citadel of Faizabad was greatly expanded and beautified by Shujauddaulah who erected a number of palaces which were dressed in stucco veneer and worked in gold, silver and coloured designs.[125] Since they do not have any traces of European impact, their description will not be part of the present discussion.

On the contrary, the city of Lucknow had a lot of European style buildings: town mansions, summer houses and country houses. Most of these were built in a style which is characterized by Fergusson as 'pseudo-Italian', while some represent a style that was in fashion in the eighteenth century. In most cases, however, several architectural styles got intermixed and emerged as a hybrid one. Consistency is also not found in the application of these architectural styles either in construction or in decoration. Instead, a particular style received predominance or receded in the background according to the personal likings of a builder. Thus, almost all the palaces of Sa'adat Ali Khan were erected in European manner. Ghaziuddin Haider and Nasiruddin Haider preferred a mixed style, while Wajid Ali Shah built in both.

The palace called Farhat Bakhsh was the first building in Lucknow to be erected by Claude Martin in European style. The design was 'unique and singular'[126] in many respects, for this villa had 'the appearance of a fortified castle', and it was constructed with a view to defence with narrow winding staircases, drawbridges and battlements.[127] The Farhat Bakhsh was designed in semi-Italian style.[128] It had beautiful arcades and spacious rooms designed to mitigate the effect of summer winds.[129] Thus, from the very beginning a design was sought for residential buildings which could accommodate the climate.

This villa was bought by Sa'adat Ali Khan after the death of Martin and a conglomeration of buildings appeared around it, which included the Qasrus Sultan, Sheesh Mahal, Khwurd Manzil, Rang Mahal, Mahalsara and Naubat Khana.[130] The Marquiss of Hastings refers to 'a large saloon in the English style and a splendid banqueting hall' in this palace complex.[131] One cannot agree with the opinion that the Farhat Bakhsh 'not a little contributed to impress the less informed of the natives of that remote part of the country with an idea of the superiority of European taste and knowledge.'[132] However, it may be said that some of its architectural features, especially its castellated form, were borrowed in Martin's own country house Constantia. It was in fact this building which became the source of inspiration to the royal builders of Lucknow.

The Constantia, better known as La Martiniere, was 'the first large building of European order to be erected in upper India.'[133] Like the Farhat Bakhsh, it was designed in the form of a palace-fortress. Some found in it the semblance of a Gothic castle, while it reminded Marquiss of Hastings of the 'Castles Pastry which in former days used to adorn the desserts.'[134] The Constantia struck a new note in the construction technique, design and decoration. The design seems to have been impressed by the Palladian style,[135] though in its 'silhouette and in certain details' it reminds one of Mughal architecture.[136] Thus, it was hybrid in style. Fergusson regards it a 'quaint admixture of

Greek, French, Indian and Italian elements.'[137] Here are to be seen Gothic towers indifferently rising amidst clusters of indigenous kiosks, and Grecian pilasters,[138] arabesque and bas-relief ornamentation on the walls illustrative of classical subjects, European fountains set against Indian turrets, Indian verandah running beside the court of western type, and Indian blinds projecting from an Italian facade. The central tower was crowned by flying buttresses shaped like a dome.[139] While the gardens were French having some semblance of the Versailles, the lawns were adorned with statues of Greek, Indian and Chinese subjects.[140]

The Constantia 'sins' against most of the rules of Palladian art. The reasons are simple: Claude Martin was a soldier and not an architect. He had some notions of French architecture, but he was not adept in its particulars. Besides, his buildings were constructed by those masons who had no knowledge of European art. Neither they had any visual model before them:[141] they were merely imitating the pattern books and the sketches which Martin provided to them.[142]

Secondly, the details were executed for the most part in the native fashion. This appears to be a substantial cause for the inability of Indian masons to produce classic details in their purer form, and the jumbling of different styles and modes of construction. The buildings did not strictly follow European planning because it was designed in view of the hot climate of the country. Taken altogether, as Thornton opines,[143] it was a far reasonable edifice than the 'Italian rural capricio'. The building is not a proof of 'the builder's eccentricity', as Valentia regards it. Instead, it reflects well the problem and confusion of local mason who was not yet exposed to European designs and constructional techniques fully.

The Constantia was regarded a great achievement in the building art.[144] It introduced an entirely new orientation in Awadh architecture: all the principal palaces followed the course which it pointed out. Practically, every detail of this building was copied in the building of Lucknow. Also, it led to the development of a style 'of a pronounced hybrid character' which had a Mughal framework and garnishing of 'pseudo classical details'.[145]

European influence may be observed in the following buildings: Qasrus Sultan,[146] Khurshid Manzil,[147] Moti Mahal,[148] Chatar Manzil complex (which included the *Bara* Chatar Manzil, Chatar Manzil *khwurd,* Darshan Bilas and Gulistani Iram),[149] Qaisar Pasand or Kothi Roshanuddaulah,[150] Begum Kothi,[151] and Qaisar Bagh.[152]

Among these, the two Chatar Manzils represent the second phase of transition. For the first time native decorative elements, such as turrets, minarets and *kangura* (battlement motif), were discarded in favour of constructional simplicity. The design is eclectic, as Nevill remarks: 'A glance at the exterior suffices to say that the architect responsible for the design sought to reconcile late eighteenth century French influence with the Mohammadan tastes and prejudices. The effect being that of a French chateau to which...masons added cupolas and kiosks intended for an oriental palace.'[153]

The Darshan Bilas is a piece of remarkable originality: it shows the local masons successfully experimenting with Western traditions. Its four facades represent four different styles borrowed from the Dilkusha, Farhat Bakhsh, Khurshid Manzil and Moosa Bagh. These facades are well assimilated to produce a pleasing effect which gave it the name Darshan Bilas. The Gulistani Iram is a Westernised building in all its appearances; dome, minarets and turrets disappear in it. These buildings represent a style which was not merely imitative or 'avowedly and openly copied from debased European models'.[154]

Of much Westernised appearances are the Qaisar Pasand and the Begum Kothi. The latter has a huge portico surmounted by a triangular pediment and the side wings are composed of Ionic columns. Cusped *shahjahani* arches are absent in it. Even the two shapely domes surmounted by mini *chatar*, complementing the view of the pediment, lose their native identity in the ensemble of European features.

The Begum Kothi was a magnificent edifice with garland motifs, ornamental gables, Corinthian columns with beautiful entablatures, minarets and gilt spires. The building was very imposing in appearance. Fergusson regards it as a fine specimen of Italian architecture in Awadh.[155] In the opinion of Goetz, however, it displays the Gothic admixture of the Romantic period.[156] The Begum Kothi displays very well that an eclectic style was on the verge of emergence with Italian, Gothic and Indian features.

The Qaisar Bagh palace complex invites our special attention as an amalgam of heterogeneous architectural styles. It makes an interesting study in the transformation of the native fashion of Awadh into a highly Europeanised one. One could find enough material evidence on this change even though most of its buildings could not stand the ravages of time and are extinct now. There are, on the one hand, the tombs of Sa'adat Ali Khan and Murshidzadi representing the regional variations of the later Mughal architecture. On the other hand, the Lunka palace bears the impress of a builder who might have been schooled in the Vatican and French architecture of the eighteenth century. In between these fall the Lakhi Darwaza, the Sufaid Baradari and a host of quadrangular abodes of the ladies of the *harem* (*mahal sara*), all built in an eclectic manner with varying degree of foreign influence. However, the French influence appears to be most pronounced on its style, extent and arrangement. In the opinion of Reene, it was a 'stucco Louvre', while Goetz regards it a copy of Trianan.[157]

The Lakhi Darwaza represents the final stage of transition where European elements found considerable vogue, though indigenous elements also persist. The Sufaid Baradari, with its Adam-style fanlights, cut-glass screen, wooden mullians and trifoliated arches, bears the appearance of an English villa. However, it also employs cusped *shahjahani* arches, bell turrets and a pair of kiosks which appear to be well assimilated in the design. These motifs were frequently employed in the European style town mansions of the period.

The strangest of all the buildings was the Lunka palace at the Qaisar Bagh. It has eight octagonal battlemented two-storeyed towers in the fashion of the baronial castle of the European Middle Ages, the like of which is seen in the Khurshid Manzil. These towers are designed on two blocks of buildings which are combined by flying buttresses arranged in the shape of a dome. The blocks of building have a colonnaded verandah. In the interior one finds trifoliated arches, as seen in Gothic cathedrals. The local decorative elements are completely absent in this structure.

The Qaisar Bagh is greatly criticised for two reasons. In it mostly those details are employed which were in disuse at the time of its erection.[158] Secondly, the details are only partially copied. There is a great element of truth in it, but one should not forget that a stagnation appeared in the building of fine architectural monuments in Lucknow after the eighteenth century, and they had no model other than the buildings of Martin which employed these details.

BUILDINGS IN NEO-CLASSIC STYLE

A good many buildings, summer resorts and country houses were erected in neo-classic style as it developed in England towards the end of the eighteenth century. The plan generally consists of a portico with Ionic or Corinthian pillars leading to the drawing room or a central hall. Instead of arched openings, they have shuttered doors and Adam-style fanlights with stained glasses. Casually one comes across some Gothic features. The roofs are either flat or sloping, or both. Most of these are double-storeyed structures surrounded by gardens. These are marked out for their simplicity and rarification of ornamental superficialities. One might think after viewing these buildings (*kothi* as they are called) that Awadh architecture was totally transformed within a period of hundred years. These are a pointer to the future course of architectural development of residential buildings in India. Presumably their style was derived from the cottage. The Bibiapur Kothi,[159] Kothi Dil Aram,[160] Kothi Hayat Bakhsh,[161] Kankarwali Kothi,[162] Tarawali Kothi,[163] Residency,[164] Kothi Dilkusha,[165] Moosa Bagh[166] and Alam Bagh are instances of it.[167]

Lucknow was equally famous for its gardens, parks and avenues. Quite a few were laid out in French and English styles.[168] These were surrounded by high wall and pierced with lofty gateways. The most significant architectural structure was the gateway of Sikandar Bagh,[169] which was shaped after the Roman round arch and decorated on either side by two octagonal towers. The surface was decorated with minute stucco ornaments and swags. The spandrels have the crest of fish. What distinguishes it from other structures is a conscious effort of the builder to effect a synthesis of the native and European elements.[170] This structure designed by Husain Ali Khan shows that the phase of transition and experimentation was over, and that local craftsmen had succeeded in availing the best of the two traditions. Unfortunately, this process was interrupted as the dynasty came to an end. One can agree with Havell that 'there is no doubt that Indian craftsmanship...would sooner or later have evolved a new tradition of building practically and aesthetically more worthy of Anglo-India which Anglo-India made for itself.'[171]

MUSIC

Contrary to painting and architecture, musical arts in Awadh are completely free from European impact. Evidence shows that nobles used to have French organs[172] but these were merely curiosities. The keyboard instruments also never became popular in India.

However, in drama we can see European traces. Although there is no evidence to suggest the impact of Western drama on the *rahas* performances of Wajid Ali Shah, there is a strong possibility that he was inspired, to some extent, by Western theatrical performances. There were theatres in Calcutta as early as 1756, and the Bengal theatre was established on their model.[173] Lucknow had no theatre like Calcutta and Kanpur. However, theatrical performances were given by touring actors.[174] Surely, the court circle was familiar with these.

It appears that Western theatrical performances did not have a direct impact on the rulers of Awadh, though the desire to enact drama was derived from them. The *jalsa* performed by *jalsewaliyan* (a group of female performing artists patronized by Nasiruddin Haider and his mother Badshah Begum) was probably an 'Indianised version of these theatrical performances'.[175]

Wajid Ali Shah established *Parikhana* for imparting training in dancing and singing to female artists who were designated as *pari* (fairy). It was a prototype of opera house or play house where the *paris* enacted the first Urdu drama, the *Radha-Kanhayya ka Qissa.*[176] Several other *jalsas* were also performed here. For the first time professional artists like *sangiya* or *rahasdhari* were not employed in these theatrical performances, which makes a break from Indian tradition.

These *jalsas* inspired the people outside the Awadh court circle. Mirza Amanat's *Indar Sabha* (written in A.D. 1851-2) was also performed on the line of *jalsa.* It had some of the characteristics of Western theatre. It was performed on an improvised stage at night. A red screen (*surkh dupatta*) was used as drop curtain and the orchestra was played behind it. The screen was draped or raised to signify the change of scene. Costume was also defined.[177] The *Indar Sabha* paved the way for the Parsi theatre.

INDUSTRIAL ARTS

The industrial arts at Lucknow are free from the strains of European influence. This appears curious in view of the fact that Lucknow had a large European population. This was due to a cautious policy followed by the Awadh rulers, especially Shujauddaulah and Sa'adat Ali Khan. Shujauddaulah was fully aware of the commercial policies of the East India Company. Article 8 of the Treaty of Allahabad had provision of free trade in Awadh, which could be ruinous to the trade network and industries of the State. Shujauddaulah strongly and consistently resisted it and finally in 1773 a trade barrier was established that closed the commercial penetration of the East India Company into Awadh. Sa'adat Ali Khan, by creating a high tariff wall, restricted Company's trade and took every step to safeguard the interests of the local mercantile community and professionals.[178] This resulted in the blooming of industries in the capital without the involvement of European capital or supervision. There are no indications to suggest introduction of Western technology for production of such items which were in demand locally. For instance, glass industry was totally absent in Awadh.[179] The traditional crafts retained their local techniques of production. There are, however, some exceptions. At Tanda, textile printing and bleaching was supervised by 'two or three agents of the East India Company'.[180] Tanda was the largest seat of cotton manufacture in Awadh, which catered mainly to European markets. Several European firms existed there,[181] and European merchants made efforts to improve the quality of its products. The names of Scott, James Orr and Johannas are important in this context. Scott had an immense washing centre and Orr was associated with textile designing and printing. He is said to have introduced European patterns for table cloths, towels and other articles.[182] In *jamdani* (flowered muslin) European style crown is used as a motif which was known as *Tajbati.* It is flanked on each side with mermaids holding flags in their hand. This motif is also seen on the Lakhi gateway of the Qaisar Bagh and the coins[183] of Wajid Ali Shah. The mermaids probably were employed as a variant of fish motif.

The wood-carvers of Lucknow used to produce furniture articles after the European fashion, though on a very limited scale since the use of furniture was very rare and confined exclusively to the male apartments.[184] These articles had a distinct touch of local artistic skill. Indian floral designs, human figures and animal motifs were carved out in relief or independently, which were mostly employed on the legs of the chairs, coaches and the tables. A superb example of the artistic genius of Lucknow was the throne-chair presented to the first Earl Amherst, Governor-General of India (1823-8), by Ghaziuddin

Haider. While the design was based on 'a European prototype of the Egyptian Revival', the decorative details were typical of Awadh. It had on its back, in bold design, the fish symbol of the Awadh rulers.[185]

Lucknow was especially famous for its coaches. In these was employed the fairy motif which gave an entirely Indian look to European coach design. It also suggests that in decorative details the wood-carvers retained their traditional art vocabulary. Lucknow was famous for the 'flying' coaches.[186]

The art of clay modelling developed in Lucknow 'as a direct result of Martin's sculptural movement', who introduced the art of figure sculpture in stone and stucco after the Greek and Italian style in his Constantia. The gardens and palaces of Lucknow were adorned with statues in the fashion of Constantia. The form of statuary found expression in yet another medium (clay). The European impact is more apparent in the red ochre coated smaller human figures which resemble the Italian terracotta.[187] Busts were also produced in this style.[188] A special type of terracotta was produced in Lucknow by a small group of moulders. In it, the working process was that of 'tooling and carving than actual moulding'. The figures were modelled when the clay was in a green stage (a stage between wet and dry). This work was costly and reflected fully the stone-carver's art. It vanished after the annexation of Awadh.[189] These represented the highest form of fine art in India.[190] Besides clay figures, glazed tiles, flowerpots, jars, clock cases and wall brackets were also produced in Lucknow. A special notice should be taken of the glazed roof finials which were frequently employed in the palaces of Lucknow. The glaze was given by adding copper. Tiles and finials were produced in pale, purple green and blue shades.[191]

One can conclude on the basis of the above discussion that although traditions in art and architecture were operating within the European sphere, its influence was often superficial and always limited. There was no lack of artistic dynamics. The Nawabs, too, as patrons, were dynamic. They encouraged experimentation which resulted in the combined use of foreign and native traditions and styles. In spite of this, any new or vibrant artistic tradition could not emerge. It was possibly due to the fact that the life-span of the dynasty was too short; therefore, the experimentation remained individualistic. At local levels, artistic traditions retained their vitality and the roots of local traditions continued. Even in painting and architecture, the layer of Western influence remained overshadowed by powerful local traditions.

NOTES

1. Cf. Walter Kelly Firminger, *Historical Introduction to the Bengal Portion of the Fifth Report,* Calcutta, 1877, Vol. I, pp. 89-90.

2. Muhammad Faiz Bakhsh, *Tarikh-i Farah Bakhsh,* Abdus Salam Collection, MS No. 172/38, Maulana Azad Library, Aligarh Muslim University, Aligarh, f.225a.

3. Ibid.

4. Lalji, *Mirat-ul Au'za* (1851 A.D.), Persian MS, Maulana Azad Library, Aligarh Muslim University, Aligarh, f.110b. In mid-nineteenth century Lucknow was the largest and the most prosperous pre-colonial city in the sub-continent. Only Madras, Calcutta and Bombay surpassed its size or affluence (see Veena Talwar Oldenburg, *The Making of Colonial Lucknow,* Delhi, 1989, pp. 3-4).

5. John Guy and Deborah Swallow (ed.), *Arts of India: 1550-1900,* Victoria and Albert Museum, London, 1990, p. 180.

6. Ghulam Ali Khan Naqvi, *Imad-us Sa'adat* (A.D. 1808), Naval Kishore Press, Lucknow, 1864, pp. 5, 30.

7. See *Modern India with Illustrations of the Resources and Capabilities of Hindoostan,* London, 1837, Vol. I, p. 229.

8. Walter Hamilton, *The East India Gazetteers of the Hindoostan and the Adjacent Countries,* London, 1828, Vol. II, p. 350.

9. Ibid., Vol. II, pp. 351, 352, 353.

10. Ibid., p. 352. It was in the Company's interest.

11 Cf. Captain Mundy, *Pen and Pencil Sketches, being the Journal of a Tour in India,* London, 1833, Vol. I, p. 13.

12. A contemporary statement records that Shujauddaulah is quoted to have said that he was adopting measures by which 'he is so desirous to convince the world that there is no difference between the English and him' (Harper to Cartier, 7 February 1770, India Office Library, London: Orme MSS *Orme Various Collections,* LXIX, p. 33, cited in Richard B. Barnett, *North India Between the Empires,* Delhi, 1987, p. 77).

13. P. Carnegy, *A Historical Sketch of Fyzabad Tahsil including the former Capital Ajudhya and Fyzabad,* London, 1896, Appendix, p. 18.

14. The mud fort was so big that it embraced an area equivalent to 19 villages and was surrounded by a moat 10 miles in perimeter (see H.R. Nevill, *District Gazetteers of the United Provinces of Agra and Oudh,* Lucknow, 1922, Vol. XLIII, pp. 220-1). The walls of the fort are said to have been 60 feet thick and so well beaten 'that elephants made to tread on this left no impression of their feet' (see Col. Allen Macpherson and John Macpherson, *Soldiering in India (1764-1787): Extracts from their Journals and Letters left of the East India Company by Col. Allen Macpherson and John Macpherson,* ed. Charles Macpherson, London, 1928, p. 102).

15. *Imad-us Sa'adat,* op. cit., pp. 101-2. He also employed Armenian and Abyssinian officers who had previously worked with Mir Qasim.

16. Comte de Modave noted in 1773 that guns and bayonets manufactured in the Nawab's arsenal were 'almost as well as in our workshops in Europe' (see *Voyage en Inde du Comte (1773-1776),* ed. Jean Deloche, Paris, 1971, p. 155. I am indebted to Mrs. N. Kamala, Assistant Professor, Centre of French Studies, Jawaharlal Nehru University, Delhi, for this reference).

17. Ibid., p. 156. Also see the report of Galliez, the Company's commander posted in Bihar, to the Council, 12 Feb. 1775, Foreign Department (Calcutta Council, East India Company) in *Select Committee Proceedings* (Henceforth *FDSC),* National Archives of India, Delhi.

18. S.P. Sen, *The French in India, 1763-1816,* Delhi, 1971, pp. 120, 124, 128, 144, 150.

19. Ibid., p. 155. He thus had an opportunity to interact with the upper layer of society and to come in contact with the best of the Mughal traditions which made an immense impact on him. He virtually began Indological studies in France.

20. Comte de Modave, op. cit., p. 18.

21. S.P. Sen, op. cit., pp. 116-17, 120, 128, 129.

22. Ibid., p. 113.

23. See Rosie L. Jones, *A Fatal Friendship,* Delhi, 1985, p. 33.

24. Gulliez to Council, 3 March 1775, *FDSC* 6, 20 March 1775; Bristow to Council, 4 May 1775, *FDSC* 4, 22 May 1775, *FDSC* 10, 31 May 1775 (National Archives of India, Delhi). He was allowed to employ craftsmen, carpenters and 'repairers of his musical clocks' but no 'Gentlemen except Colonel Martin' (cf. Rosie L. Jones, op. cit., p. 34).

25. *Asiatic Annual Register,* London, 1814, p. 11 (compiler's name is not given).

26. Thomas Twining, *Travels in India a Hundred Years Ago,* London, 1893, p. 311 (the author visited Lucknow in 1792). Abu Talib, *Tafzih ul Ghafilin,* tr. W. Hoey, *History of Asafuddaulah,* reprint, Lucknow, 1971. Abu Talib wrote this work in 1211 A.H./1796-97 A.D., during his stay at Calcutta.

27. *Asiatic Annual Register,* op. cit., p. 11.

28. See *Sketches of the Field Sports as Followed by the Natives of India,* London, 1822, p. 163; Viscount George Valentia, *Voyages and Travels in India, Ceylon, the Red Sea, Abyssinia and Egypt in the years 1802-1806,* London, 1809, Vol. I, p. 164.

29. Twining, op. cit., p. 311; Valentia, op. cit., Vol. I, p. 40.

30. Twining, p. 311.

31. The aristocratic circle used to have in their collections such articles as ornate mirrors, French organs, fancy clocks of the most costly description (see Captain Mundy, op. cit., Vol. II, p. 29).

32. Valentia, Vol. I, p. 164.

33. Comte de Modave, p. 439.

34. See Ann Deane, *A Tour through the Upper Provinces of Hindostan, between 1804 and 1814,* London, 1823, p. 103.

35. Ibid., p. 103.

36. *Calcutta Review,* Calcutta, 1845, p. 78. In some of the paintings he is shown in English riding suit.

37. Cf. Madhu Trivedi, *nee* Sharma, 'Costume and costume craft in the kingdom of Awadh', *Proceedings of the Indian History Congress,* 1970, p. 178.

38. Valentia, Vol. I, p. 144.

39. Ibid.

40. *Bengal, Past and Present,* Calcutta, 1992, Vol. 24, pp. 95-102.

41. Guy and Swallow, op. cit., p. 184.

42. Captain Mundy, p. 30.

43. *The Asiatic Journal,* New Series, Vol. 22, pt. 2, London, 1837, p. 34.

44. William Knighton, *Private Life of an Eastern King,* ed. S.B. Smith, Oxford, 1921 (First published in 1856).

45. F.J. Shore, *Notes on Indian Affairs,* London, 1857, p. 275.

46. This fact is acknowledged by Captain James Herbert, the superintendent of the observatory till 1831 (cf. D.B. Diskalker, 'Foundation of an observatory at Lucknow', *Journal of the United Provinces Historical Society,* Vol. X, pt. 1, 1937, pp. 10-11). For a detailed account of the observatory, college and the hospital, see Rosie L. Jones, chapter 2.

47. Archer regrets that their love of novelty had gone beyond some idle gratification or indulgence, and that 'their minds have not expanded or their views became more enlightened by constant intercourse with the people who had so much knowledge, both oral and political...' (see Major Archer, *Tours in Upper India and in parts of Himalayan Mountains,* London, 1833, Vol. I, p. 26).

48. Ahsan Jan Qaisar, *The Indian Response to European Technology and Culture,* Delhi, 1992, p. 85.

49. Ibid.

50. Luber Hajek, *Indian Miniatures of the Mughal School,* London, 1960, pp. 49-50.

51. Mario Bussagli and Calembus Sivaramamurti, *5,000 Years of the Art of India,* Bombay, p. 295.

52. For details see Qaisar, op. cit., pp. 91-2.

53. For details, see Madhu Trivedi (*nee* Sharma), 'Cultural History of the Kingdom of Awadh' (Ph.D. thesis, Aligarh Muslim University, Aligarh, 1977, unpublished, chapter 2).

54. S.N. Gupta, 'European influence on Indian painting', *Rupam,* ed. O.C. Ganguly, Calcutta, January, 1921, p. 20.

55. Bahadur Singh Nami, *Yadgar-i Bahaduri* (written in 1837), Persian MS No. 255, The State Archives, Allahabad, f.325a.

56. Most part of the Gentil's Collection is in the Cabinet des Estampes at the Biblitheque Nationale, Paris (albums of miniatures are od. 36, 39, 43, 44, 49, 50, 51, 52).

57. Muhammad Faiz Bakhsh, *Insha-i Faiz Bakhsh* (1205 A.H.), Persian MS No. 1205, Maulana Azad Library, Aligarh Muslim University, Aligarh, f.51a.

58. Leigh Ashton, *The Art of India and Pakistan,* London, 1950, p. 183.

59. J.D. Milner, 'Tilly Kettle, 1735-1789', *The Walpole Society,* Vol. XV, 1926-7, pp. 47-103.

60. Cf. J.J. Gentil, *Memoires Sur L'Indoustan ou Empire Mogol,* Paris, 1822, p. 310 (I am indebted to Mrs. N. Kamala for the translation of the French text related to painting).

61. Ibid.

62. Mildred Archer and W.C. Archer, *Indian Painting for the British (1770-1800),* Oxford, 1955, pp. 34-5; Guy & Swallow, p. 181. These miniatures are in the collection of Victoria and Albert Museum (India Section), 1, a 287-1951; British Museum, 1946-10-10-03.

63. Mildred & W.C. Archer, op. cit., p. 35.

64. Valentia, p. 133.

65. L.F. Smith, *The Asiatic Annual Register for the 1804: Miscellaneous tracts,* 10-12, London, 1806 (cited in Major Archer, op. cit., p. 56).

66. Fancy Parkes, *Wandering of a Pilgrim in Search of Picturesque during Four and Twenty years with Revelation of Life in Zenana,* London, 1843, Vol. I, p. 181. According to P.C. Mookherji, 'the original painting is lost and only the prints remain' *(Pictorial Lucknow,* Lucknow, 1883, p. 177).

67. One copy by a bazar artist is located at Husainabad Art Gallery, Lucknow.

68. 'These pictures are superb', he remarks, 'and more life like than most pictures, having the touch of Titian and the flesh of Etty' (see William Knighton, op. cit., p. 219).

69. The 'View of Daulat Khan Palace' was painted by him and this is perhaps the only picture of this complex.

70. Daniel Johnson mentions 47 portraits of Martin by Zoffany (see *Sketches of Field Sports & C,* op. cit., p. 188). Martin had a fabulous collection of paintings which was auctioned after his death. Many of these were bought by Ghaziuddin Haider for decorating his palace (see *Yadgar-i Bahaduri,* f.326a).

71. Mildred & W.C. Archer, pp. 60-3.

72. The above analysis is based on the study of the reproductions of the original paintings given by the Archers in their monograph.

73. Mildred & W.C. Archer, pp. 60-3. No illustrations are available which may be called representative of this style.

74. T.G.P. Spear, *The Nabobs,* Oxford, 1932, pp. 180-1.

75. Knighton, p. 18.

76. Bishop Reginald Heber, *Narrative of a Journey through the Upper Provinces of India from Calcutta to Bombay, 1824-25,* London, 1828, Vol. I, p. 122.

77. Ibid., pp. 216, 219. Also 'Lord Maira's letter', printed in *Calcutta Gazetteer,* June 1815, p. 66.

78. Emily Eden, *Up the Country,* London, 1866, Vol. I, p. 387.

79. Mildred & W.C. Archer, p. 119.

80. Knighton, p. 16.

81. Ibid.

82. Mildred & W.C. Archer, p. 61. This monograph is indispensable for the study of the bazar paintings produced at Lucknow. However, their description is rather sketchy and they do not discuss at length the characteristics of these paintings.

83. I am grateful to Professor S.P. Verma, Department of History, Aligarh Muslim University, Aligarh, who helped me in the delineation of these technical details.

84. Mildred & W.C. Archer, p. 61.

85. Ibid., p. 62.

86. Ibid.

87. *Yadgar-i Bahaduri,* f.325a.

88. Ibid.

89. P.C. Mookherji, op. cit., p. 179.

90. Knighton, p. 219.

91. *Yadgar-i Bahaduri,* f.325a.

92. *The Indian Travels of Thevenot and Careri,* tr. & ed. S.N. Sen, Delhi, 1949, p. 65 (cited in A.J. Qaisar, p. 102).

93. *Tarikh-i Farah Bakhsh,* f.222a.

94. Antonie Louis Polier, *Shah Alam and His Court,* ed. Pratul C. Gupta, Calcutta, 1947, p. 5.

95. Ibid.

96. Rosie L. Jones, p. 162.

97. The house of Raja Mehra 'puts one in mind the Louvre at Paris' *(The Asiatic Journal,* London, 1816, p. 579). Raja Mehra was the chief palanquin bearer of Asafuddaulah (see translator's note in *Tafzih ul Ghafilin,* p. 39).

98. *Yadgar-i Bahaduri,* f.607a.

99. See William Hodges, *Travels in India, 1780-3,* London, 1793, p. 101.

100. Valentia, pp. 143, 173.

101. Anon., *Sketches of India,* London, 1816, p. 145.

102. Heber, Vol. I, p. 386.

103. See Hamilton, *East India Gazetteer,* Vol. II, p. 131; also see Heber, p. 383.

104. Henry Lawrence, 'The Kingdom of Oude', *Calcutta Review,* 1845, p. 380.

105. Hamilton, op. cit., p. 131.

106. Ibid. Travellers have compared the palaces of Lucknow with those of Moscow and Constantinople (cf. H. Lawrence, p. 350).

107. Fancy Parkes, p. 163.

108. See Heber, p. 386.

109. *Yadgar-i Bahaduri,* ff.606a, 607a.

110. Ibid., f.607a.

111. Rosie L. Jones, p. 162.

112. Ibid., pp. 163, 164-5.

113. James Fergusson, *History of Indian and Eastern Architecture,* reprint, Delhi, 1967, Vol. II, pp. 327-8. An order consists of a column and its entablature. The column has three parts: the base, the shaft and its capital; the entablature's three parts are the architrave, the frieze and the cornice.
There are five orders or types of columnar architecture known as Tuscan, Doric, Ionic, Corinthian and Composite. The Composite developed in the later Roman times. It was called Composite because its capital contained two superimposed rows of acanthus leaves of Corinthian, while its column was borrowed from the Ionic.

114. Percy Brown, *Indian Architecture (Islamic Period),* reprint, Delhi, 1968, p. 114.

115. Sten Nilsson, *European Architecture in India, 1750-1858,* London, 1968, p. 131.

116. A. Fuhrer, *The Monumental Antiquities and Inscriptions in the North-Western Provinces and Oudh,* reprint, Delhi, 1969, p. 266.

117. Ibid.

118. A style associated with Andre Palladio. He was a famous architect of the later Renaissance period of art and architecture and erected classic architecture in its purest form. He was known as the father of the classical revival and the style of later Renaissance was regarded Palladian after him.

119. Murray Kidson and Thompson, *A History of English Architecture,* London, 1965, p. 238. Also see Rosie L. Jones, p. 149.

120. In classic or Renaissance architecture, the moulded horizontal superstructure of a wall colonnade or opening consisting of an architrave, frieze and cornice is called an entablature.

121. See Catherine B. Asher, *Architecture of Mughal India,* Cambridge, 1992, p. 322.

122. Lt. Col. Forrest, *A Picturesque Tour Along the Ganges and Jumna,* London, 1824, p. 164.

123. Sten Nilsson, p. 132.

124. Claude Martin's will, dated 1 Jan. 1800, La Martiniere copy, Lucknow (I am thankful to Mr. Shaw, Principal, La Martiniere, who kindly allowed me to consult the above document). Also see Rosie L. Jones, p. 134.

125. *Tarikh-i Farah Bakhsh,* f.222a; Har Charan Das, *Chahar Gulzar Shuja'i,* 1786-7, Persian MS, British Museum Or. 1732 (rotograph No. 35, Seminar Library, Department of History, Aligarh Muslim University, Aligarh. For details, see Madhu Trivedi, 'Palace Architecture in the Kingdom of Awadh' (mimeograph) presented at the Indian History Congress, Muzaffarpur, 1972).

126. Anon., 'An Account of Colonel Martin's Villa, near Lucknow', *The European Magazine,* London, 1790, Vol. XVII, pp. 86-7.

127. Twining, p. 309; Valentia, p. 166.

128. P.C. Mookherji, p. 202; Fergusson, Vol. II, p. 324.

129. Edward Thornton, *A Gazetteer of the Territories under the Government of the East India Company and of the Native States of the Continental India,* London, 1854, Vol. IV, p. 25.

130. *Mirat ul Au'za,* f.108a; Babu Himmat Prasad, *Tarikh-i Awadh* (A.D. 1849), Urdu MS, Raza Library, Rampur, f.12.

131. The Marquiss of Hastings, *Private Journal of Marquiss of Hastings,* ed. Marchiones of Bute (1907), Vol. I, p. 104.

132. Anon., 'An Account of Colonel Martin's Villa', op. cit., pp. 86-7.

133. Percy Brown, p. 114.

134. *Hastings' Journal,* op. cit., Vol. I, p. 106.

135. Fergusson, Vol. II, p. 324; Percy Brown, p. 106.

136. Sten Nilsson, p. 131.

137. Fergusson, Vol. II, p. 324.

138. Pilaster is a shallow pier attached to wall.

139. Flying buttress is an arch or half arch transmitting the thrust of a vault or roof from the upper part of the wall to an outer support or buttress.

140. Valentia, p. 162.

141. Indian mason's exposure to European architecture was confined to coastal regions only (see Qaisar, p. 105).

142. Claude Martin had a vast collection of books on architecture (cf. the list given in Rosie L. Jones, pp. 156-59).

143. Thornton, Vol. IV, p. 308.

144. Mirza Muhammad Taqi, *Tarikh-i Aftab-i Awadh,* 1874, Urdu MS, Lucknow University, f.70.

145. Percy Brown, p. 114.

146. It was initially built in the Mughal style by Sa'adat Ali Khan. Later some 'improvements' were made under the supervision of James Lock. As a result, its lower storey imparted the impression of an English villa.

147. It was a palace fortress with huge towers like a baronial castle and surrounded by a ditch. It was built by Sa'adat Ali Khan (*Mirat ul Au'za,* f.107a; *Hastings' Journal,* Vol. I, p. 341).

148. Constructed by Ghaziuddin Haider (*Mirat ul Au'za,* f.108a). It was the strangest of the palaces of Lucknow. Contemporary observers regard it a curious mixture of distorted Gothic, Saracenic and Roman elements; while in the opinion of Hermann Goetz, it represents 'English classicism' (see 'Later Mughal Architecture', *Marg,* September, 1958, p. 17).

149. Bara Chatar Manzil was begun by Ghaziuddin Haider and completed by Nasiruddin Haider (see Tota Ram Shyam, *Tawarikh-i Nadir ul 'Asr,* Lucknow, 1863, p. 152).

150. It was built in a predominantly Italian style and is the largest and the most beautiful palace of Lucknow.

151. The Begum Kothi was built in 1844 by King Amjad Ali Shah. It was badly damaged during the Mutiny.

152. It was built in 1850 at the cost of more than a hundred million pounds sterling (*Lucknow Album,* pp. 25-6). According to Lalji, there were more than 30 buildings inside it. It also included in its premises the palaces of earlier period, for instance *Makan-i Chaupahlu,* Qaisar Pasand and Badshah Manzil, etc. (see *Mirat ul Au'za,* ff.110a-111b).

153. H.R. Nevill, *District Gazetteer of the United Provinces of Agra and Oudh,* Lucknow, 1922, Vol. XXXVII, p. 34. In the opinion of Fergusson, however, the Farhat Bakhsh and Chatar Manzil 'display all the quaint picturesque irregularity of the age of Francis I, combined with more strange details that are to be found in the buildings of Henry IV' (see Fergusson, Vol. II, p. 325).

154. This opinion is held by A. Fuhrer, op. cit., p. 267.

155. Fergusson, p. 325.

156. See *Marg,* September 1958, p. 17.

157. H.G. Reene, *A Handbook for Visitors to Allahabad, Cawnpore and Lucknow,* Calcutta, 1899, p. 58; also, *Marg,* September 1958, p. 17.

158. According to Fuhrer, 'All the mongrel vulgarities which were applied in Vaux Hall, Rosher Ville and the Sarrey gardens took refuge in the Qaisar Bagh and the Chatar Manzil when expelled from thence', op. cit., p. 267.

159. These country houses were erected by Martin

for Asafuddaulah (see *Mirat ul Au'za,* f.105a).

160. It was erected by Sa'adat Ali Khan. Its style reminds one of an improvised bungalow (see *Mirat ul Au'za,* f.107a).

161. It was a summer house erected by Sa'adat Ali Khan (see *Mirat ul Au'za,* f.107a).

162. Its style suggests that it was Sa'adat Ali's creation.

163. It was built as an observatory for Nasiruddin Haider under the supervision of Col. Wilcox.

164. Built by Sa'adat Ali Khan in 1800 for the British Resident (E.H. Hilton, *Guide to Lucknow and the Residency,* Lucknow, 1934, p. 75). Lalji attributes its erection to Asafuddaulah, op. cit., f.105a. It is considered to be the best example of the neo-classic style of Lucknow. In the opinion of Hermann Goetz, it represents a style which is a Gothic admixture of the Romantic period (*Marg,* September, 1958, p. 17).

165. It was a summer resort of Sa'adat Ali Khan (*Mirat ul Au'za,* f.107a). It was an attractive building with a colossal front and reminded one of the 'eighteenth century French Chateau enlivened by the touch of an Italian hand' (William Howard Russel, *My Diary in India,* London, 1860, Vol. I, p. 307). This building was completely damaged during the Mutiny.

166. It was a commodious villa in the English style which was erected by Martin for Asafuddaulah (Valentia, p. 147). According to Henry H. Spray, it was 'the only fascimile of an English mansion in the plains of Hindoostan' (see Spray, *Modern India with Illustrations of the Resources and the Capabilities of Hindoostan,* London, 1817, Vol. I, p. 234).

167. This summer house was erected by Wajid Ali Shah (*Lucknow Album,* p. 6). Its style had a blending of Gothic and Grecian features.

168. *Lucknow Album,* p. 17. The Nasiri Bagh was in French style (see Leopold Von Olrich, *Travels in India including Sinde and the Punjab,* London, 1845, Vol. II, p. 96), while the Dilkusha Park resembled the Needwood Forest (Heber, Vol. I, p. 214). The Wilayat Bagh, as the name suggests, was a garden in the English style built by Nasiruddin Haider.

169. The Sikandar Bagh originally belonged to Sa'adat Ali Khan known as Bibi Bagh. It was renovated by Wajid Ali Shah (see *Mirat ul Au'za,* f.107a).

170. Nandlal Chatterjee, 'The Nawabi Architecture of Lucknow'. *Journal of U.P. Historical Society,* Vol. 9, pt. ii, 1936, p. 48.

171. E.B. Havell, *Indian Architecture,* London, 1927, p. 222.

172. Captain Mundy, p. 29.

173. O'Malley, *Modern India and the West,* England, 1941, p. 490.

174. Martin refers to a play by the touring actors at Lucknow (Rosie L. Jones, *A Very Ingenious Man, Claude Martin in Early Colonial India,* Delhi, 1992, p. 76).

175. *Mirat ul Au'za,* f.92b.

176. Wajid Ali Shah, *Bani* (Urdu), Lucknow, 1885, pp. 103-5.

177. *Sharahi Indarsabha,* 1270 A.H. It was the *muqaddama* of *Indarsabha,* written independently by Syed Agha Husain Amanat (cited in Syed Masud Husain Rizvi, *Urdu Drama aur Stage, Ibtadaai daur ki mufassil Tarikh,* Lucknow, 1957, pp. 159-64).

178. William Hoey, *A Monograph on Trade and Manufactures in Northern India,* Lucknow, 1879-80, p. 28; Anon., *A Gazetteer of the Provinces of Oudh,* Lucknow, 1877, Vol. I, p. xvii.

179. *A Monograph on the Pottery and Glass Industry in the North Western Provinces and Oudh,* Allahabad, 1896. As late as 1888, the industry was 'in its most primitive state' confined only to the manufacture of bangles and beads (cf. T.N. Mukharji, *Art Manufactures of India,* Calcutta, 1888, p. 294).

180. Nevill, op. cit., Vol. XLIII, p. 41.

181. Thornton, op. cit., Vol. IV, p. 647; C.A. Silberrad, *A Monograph on Cotton Fabrics produced in the North Western Provinces and Oudh*, Allahabad, 1896, p. 32.

182. Nevill, op. cit., Vol. XLIII, p. 41.

183. The coins and the specimens of *tamdani* are in the State Museum, Lucknow.

184. Knighton, pp. 241-2. Mrs. Meer Hasan Ali remarks that 'chairs and sofa are produced when English visitors are expected' (see her *Observations on the Mussalmans of India, description of their manners, customs, habits and religious opinions & C*, Vol. I, London, 1832, p. 310). Even the dressing rooms of the *harem* had no shelved closets, almirahs or chest of drawers. The ladies preferred the old mode of squatting and lounging on carpets (ibid., Vol. I, p. 310).

185. Guy and Swallow, op. cit., p. 182. The design was prepared by Robert Home. This throne chair is in the Victoria and Albert Museum.

186. P.C. Mookherji, p. 175.

187. *Monograph on Pottery & C*, op. cit., p. 16.

188. P.C. Mookherji, p. 174.

189. Anon., 'Terracotta Figures from Lucknow', *Journal of Indian Arts and Industries*, London, 1903, p. 50.

190. A. Coomaraswamy, *Introduction to Indian Art*, Calcutta, 1956, p. 54.

191. *Monograph on Pottery & C*, p. 16.

4

Some Problems of the Mughal School of Art: Ascriptions, Duplicate Versions and Modern Attributions

SOM PRAKASH VERMA

The Mughal school of art flourished under the patronage of the Mughal Emperors, princes and nobles with a regular scheme, first formulated at the imperial atelier. We have no definite information whether Babur and Humayun maintained regular studios (*taswirkhana, naqqashkhana*) which became an integral part of the royal library (*kitabkhana*) since Akbar's reign. But there are references to establish that even during the most difficult times (August-September 1542 at Amarkot) Humayun had painters in his retinue. One account tells us that when a beautiful bird flew into Humayun's tent, he had a picture taken of the bird.[1] Another source also furnishes evidence of Humayun's painters at Kabul and Delhi.[2] Among the officials who accompanied him from Kabul to Delhi in 1555, Hashim Haini, *darogha-i kitabkhana* (superintendent of royal library), was one of them.[3] In the same list we also find names of two famous painters Mir Sayyid Ali and Khwaja Abdus Samad.[4]

The organization of the imperial atelier received its particular stamp during Akbar's reign. The earliest reference to Akbar's studio is available in Monserrate's account (1580-82).[5] Abul Fazl gives some details. He tells us that the works of all painters were weekly laid before His Majesty by the *daroghas* and the clerks; he then conferred rewards according to excellence of workmanship, or increased the monthly salaries.[6]

Under this system, special care was taken at the atelier to inscribe the names of artists on the works executed by them. It must have become necessary for evaluating the merit of the individual painters in support of their promotion or increase in salary. As a result, quite a large number of painters are known through inscriptions given on the miniatures[7] compared to those from the contemporary literary sources.[8]

Thus, the inscriptions are very important to identify the paintings as the work of a particular artist. Even the historicity of many Mughal miniatures depends on the ascriptions given on them. On the other hand, the genuineness of the ascriptions may sometimes be questioned due to various reasons. For example: (a) a version may be forged in the name of the painter who executed the original. In such cases, the inscriptions (artist's name, theme, etc.) given in the original are sometimes faithfully imitated in the replicas; (b) a version of a particular artist's work may be forged in the name of his contemporary; and (c) a late miniature being forged in the name of an earlier master-painter.

To discern a forged miniature is difficult indeed. While there is no foolproof method to indicate clearly the falsely inscribed and duplicate (copy) works, it is mainly the stylistic and technical variants which help us in uncovering the genuine pieces. But in case of the Mughal painters, since specific style was not always the hallmark of a particular painter, this methodology, too, may fail us sometimes. This exercise becomes more difficult in the face of the non-availability of the stages of evolution in the style and technique of a particular painter. The task of deciphering forged works is a delicate matter: attempts have been made in this direction, but not without controversies and doubts.

But the case is not so hopeless. Often the ascriptions themselves lead us to discover the forgery. Wrong rendering of the Persian inscriptions, for example, is a direct clue to it. Besides, in case of the ascriptions intended to be artist's signature, a comparison with the genuine signatures of that artist is more relevant.

The surviving examples of replicas indicate that the work of a master-painter was of great interest since, either an individual or an institution holding an art collection, could be proud of possessing the work of great masters. Moti Chandra thinks that the great demand for Mughal miniatures encouraged descendants of the Mughal painters to prepare fake pictures signed in the name of master-painters to fetch fabulous price from the enthusiastic but ignorant collectors.[9] Rai Krishnadasa says that copies were made to replace the miniatures which were highly esteemed or got lost but the *charba* of which were still available for use.[10] Milo Cleveland Beach opines that such copies were perhaps made for British customers who accepted on trust that they were acquiring genuine royal treasures.[11]

Moti Chandra realized the problem of fake pictures and took pains to discern the fakes from the originals. He found that technical quality was inferior in the forged specimens. In this attempt, he pointed out a good number of fake examples in the Wantage Collection preserved in the Victoria and Albert Museum (London). These include the fake works given in the names of Alam, Balchand, Bishandas, Daulat, Farrukh Beg, Manohar, Mansur, Mir Hashim, Pidarath and Sahifa Bano.[12] He writes:

> As we have seen already in the paintings of Jahangir and Shah Jahan's time, colours are applied in many thin coatings so as to impart the painting depth and an enamelling effect. The fake paintings sadly lack these qualities. To amend the defects of colour the painters have taken recourse to stippling, and there is not a single spot in the fake paintings of this album where extensive stippling has not been done.[13]

Rai Krishnadasa also observes that many of the paintings in the Wantage Collection are copies done in Emperor Shah Alam's period.[14] He further notices a late eighteenth century copy with forged ascription of Bichitr's original "Portrait of Jahangir holding an orb" (*c.* 1610-20) in the Chester Beatty Library (Dublin).[15] Karl Khandalavala gave serious thought to the problem of late versions intended to be presented as the work of the sixteenth and seventeenth century artists of the great Mughal school. He detected numerous fake works of the eighteenth century published by Welch, Mehta and others as masterpieces of Jahangir and Shah Jahan's reign.[16] Khandalavala observes that copies, in general, are characterised by hard lines, and the drawing is without flow. Sometimes these copies were executed with great care. According to him, it is only the long continuous contact with Mughal paintings and an experience of seeing a number of copies that one could detect the forged ascriptions and fake pictures.[17]

Beach's attempt towards discovering late versions especially of the works of Bichitr, Balchand, Goverdhan and Mansur, needs to be pursued further since his study is confined to the paintings preserved at the Freer Gallery of Art (Washington).[18] Welch, Schimmel, Swietochowski and Thackston are amongst others who have pointed out fake ascriptions and late versions, especially from the Kevorkian Album lodged in the Freer Gallery of Art and the Metropolitan Museum (New York). Numerous pictures are forged in the names of Abul Hasan, Balchand, Bichitr, Farrukh Beg, Goverdhan, Hashim, Mansur and Muhammad Alam.[19]

The picture of 'Himalayan cheer pheasant' (Plate 1), first brought to light by Asok Kumar Das from the collection of Sawai Man Singh II Museum (Jaipur),[20] bears an inscription *'Amal Ustad Mansur'* ('Work of *Ustad* Mansur') identical to the painting of this bird in the Wantage Collection (Plate 6).[21] Which one is genuine and which fake? This problem can be tackled only if one knows the unique features of Mansur's art that lay in the development of bold sweeps of his brush strokes to build up the landscape, but distinctly contrasted and delicately balanced with minute details and delicate fine lines of the main drawing. Handling of pigments with such confidence in expression is available in Mansur's work as early as 1600.[22] This characteristic of Mansur is visibly prominent in some of his masterpieces,[23] but not altogether absent in his other works.[24] Niharranjan Ray was the first scholar who noticed it while describing the picture *'Jurz-bar'* ('Indian bustard'), executed by Mansur in 1619 (Plate 5).[25] He observes:

> Mansur's acute observation and detailed and refined draughtsmanship are noticeable in this study as well, as much as in his numerous other bird studies. But what is more striking is the seemingly casual but well-measured and balanced, flat and broad sweeps of the brush in a colour tone which is deeper than that of the light background. These flat, broad sweeps throw the bird in relief to the fore, and despite its light and subtle colour scheme, give it a vivid naturalness.[26]

These broad sweeps of brush in their mature form confirm the artist's absolute confidence in his brush and expanded sense of freedom in the execution of a painting.

The Wantage miniature has very bold sweeping strokes, so brilliantly expressive as in other works of Mansur that the Jaipur picture appears very weak and insignificant in composition. In the Jaipur copy, the brush strokes are so slight, hesitant and restricted in movement that the frank spontaneity of Mansur in the Wantage copy is conspicuously absent. This is natural when one tries to run the brush in the likeness of another painter. And that puts one in serious doubts about the authenticity of the Jaipur miniature.

The ascription given on the Jaipur miniature, too, appears fake in the sense that it is identical with the Wantage copy both in text and placement. An agreement in such detail seems to be an obvious result of conscious manipulation.

For another version of this picture in the Baron Maurice Rothschild Collection (Paris), Beach opines emphatically that it is not by Mansur but a contemporary copy of the Wantage miniature.[27] Edwin Binney 3rd has suggested its attribution to Payag, a master-painter of Shah Jahan's atelier.[28] However, the outline drawing of the bird and the background of the picture is positively at variance in the present example when compared with the original in the Wantage Collection. Deep shading, heavy modelling in the treatment of landscape and well defined details in the background, unknown in Mansur's paintings, take it to the early nineteenth century (Plate 2).

Beach's observation (in context of this particular version) that it was common practice for Mughal artists to adapt single figures and even whole compositions from the work of their compatriots,[29] appears to be a generalisation since such instances occur rarely. One rare example of it are the identical figures of the musician and his companion in the works of Bichitr and Goverdhan respectively.[30] It is remarkable that in such examples the painter who adapted the figure was a known artist. Mention may be made of a modified version of Aqa Riza's 'Seated youth', containing a late inscription.[31]

The third version of the Himalayan cheer pheasant in the collection of Bernard Quaritch (Paris) is an identical reverse of the original.[32] On the grounds of style, it seems to have been done at a later date, perhaps in early nineteenth century (Plate 3). The whole picture is finished with linear details in thin pigment after the water colour technique — a trait unfamiliar to Mansur.

The picture of 'Falcon', ascribed to Mansur (Sawai Man Singh II Museum),[33] may be discussed along with the miniature 'Himalayan cheer pheasant' (above) from the same collection (Plate 4). When we consider the background treatment of the 'Himalayan cheer pheasant' and the 'Falcon', we see an astonishing similarity of brush strokes. They are slight in execution and very thin in pigment application, almost as in water colour. The grassy ridges also look alike. We know that Mansur's repertoire does not include such techniques. Besides, the linear delineation of the drawing of the falcon is so pronounced, very unlike Mansur, who would substitute it with this shading technique, and get out of it with better results. The identical features of landscape background in the two Jaipur miniatures raise doubt about the authenticity of the ascription given on the picture of falcon, since in the case of Himalayan cheer pheasant its originality has already been rejected by its comparison with Mansur's original in the Wantage Collection, and also on the grounds of the salient features of this painter's style seen in his other works.

The inscription *'Amal Nadir ul Asr Jahangir Shahi'* is carefully placed on the perching stand of 'Falcon' intended to be artist's signature, but it is at clear variance with Mansur's identified signatures and his handwriting.[34] Besides, Mansur never mentioned his title *'Nadir ul Asr'* ('Unique of the Age') alone, without his name in his signatures.[35]

Again the picture 'Assembly of Pigeons' is also enigmatic as to its authenticity because of the inscription on it, *'Amal Mansur Jahangir Shahi'* ('Work of Mansur, (servant) of King Jahangir').[36] The entire composition is indeed very formal, and betrays many loose ends to be believed as Mansur's work. An arrangement of birds (pigeons) such as seen here in the margin painting is not found in the sixteenth and seventeenth century Mughal paintings. The margin painting and the picture in the middle have been done on two types of paper which make it clear that the two were made separately and pasted together later. The authenticity of the two pigeons in the middle is palpably dubious also. Falk and Digby's hesitant note that the two middle figures were probably done by Mansur would be unconvincing if we just take a close look at the technique and quality of the painting of the border decoration and the picture in the middle itself.[37] They are identical in form and execution. Evidently, all the pigeons seem to have been executed by the same hand, and totally lacking the soft brush strokes, fine shading and minute details of description which is Mansur's forte, but not rare in the works of other painters among his contemporaries. The toy-like woodenness and opacity in the colouration of the figures and the background in this miniature is exactly the reverse of the wonderful lyrical transparency effects in Mansur's pictures. The typical mannerism and stylization in the depiction of birds conform to the conventions prevalent towards the close of the eighteenth century.

An unascribed version of the 'Turkey Cock' is inte esting since there appears

Jahangir's seal on its illustrated margin (Plate 7),[38] which probably suggests that this folio was painted at the imperial atelier itself within close proximity of the time of the picture of this bird in the Wantage Collection with the accepted signature of artist Mansur on it (Plate 8).[39] Krishnadasa and Humayun Kabir have observed that imitations of mounts and *hashiyas* of Jahangir's period made during the nineteenth century look like originals.[40] They further say that even the authentic seals of the former Emperors were stamped on such mounts.[41] This copy may thus be an instance of this kind of misrepresentation of the original of Mansur.

Brown, Havell, Clarke, Ray and Das have attributed this version to Mansur.[42] Though, generally speaking, the main figure looks almost identical to the signed study of this bird, the deviations are sharp and apparent in the treatment of the figure drawing and the background. If we compare closely the two figures, the brush work and colour textures (especially on the head portion and the lower plumage of the original) are missing in the other one. The reason for this is simple enough to understand: in a copied version, such effects cannot be exactly brought out. If we suppose that Mansur made this repetition himself, then, at least, the head studies would have had the same texture of colour, although the patterning aspect of the plumage could show some small differences in repetition. Evidently, the head study of the unascribed version is inferior artistically. The brush strokes, the landscape, the well defined horizon line with vegetation along the undulated hillocks make the miniature alien to Mansur's art of doing backgrounds. Also, the prominently defined contouring of the hillocks and the skyline, absence of bird clusters in high margin, brush lines drawn in deep pigment with water colour effect to depict the sky, are indeed irreconcilable with Mansur's technique.

Another unascribed version (No. A.G.839, Maharaja Sawai Man Singh II Museum), too, shows the landscape background clearly at variance.[43] Here the copier has failed to imitate Mansur's method of modelling with the application of defined bold and spontaneous strokes. The puerile brush strokes seen in the version testify it.

An unascribed picture of hornbill from the collection of Geoffrey C.N. Sturt, Painswick (Gloucestershire),[44] is almost similar to another picture of this bird in the Metropolitan Museum of Art (New York).[45] The latter is ascribed to Mansur and bears the stamp of his particular soft spontaneous brush movements on horizontal strokes and along the undulations of the landscape form. The depiction of long and supple tufts of grass and other vegetation, too, is characteristic of him. A comparison of these two pictures would show that the unascribed version is clearly inferior both in draughtsmanship and colouration. The soft transparency of the pigment with tonal variations, and the minuteness of details of the original are altogether absent in the Gloucestershire version which, on the basis of its representational style, may presumably be dated to early nineteenth century—the period which is marked for its wooden treatment of objects.

The rounded ends of wing feathers of the original are distorted into conical and edgy ends, which is more a result of fancy rather than a close objective reproduction of the natural living form. Further, though a minor point, positioning of the talons of the right foot is changed in the copied version.

The comments of some noted scholars with regard to the versions of the Himalayan griffon (Freer Gallery of Art and Chester Beatty Library) invite a fresh look.[46] Beach has rightly concluded that the picture of the Himalayan griffon in the Freer Gallery of Art is a work of early nineteenth century.[47] The Freer version lacks the finesse of Mansur's brush, and does not conform to Mansur's manner of art, especially the way in which the rock contours with the springing sprigs and vegetation, and heavily shaded foreground are treated in it (Plate 9). Therefore, as a logical corollary to this, one may say that both the inscription and Mansur's title on the miniature are fake. The problem arises when Welch describes Freer version as a copy of the study of this bird preserved in the Chester Beatty Library executed, according to him, in the seventeenth century from a lost picture by Mansur (Plate 10).[48]

We find that of the two versions, i.e., Freer and Chester Beatty, the former is closer in drawing to the original one 'King vulture and Himalayan griffon' in the Metropolitan Museum of Art (New York)[49] than the Chester Beatty version which is far inferior in artistic qualities (Plate 11). It is rather of spurious origin and, therefore, it is also difficult to agree with Arnold and Wilkinson who attribute it to Mansur.[50] The Chester Beatty copy is notably inferior: the chest line and the shape of the back, legs and talons, are disproportionately thick and large, and the folds of the wings are crudely patterned. Obviously, it is both a weak drawing and an inaccurate representation of the bird when put side by side with Mansur's original in the Metropolitan Museum of Art. Variations seen in the form of the bird further suggest that the imitator copied the original by looking at it rather than from its *charba.* Nowhere can we trace the true characteristics of Mansur's style and drawing in it. The probable date of Chester Beatty version could be early nineteenth century, as it shows both decadence of form and colour generally associated with the late Mughal style in this period. These observations on its art form and colouration are at cross with Welch's contention that it was painted in the seventeenth century from a lost work of Mansur and not from the original miniature in the Metropolitan Museum of Art or the version in the Freer Gallery of Art.

It would be relevant to examine here whether there was a practice of executing identical copies of a Mughal miniature at the imperial atelier itself. If so, who did the copies: (a) one who did the original; (b) or someone else? Clarke observes that Jahangir usually ordered one or more copies to be prepared for gifts.[51] I am unaware of any evidence to support Clarke's statement who does not cite his source. Jahangir's statement, 'As these animals appeared to me very strange, I both described them and ordered that painters should draw them in the *Jahangirnama'*, might tempt one to take the view that more than one artist might have been asked to paint the same subject.[52] Thus several artists may have been employed in illustrating various copies of the *Jahangirnama*. The work of illustrating the *Jahangirnama* was in progress in 1618. It is evident from Jahangir's specific mention of the illustrated frontispiece, namely, the scene of Jahangir's accession painted by Abul Hasan in 1618.[53] Hardly two months after this event, the first copy of the *Jahangirnama* was presented to Shah Jahan[54] and a little later, in the same year, two other copies were presented to Itimaduddaula and Asaf Khan.[55] But there is no specific evidence that the gifted copies contained illustrations.

In addition to the above frontispiece, a few dispersed miniatures including those preserved at the State Library (Rampur) are supposed by Das to belong to the royal copy/ copies of the Emperor's Memoirs.[56] However, Das's identification of these paintings as illustrated folios of a MS is not beyond doubt, since none of them contains lines of text set within the picture frame — a characteristic feature of book illustration of Jahangir's reign.[57] Most likely, the miniatures belonged to the tradition of album (*muraqqa*) pictures illustrating major events described in the *Jahangirnama*.

These pictures clearly do not belong to the category of manuscript illustrations since these are executed on varying formats and lines of text are found absent. Detailed notes occurring on some of the pictures in the handwriting of the Emperor further rule out their affiliation with manuscript painting.[58] In the Mughal school, the Emperor's autographs appear only on album pictures and in no instance do they occur on book illustrations. It may thus be said that the bird and animal pictures executed during Jahangir's time, of which duplicates are available (noticed above), belong to the tradition of album pictures and have no relationship to the art of book illustration of the *Jahangirnama*.

Das in his attempt at identifying the miniatures which must have formed part of an illustrated copy of the *Jahangirnama*, says that the number of portrait studies of animals executed in conformity with their description in the Memoirs is fairly large, and that the majority of them were preserved in the albums.[59] He is doubtful that the pictures of curious birds and animals or notable events done by painters in royal entourage were incorporated in the *Jahangirnama*.[60]

It is important to note that at the imperial atelier, even when a particular theme was the subject of being repeatedly illustrated, copying was never accepted. This observation is based after comparing the miniatures on identical themes illustrated in different copies of a particular manuscript.[61] Our extensive survey shows that no contemporary, identical copy of a book illustration is known.[62] Hence, the possibility of the replicas being made at Jahangir's atelier to decorate the copies of his Memoirs is remote.

In case of album pictures, too, identical copies of portraits, etc. are rather late versions of the originals. For example, an early nineteenth century version of Abul Hasan's painting 'Jahangir shooting at the head of Malik Ambar' (*c.* first quarter of the seventeenth century)[63] is preserved at the Freer Gallery of Art.[64] Another instance from the same Collection is of an early nineteenth century copy[65] of Bichitr's famous painting '*Rubab* player, his companion and a peasant' (*c.* first quarter of the seventeenth century).[66] It is important to note that the copier's name appears in copied versions rarely.[67] As against this, the inscriptions (artist's name, theme inscriptions, etc.) given in the originals are frequently copied in the replicas with exactitude. In both the above examples, inscriptions given in original paintings are imitated which suggest that copies were often forged in the name of the painter who executed the originals. Sometimes even new works were forged in the name of old masters;[68] or a copy of the work of a master-painter was forged in the name of his compatriots.[69] From the surviving examples of the replicas it may be inferred that mainly the works of master-painters were of great attraction to the copiers.

It is true that copies of Persian miniatures were prepared at Jahangir's atelier, but it was a rare phenomenon at the royal studio. It is important to note that in such cases, the inscriptions given on the Mughal versions clearly mention that the present work was a copy. An inscription (Emperor's autograph) given on a copy of Bihzad's original, executed by Nanha in 1608-09 is significant (Plates 12-3).[70] It reads: *'Allah-u Akbar. In kar-i Ustad Bihzad ra did Nanha musawwir karda hasbul hukum man. Harrarah Jahangir bin Akbar Padshah Ghazi, san 1017* ('Allah is Great. This work of master Bihzad was seen by Nanha [and he] painted it according to my orders. Written by Jahangir son of Akbar Padshah Ghazi, A.H. 1017') [A.D. 1608-09]. Obviously, the nature of such a copy is quite different from those observed above since there appears a clear attempt to project them as original pieces.

Copies of European pictures/engravings were occasionally prepared. In all probability, it was due to the fact that for both the patrons and the painters, it was a novel experience to deal with Christian themes and the techniques of European art. Sometimes, it was also necessary to prepare copies of European example to suit the format of the Mughal albums; and, especially in case of engravings, preference was given to their coloured reproduction.[71] When a painting was brought for a short while by the Jesuits or others, it was copied for the royal collection.[72] Documentation of European pictures at the imperial atelier could have been another reason for the preparation of such replicas. It is significant to note that in rare cases some European pictures were copied more than once at the imperial atelier, since a single copy possibly did not meet the demand of the patron.[73] Could we say, then, that at the imperial atelier mere copying of the originals was not the aim of the Mughal painters?

A close scrutiny of the inscriptions, too, leads us to discover the forged works. We know that Bichitr in his signatures always wrote his name as 'Bichitr' (Plate 14).[74] However, in an inscription on a painting 'A prince on the back of an elephant' his signature reads as *"Amal ghulam ba ikhlas Bichitr, 1016"* ('Work of the loyal slave, *Bichhitr, A.H. 1016'*) [A.D. 1607-08].[75] Clearly this has been forged by someone who overlooked the fact that Bichitr never inducted a *ha* (to become *chh*) into the spelling of his name. This fact of forgery is then reinforced by the text of the preceding inscription on the same miniature: *'Shahzada Muhammad Murad farzand Shah Jahan bar fil Iqbal'* ('Prince Muhammad Murad, son of Shah Jahan, on the elephant Iqbal'). The name of Prince Murad was Murad Bakhsh, not Muhammad Murad. Bichitr, being at court, could have never made this mistake. Moreover, in A.H. 1016 (A.D. 1607-08), the year given in the inscription (artist's signature [?]), Murad was not even born. Thus, the fact of forgery suggested by style of writing is proved beyond dispute by the actual contents of the inscription.

In another example, faulty inscription is found on a nineteenth century work, 'Forktail' (bird) forged in the name of the master-painter Mansur.[76] Inscription on it reads: *'Taswir-i janwa[r] ablaq, banda-i dargah Ostad [sic] Mansur Jahangir Shahi'* ('Picture of a piebald bird. Slave of the court *Ostad* Mansur, servant of King Jahangir'). The spelling of *Ustad* has been wrongly rendered as *Ostad*. Actually, the original of this picture is by Abul Hasan (*c.* 1615-20), and the one in question is a nineteenth century copy.[77] While Abul Hasan, a great contemporary of Mansur, puts all the masterly touches in his picture, the copier fails to catch the thrilling beauty of it, or even to do it in Mansur's style and technique. These are only a few examples.

Now, let us take up the problem of modern attributions. We have already discussed some of the unascribed miniatures attributed to Mansur by Martin, Brown, Arnold, Wilkinson, Das and others. In this context, the picture of the 'Siberian crane' is of particular significance (Plate 15).[78] Here an attempt to imitate Mansur's typical sweeps of brush is apparent. The isolated figure of the crane is accepted by Das as the work of Mansur on the fact of its 'very minute brush work and the stamp of distinctiveness expressed in its [bird's] posture.'[79] Of course, the striking similarity of brush strokes in the landscape and the flight of birds on the high margin, typical of Mansur's miniatures, do tempt us into accepting this as his work. But when we closely observe the strokes we see that they are a bit too crowded and rather carefully arranged, lacking Mansur's spontaneous expressiveness, casualness, and boldness of approach in laying the background. Further, the drawing of legs is too weak to be accepted as drawn by the master (compare the study of another crane, *jurz-bar,* noticed above). Most probably, the miniature is an inspired work of imitation from some original work of Mansur, not known to us, and very likely to have been done in the nineteenth century.

Unascribed miniatures are attributed mainly to the master-painters on the grounds of close stylistic similarities found in common with the salient features of their works. The problem arises when the attribution of a picture is suggested to different painters by different scholars and, thus, the attribution becomes controversial. Even, in certain cases, scholars are found to have revised their earlier opinion. Besides, attributions are often made freely without an explanation being given in their support. One suspects that sometimes attributions to master-painters are made by modern critics, cataloguers, etc. to stress the importance or quality of a miniature, or even to enhance the status of an Art Collection. Several bird and animal drawings are attributed to Mansur for the simple reason that he is known to have been a master in this field.

There is a fairly large number of unascribed paintings whose suggested attributions have become controversial. Only a few examples are cited here to illustrate the point. The attribution of a miniature, 'Jahangir embracing Nur Jahan (?)', attributed by Stchoukine to Goverdhan (of Jahangir and Shah Jahan's court),[80] and followed by Welch[81] and Beach,[82] is disputed by Khandalavala who assigns the date of this miniature to the late seventeenth century.[83] Similarly, the miniature 'Lovers on terrace' attributed to Goverdhan[84] is also suspect: Khandalavala rightly describes this miniature of the late seventeenth century as fake.[85] In another instance, the attribution of the illustration 'The undoing of the ill-natured wazir' to Manohar as suggested by Welch, too, becomes doubtful.[86] Das suggests it to have been executed by Goverdhan.[87] Again, the unascribed picture of 'Wounded buck' noticed in the Fogg Art Museum (Cambridge) was first attributed to Mansur jointly by Welch and Beach in 1965.[88] Later, in 1973, Welch revised his opinion and attributed it to Abul Hasan.[89] Again, the picture of a bird 'Forktail' with the inscription *'Nadir uz Zaman'* (i.e., Abul Hasan) is considered by Beach as a nineteenth century work.[90] But Welch describes the same as a genuine work of Abul Hasan and assigns its date around 1610-15.[91] Welch's observation on this miniature is relevant: 'This is one of Abul Hasan's few natural history pictures, and the only one with contemporaneous inscription.'[92]

Sometimes the ascriptions recorded on the reverse of the picture, too, are of doubtful nature. The painting 'Squirrels on a chinar tree' contains an inscription on the reverse: (A) *'Nadir uz Zaman'* [i.e., Abul Hasan], and (B) *'Nadir ul Asr'* [i.e., Mansur].[93] If genuine, they indicate joint work by two very celebrated painters of the Mughal school. However, Das thinks that it is the work of Mansur alone.[94] As against this, Gray,[95] Falk and Mildred Archer[96] refer this work in the name of Abul Hasan.

We may mention here that confusion has arisen since the namesakes of the Mughal master-painters were active during the eighteenth century and, thus, their works have been mistakenly accepted as belonging to the great Mughal school. The namesake of the prolific Mughal painter Goverdhan was active during the eighteenth century. The picture of a lady (face and shoulder), based on a European example (adapted from the engraving by Cornelius Jacobsz), ascribed to Goverdhan (location not known), is accepted by Mehta as the work of Jahangir's reign.[97] Khandalavala argues that this is not by the Goverdhan of Jahangir's reign but by an eighteenth century artist.[98] Other unascribed versions of this picture are known in the Gulshan Album, Imperial Library (Teheran),[99] Johnson Album, India Office Library (London)[100] and the Victoria and Albert Museum (London).[101] It was an oft-repeated subject.

Doubts are also raised about another miniature 'King discovers the debauched Qazi' (location not known), ascribed to Goverdhan. But Falk, Digby and Goedhuis suggest that the inscription is a later addition.[102] In another instance, the miniature 'Shah Abbas with Khan Alam' (location not known), ascribed to Bishandas, is found by Coomaraswamy not quite in his best manner.[103]

Another Mughal painter Hunhar also had his namesake in the eighteenth century.[104] The picture 'Noble seated on a terrace with a lady' (Lt. Col. R.K. Tandon's Collection)[105] and 'Portrait of Khan Jahan Bahadur' (Johnson Album, India Office Library)[106] are works executed by the eighteenth century painter Hunhar, not by the Hunhar of Shah Jahan's reign. Percy Brown has listed miniatures ascribed to Hunhar of the eighteenth century under *the* Hunhar of Shah Jahan's reign.[107]

There are unfortunately many cases where the original attributions are defaced or erased for unknown reasons; in other cases, binders have cut the folios carelessly as to slice away part of inscriptions. On the other hand, there are spurious attributions added later with a view to inflating the value of a painting. Glaring examples of this are the miniatures of a *Razmnama* manuscript of the sub-imperial Mughal school lodged in the Birla Academy of Art and Culture (Calcutta).[108] These are spuriously ascribed to the painters of Akbar's school, viz., Mir Sayyid Ali, Basawan, Lal, Daswant, Mahesh, Mukund, Sarwan, Mukhlis, Jagan, Jagjiwan, Anis, Tara, Tulsi, Kesav, Kesav Gujarati, Bhagwan, Paras, Farrukh *Chela*, and others.[109] In another instance, certain art-historians hold that the *Tutinama* manuscript of the Cleveland Museum of Art (Cleveland) does not belong to the imperial atelier and the names of the sixteenth century Mughal painters (Basawan, Banwari, Ghulam Ali, Daswant, Iqbal, Lalu, Sarwan, Sarju, Tara and Gujarati given in the miniatures) are later additions.[110] Khandalavala describes it patently a provincial (not even sub-imperial) production of the late eighteenth century.[111] Similarly, the miniatures of the *Razmnama* manuscript in the Cowasji Jehangir Collection (Bombay) being described as the production of Akbar's atelier, and the illustrations of a seventeenth century *Bostan* manuscript (British Museum, London) are greatly doubtful. Miniatures of both these manuscripts belong to the eighteenth century: these lack the colour tonality and nuances of Akbar, Jahangir and Shah Jahan period.[112]

On the basis of the parameters chosen above, including the obvious norms of historical analysis and clear internal evidence of stylistic devices, certain helpful guidelines could be drawn to sift the genuine work from the forged imitations and copies preserved in different museums. To sum up:

A. In no instance, identical copies of their work were executed by the Mughal painters themselves.

B. Duplicate miniatures are not necessarily the product of imperial atelier; and the claim of their being contemporaneous is not beyond doubt.

C. Genuineness of identical copies bearing inscriptions is questionable on the grounds of internal evidence in the paintings themselves.

NOTES

1. Jauhar, *Tazkereh al Vakiat,* tr. Major Charles Stewart, Delhi, 1972, p. 43.
2. Bayazid Biyat, *Tazkira-i Humayun o Akbar,* ed. M. Hidayat Hosain, Bib. Ind., Calcutta, 1957, pp. 76-9, 177.
3. Ibid., p. 177 (no. 23).
4. Ibid., pp. 67-9, 176-87.
5. Monserrate, *The Commentary of Father Monserrate,* tr. J.S. Hoyland, London, 1922, p. 116.
6. Abul Fazl, *Ain-i Akbari,* ed. H. Blochmann, Bib. Ind., Calcutta, I, p. 116.
7. T.W. Arnold and J.V.S. Wilkinson, *A Library of A. Chester Beatty: A Catalogue of Indian Miniatures,* London, 1936, I, pp. XXVI-XXVII; P. Brown, *Indian Painting under the Mughals, A.D. 1550 to A.D. 1750,* Oxford, 1924, Appendix, pp. 195-8; Som Prakash Verma, *Art and Material Culture in the Paintings of Akbar's Court,* New Delhi, 1978, Appendix, pp. 124-9; also see his *Mughal Painters and Their Works,* Oxford University Press, New Delhi, 1994.
8. *Ain-i Akbari,* op. cit., p. 117, tr., p. 114; Mulla Alauddaula Qazwini, *Nafais al Maasir* (Aligarh MS, dated 1573), f. 51b; *Tazkira-i Humayun o Akbar,* op. cit., pp. 67-9, 177; Jahangir, *Tuzuk-i Jahangiri,* ed. Saiyid Ahmad, Ghazipur and Aligarh, 863-4, pp. 7, 75, 235, 275, 281, 299, 306; Abdul Baqi Nihawandi, *Maasir-i Rahimi,* ed. H. Hosain, Bib. Ind., Calcutta, 1910-31, pp. 753-4. Also see M.M. Haq, 'The Khan-i Khanan and his Painters', *Islamic Culture,* Hyderabad, Vol. 5, 1931, pp. 625-7.
9. Moti Chandra, *The Technique of Mughal Painting,* Lucknow, 1946, p. 79.
10. Rai Krishnadasa and Humayun Kabir, *Mughal Miniatures,* New Delhi, 1955, text and pl. 10. *Charba* is described as a thin transparent sheet of deer skin used for tracing outline drawings (see Brown, op. cit., p. 183; Chandra, op. cit., p. 39, n. 6). Steingass, *A Comprehensive Persian-English Dictionary,* s.v.
11. Milo C. Beach, *The Grand Mogul Imperial Painting in India (1600-1660),* Williamstown, Mass., 1978, p. 138.
12. Chandra, pp. 80-1. For their reproductions, see C.S. Clarke, *Victoria and Albert Museum Drawings: Thirty Mogul Paintings from the school of Jahangir (17th Century) and four panels of calligra-*

phy in the Wantage Bequest, London, 1922, pls. 2-7-10, 12, 17-20.

13. Moti Chandra, pp. 81-2.

14. Rai Krishnadasa and Humayun Kabir, op. cit., text to pl. 10.

15. Ibid. Here Rai Krishnadasa observes hard touches of brush unlike of Jahangir's painters and lack of modelling.

16. Karl Khandalavala, 'Some Problems of Mughal Paintings', *Lalit Kala,* No. 11, New Delhi, 1962, pp. 9-13.

17. Ibid., p. 12.

18. Milo C. Beach, *The Imperial Image, Paintings for the Mughal Court,* Washington, D.C., 1983, pp. 185-191 (Cat. nos. 18c, 18d, 18e and figs. 32-5, 37-9).

19. S.C. Welch, A. Schimmel, M.L. Swietochowski and W. Thackston, *The Emperors' Album, Images of Mughal India,* New York, 1987, pp. 245-6, 249-50, 254, 257-8, 261-2, 266, 269, 273, 277-8, 281-2, 285, pls. 86-7, 89, 91-2, 94, 96-100.

20. Asok Kumar Das, 'Some More Mansur's Drawings', *Lalit Kala,* No. 18, New Delhi, p. 29, pl. XIII, fig. 3.

21. For reproduction, see Clarke, op. cit., no. 24, pl. 16; Verma, 'Mansur, the Master painter of Jahangir's Epoch', *Roopa-Lekha,* No. 55 (1-2), New Delhi, p. 8, pl. on p. 7.

22. See the miniatures: (1) 'Two bufffalos' in the Freer Gallery of Art, No. 54.29 (Published in Beach, *The Imperial Image & C,* op. cit., p. 77, pl. on p. 50.

23. See the miniatures: (1) 'Himalayan cheer pheasant' (Wantage Collection, V.A., IM 136 & A-1921), reproduced in Clarke, no. 24, pl. 16; (2) 'Indian bustard' (Indian Museum, Calcutta), No. R. 31), reproduced in Niharranjan Ray, *Mughal Court Painting,* Calcutta, 1975, pl. 15; (3) 'Dipper' (Metropolitan Museum of Art, New York), reproduced in Verma, 'Mansur & C', op. cit., pl. on p. 7; (4) 'King Vulture and Himalayan Griffon' (Metropolitan Museum of Art), reproduced in M.A. Alvi and A. Rahman, *Jahangir — the Naturalist,* New Delhi, 1968, pl. 19; (5) 'Salt water fish' (Red Fort Museum, Delhi), reproduced in Das, 'Ustad Mansur', *Lalit Kala,* No. 17, New Delhi, 1974, pl. XII, fig. 1; Verma, 'Mansur & C', pp. 8-9, pl. on p. 6.

24. See the miniatures: (1) 'Himalayan blue throated barbet' (Wantage Collection), reproduced in Clarke, No. 22, pl. 15; (2) 'Turkey cock' (Wantage Collection), reproduced in Clarke, No. 23, pl. 15; (3) 'Goldfinch' (National Museum, New Delhi), reproduced in Alvi and Rahman, op. cit., pl. 17 (A); (4) 'Blue bull' (Metropolitan Museum of Art), reproduced in Das, 'Ustad Mansur', pl. XIII, fig. 5.

25. Ray, op. cit., pl. 15.

26. Ibid., p. 170.

27. Beach, *The Imperial Image & C,* op. cit., pp. 171-2, pl. on p. 173.

28. Ibid.

29. Ibid.

30. For which see Bichitr's miniature '*Rubab* player, his companion and a pheasant' (Victoria and Albert Museum, London, IM 27 & A-1925) and Goverdhan's painting in Chester Beatty Library, Dublin. For their reproductions, see E.B. Havell, *The Art Heritage of India,* Bombay, 1964, p. 91, pl. 61 (A) and Arnold and Wilkinson, op. cit., Vol. I, p. 30, Vol. III, frontispiece, respectively.
For other instances, see Robert Skelton, 'Two Mughal Lion Hunts', *Victoria and Albert Museum Year Book 1969,* No. 1, Phiadon, pl. II, fig. 16; Sir Leigh Ashton (ed.), *The Art of India and Pakistan,* London, 1948, No. 708, pl. 134.

31. Beach, *The Imperial Image & C,* pl. on p. 200.

The inscription *'Raqam Nadir uz Zaman'* in crude handwriting raises doubts on its authenticity. Beach also thinks that the inscription on it was added later (ibid., pl. 198).

32. For reproduction, see F.R. Martin, *The Miniature Painting and Painters of Persia, India and Turkey*, London, 1912, Vol. II, p. 12, pl. 220, where it is attributed to Mansur.

33. For reproduction, see Das, 'Some More Mansur's Drawings', op. cit., pl. XIII, fig. 2.

34. Verma, 'Artists' Signatures in the Miniatures of the Mughal school', *The Indian Historical Review*, Vol. X, Nos. 1-2, New Delhi, 1983-4, pp. 37-8, 43-4, where the paintings containing Mansur's signatures are identified.

35. Ibid.

36. Reproduced and described in Toby Falk, Simon Digby and Michael Goedhuis, *Paintings from Mughal India*, Colnaghi, London, n.d., p. 48, no. 22, pl. on p. 49.

37. Ibid.

38. See Clarke, text and pl. 15; Ray, p. 164, pl. XII; Das, *Mughal Painting During Jahangir's Time*, Calcutta, 1978, p. 149.

39. Reproduced in Clarke, no. 23, pl. 15.

40. Krishnadasa and Kabir, text and pl. 10.

41. Ibid.

42. See Brown, p. 139, pl. LIII; Havell, *Indian Sculpture and Painting*, London, 1908, pp. 214-6, pl. LXIII; Ray, p. 164, pl. XII; Clarke, no. 23; Das, *Mughal Painting & C*, op. cit., p. 149.

43. For reproduction, see Das, 'Mansur' in *Master Artists of the Imperial Mughal Court*, ed. Pratapaditya Pal, Bombay, 1991, p. 51, fig. 16.

44. Reproduced in Alvi and Rahman, op. cit., p. XVII (B).

45. Reproduced in Welch, Schimmel, Swietochowski and Thackston, op. cit., p. 165, no. 41, pl. on p. 167.

46. Ibid., p. 249, no. 82, pl. on p. 248, also see Arnold and Wilkinson, Vol. I, p. 45, Vol. III, pl. 80.

47. Beach, *The Imperial Image & C*, pp. 185-6, Cat. no. 18c (recto), pl. on p. 186.

48. See Welch, Schimmel, Swietochowski and Thackston, p. 249 & n. 82.

49. Ibid., p. 173, no. 45, pl. on p. 175; also in Alvi and Rahman, p. XIX.

50. Arnold and Wilkinson, Vol. I, p. 45, Vol. III, pl. 80.

51. Clarke, text and plate 16 (no. 24).

52. *Tuzuk-i Jahangiri*, op. cit., p. 105.

53. Ibid., p. 235.

54. Ibid., p. 239.

55. Ibid., p. 244.

56. Das, *Mughal Painting & C*, pp. 135-72.

57. See *Anwar-i Suhaili* (*c.* 1604-10), British Museum, Add. 18579; *Bostan* of Sa'di (*c.* 1605-10), British Museum, Add. 27262; *Diwan-i Hafiz* (1610), British Museum, Or. 7573.
For the reproductions of some of the miniatures from these MSS, see J.V.S. Wilkinson, *The Lights of Canopus: Anwar-i-Suhaili*, London, 1929; J.P. Losty, *The Art of the Book in India*, London, nos. 74-6, pls. XXVII, XXIX and fig. on p. 97; D. Barrett and B. Gray, *Painting of India*, Laussane, 1963, pls. on pp. 100-1.

58. For the reproduction of the miniatures containing Emperor's autographs, see Ray, pl. XV; Alvi and Rahman, pl. VI; Verma, 'Mansur & C, pls. on pp. 5-6.

59. Das, *Mughal Painting & C*, p. 137.

60. Ibid., pp. 136-7.

61. Verma, 'Treatment of Similar Themes — A Study based on the illustrations of Tuzuk-i Baburi', *Proceedings of the Indian History Congress*, Chandigarh, 1973, pp. 292-7.

62. A double-page illustration wrongly identified by Clarke (No. 2, pl. 2) as 'Humayun's accession-darbar at Agra, in 1530' preserved in the Wantage Collection (IM, Nos. 127 & 128-1921) in an early nineteenth century copy of the originals in the *Baburnama*, British Museum, Or. 3715 (Published in Hamid Suleiman, *Miniatures of Baburnama*, Tashkent, 1970, pls. 87-8).

63. Reproduced in Arnold and Wilkinson, Vol. I, p. 31, Vol. III, pl. 62.

64. Kevorkian Album, Freer Gallery of Art, No. 48.19 (Reproduced in Beach, *The Imperial Image & C*, pp. 185-6, Cat. no. (18c).

65. Kevorkian Album, op. cit., No. 48.21a (Reproduced in Beach, *The Imperial Image & C*, p. 191, fig. 38).

66. Miniature in Minto Album, Victoria and Albert Museum, London (IM, No. 27A-1925). For reproduction, see I. Stchoukine, *La Peinture Indienne l'Epoque des Grands Moghols*, Paris, 1929, pl. 44.

67. Beach (*The Imperial Image & C*, p. 159, fig. 30) has noticed a modified version of an unascribed miniature, 'A Mongol chieftain and attendants' (ibid., Cat. no. 16a, pl. on p. 158) given in the name of Vilayat, otherwise unknown. However, Agrawala does not mention the artist's name being given on this particular version (see V.S. Agrawala, *Indian Miniatures, An Album*, New Delhi, 1961, text and pl. XVI).
Also see Welch, Schimmel, Swietochowski and Thackston, p. 265, where Muhammad Alam is noticed as one of the early nineteenth century Delhi copyists.

68. For which see the miniature in the Kevorkian Album, No. 39.48 ('Two deer in landscape'), reproduced in Beach, *The Imperial Image & C*, p. 188, Cat. no. 18e recto. An original from which it was copied, is not known.

69. An early nineteenth century copy of a miniature 'Forktail' by Abul Hasan (preserved in the Metropolitan Museum of Art) forged in the name of Mansur is lodged in the Freer Gallery of Art, No. 39.46b. For their reproductions, see Alvi and Rahman, pl. XXII; Beach, *The Imperial Image & C*, p. 189, fig. 33; Welch, Schimmel, Swietochowski and Thackston, pp. 164-5, 254, nos. 40, 85, pls. on pp. 166, 255.

70. See miniatures: (1) 'Camel-fight' (identical copy of Bihzad's work), *Muraqqa-i Gulshan*, Gulistan Palace Library, Teheran (reproduced in L. Binyon, B. Gray and J.V.S. Wilkinson, *Persian Miniature Painting*, London, 1933, pls. 87 (A) (reproduction of Bihzad's original) and 87 (B) (copy made by Nanha)). According to Emperor Jahangir's autograph on the version, it was executed by Nanha in 1608-9 at his command; (2) 'Portrait of Abdur Rahman Jami' in the Gulshan Album, op. cit. (reproduced in Y.A. Godard, 'Les marges du Muraqqa Gulshan', *Ather-e-Iran*, Vol. I, Haarlem, 1936, p. 26, fig. 21). According to an inscription near the figure of the poet, this picture was copied by Daulat from an original by Bihzad (see Das, *Mughal Painting & C*, p. 127); (3) 'Mason at work' (copy of Bihzad's work in the *Khamsa* of Nizami, British Museum, Or. 6810, f. 154b, date 1494), Nasiruddin Album, Imperial Library, Teheran (reproduced in Godard, 'Un album de portraits des Princes Timurides de l'Inde', *Ather-e-Iran*, Vol. II, 1937, p. 266, no. 68, fig. 110 (ascribed to Sahifa Banu, a woman painter of Jahangir's reign)). For the reproduction of Bihzad's painting, see Gray, *Persian Painting*, London, 1961, pl. on p. 116. See also Das, *Mughal Painting & C*, p. 127, ns. 44-5.
See also 'Two camels' by Abdus Samad (Private Collection), inspired by Bihzad's work (reproduced and described in Michael Brand and Glenn D. Lowry, *Akbar's India: Art from the Mughal City of Victory*, New York, 1985, p. 151, fig. 58, where they observe that an exact copy (of Bihzad's work) would have been of no interest to Akbar).

71. E. Maclagan, *The Jesuits and the Great Mogul,* London, 1932, p. 248: 'The coloured Mughal picture of a Christian subject was not, as a rule, a copy of a coloured European picture, but was based on some uncoloured European print. In some few cases it is possible that colour was imposed by the Indian artist on the print itself; for Father Jerome Xavier tells us how he once saw one of the king's painters illustrating some small pictures by putting on colours and pigments.'

72. Ibid., p. 236: 'As early as 1580, we find Akbar having copies made of the pictures of the Virgin and of Christ which the Fathers had with them, and in 1597 the Prince Salim is reported to have begged for the loan of the picture of S. Ignatius Loyola that he might have it copied.' Also see pp. 232-3.

73. See Beach, 'The Mughal Painter Kesu Das', *Archives of Asian Art,* London, Vol. 30, 1976-7, figs. 7-8 (pictures of St. Jerome), 9-10 (Joseph telling his dream to his father).

74. Verma, 'Artists' Signatures & C', op. cit., p. 42.

75. Ibid., p. 41 for the reproduction of the miniature, see Havell, *Indian Sculpture & C,* op. cit., pl. LVII.

76. For reproduction, see Beach, *The Imperial Image & C,* p. 189, fig. 33; Welch, Schimmel, Swietochowski and Thackston, p. 254, no. 85, pl. on p. 255.

77. For reproduction, see Alvi and Rahman, pl. XXII; Welch, Schimmel, Swietochowski and Thackston, pp. 164-5, no. 40, pl. on p. 166.

78. Reproduced in Havell, *Indian Sculpture & C,* pl. LXI.

79. Das, *Mughal Painting & C,* pp. 197-8, pl. 58.

80. I. Stchoukine, 'Portraits Moghols, Parts I-IV', *Revue des Arts Asiatiques,* Ascona, Vol. II, pp. 168-76, pl. 56.

81. Welch, *The Art of Mughal India: Painting and Precious Objects,* New York, 1963, no. 32, p. 73.

82. Beach, *The Grand Mogul & C,* p. 125.

83. Khandalavala, pp. 9-10, fig. A.

84. Welch, *The Art of Mughal India & C,* p. 102, no. 47; Beach, *The Grand Mogul & C,* p. 125.

85. Khandalavala, p. 10, fig. B.

86. Welch, 'Early Mughal miniature paintings from two Private Collections shown at the Fogg Art Museum', *Ars Orientalis,* Vol. III, Washington, 1959, p. 142; Beach, *The Grand Mogul & C,* p. 69.

87. Das, *Mughal Painting & C,* pp. 95-6.

88. Welch and Beach, *Gods, Thrones and Peacocks,* New York, 1965, No. 10. Also see Beach, *The Grand Mogul & C,* p. 143.

89. Welch, *A Flower from every Meadow, Indian Paintings from American Collections,* New York, 1973, no. 61.

90. Beach, *The Grand Mogul & C,* p. 92.

91. Welch, Schimmel, Swietochowski and Thackston, pp. 164-5, no. 40, pl. on p. 166.

92. Ibid.

93. Johnson Album, India Office Library, London, Vol. I, F. 30 (reproduced in Welch, *The Art of Mughal India & C,* p. 74, pl. 35).

94. Das, *Mughal Painting & C,* p. 199, pl. 67.

95. Gray, 'Painting' in Leigh Ashton, op. cit., p. 163, no. 737.

96. Toby Falk and Mildred Archer, *Indian Miniatures in the India Office Library,* London, 1981, pp. 59-60, no. 34, colour pl. no. 4.

97. N.C. Mehta, *Studies in Indian Painting,* Bombay, 1926, p. 88, pl. 36.

98. Khandalavala, p. 10.

99. Beach, 'The Gulshan Album and its European sources', *Bulletin of Museum of Fine Arts, Boston,* No. 332, Boston, 1965, p. 87, fig. 11.

100. Falk and Archer, op. cit., pp. 156-7, no. 326, pl. on p. 444.

101. Victoria and Albert Museum, London (I.S. 259-1952). Unpublished.

102. Falk, Digby and Goedhuis, op. cit., p. 55, no. 25, pl. on p. 54.

103. A.K. Coomaraswamy, 'Notes on Indian Painting', *Artibus Asiae,* Dresden, 1927, p. 290, no. 12, fig. 13.

104. For the work of the latter, see Falk and Archer, pp. 145-6 (no. 269), 146-7 (no. 274).

105. Khandalavala, p. 11, pl. on p. 8.

106. Falk and Archer, pl. 98 (no. 133), pl. on p. 416.

107. Brown, p. 197. See Falk and Archer, p. 146, no. 274.

108. Khandalavala, 'A Sub-Imperial Akbari Period Razm Nama of A.D. 1605' in Karl Khandalavala and Saryu Doshi, *A Collector's Dream, Indian Art in the Collection of Basant Kumar and Saraladevi Birla and the Birla Academy of Art and Culture,* Bombay, 1987, pp. 165-80.

109. Ibid., pp. 174-177-80.

110. Khandalavala, 'Some problems & C', op. cit., p. 13; Ananda Krishna, 'Reassessment of the Tuti-Nama Illustrations in the Cleveland Museum of Art (and related problems of earliest Mughal Paintings and Painters)', *Artibus Asiae,* Ascona, Vol. XXXV, pp. 174, 246-67. Also see Verma, 'Origins of the Mughal School of Painting', *Art and Culture* (Felicitation Volume in Honour of Professor S. Nurul Hasan), ed. Ahsan Jan Qaisar and Som Prakash Verma, Jaipur, 1993, pp. 60-2.

111. Khandalavala, 'A Sub-Imperial Akbari Period & C', op. cit., p. 174.

112. Khandalavala, 'Some Problems & C', op. cit., p. 10.

5

Indian Response to Western Medicine: Vaccination in the City of Bombay in the Nineteenth Century

MRIDULA RAMANNA

Smallpox was one of the dreaded diseases that appeared frequently in epidemic form in India. In ancient India it was ascribed by the physicians to injurious food defects in diet, air and water.[1] On the other hand, popular superstitions traced its origin to a goddess Sitala Devi.[2] However, in pre-colonial India, a method of immunisation against smallpox was developed through variolation, which was the inoculation of variolous matter taken from someone who already had the smallpox. The matter was prepared from the pustules of the preceding year which indicates that there was an awareness that the virus, thus introduced, would be in an attenuated form and, therefore, less virulent.[3] It has been suggested that variolation may have developed independently in different parts of Eurasia and Africa.[4] Initially approved of by the British, this method was discouraged after Jenner's discovery, because Western vaccination was regarded more effective in controlling the disease that could spread so alarmingly.

An attempt has been made here to show Indian response to Western vaccination, taking Bombay City as a case-study. Even in the growing commercial centre that Bombay was in the nineteenth century, its acceptance was very gradual. To most, the method of arm to arm vaccination was ritually polluting, while some saw in it a British design to "Christianize" Indians. It came to be more widely used by mid-nineteenth century when Indian doctors trained in Western medicine and convinced of its efficacy actively promoted it. Noteworthy in particular was the effort of Dr. Ananta Chandroba who spent twenty-five years in this exercise. His observations in the Vaccination Reports relate the various obstacles faced by him and his team among the communities and castes in the city. Chandroba was uniquely successful in using animal vaccination, a method of inoculating calves and collecting lymph from their vesicles. After vaccination was made compulsory in 1877, the disease became more controllable.

It was in 1802, six years after Jenner's discovery, that the cowpox vaccine was transmitted through a series of volunteers vaccinated in the course of their voyage to India. In 1803, Dr. George Keir of the Medical establishment of the Bombay Presidency published a pamphlet on cowpox.[5] The Government initially wanted to immunise only soldiers, but the epidemic nature of disease made them promote vaccination as a policy. The British had first to counter inoculation which was widely used. The method was believed to be very old in India. Nana Raojee of Warneer Taluka (Nasik) and his colleague Bhadoo Nana deposed before the Magistrate at Surat thus: 'the left arm over the vein was scratched and when a little blood appeared, the variolous matter, which had been taken from someone who had smallpox earlier, was inoculated. After six days, the patient got fever and had a moderate reaction, which subsided in three days, giving immunity. The inoculators, who were *kumbhars,* received one seer of rice and one pice as payment, or sometimes nothing, from those unable to pay.'[6] J.Z. Holwell, in his account of inoculation in Bengal, observed that the inoculators there were Brahmins. The operation began by rubbing the arm with a piece of cloth for 8-10 minutes, and then inoculating with an iron instrument, four and half inches long, which had a twisted middle, a flattened end and an extremity with two sharp corners. All through the inoculators recited chants of *Sitala.* The regimen prescribed thereafter included cold baths till the fever came on and a diet of cooling foods. Holwell came to be convinced of the efficacy of this method and used it in his medical practice.[7] To the British, this method was only a little less dangerous than smallpox, particularly after Jenner's vaccine became available.

The Bombay Presidency developed an elaborate programme of vaccination under the direction of Mountstuart Elphinstone. The province was divided into circles, each under a group of Indian vaccinators, who visited the villages and provided free vaccination under the supervision of European officials. Elphinstone saw these vaccinators as probable propagators of Western medical technique.[8] But, to Indians, vaccination was unknown. The Superintendent of the Deccan, Joseph Glenn, observed that Hindus and village *patels* were particularly opposed to the innovation. He recorded that he stopped vaccinating personally for some time to gauge whether the opposition was directed against him as an Englishman, but found that hostility had not decreased. In order to disseminate its practice and discourage inoculation, Indian inoculators were encouraged to learn vaccination on a stipend of Rs. 8-9 per month.[9] But progress was slow and a proposal was actually made in 1835 to make vaccination compulsory, which was subsequently rejected.[10] Inoculation was considered more compatible to religious sentiments and remained a rival.[11] The government considered the possibility of prohibiting it, but most revenue and judicial officials opposed this move.[12] The Medical Board proposed that parents of children who may seek prospective employment with Government should be vaccinated, but this was not approved by the Court of Directors.[13]

To propagate the benefits of vaccination, a paper was prepared in Marathi, Gujarati, Kannada and Hindustani which explained Jenner's discovery that those who contracted a certain disease from their cows, causing an eruption, never suffered from smallpox and this had helped in checking the disease in England. The difference between inoculation and cowpox vaccination was emphasized, particularly pointing out that the latter never produced disfigurement, blindness or death.[14]

In Bombay City, a Superintendent was incharge of vaccination till 1845 when the Grant Medical College was set up. John Peet, Assistant Surgeon at the Jamsetjee Jejeebhoy Hospital and a Professor at the College, supervised vaccination with a staff of ten assistants. Charles Morehead, the Principal of the College, recorded his observations on smallpox in the city on the basis of his experiences in the European General and J.J. Hospitals between 1838 and 1853. He pointed out that the incidence of the disease prevailed more in March and April. He also noted that between 1848 and 1853 of 4038 deaths of this disease, 3203 were children under 7 years. Only 12 of 1177 deaths among Europeans in the same period were due to smallpox, the small number being attributed to their acceptance of vaccination.[15] In 1822-23, 3464 persons were vaccinated; the number rose to 7218 in 1854-5.[16] Soldiers were compulsorily vaccinated. However, the percentage of the vaccinated was small: it included the labour sent to Mauritius.[17] The unexpectedly poor response of the Parsis and the religious prejudice of the Hindus were both considered responsible for the slow acceptance of vaccination, while the Court of Directors characteristically attributed the inadequate progress to 'the indolence and apathy of the native character'.[18] The Medical Board wanted children to be vaccinated three months after their birth, but to Indians this was too tender an age for it.[19] Children, who did get vaccinated, had to be checked eight days later, during which period parents had to take care that vesicles were not broken. That the child was being touched without caste ceremonies being performed was regarded objectionable. In fact, children were either hidden on the eighth day or false addresses were given. Since children of lower castes or untouchables were used as vaccinators by Europeans and richer Indians, some high castes objected on grounds of caste pollution. Doubts regarding the efficacy of vaccination increased when some vaccinated cases succumbed to smallpox. This could have been because lymph, which was brought from the National Vaccine Institute in England in sealed packets, deteriorated during the humid monsoon months. Vaccination was also attempted in homes from dry lymph but it invariably proved to be a failure. Vaccinators were often ignorant and were unable to distinguish the reactions.[20] While vaccination returns were filed regularly, both Peet and Morehead regarded them unreliable. They ascribed the 'untrustworthy' nature of vaccinators to low salaries and the lack of pensions.[21]

In the 1850s, vaccination facilities were improved throughout the Presidency incurring Rs. 59,040 p.a. This increased the number of agents from 50 to 132, for which mostly graduates of the Grant Medical College were employed. Since Indians were employed up to the level of Sub-Assistant Surgeons, the Superintendents of Vaccination were now given this designation, thus effecting a saving of Rs. 14,440 p.a. for the colonial government.[22] Vaccination 'stations' were organised in the city at the J.J. Hospital; the Nagdevi Charitable Dispensary maintained by Dr. Bhau Daji and his brother Dr. Narayan Daji; the Fort Gratuitous Dispensary; the Bombay Native Dispensary; and Ardesir Jamsetji's Dispensary. The Grant Medical College's students manned all these stations. Dr. Atmaram Pandurang, who was incharge of a clinic in the Konkan (Bhiwandi), presented a paper on the obstacles in propagating vaccination at the Grant College Medical Society. He observed that even the 'intelligent' persons were unaware of the difference between vaccination and inoculation. Besides religious objections, there was the belief that vaccination provided slight immunity. He noted the 'secondary' causes of neglect among middle class Hindus (Prabhus, Shenvis and Sonars), that is, carrying the child, saved from an attack, to the Sitaladevi temple at considerable expense. The same practice was observed after vaccination which would even be deferred, till the means to observe the ceremonies were procured. *The Times of India* of 6 June 1861 describes a Parsi lady, whose child was attacked by smallpox, walking from the Fort to Bhuleswar temple on a Sunday afternoon carrying a pot of *chunam* (lime) which she allowed to drop on the ground as she walked to the temple. She performed several ceremonies, paid fees to the guardians of the temple and then returned home in the same manner.[23] That *chunam* has cooling properties is well known, and could have had a symbolic importance.

On the basis of Peet's suggestions to combat the various problems in propagating vaccination, new rules were drawn up in 1858. Some of these were: (a) operations were to be performed only by full-time vaccinators, supervised by an Honorary Inspector; (b) a full-time Indian Superintendent, familiar with native languages, was appointed; (c) the Island of Bombay was divided into divisions, each under an Assistant Vaccinator, who had to reside within its limits and check vaccinated children for failure or irregularity in the progress of the vesicle; (d) domiciliary vaccination among the poor was prohibited; and (e) the practice of sending Government Vaccinators to the houses of Europeans and rich Indians was abolished. Their children could use the weekly facility at Byculla.[24]

Dr. Ananta Chandroba, who belonged to the first batch of graduates from the Grant Medical College, was appointed as Superintendent of Vaccination in 1858 on a salary of Rs. 180 per month (Rs. 150 + Rs. 30 for conveyance allowance). Chandroba had earlier served in Central India and subsequently with the Karachi Municipality.[25] His establishment comprised a Head Vaccinator, A.M. de Monte, who was paid Rs. 39 p.m. (Rs. 24 + Rs. 15 for conveyance allowance); Caetano da Silva, First Assistant, at Rs. 18 p.m., Atmaram Abba, Hormusjee Cowasjee, Shaikh Ibrahim and Kirpa Sunder Purba Sanker, all for Rs. 12 p.m.[26] Recounting his experiences in the Annual Vaccination Reports,

Chandroba mentions his own initial diffidence in view of the lack of success over half century by the best of medical men. He supervised six stations at the Nagdevi Charitable Dispensary, the Fort Gratuitous Dispensary, the J.J. Hospital, and at Mazgaon, on the verandah of the house of his classmate, Dr. J.C. Lisboa, for want of any other accommodation. A clinic was also opened at Mahim catering to the residents of Worli, Naigaum and Sion. Due to Chandroba's sustained efforts, 7,999 persons were vaccinated in 1859. Sonars and Arabs brought their children to these clinics, while the Parsi response improved marginally.[27] The reluctance of the Parsis is frequently noted and was attributed by Chandroba to the ignorance and superstition of the women, who, he said, 'out Hindued' the Hindus in their superstitious regard for smallpox. But the Bhatias, Lohanas and Banias, Ghattis and North Indian Muslims also refused to be vaccinated. The Kolis' answer to all entreaties by Chandroba and his team was that they would rather have their children die of smallpox. He ascribed this reluctance to a 'false sense of tenderness for their little ones', religious prejudices, 'the all powerful custom, caste and pecuniary considerations', since vaccination was followed by expensive customary ceremonies.[28] The upper class parents were not only unwilling to allow their children to be vaccinated but also their servants.[29] Some even went to the extent of destroying their children's vesicles if smallpox struck: they regarded it to be *Sitala's* wrath.[30]

Inoculation was not practised in the city only, but in the neighbouring districts of Konkan, Thane, Bulsar and other parts of the Presidency also. This meant that some of the migrants into Bombay would have been inoculated.[31] The frequent prevalence of smallpox led to repeated proposals for a legislative enactment. On the basis of statistics, it was found that waves of mortality rose every second or third year. The year 1866-69 saw over a thousand deaths every year.[32] The number of patients at vaccination stations increased to 150-250 per day and therefore, evening clinics had to be set up. In 1869-70, the number of the vaccinated rose to 9222. When some employees of the Telegraph Department suffered severely from smallpox, a directive for compulsory vaccination was issued.[33]

The local press commented on these efforts. The *Akhbar-e-Sowdagar* of 15 April, 1871, reporting that there were 50 deaths a week, suggested the distribution of handbills and the propagation of vaccination by the students of the vernacular classes of the Grant Medical College in the thickly populated areas of the city. The *Native Opinion* of 19 November, 1871, commended the good work of the Department.[34] The frequent epidemics of smallpox and cholera were ascribed to the neglect of public health. The Health Officer's claims of reduced death rates, which were credited to the efforts of the Conservancy Officers, were doubted by contemporary papers, such as the *Bombay Samachar* (20 August, 1870) and *Jam-e-Jamshed* (20 December, 1870). Sickness was attributed to open gutters and night soil carts, which moved on the roads.[35] The *Bombay Chabuk* observed that since Municipal taxes were realised from all sections of the Bombay inhabitants, it was the duty of the Corporation to attend to the conveniences of all alike and contrasted the filthy condition of Indian quarters with the clean thoroughfares and roads used by Europeans.[36]

The medical fraternity had to counter speculations about syphilis being communicated through vaccination. The Superintendent General, Pinkerton, assured his colleagues that he had not come across such a case. It also came to be known that infantile vaccination did not give lifelong immunity or that one attack could not protect from another attack.[37]

In 1869, Dr. Blanc, the Vaccination Superintendent of the western circle, learnt the method of animal vaccination in London and instructed Ananta Chandroba on how to inoculate the calf and collect lymph from the vesicles. This method of animal vaccination to obtain lymph was introduced either by punctures or incisions. The latter gave elongated vesicles and, being large, provided a larger supply of lymph but often with a mixture of serum; while punctures gave round vesicles and contained lymph which was less in quantity but better in quality. On the third day of the operation, papules appeared; on the fourth they become vesicular; on the fifth the lymph was fit for use and on the sixth the vesicles were perfect.[38] The Health Officer, Dr. Hewlett, recommended to Crawford, the Municipal Commissioner, that five calves would be required every month costing Rs. 1121/2 p.m., which amount could be recovered by the sale of the calves, after their use. In 1869, the first heifer was inoculated from English lymph, each successful heifer giving enough lymph to vaccinate 100 persons; and, in 1870, 115 heifers were used. Cowasjee Jehangir made a donation of Rs. 540 to meet the initial expenses.[39] The Municipality also gave some financial support, perhaps grudgingly, because the *Bombay Chabuk* (24 August, 1870) remarked that the former could be more generous when several *lakhs* were being spent in the name of public health and comfort. The *Rast Goftar* also commented that when the Municipal income was half a *karor*, the government must provide the necessary assistance.[40] Animal vaccination came to be accepted mainly due to the 'commendable efforts' of Chandroba, who found the adequate supply of lymph a boon.[41] Some of the hitherto reluctant Bhatias and Banias now came forward. It seems that cow lymph was preferred to human lymph as less polluting.[42] On the other hand, some Europeans objected because of protests in Europe that animal vaccination caused fatalities due to localised irritation.[43]

Two sub-assistant surgeons, Balkrishna Chandroba and Ruttonjee Hormusjee, tried animal vaccination at Pune and Ahmedabad, but found that the public would not initially accept this method. However, it was used at Pune later on a regular basis along with 'human' vaccination. The method was also practised at Surat as long as Muslims and *Dheds* supplied heifers; some Hindus refused to provide their calves.[44] In fact, some municipalities did not sanction funds and individual contractors were subjected to such pressure that they declined to supply animals; the objection being the harm caused to the calves. Animal vaccination was introduced in 1882 at Broach, Ankleswar, Nadiad and the lymph was supplied to British Burma and Goa.[45] This was the only method in use in Bombay, each calf having as many as 185 insertions.[46] The success rate was ninety per cent on an average.

At the time of epidemic in 1872, an unsuccessful attempt was made to introduce compulsory vaccination. The Bombay Association had petitioned for this despite fears being expressed that Brahmins might object to compulsion on religious grounds. However, there was great support for the move and a plea for its extension to other cities of the Presidency was made.[47] There were 1854 deaths in 1872, and in fifteen months, 892 children succumbed to the disease. The highest mortality was in crowded areas like Kamatipura. The population of the city was 644,405 according to the census of 1872, while successful primary vaccination was 1.8% of the population in 1872 and 2.02% in 1873. The inadequate response of the Kamatis, Muslims, Lohanas, Kutchi Hindus and Parsis was particularly noted. Of 156 deaths in Kamatipura, 80 were Muslims, 20 lower caste Hindus and 48 of 165 deaths in Dhobhi Talao and 68 of 103 deaths on the Fort were of Parsis.[48] It was observed that the disease was endemic to Bombay as it was constantly imported from the African coast or Persian Gulf. Christians from Goa fled to Bombay to escape the epidemic there.

Smallpox recurred in 1876 which took away 3174 lives, though some cases of measles and chickenpox were confused with smallpox. Vaccinations were carried out on ships docked in harbours, in public offices, workshops, hotels, schools and colleges. Ananta Chandroba particularly commended the work of the Head Vaccinator, Sadashiv Balshet, and his team who worked round the clock: the number of the vaccinated and re-vaccinated ones that year being 35,658. Yet Chandroba encountered opposition even among his acquaintances. He relates the case of a family, whose womenfolk resisted vaccination of the other non-vaccinated children as long as there was a case of smallpox in the house. At such times, doubts and criticisms seem to have been voiced over animal vaccination as well, but Chandroba reiterated his faith that the method was sufficiently prophylactic.[49] Death figures from smallpox between 1850 and 1878 suggest recurring cycles of intensity which were, nevertheless, irregular. There were fourteen epidemics during this period. Their occurrence was linked with pilgrims passing through the city from regions where vaccination was not practised. The government subsequently erected pilgrim camps and tried to restrict their mobility in the city.[50] To bring about coordination in public health tasks, the government amalgamated the Sanitary Department with the Vaccination Department. The Superintendents of Vaccination were given extra duties as Health Officers and designated Deputy Sanitary Commissioners.[51]

The proposals for legislative enactment were finally put into effect through the

Vaccination Act of 1877. Some of the main provisions were: (a) the City was divided into six districts, each under a Public Vaccinator and two Public Stations were to serve two or more wards providing free vaccination once a week. Only animal lymph was permitted; (b) children born in the city had to be vaccinated within six months of birth; while unprotected children under 14 years, brought to the city temporarily or permanently, were to be vaccinated within three months of their arrival; (c) children were to be inspected after vaccination, and, if the operation had been unsuccessful, the child had to be re-vaccinated; (d) a magistrate could order vaccination of unprotected children under 14 years of age; and the penalty for refusing to do so was Rs. 50. And for intentionally not producing the summoned child the penalty was Rs. 1,000 or 6 months simple imprisonment; (e) penalties for signing false certificates or accepting illegal fees were also laid down; and (f) a fine of Rs. 200 was to be levied to discourage inoculation.[52]

The government also passed a resolution that no one would be admitted into public service, unless he had been vaccinated.[53] Vaccination was extended to the Jail and the House of Correction and the Mental Asylum. Private vaccinators were also licensed to encourage its practice. With amendments in 1882, vaccination had become free, but a fee of Rs. 2 was to be charged for the use of a heifer at a private house. Medical practitioners were supplied with lymph in capillary tubes or on ivory points.[54]

In 1883, the epidemic reappeared. The *Yazdan Parast* noted that it raged among the poor and in the overcrowded areas and contrasted their neglect with the areas inhabited by the rich which were kept clean by the Municipal Corporation.[55] Out of 1566 deaths reported, it was found that 840 persons had not been previously vaccinated. It reveals that people were evading the Vaccination Act or providing false information. Resistance to vaccination persisted and sometimes the staff was assaulted. When three of his *karkuns* were physically attacked, Chandroba appealed to the government for protection. The guilty were tried and convicted. The Vaccination Act was consequently amended to include *karkuns* or peons in addition to public vaccinators who had the authority to search unprotected children. Some deaths were reported among the vaccinated but, on enquiry, Chandroba found that there were only six cases. He called for information from other parts of India, regarding smallpox among the vaccinated. Most Sanitary Commissioners agreed with Chandroba that these failures were due to the incompetence of the vaccinator or the quality of the lymph.[56] Besides, inoculation was not an offence against law elsewhere in Bombay Presidency.

Chandroba's successor in the Vaccination Department, Dr. Sakharam Arjun, carried on his work. Others like Dr. Shantaram Kantak conducted regular classes for animal and human vaccination for subordinate staff of the Sanitary Department from 1890. The graduates of the Grant Medical College, including two women, were also trained.[57] In vaccination, the lancet was replaced by the vaccinating needle in the 1870s, and the method of the single puncture by multiple punctures in the 1890s.[58] Animal vaccination had problems like foot and mouth disease among calves, want of good stabling and severe reactions in young children during the development of vesicles, but not in the case of human lymph.[59]

A special smallpox hospital functioned between March and August 1889 under the charge of Dr. Choksey. An Infectious Diseases Hospital was set up at Grant Road under government control in 1892. The hospital at Arthur Road (which is still functioning), also established in 1892, provided additional facilities. Two hundred and nineteen patients of smallpox were treated here, of whom 184 were cured. The treatment comprised Cerolin applied externally (1 part of Cerolin to 14 parts of sweet oil) and found to be more effective than Carbolic acid.[60]

By the end of the century, the number of deaths from smallpox and the frequency of epidemics had declined and, when they did occur, they were more manageable than in the period preceding compulsory vaccination. The highest mortality was among children under four years. Death rate was high among 'Negro Africans' whose population was small and uncertain, and among Goan Christians who migrated to Bombay unvaccinated. Eurasians, Brahmins, and Hindu 'low castes', in that order, had high mortality. Female mortality was higher than male.[61] A major handicap was the defective registration of births. The police registered births from 1850-1867, after which the Health Department of the Municipality did so.[62] The Vaccination Department was amalgamated with the Health Department for coordination. Local newspapers urged compulsory registration of births (*Jam-e-Jamshed,* 4 December, 1885). It was suggested that other means should also be adopted to persuade people, like the circulation of handbills, public notifications and the beating of the drum (*Yazdan Parast,* 6 December, 1885).[63] Many births were not registered as women left the city for delivery, while some children were brought by their parents who came for work. A survey conducted by Kantak among migrant mill-workers showed a number of them susceptible to diseases. Besides, most female workers refused to be inspected. The numbers of those who were re-vaccinated were smaller than those who received primary vaccination. Vaccinated males outnumbered the females. This was attributed to parental reluctance in bringing grown up girls out in the public. During the last few years of the century, plague outbreak interfered with vaccination though a peak of 65% had been reached in 1890.[64]

The success of vaccination is apparent from the fact that in the years 1905-1909 the average annual number of deaths from smallpox shows 1.8% of total mortality, while it had been about one-fifth in the middle of the nineteenth century.[65] Arnold has shown that fear of the consequences of medical intervention had been an important check on the government which had to rely on Indian intermediaries, and the art of persuasion. The role of Indian doctors and their assistants is greatly laudable who had to work in the face of apathy and opposition which occasionally took the form of physical assaults. They worked hard in spite of their low salaries. The powerful belief in Sitala Devi was an irritating hindrance. The local Indian press, however, not only supported vaccination but brought to light the negligence of public health issues by the government. The achievement is all the more creditable because of the popular view that arm to arm vaccination caused caste pollution, and the fear that animal vaccination might lead to the sprouting of horns.

NOTES

1. Julius Jolly, *Indian Medicine*, tr. by G.G. Kashikar, Pune, 1951, p. 137.
2. See Ralph W. Nicholas, 'The Goddess Sitala and Epidemic Smallpox in Bengal', *Journal of Asian Studies*, XLI, No. 1, 1981, p. 26; *Bhavaprakasha* of Sri Bhavamisra, ed. Pant Sri Brahma Sankara, pt. II, Benaras, 1949, p. 546 (Bhavamisra was a physician, for which see *Bhartiya Sanskrit Kosh,* ed. Mahadev Shastri Joshi, Pune, 1976, Vol. IX, p. 397); *Vaccination Reports,* Bombay Presidency, Bombay (hereafter *V.R.*), 1874-5, p. 30.
3. Cf. J.Z. Holwell, *An Account of the Manner of Inoculating for the Smallpox in the East Indies,* 1767, p. 151.
4. See David Arnold, 'Small Pox and Colonial Medicine in Nineteenth Century India' in Arnold (ed.), *Imperial Medicine and Indigenous Societies,* Delhi, 1989, p. 49.
5. *Gazetteer of Bombay City and Island,* ed. S.M. Edwards, Bombay, 1909, Vol. III, p. 199 (henceforth *City Gazetteer*).
6. See *V.R.*, 1874-5, p. 30; *General Department Volumes,* Government of Maharashtra Archives (hereafter *G.D.*), Vol. 26, 1824, pp. 171-180.
7. Holwell, op. cit., pp. 150-3.
8. G.W. Forrest, *Writings of Mountstuart Elphinstone,* London, 1894, p. 92.
9. *G.D.*, Vol. 26, 1824, pp. 223-37.
10. *G.D.*, Vol. 40, 1838, p. 170.
11. *Selections from Records of Bombay Government: Vaccination,* Bombay Presidency, Bombay, 1854.
12. *G.D.*, Vol. 106, 1854, pp. 61-2.
13. *G.D.*, Vol. 88, 1857, p. 217.
14. *G.D.*, Vol. 101, 1856, p. 157.
15. Charles Morehead, *Clinical Research on Disease in India,* London, 1860, pp. 182-190. Morehead quotes Leith's registers to show that mortality from smallpox was 60 out of 1000 persons.
16. *G.D.*, Vol. 101, 1856; *V.R.*, 1854, p. 5. The number 7218 included 4403 males and 2815 females of which 4922 were Hindus, 1289 Muslims, 830 Christians and 177 Parsis. The percentage of successful vaccination was 85.7% (*V.R.*, ibid.). Dr. Hewlett, Health Officer, compiled statistics to show that there were more deaths in the second and third quarters of the years 1850-1869 (*V.R.*, 1870-1, p. XXVII).
17. Morehead, op. cit., p. 190; *G.D.*, Vol. 88, 1857, p. iii. Between 1853 and 1857, 1169410 persons were vaccinated—647121 males and 522289 females (*G.D.*, Vol. 82, 1858; *V.R.*, 1856-7, p. 85).
18. *G.D.*, Vol. 88, 1857, p. 478.
19. *G.D.*, Vol. 101, 1858, p. 157; *V.R.*, 1862, p. 2.

20. *G.D.*, Vol. 88, 1857, pp. 111-73.

21. *G.D.*, Vol. 82, 1858, p. 3. Morehead, p. 189. Peet's Assistant was paid Rs.24 p.m. after twenty years of service. The Head Vaccinator was like a *karkun* who performed office work as well (*G.D.*, Vol. 88, 1857, pp. 111-73; *G.D.*, Vol. 82, 1858, p. 8).

22. *G.D.*, Vol. 106, 1854, pp. 61-5.

23. *G.D.*, Vol. 88, 1857, pp. 111-73; *City Gazetteer*, Vol. III, p. 200.

24. *G.D.*, Vol. 82, 1858, pp. 71-4.

25. Ibid., p. 63; Mridula Ramanna, 'Professional Education—A Study of Grant Medical College, 1845-1858', *India, Past and Present*, Vol. V, 1988, Nos. 18-20, pp. 165-6.

26. *G.D.*, Vol. 82, 1858, p. 103.

27. *V.R.*, 1859, pp. 2-5.

28. *V.R.*, 1872-3, p. 54.

29. *V.R.*, 1868, p. 47.

30. *V.R.*, 1865, p. XII; *V.R.*, 1870-1, p. 52.

31. Morehead, p. 189.

32. *City Gazetteer*, Vol. III, p. 202.

33. *V.R.*, 1869-70, pp. XII, 56-7.

34. *Report on Native Newspapers*, Bombay Presidency, Bombay, 1871.

35. Ibid. (*Jam-e-Jamshed*, 6 June, 1870 and 18 February, 1873).

36. Ibid. (*Bombay Chabuk*, 18 June, 1870 and 12 October, 1870).

37. *V.R.*, 1869-70, p. XXXII.

38. *V.R.*, 1869-70, p. XVIII; *Reports of the Sanitary Commissioner for Government of Bombay* (hereafter *R.S.C.*), 18th Report, p. 33.

39. *V.R.*, 1869-70, pp. 56-62.

40. *Report of Native Newspapers*, Bombay Presidency, Bombay, 1870.

41. *V.R.*, 1869-70, p. XIX.

42. *V.R.*, 1872-3, p. XVI; *V.R.*, 1873-4, p. XXVII.

43. *V.R.*, 1870-1, p. 60.

44. *V.R.*, 1875-6, p. 16; *R.S.C.*, 15th Report, p. 52.

45. *R.S.C.*, 19th Report, p. 20.

46. *V.R.*, 1889-90, p. 36; *V.R.*, 1895-6, p. 16.

47. *Jam-e-Jamshed* (5 August, 1872); *Dayan Prakash* (12 August, 1872); *Rast Goftar* (11 August, 1872).

48. *V.R.*, 1872-3, pp. 47-55.

49. *V.R.*, 1875-6, pp. 5-7, 21.

50. *R.S.C.*, 15th Report, p. 30; *City Gazetteer*, Vol. III, pp. 172, 202.

51. *R.S.C.*, 13th Report, p. 3.

52. *Vaccination Act*, 1877, Bombay, pp. 1-12.

53. *G.D.*, Vol. 160, 1885, p. 169.

54. *G.D.*, Vol. 127, 1882, p. 345; *G.D.*, Vol. 128, 1882, p. 187.

55. *Report on Native Newspapers*, Bombay Presidency, Bombay, 1883.

56. *G.D.*, Vol. 154, 1883, pp. 5-10, 49, 52, 81.

57. *V.R.*, 1889-90, p. 16; *V.R.*, 1890-1, p. 6.

58. *City Gazetteer*, Vol. III, pp. 200-1.

59. *V.R.*, 1892-3, p. 15; *V.R.*, 1889-90, p. 20.

60. *Administrative Report of Municipal Commissioner*, Bombay, 1889-90, p. 327; also see ibid., 1892-3, pp. 597-8.

61. Ibid., 1893-4, p. 497.

62. *City Gazetteer*, Vol. III, p. 177.

63. *Report on Native Newspapers*, Bombay Presidency, Bombay, 1885.

64. *V.R.*, 1889-90, p. 20; *V.R.*, 1898-9, pp. 4, 10.

65. *City Gazetteer*, Vol. III, p. 170; Morehead, p. 190.

6

Muhammad Zaman: A 17th-Century Controversial Artist

AHSAN JAN QAISAR

If there was any artist in the medieval Indo-Persian context who has puzzled modern historians of Art for long, certainly he was none other than Muhammad Zaman, the son of Hajji Yusuf. Did he belong to the Persian or Mughal School of Art? Or both the Schools could claim him at one and the same time? Right from the first decade of the twentieth century Zaman holds the enviable position of being made the focus of debate within the framework of the above two queries. Is there really some mystery about this painter which has blurred his "provenance"?

The root of the controversy or misunderstanding about Zaman could be traced to one well-known European traveller who was in India during the second half of the seventeenth century. He is Niccolao Manucci from Italy whose rambles and recollections were translated into English by William Irvine in four volumes, and published in 1907-8. It is necessary to quote Manucci at length for a fair judgement:

> It was a custom introduced by Akbar, and maintained by his successors, to receive and to favour those who justly or unjustly were persecuted by the king of Persia, when they took flight and sought the protection of the Mughal kings...pay was given to them as *mansabdars*...they were sent to the province of Kashmir...when one of these dropped out, the others appropriated the dead man's allowances.
>
> Aurangzeb desired to remedy this abuse, and therefore ordered all the *mansabdars* of Kashmir to attend at court. There was a great number of them. Among them I had the opportunity of making the acquaintance of Muhamedzama, a man of great intelligence, whom Shah 'Abbas, King of Persia, sent to Rome as a student early in his reign. He had to learn how to answer our missionaries, who in Persia confounded the mullas and doctors of the Mahomedan faith. This Muhammad Zaman, well acquainted with his own faith, by study came to know the truth; and instead of becoming more stubborn in the faith of Muhammad and of 'Ali, he

> renounced it and turned Christian, and taking the name of Paul, called himself Paulo Zaman. He then went back to Persia. There the learned men of Persia became aware by their talk with him that he was more favourable to the Christians than the Mahomedans (although he concealed his being a Christian). They began to speak against him, and fearing some harm, he fled from Persia and claimed protection from Shah Jahan. He was given the pay of a *mansabdar* and sent to Kashmir to join the other Persians. On the occasion when they were sent for by Aurangzeb, he came to Dihli and made friends with the Christians, chiefly with Father Buzeo Busee. They discussed theological books, he having several Latin books; yet, although he was, and declared himself to be a Christian, his way of life differed in no respect from that followed by Mahomedans.[1]

The above text must be read along with the footnote by the translator on page 17, Vol. II:

> It is not clear which Shah 'Abbas is intended; the first reigned from 1587 to 1629, the second from 1642 to 1667. I have been unable to find any confirmation of the presence of these students at Rome, either from Oriental or European sources. The date of the party sent in the time of the Sherleys, about 1606, seems too early. One of them became a Christian, and published a book under the name of Don John of Persia. Mr. A.G. Ellis suggests that Manucci's Muhammad Zaman is possibly identical with the painter of that name, by whom there are three beautiful signed and dated pictures in a copy of Nizami's *Khamsa,* BM Or. MS No. 2265, fols. 203b, 213a, and 221b. The influence of European art is almost unmistakable; the date however — 1086 A.H./1675-76 — is somewhat late to suit Manucci's story (*circa* 1660). But he may have returned to Persia after the death (1667) of Shah 'Abbas II.

> Sir Caspar P. Clarke, C.I.E., whose article in the *Journal of Indian Art,* Vol. vii, Oct. 1896, No. 56, bears on the subject of Raphael's influence on Persian art, tells me that when he was in Persia in 1874, the book illuminators had a tradition that twelve young Persians were sent in the time of Shah 'Abbas to study in Rome. Of the twelve, eight or nine only returned; some died, and some, on becoming Christians, remained in Europe. At Rome he was told that they lived in the Borgo.

Thus, A.G. Ellis[2] was the first person to float the view in 1907 that Manucci's Paolo Zaman may be identified with Muhammad Zaman, the Persian painter. Ellis did not substantiate his opinion: it was merely a suggestion. But this unwarranted suggestion gained favour with many scholars one after another till 1962. It is no accident, then, to find even a cautious scholar like Vincent A. Smith[3] to repeat the same story in 1911. He admits that the 'strange story of the Persian mission to Rome' is pieced together from Manucci (tr. Irvine) and Clarke's article[4] (see *supra*). Quite obviously, Smith accepted the suggestion of Ellis for Zaman's identity.

F.R. Martin in his monumental work in 1912 summarizes the same story, yielding submissively to Ellis and Smith.[5] Later, in 1924, Percy Brown readily swallowed Manucci's version of Paolo Zaman's story. Since Brown's work is very popular and widely read by students and scholars alike, especially in the Indian sub-continent, we reproduce a part of his comments below:

> Towards the middle of the seventeenth century Shah Abbas II of Persia (1642-67), whose leanings towards Western culture were most marked, had dispatched from his capital a group of young Persians to study various subjects in some of the centres of learning in Europe. Among these was a painter, who proceeded to work for a considerable period as a student in Rome. While there he became converted to Christianity, so that on his return he was compelled to leave Persia, and eventually to seek the protection of the Mughal. The painter was most probably Muhammad Zaman.[6]

Undoubtedly, Brown was writing under the spell of Manucci and his own contemporary scholars whose works were available to him. Again, in 1925, Nicholas N. Martinovitch (Columbia University) wrote a short article.[7] Though he based his verdict primarily on Manucci and Martin, he went further and embellished the story by proposing that in the beginning Zaman obtained the protection of Shah Jahan and later that of his son Dara Shukoh who was a freethinker with 'a leaning to Christianity', and when Aurangzeb succeeded Shah Jahan after vanquishing Zaman's second patron Dara, the artist was 'obliged to escape from India' to his homeland because Aurangzeb was a 'stern puritan' and a 'bigoted Musulman' under whom 'the existence of Christians' had become unendurable. This tailpiece to Zaman's story had to be *invented* by Martinovitch to suit his purpose which we will come to presently. We would only remind the reader that Manucci does not say anything about Zaman's return to Persia. Moreover, to resolve one difficulty in his thesis, he had to invent yet another piece, that is, Zaman's reconversion to Islam after his departure from India to reestablish his 'Moslem reputation' for which he 'made Moslem pilgrimage' and 'received the title of haji'.

Pursuing this 'lineage' of commentators on our artist, let us now turn to T.W. Arnold, who, in his celebrated tome in 1928, builds up the core of Zaman's biography out of Manucci and his own predecessors.[8] He, however, adds one information that Zaman translated two chapters of Matteo Ricci's book *De Christiana Expedicione apud Sinas* into Persian under the title *Tarikh-i Chin* (History of China). Arnold's source is Wladimir Ivanov.[9]

No student of Mughal history can feign ignorance of E. Maclagan whose *The Jesuits and the Great Mogul* published in 1932 is now a classic.[10] But, like others, he too fell a prey to the suggestion of Ellis. Maclagan says: '...this man appears almost certainly to have been identical with a Persian of that name who was sent as a student by Shah Abbas to Rome and was there converted and changed his name to Paolo Zaman.'[11] He is the only scholar till his time who gives the date of Paolo Zaman's arrival in India in 1646. This date is based on an account of the four Jesuits residing at Agra during this period.[12] Our author is not certain whether Paolo retained his new faith when back home, but he thinks that 'there is reason to believe that he relapsed into Muhammadanism and performed the pilgrimage to Mecca.'[13]

Thus we find that since the publication of Irvine's translation of Manucci's work to 1932, all scholars accepted Ellis's suggestion that Muhammad Zaman was identical with Paolo Zaman.[14] Such an uncritical submission to an unsubstantiated suggestion for such a long time by grand scholars is simply amazing. To say the least, it is faulty historiography: it is a case of one blind man leading the other.

The greatest blunder that has been committed is that none paused for a moment to ponder over the simple fact that Manucci does not even hint at Paolo as a painter. Manucci, like Bernier, was very much familiar with Mughal paintings which is testified to by their comments in this regard:[15] the fact is that his Paolo was never a painter. Hence, the entire exercise of identifying Muhammad Zaman with Paolo Zaman is futile: it is like chasing a wild goose that does not exist.

But who was, then, Paolo Zaman? Manucci tells us that he was a *mansabdar* during the reign of Shah Jahan. A letter of the Jesuits at the "Agra College" (1648-9) reveals that he had come to the court of 'Mogor' in 1646 from Persia and was counted among the officials of 'minor grade'.[16] When still a child in Persia, he was baptized by the Carmelite Fathers. Once he was summoned to the Mughal court to explain a certain theological concept when other priests failed to satisfy the emperor (Shah Jahan). He was trained in 'liberal art and sciences...[possessed] acute mind and excellent disposition...made progress in Rhetoric, Philosophy, Mathematics and Theology... [and] acquired a wonderful knowledge of several European languages.' The letter adds that Paolo professed Christianity 'though not openly'. In 1649, he received 'fresh honour' from Shah Jahan. The Jesuits entertained great hopes that one day, like Mirza Zulqarnain, 'Paul Zaman too (as he is called)' will be another 'most firm pillar of this mission'.

We are not told about Paolo's rank in the *mansab* system. But the question is whether there was really a *mansabdar* bearing his name under Shah Jahan? No one ever endeavoured to explore this aspect because Manucci's statement was taken as gospel truth (although Arnold calls him 'gossipy traveller'). In this connexion, the best guide to date is Athar Ali's *The Apparatus of the Empire* which carries the names of almost all the *Mansabdars* from Akbar to Shah Jahan, giving their ranks, promotions, ethnic affiliations, etc.[17] Turning to the reign of Shah Jahan, we find six persons bearing the name Muhammad Zaman. Two were Turani (nos. S. 1714 and S. 1831) and another Afghan (no. S. 1865); therefore, they are not relevant to us. The third one's ethnic identity remains unknown, but it does not matter as he died in 1648.[18] The rest two were Irani — Muhammad Zaman Tehrani (no. S. 161) and Muhammad Zaman Turbati (no. S. 6348). The former seems to have received his *mansab* for the first time in 1628[19] and the latter in 1655.[20] But Tehrani died in 1651[21] and Turbati in 1656.[22] These facts do not lend support to Manucci's story. On the other hand, the Jesuits of the 'Agra College' report they met Paul Zaman in 1648 at the Mughal court as an official of 'minor grade'. We do not intend to reject Manucci's story *in toto.* Perhaps Paolo was not a *mansabdar*: he might have received stipend (*wazifa* — cash grant) from the Emperor. Maclagan is perhaps right when he says that Paolo was 'given a stipend by Shah Jahan'.[23] Being a stipendiary, then, he will not find a place in Athar Ali's list of *mansabdars.* Also, it would fit in with the episode of summoning the Irani immigrants for verifying their documents since such verification was not called forth in case of *mansabdars.* At any rate, this act of Aurangzeb to rectify malpractice allegedly committed by the Irani immigrants in Kashmir is not recorded in Mughal sources. But, surprisingly, the modern scholars did not take notice of Manucci's account in this regard.

It was in 1962 that a blow was given to Ellis's suggestion by A.A. Ivanov who departed from the usual line and dismantled the view propagated for long that our Persian painter journeyed to Rome, embraced Christianity and then left for India, etc.[24] He argues that Manucci's story pertains to another Muhammad Zaman who was called Farangi Khan, more correctly *khwan,* that is, one who knows European languages.[25] That Paolo knew many European languages is corroborated by the Agra Jesuits. The Persian translation of Ricci's Latin work testifies to this fact. The evidence for the 'title' Farangi Khan is available in the manuscript of the Persian translation itself which is lodged in the library of the Asiatic Society of Bengal.[26] It is unfortunate that Maclagan tacks this evidence to a note instead of placing it in the text of his book. Further, he gives the same treatment to the Jesuits' statement that Paolo was baptized by the Carmelite Fathers in his childhood. Arnold, too, withholds these two dimensions of Paolo's story. This is a serious histographical error that leads to distortion.

Ivanov enumerates nineteen persons of Persia who bore the name Muhammad Zaman during the seventeenth and eighteenth century. None of them ever came to India during the seventeenth century except Farangi *khwan*/Khan. This is one set of Ivanov's methodology to unravel the mystery of our painter. His another approach is to examine the painter's compositions to settle whether, on artistic grounds, the artist could have been *trained* in Italy if he resided at Rome at all. We will take up this aspect in the next section.

Above we promised to find out the reason why Martinovitch had to *invent* the legend of Paolo Zaman's departure from India. Since there is no evidence for

Muhammad Zaman's artistic activity under Shah Jahan or Aurangzeb, he must be sent back to Persia because examples of his artistic output are available only from 1575-76 in Persia. And the readymade reason for his 'forced' departure was Aurangzeb's puritanism and bigotry. Further, he must be reconverted to Islam and also made to perform the *hajj* because he calls himself *hajji* in the inscriptions on some of his paintings. It is a strange case of *history by assumption* to suit the arbitrary thesis that Paolo Zaman and Muhammad Zaman the painter were identical.

II

Such somewhat detailed examination of the debate over our painter's identity is definitely warranted, else we might fall into an error like Percy Brown who made the following fantastic remarks:

> ...Muhammad Zaman, whose work may be examined in three pictures in the British Museum copy of *Khamsah,* Or.2265, folio 203b, 213a, and 221b. Manifestly Occidental in character, they leave no doubt as to the course of study that the young Persian adopted; and if, as he appears to have done, he became a protege of the Mughal Emperor, the growth of the European element in the painting of Shah Jahan's reign is readily explained. The result of Muhammad Zaman's presence in Delhi and the influence of his Occidental training on those around him may be observed in many of the pictures of the time of Shah Jahan, as for example in the borders of the portrait album produced under the supervision of Faqirullah Khan. On the upper part of the mount of most of these there is a design of flying angels on billowy clouds, with a background of rainbows and radiant suns which, while fantastic in some respects, is not unconnected with the art of Raphael or his school.[28]

This entire statement of Percy Brown is not only whimsical but absolutely misleading in view of the fact that Zaman the painter never came to India. The European motifs like 'flying angels' and 'billowy clouds' were extensively employed by Jahangir's artists. Thus, there was no question of Zaman's impact on Mughal painters in Occidental terms under Shah Jahan. Brown's enthusiastic kudos in this respect to Zaman are totally meaningless.

The view that Muhammad Zaman was trained as a student of art at Rome has been examined and rejected by Ivanov. His approach is that if the artist was ever sent to Rome by Shah Abbas II to learn European art, then his compositions must exhibit exclusive influence of the art traditions of the Italian masters.[29] Ivanov is not convinced that Zaman's work overwhelmingly bears Italian stamp. He holds that the artist's pictures 'Venus and Cupid' (Plate 16), 'Abraham's Sacrifice' (Plate 17), 'Holy Trinity/Family' (Plate 18) and 'Mary and Elizabeth' (Plate 19) actually display Flemish impact.[29a]

Zaman's 'The Flight into Egypt' (Plate 20) has been copied from an engraving of a similar composition by Rubens.[30] Moreover, almost all his paintings were completed after 1674-5 in Persia: actually, no painting of Zaman prior to this date has been noticed. This establishes Ivanov's thesis that our artist did not come to India at all. We may strengthen his opinion by pointing out that Manucci does not say that Zaman was sent to Rome to get training in European art: he visited Rome, according to Manucci, 'to learn how to answer our missionaries, who in Persia confounded the mullas and doctors of the Mahomedan faith.'[31]

Not all of Zaman's work has yet been published, but whatever has been reproduced in books and journals offers substantial evidence of the artist's versatile and innovative predilection. Parallel to the Mughal painters, Zaman, too, was not only an illustrator of manuscripts but he has also left examples of his pictures unconnected with manuscripts as *muraqqa* paintings, that is, for the patron's album. He illustrated a few folios of the two copies of Nizami's *Khamsa* lodged in the British Museum[32] and the Morgan Library (New York).[33] He also illustrated two folios of a copy of the *Shahnama* of unusual size obviously for a royal library.[34] Besides, there are a number of separate miniatures. These paintings carry Zaman's signature, sometimes with dates, and the place of work (Isfahan), etc. In one inscription he gives himself the title '*hajji*' signifying that he had performed the Islamic pilgrimage to Mecca (*hajj*).[35] One gathers from these inscriptions that he was the son of one Hajji Yusuf. The period of Zaman's vigorous artistic output was between 1675 and 1685. Perhaps he continued working till 1702. As shown above, none of his compositions was executed in India which was out of the question; nor do we find any example prior to 1674 in Persia. This latter fact led Irvine to observe that 'the date...is somewhat late to suit Manucci's story' (*c.* 1660). But, unfortunately, Irvine misfires when he says that 'Zaman may have returned to Persia after the death (1667) of Shah Abbas II.'[36]

That Zaman's paintings zealously reveal a deep impact of European art cannot be denied. He, along others like his compatriot 'Ali Quli Jubadar,[37] experimented with European art traditions. This response could be divided into two categories: a) imitation of or copying from European specimens that were available to them privately or at the court, and b) adopting/adapting European motifs like angels, cupids, cherubs, billowing clouds, God the Father, etc. Zaman's two compositions 'Mary and Elizabeth' and 'The Flight into Egypt' can be put in the first category (Plates 19 and 20). Billowing clouds in Pl. 20 have been obviously borrowed from Europe. The folds in the drapery of the figures of both the above copies are characteristic of the non-Asian art. Besides, one can notice the employment of distant perspective, too. These two are, by and large, faithful copies. Martin notes that they are from Italian prints. But he abstains from linking them with definite European specimens as he does for the copies by 'Ali Quli Jubadar. It is a very delicate matter to decide the provenance of the compositions being imitated unless positive evidence is adduced. Basic artistic elements in European art were shared in common by the diverse Schools like the Italian, Flemish, German, etc. That is perhaps one of the reasons why Ivanov is not inclined to accept Zaman's paintings to have been executed *exclusively* under Italian influence. For that matter, then, many Mughal painters who copied or adopted European prints should have gone to Europe. Martin, Brown and others forget the fact that European engravings were available in Iran (and India) which the native artists were constantly exposed to.[38]

As for the second category, the artist was free to interpret European themes even when using European motifs and symbols. One such work by Zaman is his 'Holy Trinity/ Family' (Plate 18). Elsewhere we have analyzed this painting in a little detail.[39] According to the inscription, Zaman took fourteen months to complete it. One can understand why he had to spend such a long time over it. It was not a mere copy: our artist was endeavouring to interpret the theme independently. In fact, he tried to combine two themes into one, that is, 'Holy Family' and 'Holy Trinity'. In Europe, the former invariably displayed Mary, her husband Joseph and infant Jesus, while the picturization of 'Holy Trinity' was done in the background of Crucifixion, God the Father and the Dove signifying the Holy Spirit. But Zaman conveniently ignores Crucifixion, perhaps to suit the Muslim belief that Christ was not Crucified. We strongly believe that this painting is intensely innovative in the sense that such combination is without parallel in European art. Moreover, depiction of God the Father was attempted for the first time in Persian art. Indeed, it was a very bold job by a Muslim artist, and it was never repeated afterwards in Persia.

Muhammad Zaman was also interested in Greek mythology. His 'Venus and Cupid' is one such example (Plate 16). His model was a painting by Paris Bordone (Plate 21). But Zaman did not copy it faithfully. For some reason, he departed from the original by introducing a few changes. The posture of the sleeping Venus is much different. Bordone picturized Venus reclining on her right hand, but Zaman changed the position to the left, the head being given support by the left palm. Bordone fully bares the ample breasts of Venus, while the copy tries to hide them partially by putting her right hand over them. This change in posture is followed by reverse positioning of the tree also beneath which Venus lies on bed. In Zaman's experiment, the tree (in Persian idiom) moves to the right. Even the details of the bed are dissimilar. The most interesting alteration is in the figure of Cupid whom Zaman gives wings which is absent in Bordone's composition. Again, Cupid's conventional prank of playful naughtiness in disrobing Venus goes unrepresented in Zaman's copy. Bordone draws Cupid in the nude displaying his tiny pudendum, but our artist's prudery bestows on him a loin-cloth. In doing so, Zaman practically takes away the 'soul' of Cupid's personality! However, rolling clouds in the distant background retain European taste. Thus, our artist was not a blind imitator: he often tampered with the original specimens during the course of his interpretive exercise, most probably in conformity with the *values* of his milieu.

It is appropriate to emphasize here that Ivanov erred in thinking that this work by Zaman does not show Italian influence: he takes it to have been done under Flemish inspiration.[40] The fact is that Ivanov did not know that Zaman's model was Bordone's print. Since the latter was an Italian finally working at Venice (b. 1500; d. 1571), Ivanov's verdict suffers from infirmity. But this ignorance is shared by Ivanov in common with other modern scholars of Persian art to date.

Yet another example of Zaman's interpretive exercise is his excellent depiction of Prophet Abraham sacrificing his son (Plate 17). The story is narrated in the Old Testament thus (Genesis: 22:1-13):

> And it came to pass after these things, that God did tempt Abraham, and said unto him, Abraham: and he said, Behold, *here I am.*
>
> And he said, Take now thy son, thine only son Isaac, whom thy lovest, and get thee into the land of Mo-riah; and offer him there for a burnt offering upon one of the mountains which I will tell thee of.
>
> And Abraham rose up early in the morning, and saddled his ass, and took..., Isaac his son, and clave the wood for the burnt offering, and rose up, and went unto the place of which God had told him.
>
> Then on the third day Abraham lifted up his eyes, and saw the place afar off.
>
> And Abraham said...I and
> the lad will go yonder and worship...
>
> And Abraham took the wood of the burnt offering, and laid it upon Isaac his son; and he took the fire in his hand, and a knife; and they went both of them together.
>
> And Isaac spake unto Abraham his father, and said, My father...Behold the fire and the wood; but where is the lamb for a burnt offering?
>
> And Abraham said, My son, God will provide himself a lamb for a burnt offering...
>
> And they came to the place which God had told him of; and Abraham built an altar there, and laid the wood in order, and bound Isaac his son, and laid him on the altar upon the wood.
>
> And Abraham stretched forth his hand, and took the knife to slay his son.
>
> And the Angel of the Lord called unto him out of heaven, and said, Abraham,

Abraham: and he said, Here *am* I.

And he said, Lay not thine hand upon the lad, neither do thou any thing unto him: for now I know that thou fearest God, seeing thou hast not withheld thy son, thine only son, from me.

And Abraham lifted up his eyes, and looked, and beheld behind *him* a ram caught in a thicket by his horns: and Abraham went and took the ram, and offered him up for a burnt offering in the stead of his son.[41]

The most significant difference between the Biblical account and the belief of the Muslims is that the former mentions Abraham's son Isaac (Ar. Ishaq) as the object of sacrifice, while the Muslims believe him to be Ismail (Ishmael), another son of the Prophet. But this is not material for the moment.

The model before Muhammad Zaman was Rembrandt's work on this theme. But the latter had executed two versions of this theme: let us call these 'A' (Plate 22) and 'B' (Plate 23). Rembrandt has altered the actions of the characters concerned in the two versions. In 'B' the figure of the Patriarch's son on the altar has been reversed: it moves from the right to the left. What is surprising is that in 'A' Abraham is right-handed while in 'B' he becomes left-handed! Also notice that in 'A' his left hand covers his son's face, holding the knife in his right which is falling from his hand; this is reversed in 'B'. The face of the Patriarch in both the versions remains similar. Alteration occurs also in the figure of the angel, especially his depiction in 'A' restraining Abraham from carrying out the sacrifice by holding the latter's right hand, and in 'B' his left hand. Strangely, 'A' does not display the ram: the miraculous presence of the ram is a very important part of the story; in fact, the animal symbolizes anti-climax of the episode!

At any rate, this subject was not alien to Islamic art (Plate 24).[42] But we are quite definite that Zaman's composition must have been inspired by the European master. Once again, we discover our artist's innovative urges in operation in choosing the positioning of figures and actions differently from his model, albeit the European flavour is unquestioned. Zaman's Patriarch is right-handed but, instead of holding a knife, he wields a straight sword. Abraham's sleeves are expectedly rolled up for the act, and his left hand forces the son's head downwards. This structure is in absolute contrast to Rembrandt's handling. Actually, Zaman was partially following the Qur'an's version which runs thus (*Surah* XXXVII: 102-107):

And when [his son] was old enough to walk with him, [Abraham] said: O my dear son, I have seen in a dream that I must sacrifice thee. So look, what thinkest thou? He said: O my father! Do that which thou art commanded. Allah willing, thou shalt find me of the steadfast.

Then, when they had both surrendered [to Allah],
and he had flung him down upon his face [*jabeen*].
We called unto him: O Abraham!
Thou hast already fulfilled the vision. Lo!
thus do we reward the good.
Lo! that verily was a clear test.
Then We ransomed him with a tremendous victim.[43]

The Arabic word *jabeen* actually means forehead and, therefore, the translation should be 'he had laid him prostrate on his forehead'. It seems that Zaman desired to display the boy's composed face in surrendering to God's will: this restrained him from putting his forehead totally downwards. The Old Testament does not indicate the manner in which Isaac's face was placed. Perhaps Rembrandt had justifiably taken the cue from animal slaughter as offering to God by the Jews. The popular version among the Muslims is that Abraham did not want to see his son's traumatized face at the crucial moment else it generated filial feelings to stop his act. But that purpose is fulfilled in Rembrandt's paintings also when he makes Abraham cover the face of his son with his hand.

The different manner of tying the boy's hands should not go unnoticed. But this has nothing to do with either of the Holy Books. Again, Zaman fully dresses the boy, but his counterpart does it only partially. This is a matter of personal choice.

Another interesting difference between the two artists' compositions is the gesture of the angel's hands. In both 'A' and 'B', angel's one hand holds Abraham's hand, and the other very meaningfully points upwards signifying the call of God to stop the enjoined sacrifice. On the other hand, Zaman's angel grabs the Prophet's sword with the right hand while the forefinger of his left points towards the ram in the thicket in the foreground (left bottom corner). This last gesture is in keeping with the Islamic legend: to sacrifice the ram as a symbol of the intended offering of his son. But the placement of Zaman's ram does not agree with the Biblical narration which Rembrandt follows in 'B', that is, the ram should be at the back of Abraham. Moreover, Zaman finds a place for fragrant smoke in the foreground (right bottom corner) near the altar which was the practice to sanctify the offering, but this is not represented in Rembrandt's work. However, faggots on the altar are visible in the three compositions in consonance with the Biblical story. In spite of some basic dissimilarities, Zaman's picture is technically outside the orbit of the then Islamic art traditions. The European cloud motifs, the landscape, the folds of drapery, the thick bands of rays issuing forth from the heaven, etc. quite easily betray European impact. But it must be conceded that, contentwise, Zaman makes efforts to keep himself close to Islamic version of the legend.

To sum up, A.A. Ivanov's initial blow in 1962 to the long nourished view that Manucci's Paolo Zaman and Muhammad Zaman the painter were identical should be considered a watershed in this debate.[44] What we have done here is to present fresh arguments to reinforce Ivanov's opinion, and, also, to examine three compositions of Muhammad Zaman in detail. It is quite striking that while Zaman broadly accepted European art traditions, he did not hesitate to exercise his discretion in interpreting the subject/theme to adjust his work to the cultural values of his society to the extent his *own* perceptions permitted him to do so. Therein lay the beauty of his paintings.

NOTES

1. Niccolao Manucci, *Storia do Mogor, 1653-1708,* tr. William Irvine, Vol. II, London, 1907-8, pp. 16-8.
2. Ellis was the cataloguer of Arabic books at the British Museum.
3. See Vincent A. Smith, *A History of Fine Art in India and Ceylon, & C,* Oxford, 1911, p. 466; also *n.* 1.
4. Sir Caspar Purdon Clarke, 'A Tradition of Raphael in Persia', *Journal of Indian Art,* Vol. vii, No. 56, 1897.
5. F.R. Martin, *The Miniature Painting and Painters of Persia, India and Turkey, 8th-18th Centuries,* Vol. I, p. 124.
6. Cf. Percy Brown, *Indian Paintings under the Mughals,* Oxford, 1924, p. 174.
7. Nicholas N. Martinovitch, 'The Life of Mohammad Paolo Zaman, the Persian Painter of the XVIIth Century', *Journal of the American Oriental Society,* Vol. 45, 1925, pp. 106-9.
8. T.W. Arnold, *Painting in Islam: Study of the Place of Pictorial Art in Muslim Culture,* London, 1928, pp. 148-9.
9. See Wladimir Ivanov, *Concise Descriptive Catalogue of the Persian Manuscripts in the Curzon Collection (Asiatic Society of Bengal),* Calcutta, pp. 96-8.
10. E. Maclagan, *The Jesuits and the Great Mogul,* London, 1932, pp. 235-6.
11. Ibid., p. 235.
12. See Rev. H. Hosten, S.J., 'Annual Letter of the Agra College and of Mogor Mission, collected for part of the year 1648 and part of the year 1649', *Journal of Indian History,* Vol. 1, part 2, Feb. 1922, pp. 226-48.
13. Maclagan, op. cit., p. 236.
14. L. Binyon, J.V.S. Wilkinson and Basil Gray, *Persian Miniature Painting (Including a Critical and Descriptive Catalogue of the Miniatures Exhibition at Burlington House, Jan.-March, 1931),* London, 1933, pp. 161-2, wherein the same story is repeated.
15. F. Bernier, *Travels in the Mogul Empire, 1656-68,* tr. A. Constable, reprint, New Delhi, 1968, p. 255; Manucci, Vol. 1, p. liii.
16. See Hosten, op. cit., p. 226.
17. Athar Ali, *The Apparatus of the Empire: Awards of Ranks, Offices, and Titles to the Mughal Nobility, 1574-1658,* Delhi, 1985.
18. Ibid., p. 210.
19. Ibid., p. 100.
20. Ibid., p. 292.
21. Ibid., p. 260.

22. Ibid., p. 292.

23. Maclagan, p. 235.

24. A.A. Ivanov, T.B. Grek, O.P. Akimushkin, *Album of Indian and Persian Miniatures, XVI-XVIII Centuries* (Russian text), Akademi of Sciences, Institute of the Peoples of Asia, Moscow, 1962, pp. 44-55.

25. Ibid., p. 48.

26. Cf. Wladimir Ivanov, op. cit., p. 96.

27. A.A. Ivanov, op. cit., p. 47, *n.* 18. Some of these were poets, merchants and calligraphers.

28. Brown, op. cit., p. 177.

29. A.A. Ivanov, p. 53.

29a. Ibid.

30. Ibid. The engraver was Lucca Vorsterman.

31. Manucci, op. cit., p. 17. This statement has been noticed by Smith and Arnold, etc., but they comfortably ignored it charmed as they were by Ellis.

32. See Manucci, p. 17, *n.* 1 (MS no. Or.2265, fols. 203b, 213a and 221b). Also Brown, p. 177 and Arnold, op. cit., p. 149.

33. Cf. Martinovitch, op. cit., pp. 108-9. He was the first to examine this manuscript of the Morgan Library, New York (M 469). Out of 36 miniatures in this copy, 15 were painted and signed by Muhammad Zaman.

34. See L. Binyon, et al, op. cit., p. 162 (these were lent by Chester Beatty).

35. Martinovitch, p. 109.

36. Manucci, p. 17, *n.* 1.

37. F.R. Martin, op. cit., pl. 172; A.A. Ivanov, pls. 95a and b.

38. Bernard Lewis, *The Muslim Discovery of Europe,* New York, 1982, pp. 243-5 and 256; Ahsan Jan Qaisar, *The Indian Response to European Technology and Culture, A.D. 1498-1707,* pp. 93-102.

39. A. Jan Qaisar, 'The Profane and the Sacred: "Judgement of Paris" and "God the Father" in the Mughal School of Art' in *Art and Culture: Felicitation Volume in Honour of Professor S. Nurul Hasan,* edited by Ahsan Jan Qaisar and Som Prakash Verma, Jaipur, 1993, pp. 81-9.

40. A.A. Ivanov, p. 53.

41. I have used the King James Version.

42. See Arnold, op. cit., Pl. XXXI.

43. I have used Marmaduke Pickthall, *The Meaning of Glorious Qur'an, Text and Explanatory Translation,* Taj Company, Karachi, n.d., p. 673. I am beholden to my colleague Dr. Ishtiaq A. Zilli who kindly helped me in this context.

44. Despite Ivanov's laudable endeavour, Robert Skelton recently tried to keep up a brave face as a last-ditch battle by coming out with a 'Persian copy of an Indian painting of about 1630, signed by Muhammad Zaman, which was executed in Kashmir about 1660 — exactly the period in which Manucci met a Paolo Zaman in Kashmir.' Skelton produced it in a communication, perhaps yet unpublished, to the VIth International Congress on Persian Art and Archaeology in 1972 (see Eleanor G. Sims, 'Five Seventeenth-Century Persian Oil Paintings' in *Persian and Mughal Art,* Colnaghi, London, 1976, p. 224, *n.* 4 and p. 229, *n.* 28). Sims adds: 'The problem has evidently not been adequately resolved' (p. 229, *n.* 28). Since we have not seen the above painting, we can only say that Skelton must have erred in evaluating it. As shown above, no work of Zaman is available prior to 1675 in Persia and India. Again, in the text on p. 229, Sims is elusive and equivocal with regard to the question of the identity of Paolo Zaman and Muhammad Zaman the painter. In case we yield to Skelton's stubbornness, we will be back to square one, that is, Paolo and Muhammad Zaman were one and the same

person, a view that has been fairly blasted once for all. Indeed, the obsession with Ellis is hard to shed off! If it continues in future, it will sound the death-knell of scientific historiography (see also Som Prakash Verma, *Mughal Painters and Their Work — A Biographical Survey and Comprehensive Catalogue,* New Delhi, 1994, p. 302).

7

Popular Religion: Local Tradition in the Hills of Himachal Pradesh

MAHESH SHARMA

This article presents a documentation of popular religion in the hills of Himachal Pradesh which, to a large extent, corresponds with the hill society of the Himalayas. Research on such a subject has a feeble intellectual past and little has been done except in terms of articles in newspapers or popular and local magazines. This article, too, while not aspiring for much, hopes to introduce the local belief pattern in the hills of Himachal Pradesh. The focus is essentially on the nineteenth and twentieth century, though, at points, reference to earlier times has also been made. However, it should be borne in mind that irrespective of contemporary observations, popular religious beliefs always existed and the past-present continuum can be inferred.

I

The category of popular religion emerges from folk-peasant societies which define the lives of their members in the context of ecological niche and modes tied to specific traditions and sentiments. The group and its ecological structure defines a continuous relationship in which moral order and identity becomes synonymous with meaning of their belief system.[1] The rise of such a category also depends on increased mental and physical insecurity giving rise to emotional trauma. Deficient agriculture, imprecise knowledge of the world, physical coercion and exploitation by the force of state naturally enhance this psychotic anxiety. Popular religion, here, functions thus as a 'system of survival', a desperate search for security amidst environment and emotional stress.[2] As a result, men through the practice of magic and ritual tried to control the world by supernatural means. Hence, they were able through fantasy to augment technical ambitions and reduce the emotional tension created by the increased gap between intention and potency. Popular religion in peasant societies 'fulfilled the dual psychological function of the cathartic discharging of stress and the recharging of psychic energies for future activity.'[3]

Such religious beliefs are generally the product of an unstable past: they are homogeneous in their modes of expression and are loosely modelled after the Great Tradition beliefs of the area. From this emanates an *a priori* process whereby the Great or Classical Tradition of the region is carved out of the Local Tradition.[4] The former received the patronage of a learned clergy and royalty which helped its spatial expansion and in becoming a time-stabled belief. This resulted in spatial homogenization while the local cults remained apparently heterogeneous in character and, hence, of limited usage and import. Though the mode of worship in a particular locality defied reason and speculation, it remained close to the initial impetus of the same civilization in spite of overwhelming social change over the years. The people could change their gods, but not the spirit in which they worshipped them.[5] This would be clear if we sympathetically read Harcourt's confusion.

> Throughout Kooloo the faith is Hinduism, but it is not the religion of the orthodox, who, however, visit all the celebrated Kooloo shrines, though they have but small regard for the creed of their hill brethren, whose tenets they hold in derision...The religion of the majority of the Kooloo people is a sort of demon-worship, which may be deemed an offshoot of the Hindoo mythology, and reverence for the temples that contain statues of the noticeable gods; but their affections are more particularly concentrated on their own local deities, whose help they invoke in trouble, and by whom they swear when taking an oath.[6]

This passage shows that while people believed in the Hindu pantheon, they continued to worship their local deities. It is the latter which were more personal and emotive compared to the former. This formed the basis for all plural practices while adhering to one or the other faiths of the Classical Tradition. The autonomy of the categories hence arising depended upon the density of the local cults vis-a-vis the classical cults.[7] This also depended upon the demands imposed upon the worshippers and the benefits given. The greater the efficiency of reward, the greater shall the density be. This explains the solidarity and readiness for a collective organisation. This principle holds good in determining the causal efficacy of both the Great and the Local Tradition cults. Hence, it is the foremost operational entity in determining the relation between the two.

The categories of popular religion in Himachal Pradesh border between deism and theism. Following the Indian pantheism, people are generally polytheistic but particularly and specifically they are henotheistic. In this conceptual framework, their beliefs may be conveniently classified as animism, animatism, demonolatry, Hero (Vir) worship, Deota (area specific demi-gods) and the worship of sacred personalities (*faqirs, sannyasis,* etc.).

Before discussing these categories briefly, it would be worthwhile to state that these beliefs, cults and faiths developed in specific 'pockets', characterized by the isolation of the state for a considerable length of time from the larger (Indian) socio-political developments. Though Kulu and Trigarth (Kangra) as well as many small republics such as the Audambars, the Kunindas, etc. figured in early Indian literature,[8] the political and social organisation throughout the hills remained 'primitive'. Also these 'pockets' of beliefs were of the people who practised different occupations along with subsistent agriculture, i.e., they were economically backward. At the same time, the history of these beliefs is preserved in myths which are arbitrary but confirm our hypothesis that the genesis lies in physical coercion, stress-strain factor and emotional trauma.[9]

II

The concept of soul and life after death is universal. This resulted in the creation of the concept of ancestor worship, of malignant spirits and guardian spirits. The latter two need to be distinguished on their territorial extent. While ancestor worship pertains to a family only, the guardian spirit may be of a family, specific village or a region.[10]

Ancestor worship is very common in the hills. In Kangra, *Pitr* (ancestor) stones are found near the water-springs, as are fountain stones in Chamba and *Barselas* in Mandi. In Kulu and Suket, *Barselas* were a royal prerogative.[11] Moorcroft noted that the *Barselas* were erected on the death of each Raja or his relatives, 'Each is sculptured, also, with the figures of his wives who have been burnt with him...', and on several occasions 'the number of these victims of superstition has exceeded thirty'.[12] Usually in a Barsela the deceased Raja occupied the topmost position with his queens who became sati. Immediately below him were the figures of *Khwasis* (concubines) and *rakkalis* (slaves) burned with the king. The inscriptions recorded the names of the deceased and the burned ones.[13]

In many parts of the Shimla hills, the *nagas* (snakes) were connected with the deceased ancestors as water spirit.[14] In Pangi and Lahul, in memory of the ancestors, bridges, water-springs or 'cisterns' and even simple temples were built.[15] the ancestors metamorphosed into the guardian spirits of these edifices and water sources, and were propitiated adequately.

These *pitrs* were also worshipped regularly through the ritual of *srada*. The spirit of an issueless known as *autar* in Chamba supposedly harassed the surviving relations until appeased adequately. An *autar* pendant of silver, with a human figure etched on it, was worn in a necklace to ward off the malignant spirit, acknowledging the protection afforded. A necklace consisting of many *autar* tablets acted as a mnemonic device for the number of issueless ancestors in the family genealogy. It acted also as an amulet which warded off evil influences. This was a practical way to depict ancestral solidarity and utility in the most personalized terms. The *autars* harassed or benefited only that family which they belonged to. This, perhaps, was an extension of the father image, whereby the imagery concerns the relation of human father analogous to the ancestors (god's) relationship.[16] Thus, the *autar,* like a father and elder, punished the family of his offsprings and collaterals when they tried to tamper with the socio-cultural continuity; and rewarded their good behaviour, also measured in terms of socio-cultural dimensions.

While ancestor worship was a mode of appeasing benevolent spirits, the malevolent spirits who were worshipped out of fear and awe, could not be ignored. The deification of these spirits can be inferred from the myth of Bharmani Devi. She was a brahmin lady whose son was extremely fond of a pet-partridge. The latter was killed by a peasant and the aggrieved boy died due to shock. His mother immolated herself beside the corpse of her son and her spirit started afflicting the people. So they raised her to the status of the presiding deity of Brahmaur and built her shrine where she is regularly propitiated. It is clear from this myth that while the benevolent spirits were concerned with the family, the locus of malevolent spirits was over and above the familial sector. This is a paradox, as 'good' becomes a monopoly of the few but 'evil' a prerogative of all.

Most of the hill societies have their own guardian spirits who are propitiated in return for the gift of protection. These guardian spirits are both malevolent and benevolent and are feared for their ambiguous character. Local myths attribute to them many special powers which usually respond to acts of appeasement. The concept of guardian spirit, perhaps, arose from a helpless state of mind, or orthodoxy and superstition.[17] In Kangra, Kripal Chand was the guardian spirit of a water canal that was built in his honour, as was Suhi Devi in Chamba. Like Suhi, a local ballad from Chamba speaks of cruelty to a Gaddi belle by a 'baronial Rana'. She was sacrificed to ensure the success of a water canal that was being built. Later on she was elevated to the status of a *sati* goddess, the guardian spirit of that canal. In this capacity she became the fertility deity, propitiated regularly to escape her retributive wrath.[18]

Boni Devi, the lineage deity of a Gaddi hamlet near Paprola, fought the establishment to save her honour while alive. She burnt herself and her molesters to set the example of revolt against oppression. Her courageous act was commemorated by the people, seeking her protection as the guardian spirit of the area. The Gaddis of Ghasni worship a female deity (also called *Ghasni*) who was earlier a *churel* (demon seductress). She had fallen in love with a man, and taking an anthropomorphic form she settled into a householder's life. She possessed an extra-sensory perception which was a common attribute of her kind. Thus, on a fateful day she knew in advance the impending calamity from an avalanche. Transformed towards goodness due to her emotional attachment, she set out to stop the avalanche by sacrificing herself. For her deed she was elevated in the hierarchy as the guardian spirit of Ghasni.

It must be noticed that both Boni Devi and Ghasni approximated to the masculine character of courage and action as opposed to Suhi Devi, on the sacrificed Gaddi belle, whose femininity was exploited in terms of a ritual-murder, before their metamorphosis into guardian deities.[19]

An interesting feature of the Himalayan tradition was the variety of beliefs that people entertained. While ancestor worship arose from the metaphysical understanding of life after death, the concept of guardian spirit was invented from the sense of insecurity and helplessness in the face of natural or ecological calamity. For the propagation of their community, people entertained the concept of fertility deities ranging from human, supernatural to the world of nature. In the natural world, animals and trees form a major group which was worshipped all over the hills.[20] In this category, the cult of snake worship was the most popular.

Ophiolatry was noticed in the hills fairly early by the historians of Alexander in the 4th century B.C.[21] Snakes were worshipped as water spirits, as the lord of hidden treasures,[22] as the deified rulers of the country tracing their pedigree from Taksaka, the Mahabharata hero,[23] and also in association with Siva. The character of these *Naga* (snake) deities is capricious, alternating between the destructive and beneficial.

The live serpent was rarely worshipped, except that of *Rahla* in Kulu,[24] and the cult of *Naga* and *Nagini* in various places in the Kangra district. Popular myths associate these with Saivite tradition: for instance, Bhagsu *Naga* near Dharamsala, which is supposed to have cured people of many diseases and afflictions.[25]

The *Naga* deities were more popular with the Hindu population, who migrated or were pushed out from Lahul when Lamaic religion was established there. An example from the hills corroborates this view: *Kailung Naga* migrated to Kugti in Brahmaur, where he was elevated to the rank of *wazir* to Siva (the king), i.e., to the second place in local hierarchy of gods.[26] Similarly, *Khangsar Naga* and *Keylang Naga* of Jobrang migrated to Brahmaur. *Khangsar Naga* was a major *Naga* deity who was appeased by human sacrifice in his abode at Kolang Kothi in Lahul.[27]

Other important shrines of *Naga* were at Khajjiyar; *Indru Naga* at Kanhiara; *Naga Jamwalan* near Ranita; *Nagini Mata* near Nurpur,[28] etc. Many of the *Naga* deities were associated with the Puranic legends, for example, Karkota, Vasuki, etc. These were popular in Chamba, Mandi, Suket, Kangra and the Shimla hills, where they were worshipped on the *Naga*-Panchami festival.[29] Their shrines were the centres for the cure of snake-bite and, thus, attracted many afflicted devotees every year.[30]

Other animals popularly worshipped in the Hill States were the cow, the monkey and fish. In the hills, on religious grounds, the cow and the oxen were even exempted from grazing tax and the exemption was called *gai ka pun* (merit of the cow).[31] The Ghiraths (peasant caste) worshipped the cow by throwing a cloth over it and washing its feet placing a red *tilak* on her forehead.[32] Vigne (1892) testifies that the sacred cows were allowed to roam about in the temple of Jwalamukhi.[33] The fish was also held sacred as Baron Hugel (1845) observed a Javali near Haripur, a Machhyal (fish pond) near Samloti, Panchrukhi and one near Jogindernagar. Fishes were associated with the Matsya Avatara (Fish incarnation of Vishnu) and with Matsendra Nath, the *guru* of Gorakh Nath.[34] Monkeys were seen as incarnations or representatives of Hanuman, the god who helped Rama with his monkey army against Ravana. Hugel testifies that he saved his life with difficulty when people collected in large number to avenge the monkey he had killed at Nurpur.[35] The Jakhu temple at Shimla also associates the monkeys with *sannyasis,* and holds them in veneration as representatives of the 'devoted' army of Hanuman.[36] Opposed to the practice of zoolatry, people were wary of the owl, the crow, the black dog, cat, etc. These were considered inauspicious and heralders of illness and were therefore considered ominous.[37]

Possessing the significance of fertility, the people in the hills held the *pipal* (*Ficus religiosa*) and the banyan tree (*Ficus bengalensis*) as being the most sacred. Women worshipped these to ensure fertility and longevity of their husbands in the hope that the traits similar to those present in these would be transferred to the humans concerned.[38]

Pomegranate and *deodar* (*Cedrus deodara*) were also considered sacred.[39] The shoots and leaves of *ak* (*Cleoptropis procera*), *dhak* (*Butea frondosa*) and mango were used during auspicious occasions like marriage. A ceremony of *Panch Pallay,* or the five leaves, testifies to their usage for auspicious occasions.[40] *Tulasi* (Occymum) was grown in every household in Kangra and was held sacred. The worship of *tulasi* formed a part of the Vaisnava ritual:[41] it was also known as *bhutaghi* (destroyer of evil spirit).[42] In Kulu and Lahul the pencil-cedar and the cypress were also the objects of adoration.[43]

An important category of popular religion in the hills was that of *bir/vir* (Hero) Worship. *Birs* were seen as a class of minor deities and were impediments as well as upholders of the socio-moral order in the folk-peasant society of the hills. Their status bordered between that of demi-gods and demons. *Sindu bir,* or the 'whistling demon', was the most commonly worshipped *bir* in Chamba and Kangra.[44] He was a protector of harvests and was also a fertility deity, appeased by the sacrifice of goat or ram. He was believed to indulge in the theft of corn, milk and butter, which he transferred to his especial worshippers. He was known by different names as Lokapal, Bhumipal, Sanglipal and Chhatar pal.[45] His principal shrine was at Gangath in Kangra. People also worshipped *ban bir* or the spirits of the forest.[46] These were the deified heroes living in pomegranate, lime, fig and walnut trees.[47] They were supposedly capable of causing sickness if not properly propitiated. *Naarsing*[48] and *Kailu bir* were seen as fertility deities as well as seducers. *Naarsing* was believed to visit women in the absence of their husbands and was considered to be the deity of women.[49] *Kailu* was the deity of abortion and pregnancy.[50] *Gunga* was another *ban bir,* demon spirit of cattle, for whom a sheep was usually kept aside for sacrifice.[51]

Similar to *birs,* people in the higher hills (Kulu and Shimla especially) venerated the demi-gods of local origin who were broadly classified as *deotas.* These were the village godlings to whom specialized functions and powers were attributed with the passage of time.[52] They were the rulers of the territories they protected and any type of social change or religio-economic and cultural action required their prior consent.[53]

These *deotas* were territorially organised and placed in a certain regional hierarchy.[54] Small shrines were devoted to them and the *deotas* were generally represented by masks of copper or brass.[55] Their popularity can be gauged from Harcourt's observation that 'there is scarcely a village that has not its shrine or idol home' in Kulu.[56] If not fully propitiated, these *deotas* sometimes took on the character of spirits or demons.[57] Fairs or *jatras* and festivals were held in their honour to appease them and to escape their wrath.

These *deotas,* who were also the presiding deities of the area, owed their origin to the fear harboured by the family or villagers who initiated the process of deification. Sukhchain (1925) informs us about the *deotas* who possessed people in the Shimla hills.[58] Interestingly, one of the *deotas* delighted in breaking pitchers of village women,[59] while another refused to enter habitation declaring that he was a hermit.[60] Even the 'death' of a *deota,* throwing the village into consternation at being left godless, is recorded.[61] Thus the *deotas,* while awaking an emotional response in their subjects, become intimately connected with their daily lives and amusements. Most of the *deotas* were transformed into 'village institutions, in a way, owned and managed by the men of one or more hamlets.'[62]

The deities discussed above were worshipped because they were known to remove illness, avert natural calamities of demonic characteristics out of fear and awe. Belief in these demonic spirits was widespread and even their nomenclature and characteristics were similar throughout the hills.[63] These were classified as *bhut* (ghost), *pari* (fairy), especially *jalpari* or water spirits (also known as *jal malris*), the *chhidras* and *banshira.* The *chhidra* was conceived as a terrifying spirit and was propitiated with the incense of mustard. The *banshira* haunted old buildings, valley and peaks. It was appeased by the sacrifice of a goat, or in some places by offering dust or gravel.[64] The *dags* were the demons specially associated with the fields. If the crop failed to yield the optimum produce, it was believed that they had been taxed by the *dag.* The *dudhadhari* or *manasheri* (milk or man-eater) haunted crematoriums and was averted by wearing a silver amulet.

If possessed by these spirits, one had to renounce the consumption of flesh. *Ghatiahr* was a demon known in Dhami. He was said to possess people and was propitiated by the sacrifice of a *khadu* (ram). A stone tablet with his figure carved was kept in homes to protect cattle from harm.[65]

The *pap* was a ghost in the Shimla hills to whom small shrines (*dereoti*) amidst fields were built. This was a preventive measure against the fear of torment or affliction by the concerned ghost. The *pap* was also elevated to the status of *deota* at certain places in the course of time.[66] In Chamba, the *char* or spring festival used to be celebrated, indicating the defeat of winter personifying the evil demon Kulina.[67]

The Muslims, too, had similar beliefs, especially in *jinn* (ghost) and *ghul* who could transform themselves into any form. They haunted graveyards. The *jinn* haunted ruined wells, caused cattle sickness and robbed people of their grain. Khwaja Khizr was a water deity worshipped both by Hindus and Muslims. Parched grams were distributed and lights were placed in wells in his honour. He was also the lord of fertility and of traders, and was believed to haunt the *bazar* in the early morning to fix prices for the day.[68]

The *bhuts* had no temples[69] but were propitiated by offerings, especially during sickness or misfortunes. The *churel*, a female malignant spirit with inverted feet, was believed to long for a child in Kangra and was operational at noon and midnight.[70] All these spirits would possess an unfortunate victim characterized by the trance syndrome.[71] The *chela* (healer), usually of the lowest castes (*chuda*, for instance), by successive phases of sacrifice and faith healing helped in warding off the possessed spirits.[72]

A society, where such supernatural beliefs existed, also had the agency of warding off or inducing affliction by effective control over these spirits. Thus, the evil eye (*dagis*), witchcraft and sorcery were in vogue all over the hills. While sorcery was used for the benefit of the society, witchcraft was used for opposite purpose: the former cured, the latter afflicted. In Chamba, witches were supposed to cause cattle disease.[73]

Witchcraft was not approved by society and witches were hunted down.[74] Despite his bias, Rose's observation is vital in this context as it paints a graphic picture of popular mentality on such issues:

> Formerly when witchcraft was suspected, the relatives of the person affected complained to a court or to the Raja. An order was then issued to a Chela who was reputed to have the power of detecting witches. Accompanied by a musician and a drummer he went to the place...The musicians played, and when the Chela had worked himself into a state of afflatus, he asked the people standing by if they wished the witch to be caught, warning them that she might be one of their own relatives. They would, however, assent. This went on for three days, and on the third the Chela

standing by the Kumbh (water pot) would call out the witch's name and order his attendants to seize her. Picking up the ropes they would at once execute his orders and she would be seized and bound.[75]

The category of supernatural symbolism, discussed above, aroused emotions and stirred people to action. Such a semiotic exercise by people was their way of expression of their experiences which could not be expressed by the literal use of language. Such expressions evoked and clarified the human experience of an aspect of the world which stimulated cooperative action and hence acted as a binding force in a community.[76] But supernatural agency was not the only binding force. The belief in spiritual attainment and its symbols also had a strong influence over popular mentality,[77] e.g., in the institution of *pirs, faqirs,* etc.

Of ascetic leaning was the cult of Lakhdata (the bountiful), which was popular in Chamba and recognized to be the same as that of Sakhi Sarwar Sultan.[78] His shrines in the hills were frequented both by the Hindus and the Muslims. Muslim *mujawars* were the incumbents of his temple in most cases. But at Bari, in *pargana* Chanju, the priest was a *brahmin,* while at Rhurla, in Himgari *pargana,* a Rathi (low caste Rajput) was the priest along with a Muslim Chela.[79] A *khanqah* of Sakhi Sarwar in Nahan was worshipped by a sect of Jogis called *Far Vai,* as also in Saharanpur.[80] The Shimla hills provide an interesting cult of the followers of *Panj Pir* (Five Saints), with a strong syncretic symbolism. Placed in a shrine together these are Khwaja Khizr, Durga Devi, Vishnu, Sakhi Sarwar and Guru Gobind Singh or Gugga Pir, Balaknath, Thakur, and Siva.[81] The *Panj Pir* were also popular in Churah and Tissa *parganas* of Chamba where they were worshipped by the Hindus, Muslims and Sikhs alike.

The *khanqah* of Bhikhah Shah in Kangra was also important as a reference point to a 'secular' outlook in the popular mentality of the area. According to the story, Bhikhah Shah was a *brahmin* of Jaisimhapur who became a disciple of Mast Ali. He miraculously revived a dead person once which drew the wrath of his *guru* who chastised him. But Bhikhah Shah buried himself into the earth. A shrine was built and a fair is celebrated every year since 1907 at this place in his honour.[82]

People in these popular shrines not only worshipped the concerned deities but also brought their grievances to the lodged *faqirs, sadhus* or *mahant* of the shrine. These mystic figures were venerated for the austerity and 'counter culture' symbolism.[83] Such ascetics were not always lodged in regular monasteries. They travelled through the length and breadth of the country, apparently on pilgrimage, to all major places of worship (*tirtha yatra*).[84] The professed ascetics were known as *sadhus* and *pirs* throughout the hills.[85] The devoted villagers provided them food and alms, while some of these ascetics were invited to settle in an unoccupied shrine in or near the village. The *Udasis,* Ramanandis,

Dadupanthis, *bairagis* and *aghoris* also captured the popular imagination.[86]

The district of Lahul-Spiti[87] and Kinnaur venerated Buddhist monks as devotedly as the people of the lower hills respected ascetics. However, the monks in these districts directed their energies to help people, perhaps out of political motivation. While proselytising the masses, they imparted primary education and fashioned the worldview.[88] Some monks became popular through the practice of divination and faith healing. The popularity of monks and monastic institution was such that people contributed to the best of their capabilities.[89] The monastic lands were also exempted from tax.[90] The eldest member of every family became a monk so that the monastic order may continue.

The Buddhism of Lahul followed 'left-hand' practices and probably was a peculiar blend of the supernatural as well as of Hindu and Buddhist rites. Harcourt observed:

> In Lahul the religion is essentially Buddhism, with an admixture of Hinduism, but the former has not always existed; for before it became the popular creed there was a species of belief that went under the title of Long-pai-chos (or the religion of the valley), which appears to have been consisted mainly of bloody human sacrifices to evil spirits; nor has Buddhism, a faith which tolerates no blood shedding, ever been able to entirely drive out this system of worship. It is true that no human sacrifice at this time takes place, but goats and sheep are offered up before trees when water courses are opened in the spring, or in festivals at the beginning of harvest: all this is quite contrary to the spirit of Buddhism.[91]

III

Berreman argued that social structure, caste relationship, dietary habits[92] and modes of worship were similar throughout the hills. Hence he perceived a sort of 'cultural homogeneity' throughout the Pahari localities. The divergences that he could think of were only due to economic factors and the sanctions of high castes 'to maintain the caste hierarchy'.[93] This 'homogeneity' can be extended to the study of religion in the hills where it evokes similar sentiments, respect and awe. Again the differences lie in their respective economy and the priestly hierarchy.[94]

The Sanskritic cults were suitably organised with an established patronage, literature, modes of propagation of the cult; and the priests from the high castes had predominant right over the deity and devotees. Opposed to this, the cults of the masses remained as 'congregational religion' with a loose, undefined organisation, autonomously managed by devotees having equal rights and capabilities. While the former was a function of historic time, the latter was a function of instantaneous time but in continuum with the past. The Classical cults controlled the subjects within a socio-ethical order; the popular cults gained strength from democratisation, autonomy and revision. The former restricted self-expression and leadership opportunities while the latter thrived on the structural and personal aspects of change.

In spite of these differences, both the Great and the Local Tradition cults continued to co-exist physically and in the mentality of people as well. It is a paradox that people continued to follow the ethical order of the Great Tradition (they married into the locally prescribed castes, according to their religion, officiated by proper priests, following all rites, etc.), but they invoked the popular local deities to help them in their daily lives. While they believed in the potency of the Great Tradition cults, they also worshipped at places which, in a theological sense, were against the very tenets of the concerned religion. Thus, a Muslim visited the shrine of *Bankhandi Devi* (Forest goddess) or *Sitla* (Goddess of pox) more than he visited a mosque, yet he always married a Muslim, and supposedly led his life as enunciated in the *shari'at.* Similarly, a Hindu visited the local *pir* or *deota* more than he visited the temple of Sakti, Siva or Vishnu, and yet he adhered to the social-moral order associated with Hinduism. Thus, the cults of local origin approximated to those of the Classical Tradition, while they were in turn themselves localized. Despite these convergences at the local level, the distinctions between religion, faith and belief were clearly upheld.

NOTES

1. C.H. Long, 'Popular Religion' in the *Encyclopedia of Religion,* ed. M. Eliade, Vol. 8, New York, 1967, pp. 444-45.
2. Stuart Clark, 'French Historians and Early Modern Popular Culture', *Past and Present,* Vol. 100, 1983, pp. 60-70.
3. Ibid., p. 74.
4. M. Singer, *When a Great Tradition Modernizes,* New York, 1972, p. 67.
5. G. Santayana, *Reason in Religion,* New York, 1962, p. 73.
6. Capt. A.F.P. Harcourt, *The Himalayan Districts of Kooloo, Lahoul and Spiti,* London, 1871, p. 59.
7. David Hunt, 'The Measure of Popular Culture', *Comparative Studies in Society and History,* Vol. 31, no. 2, 1989, p. 368.
8. M. Postel, A. Nevins and K. Mankodi, *Antiquities of Himachal,* Bombay, 1985, pp. 17-21; J. Hutchinson and J.Ph. Vogel, *History of the Punjab Hill States,* Lahore, 1933 (reprint Chandigarh, 1982).
9. Mahesh Sharma, 'Tribal Group's Sense of History: A Study based on Tradition Recorded from the Gaddis of Himachal' (Unpublished M.Phil. Dissertation, Punjab University, 1991); S.R. Harnot, *Himachal Ke Mandir Aur Un Se Judi Loka -Kathayen,* Simla, 1991.
10. J.C. Campbell, *Saints and Householders: A Study of Hindu Ritual and Myth among Kangra Rajputs,* Kathmandu, 1976, pp. 21-52; R.P. Werbner (ed.), *Regional Cults,* London, 1977.
11. H.A. Rose, *Glossary of Tribes and Castes of the Punjab and North-West Frontier Province* (henceforth *Glossary*), Vol. I, p. 198. Also S. Setter and G.D. Sontheimer (ed.), *Memorial Stones,* Heidelberg, 1982. See also Karuna Goswamy, 'Sati Stones in Himachal' in *B.K. Thapar Felicitation*

Volume, ed. M.C. Joshi (forthcoming).

12. W. Moorcroft and G. Trebeck, *Travels in Himalayan Province of Hindustan and the Punjab & C,* London, 1841 (Sagar, reprint, 1971, Vol. I, p. 172).

13. Mian Govardhan Singh, *Art and Architecture of Himachal,* Delhi, 1978, pp. 28-9.

14. Rose, *Glossary,* op. cit., p. 197.

15. Ibid., pp. 198-99.

16. See John Hick, *Philosophy of Religion,* Delhi, 1983, p. 36.

17. *Village Survey Report, Brahmaur* (in *Census of India,* Vol. XX, Part V, No. 5, p. 5).

18. Rose, *Glossary,* p. 198; *Village Survey & C,* op. cit., pp. 8-9; Hutchinson and Vogel, op. cit., Vol. I, p. 284; M. Sharma, 'Women Sacrifice and the Goddess: An Enquiry into the Chamba Society' in *Women in Indian History,* ed. K. Pawar (forthcoming).

19. M. Sharma, 'Tribal Group's Sense & C', op. cit., p. 223; D. Kinsley, *Hindu Goddesses, Vision of the Divine Feminine in the Hindu Religious Tradition,* Delhi, 1987.

20. Kashinath, 'Serpent Worship', *Indian Antiquary* (henceforth *IA*), Vol. II, 1982, p. 124; Esther Cohen, 'Law, Folklore and Animal Lore', *Past and Present,* Vol. 110, 1986, pp. 6-37.

21. J.Ph. Vogel, *Indian Serpent Lore,* London, 1926, p. 1.

22. G.H. Sutherland, *The Disguises of the Demon,* New York, 1991, p. 18.

23. C.F. Oldham, 'Serpent Worship in India', *Journal of Royal Asiatic Society,* 1891, pp. 88-92.

24. *Annual Report of Archaeological Survey* (*Punjab and U.P.*), 1904, p. 67.

25. Rose, *Glossary,* p. 132.

26. M. Sharma, 'Tribal Group's Sense & C', p. 217; Rev. J.H. Knowles, 'Kali Nag, A Kashmiry Legend', *IA,* Vol. XXVIII, 1909, p. 56.

27. M. Sharma, 'Tribal Group's Sense & C', p. 218.

28. Rose, *Glossary,* p. 154; *Kangra District Gazetteer,* Part A, 1924-25, p. 233.

29. Vogel, op. cit., pp. 275-80.

30. *Punjab Notes and Queries,* Vol. II, No. 14, 1884, p. 19 (also Vol. III, 1885, p. 78); *Kangra District Gazetteer,* 1924-25, p. 211; Lall Douie, 'Guru Gugga as a Snake God', *IA,* Vol. XXVI, 1906, p. 84.

31. B.N. Goswamy, 'Social Background of the Kangra Valley Paintings' (Ph.D. Thesis, Punjab University, 1961, p. 229).

32. Edward O'Brien, et al, *The Kangra Ghirths,* Lahore, 1900, p. 34.

33. G.T. Vigne, *Travels in Kashmir, Ladhakh & C,* London, 1842, p. 134; also Moorcroft, op. cit., Vol. II, p. 72.

34. Baron Charles Hugel, *Travels in Kashmir and the Punjab,* tr. J.B. Jervis, London, 1945, pp. 52-3; G.W. Briggs, *Gorakhnath and the Kanphata Yogis,* Delhi, 1938 (reprint 1988).

35. Hugel, op. cit., pp. 58-9.

36. *Simla District Gazetteer,* Lahore, 1988-89; S.R. Harnot, op. cit., pp. 176-79.

37. Rose, *Glossary,* pp. 479-80.

38. W. Crooke, *The Popular Religion and Folklore of Northern India,* Vol. II, 3rd reprint, New Delhi, 1986, pp. 97-100; J.G. Campbell, op. cit., pp. 31-2.

39. *Chamba State Gazetteer,* Part A, 1904, p. 192.

40. *Kangra District Gazetteer,* Part A, 1924-25, pp. 211-12.

41. B.N. Goswamy, op. cit., p. 229.

42. Crooke, op. cit., Vol. II, p. 110.

43. Ibid., p. 210.

44. Sardaru Balhari, 'Sindhu Bir: The Whistling Spirit of Kangra and Kashmir', *IA,* Vol. XXIV, 1905, p. 176; 'A Charm for the Whistling Spirit of Kangra', *IA,* Vol. XXV, 1906, p. 286.

45. H.A. Rose, 'The Song of Sindhu Bir', *IA,* Vol. XXVIII, 1990, p. 286.

46. Rose, *Glossary,* pp. 210-5, 480-85.

47. Ibid., p. 212.

48. Sardaru Balhari, 'The Worship of Narsing in Kangra', *IA,* Vol. XXIV, 1905, p. 176.

49. Rose, *Glossary,* p. 469.

50. M. Sharma, 'Tribal Group's Sense & C', pp. 138-39.

51. Ibid., p. 238.

52. Crooke, Vol. I, Chapter II. See also Sir D. Ibbetson, 'Aspect of Hindu Worship', *IA,* Vol. XXIX, 1910, p. 272.

53. Crooke, Vol. I, Chapter II.

54. J.B. Lyall, *Report of the Land Revenue Settlement of the Kangra District,* Lahore, et al, op. cit., pp. 205-21.

55. Postel, et al, op. cit., pp. 205-21.

56. Harcourt, op. cit., p. 191.

57. Lyall, op. cit., pp. 83-4.

58. Pt. Sukhchain, 'Legends of the godlings of the Simla Hills', *IA,* Vol. LIV, 1925, p. 101.

59. Ibid., p. 136.

60. Ibid., p. 129.

61. Ibid., p. 135.

62. Lyall, pp. 83-4.

63. Sir J.M. Campbell, 'Notes on the Spirit Basis of Belief and Custom', *IA,* Vol. XXIII, 1904, pp. 333-74; Vol. XXIV, 1905, p. 17; Vol. XXV, 1906, p. 235; Vol. XXVI, 1907, p. 7 and Vol. XXX, 1911, p. 97.

64. H.A. Rose, 'The Legends of Banasira', *IA,* Vol. XXII, 1913, p. 312.

65. Rose, *Glossary,* p. 471.

66. *Shimla Hill State Gazetteer, Bashaher,* Lahore, 1954, p. 33.

67. *Chamba State Gazetteer,* p. 45. Also see Rev. A.H. Franke, 'The Spring myth of the kesar saga', *IA,* Vol. XXX, 1911, pp. 32, 147.

68. Rose, *Glossary,* pp. 560-65.

69. Gurdyal Singh, 'Bedsteads and Spirit Haunts', *IA,* Vol. XXVI, 1906, p. 224.

70. R. Richardson, 'Spirit-seeing in the Punjab', *IA,* Vol. XXVIII, 1909, p. 56.

71. Rose, *Glossary,* pp. 204-08. Parallels can be seen in H.G. Barnett, *Indian Shakers: A Messianic Cult of the Pacific North-West,* Carbondale, 1957; Belo Jane, *Trance in Bali,* New York, 1960.

72. H.A. Rose, 'Inherited Power of Curing Disease or Curing Evil in the Punjab', *IA,* Vol. XXI, 1912, p. 475. See also Sudhir Kakar, *Shamans, Mystics and Doctors: A Psychological Inquiry into India and its Healing Tradition,* New Delhi, 1986.

73. Rose, *Glossary,* p. 208; *Punjab Notes and Queries,* Vol. III, pp. 198-99; M. Sharma, 'Tribal Group's Sense & C', p. 239.

74. For a significant study of Rajasthani superstition and witches, see G.M. Carstairs, *Death of a Witch: A Village in North India, 1950-1981,* London, 1983.

75. Rose, *Glossary,* p. 213.

76. J.H. Randall, *The Role of Knowledge in Western Religion,* Boston, 1958, pp. 128-29.

77. Lawrence A. Babb, *Redemptive Encounters: Three Modern Styles in the Hindu Tradition,* Delhi, 1987, pp. 1-6.

78. Rose, *Glossary,* p. 566.

79. Ibid., p. 571.

80. *North Indian Notes and Queries,* Vol. IV, p. 60.

81. Rose, *Glossary,* p. 572. Is the number five a 'magical number' modelled on five Pandavas or Panj Pyare among the Sikhs?

82. Ibid., p. 626.

83. Romila Thapar, *Ancient Indian Social History: Some Interpretations,* Bombay, 1978, pp. 63-104.

84. S.M. Bhardwaj, *Hindu Places of Pilgrimage in India,* Berkeley, 1973.

85. Rose, *Glossary,* Vol. II, p. 360.

86. G.S. Ghurye, *Indian Sadhus,* Bombay, 1953.

87. H. Calvert, 'Notes on Customs and Beliefs in Spiti', *IA,* Vol. XXXVIII, 1919, p. 49.

88. M. Sharma, 'Buddhist Monastic Organization in Lahul, *Punjab Research Bulletin (Arts),* Vol. XXII, no. 2, p. 168.

89. G.C. Barnes, *Land Revenue Settlement of the Kangra District, 1883-84,* Lahore, 1889; O.C. Handa, op. cit., p. 131; Harjeet Singh, *Ladakh—Problem of Regional Development in the Context of Growth Point Strategy* (Ph.D. Thesis, Jawaharlal Nehru University, 1978, p. 130).

90. *Gazetteer of the Kangra District,* Vol. II, Lahore, 1885, p. 100.

91. Harcourt, p. 65.

92. B.K. Smith, 'Eaters, Food and Social Hierarchy in Ancient India: A Dietary Guide to a Resolution of Values', *Journal of the American Academy of Religion,* Vol. 58, No. 2, 1990, pp. 177-206.

93. G.D. Berreman, 'Cultural Variability and Drift in the Himalayan Hills', *American Anthropologist,* Vol. 62, No. 5, 1960, p. 783; also see his *Hindu of the Himalayas,* Bombay, 1963.

94. Cf. C.F. Oldham, 'Non-Brahmanic Hinduism in the Himalayas', *Punjab Notes and Queries,* Vol. III, 1886.

8

Perceptions of British Rule in Maharashtra: A Selective Study

J.V. NAIK

The expression 'Divine Providence' occurs frequently in connection with British rule in India in historical literature, especially in the speeches and writings of the 19th century social reformers of India. The Moderate School of politicians was so firm in this belief, that is, the 'British connection was ordained in the inscrutable dispensation of Providence for India's good' that Gokhale incorporated it in the Preamble to the Constitution of the Servants of India Society. However, this view was not accepted by all. In fact, the early Maharashtrian critics of British rule looked upon it as 'the most bitter curse'. The Extremists disdained the concept of 'Divine Providence' altogether and severely criticised it as savouring of slave mentality. As the volume of criticism grew in its intensity, even the Servants of India Society, some years after Gokhale's death, felt obliged to delete the statement from the Preamble.

This paper seeks to trace the genesis of the concept of 'Divine Providence', examine its use in different historical contexts, and to offer historical explanations for and against it, with special reference to the Maharashtrian response to British rule.

THE CONCEPT OF 'DIVINE PROVIDENCE'

The basic assumption behind the concept of 'Divine Providence' was a theistic belief that God willed British rule to rescue India from her plight and to promote her moral and material welfare. It had its origin in the contrast which its proponents saw between the 'prodigal anarchy', the 'colossal ignorance' that immediately preceded the establishment of British rule in India, and the Rule of Law, security of life and property and the opportunity to acquire the Arts and Sciences of Europe under the British Government. None of the major propounders of this theory of 'Divine Dispensation', however, expected, or wanted, British rule to be permanent; the British were to hold

India in trust until such time that she became fit to reclaim her political independence. Therefore, their pronouncements in this regard were not absolute but relative. Inherent in this belief of dispensation was a vision of a new life and a new society — humane, democratic, secular — to be achieved through the instrumentality of British rule. Also inherent in this belief of 'Divine Dispensation' was the presumption that India, on her own, was incapable of improvement and, hence, God willed 'enlightened' British intervention. This view, whatever be its intellectual basis and ideological premises, was repugnant to those who saw a clear contradiction between colonial rule and the interests of the Indian people. To them, the whole idea of the 'civilising mission' of Great Britain was a myth, for they asserted that there was no such thing as beneficent imperialism and there could not be anything altruistic about colonial rule. To such critics, British rule in reality was not a 'Divine Dispensation' but the 'most bitter curse'. The conflict that ensued between these two contrasting strands of thought constituted the essence of India's struggle for political freedom.

I

Although it cannot be said with any certainty as to who first used the expression — 'British rule was a divine dispensation' — the generally acknowledged originator of the idea in its articulate form was Raja Rammohun Roy, who is regarded as the political *guru* of modern India. On December 11, 1821, the *Sambad-Kaumudi* ('Moon of Intelligence'), a Bengali weekly owned by Rammohun Roy, carried an article 'On the Trial by Jury in India', which, among other things, stated: 'From such intolerable hardships and oppression [with reference to the previous Mughal administration of justice], we have, by the mercy and blessings of the Almighty God, been relieved, by placing under the mild and equitable sway of the Rule of England, since the establishment of which Government in this country, we have been enjoying every happiness without the least obstruction, having the protection of our persons and property perfectly secured to us.'[1] Rammohun Roy incorporated the same idea in the Prospectus of *Mirat-ul Akhbar* ('Mirror of News'), the Persian weekly started by him in April 1822: 'Thanks to God', he wrote in the Prospectus, 'that in these days the inhabitants of Calcutta enjoy under the Government of English nation, the freedom and security which is considered by rational and social beings as the grand object of all civil and religious institutions.'[2]

A more pointed reference to British rule as 'Divine Providence' is to be found in the memorial which Rammohun Roy and five other Bengali worthies submitted to the King-in-Council against the Press Ordinance passed by Mr. Adams, the Acting Governor-General in Council in 1823:

> We, your Majesty's faithful subjects, Natives of India and inhabitants of Calcutta, being placed by Providence under the sovereign care and protection of the august

> head of the British nation, look up to your Majesty as the guardian of our lives, property and religion...Divine Providence at last, in its abundant mercy, stirred up the English nation to break the yoke of those [Muslim] tyrants, and to receive the oppressed Natives of Bengal under its protection...your dutiful subjects consequently have not viewed the English as a body of conquerors, but rather as deliverers, and look to your Majesty not only as a Ruler, but also as a father and protector.[3]

Earlier, Rammohun Roy had expressed the same sentiment in the concluding part of his 'A Final Appeal to the Christian Public' published on January 30, 1822, the relevant portion of which was dutifully incorporated in the memorial. In this particular instance, Rammohun Roy, the famed champion of liberty, was humouring the British authorities with a specific end in view, namely, securing the freedom of press. Even so, his virulent attack on and wild generalisation about the preceding Muslim rule is historically indefensible. In contrast, as it will be shown later, a small band of Maharashtrian intellectuals in the 1840s cogently argued that Muslim rule in India was in many respects better than British colonial rule.

His quest for liberty and ardent sense of patriotism notwithstanding, Rammohun Roy genuinely believed that British rule was for the good of India and that it was a 'Divine Dispensation'. So did many other notables of Bengal. Prasanna Kumar Tagore, a close associate of Rammohun Roy, in July 1831, published in his famous English weekly, the *Reformer,* an article, 'Political Faith of the Hindoos', which declared: 'If we were to be asked what Government we would prefer, English or any other? We would one and all reply, English by all means — aye, even in preference to a Hindoo Government.'[4] Even the radical Derozians, who contributed a lot to the Bengal renaissance, did not categorically recognise the exploitative nature of British rule as some of the contemporary Maharashtrian intellectuals did.

During the Revolt of 1857, the Bengali *literati* and the landed gentry, both Hindu and Muslim, were vociferous in professing their loyalty to the British Raj. The Queen's Proclamation was hailed almost as a divine document. Ram Gopal Ghose, speaking at a public meeting of the inhabitants of Calcutta held on 3rd November, 1858, 'for the purpose of considering the propriety of presenting an Address to H.M. on the occasion of Her assuming the Government of British India, expressive of their devoted loyalty', said amidst cheers: 'Let us kneel down before her with every feeling of loyalty; let us welcome the new reign with the warmest sentiments of gratitude — the deepest feelings of devotion.'[5] Through all this ran the idea that 'British rule was a divine dispensation' which found a clearer expression in the speeches of the great Brahmo leader Keshav Chandra Sen who said that 'the Lord in His mercy sent out the British nation to rescue India. In obedience to God's injunction, England came and knocked at the door of

India, and said, "Noble sister, rise! Thou hast slept too long." And India arose. The invitation was providential and the response too...I see in history God employed special agencies to elevate and exalt my countrymen. England and India became thus connected by an overruling Providence.'[6]

Such, then, was the origin and development of the concept of 'Divine Providence' which generally remained an article of faith among the mainstream of not only Bengali but Indian thought for long as vouchsafed by the Presidential Addresses of the Indian National Congress in its moderate phase.[7]

II

For historical reasons, as compared to Bengal, the Maharashtrian response to British rule was more complex. Though the British takeover from the effete Peshwa rule was relatively smooth and the new regime under the benevolent administration of Mountstuart Elphinstone started on a promising note, Maharashtra, given its political past and traditional pride, never fully reconciled to British rule.[8] Within a short time, two contrasting currents with regard to British rule emerged: the one tending to regard it as 'Divine Dispensation', the other looking on it as the 'most bitter curse'. This dichotomy is, of course, an oversimplification, for between these two extreme viewpoints there were several other shades of opinion on British rule depending upon the individual or group perception of the given political and social reality.

In Maharashtra, the view that British rule was a 'Divine Dispensation' was first cautiously expressed in the Public Address presented by the local leaders of the Bombay Presidency to Mountstuart Elphinstone on the occasion of his departure for England in 1827. In their Address, the leaders, while eulogising Elphinstone's services to the promotion of moral and material betterment of the people, declared: '...we are led to consider the influence of the British Government as the most desirable blessing which the Supreme Being could have bestowed on our native land.'[9] The Addresses presented on such occasions are often contrived and, ordinarily, they are not treated as serious documents of history. But it was not so in the case of Elphinstone whose conservative liberalism made a deep impression on the rising Maharashtrian intelligentsia, and about whom Bal Shashtri Jambhekar, the noted scholar and social reformer, wrote in the *Bombay Durpun,* 'India has not seen a greater statesman or a more enlightened and liberal-minded man',[10] an opinion which was fully shared even by the later day militant nationalists such as Tilak.[11]

Elphinstone's successors, however, did not and could not live up to his ideals, for imperialism runs its own course. As the fuller impact of colonial policies began to be felt, the earlier views on British rule underwent a radical change. This is amply demonstrated in the small but powerful pre-*Shatpatre* (1848) political and economic literature produced, both in Marathi and English, by a small band of Maharashtrian intellectuals in the early 1840s. These critics of British rule wrote under various pen-names, such as 'Philanthropy', 'A Fairheart', 'A Hindoo', 'A Second Hindoo', and 'A Third Hindoo'.[12] Prominent among them were: Bhaskar Pandurang Tarkhadkar (1816-1847) who wrote under the pseudonym 'A Hindoo'; Govind Vithal Kunte alias Bhau Mahajan, the founder-editor of the *Prabhakar* started in 1841; and Ramkrishna Vishwanath who wrote in 1843 a remarkable book, *Hindusthānāchi Prāchin Va Sāmpratāchi Sthiti Va Pudhen Kāi Tyāchā Parinām Honār Hyāvishyin Vichār.*[13] Their perception of the Indian situation under British rule significantly differed from their better known contemporaries. They found the destructive side of the British rule to far outweigh its regenerative role.

These critics, taking advantage of the short-lived freedom of the press granted by Charles Metcalfe in 1835, made a penetrating analysis of British rule in all its aspects, especially in regard to 'draining India of its wealth and reducing it to poverty', and arrived at the conclusion that it was not a 'Divine Dispensation', but 'the most bitter curse India has ever been visited with'.[14]

Their criticism was neither shallow nor one-sided. It was not merely the exploitative nature of British rule that came under the lash of their bitter attack, but even more the fossilised Indian religious and social tradition which, they rightly held, was primarily responsible for alien political domination and the consequent economic ruination of the country. In this regard they wrote: 'It is the priestcraft of the Brahmins that have so far lowered the national character of the Hindoos as to be easily governed and even tyrannised over by a handful of foreigners [English] which is to be greatly lamented, but it is the political craft of the latter that has now impoverished them, which is still more to be lamented.'[15] They were generous in giving credit to the British rulers for their humanitarian work, such as the abolition of the practice of *Sati,* infanticide and the suppression of Thugee; but they also said that 'all these acts of common humanity vanish away in the vortex of your [British] political cruelty.'[16]

In forming a comparative estimate of Muslim and British rule in India, they made two significant observations: first, unlike the British, the Muslim rulers did not make any racial discrimination in matters of state employment; and more importantly, they did not carry the treasures of India to the countries of their origin as the British were doing 'at the sad expense of the prosperity and happiness of the poor and inoffensive inhabitants'.[17]

This stinging criticism was at once challenged by a group of pro-British writers who wrote under the pen-name of 'A Parsee Boy' and 'A Fourth Hindoo'. They lavished high praise on 'the moderation, clemency and excellence of the British Government'. Their tribute to the British rulers runs as follows:

> There is neither tyranny nor injustice in the countries, where the British flag is flying. To use an Oriental idiom, in the countries under their protection, the Lion and the Lamb drink from the same fountain — May the Almighty ever be its supporter, may its army be always successful in every country, where they direct their marches. This is humble prayer of...its loyal subjects.[18]

The critics treated this eulogy as nothing but 'shameless flattery'.

Marshalling facts of history to their aid, they demolished the arguments of the pro-British writers in a manner which is at once condemnatory and convincing. They admonished the 'Parsee Boy' for his un-Indian attitude born out of gross ignorance of the true nature of things and dismissed his pro-British eulogistic writings heavily loaded with quotes from James Mill's *History of British India,* as 'downright nonsense'. They especially pitied the man who called himself 'A Fourth Hindoo', for being 'so base and shallow-minded' as to support the 'Parsee Boy' in his justification of foreign political domination.[19]

Such was the first public debate for and against the British rule in Maharashtra. Though it lasted barely six months from July to December 1841, it marked the beginning of two contrasting trends of thought which, in the years to come, were to dominate in varying degree the two principal schools of Indian politics: the Moderates and the Extremists. It should, however, be pointed out that the early nationalist critics of British rule, unlike the later day Extremists, were radical not only in matters political but social as well. But their number was too small to make any significant impact. Nevertheless, it dawned on the thinking section of the people that British rule was not only the cause but the consequence of the evils from which India suffered in the past. It compelled them to re-examine the traditional beliefs and ideas. By the middle of the nineteenth century, there arose a group of reformers who firmly held the view that social reform was a condition precedent to political reform: 'Our social institutions must improve and become rational and just. There can be no advancement politically...without social and moral advancement.'[20] To them 'the British conquest of India was not a calamity to be lamented, but an opportunity to be seized.'[21] The new social order can best be achieved through the instrumentality of British rule, and the new forces that came in its wake. It was in this sense that they regarded British rule as a 'Divine Dispensation'.

The first and the foremost exponent of this concept in Maharashtra was Lokhitwadi Gopal Hari Deshmukh. His *Shatpatre,* written during the period 1848-50, contained not only an outspoken, impatient, penetrative analysis of the social and intellectual slavery of the caste-ridden Hindu society, but also suggestions for its improvement. Four of these letters are devoted specifically to outline the blessings of British rule and affirm that it was a divine dispensation.[22] In his letter No. 46, he wrote: 'The English owed their conquest to the stupidity of the Hindus. To remove the increasing foolishness among the Hindus, God sent these *Gurus* [English] to this country from a distant land. In fact, God wisely planned British rule to awaken the people from their deep slumber. There was no other alternative. The evil customs like Sati, infanticide, etc. practised by the people aroused God's wrath. It was to bring the people to their proper senses that God planned the British takeover.'[23] The same idea he elaborated in his letter No. 54 in which he referred to the pitiable condition of the lower caste people and attacked the dominance of Brahmins, their extreme conceit, their faulty education, their exaggerated sense of self-importance and their attitude of holding all others in total disdain. Further, in order to demolish these stupid notions and bring sanity to the people, there was no other alternative but to bring them into contact with the civilised foreigners. And it was for this purpose that God planted British rule in India.[24] The English, he said, were to hold India in trust. If the British misused this divine trust by doing things which are detrimental to the people's interests, 'the people will declare themselves independent and tell the English to quit.' It would take more than two hundred years for Indians to free themselves from British domination, 'but there was no doubt about the ultimate end', and 'the transfer of power was inevitable'.[25]

The *Shatpatre,* which constitute Lokhitwadi's chief title to fame as a social critic, were written when he was young and relatively immature. He had high hopes about the liberalising Western civilisation and, therefore, unlike Bhaskar Tarkhadkar and his anti-British associates, he generally overlooked the seamier side of British rule. While his attack on the social evils was fully justified, he was somewhat naive in his unqualified praise for the British. At this point of time, he justified almost every British action, including their well-known political treacheries in pursuit of imperial expansion. Therefore, one cannot help thinking that, amidst his manifold virtues, he had one faulty fixation: Anglophilia. At the time of the conferment of the title of 'Rao Bahadur' on him in 1877, Lokhitwadi, in his formal reply to the Address presented to him, said: '...My humble prayer and hope is that the Government of the Empress may be perpetuated in this country...'[26] This was perhaps routine protocol. But later, Lokhitwadi was disillusioned with British rule as testified to by some of his post-*Shatpatre* writings, especially his book *Hindusthānās Dāridraya Ynāchi Kārane Va Tyānchā Parinām* written in 1876.

Easily the most pragmatic and sociologically the most appealing view of the British rule as divine dispensation is to be found in the writings of Jyotiba Phule. The idea prominently and poignantly appears in three of his books: *Gulāmgiri,*[27] *Ishārā,*[28] and in the introduction to *Chatrapati Shivāji Rāje Bhonsle Yānchā Pawādā.*[29] The British Rule of Law, implying equality before law with its natural corollary of human rights, provided the hope of liberation to the millions of downtrodden whose cause Phule earnestly championed. Phule's approach was not nationalistic but intensely humanistic. The *Shudras* and anti-*Shudras* lived for centuries in a state of utter social degradation. If the past history was any index, then, there was absolutely no hope for any kind of social justice under the Brahmanical order. For the first time British rule brought a glimmer of hope to the socially enslaved. It was, therefore, quite natural for Phule to offer thanks to God for sending the British to rescue the oppressed humanity 'from the clutches of the Brahmin demons'.[30]

It was for this reason that Phule hailed the failure of the Revolt of 1857, and made it obligatory on the part of every member of the Satya Shodhak Samaj to 'take an oath in the name of God Khanderao and declare his allegiance to British rule'.[31] Tarkateertha Laxman Shashtri Joshi is absolutely right in saying that no scientific historian can disregard Phule's views on the Mutiny. Phule's argument was that 'history would have repeated itself...if the British rule had collapsed; the rule of the Brahmin Peshwa would have been restored; the traditional Hindu religion would have gained upper hand, and the little hope of liberation of the millions of downtrodden would have been completely destroyed.'[32] Not that Phule liked everything about the British rule: what he cherished was the liberating ideas that came in its wake and in that he read the divine message of human freedom.

Similar views on British rule were held by R.G. Bhandarkar, the well-known Indologist and social reformer, who once candidly said: 'I believe it to be an act of Divine Providence that English alone of all the candidates who appeared about the same time for the empire of India should have succeeded. The Marathas, the Portuguese, the Dutch and the French were all weighed in balance and found wanting and the empire was given to the English.'[33] So much pleased he was with 'all the benefits of a higher civilisation' gained by India under the British rule that he thought it to be an act of God. As an ardent social reformer, he pressed for the removal of social distinctions, agreeing with Jyotiba Phule that 'if we ask England to remove our disabilities, we must as a necessary preliminary show that we are worthy of the favour by removing the disabilities of the oppressed classes of our society.'[34]

Justice Ranade, as noted by his biographer N.R. Pathak, himself never used the expression 'Divine Dispensation', nor did he ever hint that British rule should be permanent.[35] His was a comprehensive vision, and he firmly held that for the achievement of national emancipation the various aspects of reform—political, economic, social and religious — were inseparable and had to be pursued simultaneously. He did not regret Indo-British connection; he rather welcomed it for the sake of national reconstruction on higher and 'more elevating' lines. In this he saw 'the guiding hand of God in History'.[36] He had a high regard for the British nation whose character, he said, had been 'formed by ages of struggle and self-discipline which illustrates better than any other contemporary power the supremacy of the reign of law.'[37] He discerned a 'moral element' in the British people which 'inspires hope and confidence in colonies and dependencies of Great Britain that whatever temporary perturbation may cloud the judgement, the reign of law will assert itself in the end.'[38]

Mahatma Gandhi, like Ranade, never used the expression 'Divine Dispensation', but he, too, till 1918, held that 'partnership in the Empire was India's definite goal', and that 'it was clearly the duty of every Indian to suffer for the Empire. If the Empire perishes, with it will perish our cherished aspirations...If we want 'Swarajya', it is our duty to help the Empire and we shall undoubtedly get the reward for this help.'[39]

Such was the political faith of the nineteenth century Indian liberals. With the ideal of English Government before them, they asserted that only a democratic rule could make the country strong and prosperous. Such a thing was to be achieved in India on liberal, democratic and constitutional principles through the instrumentality of British rule. It was in this sense that they regarded British rule as a 'Divine Dispensation'.

What Dadabhai Naoroji, Pherozeshah Mehta, Justice Ranade and many other liberals affirmed, Gokhale officially inserted in the Preamble of the Constitution of the Servants of India Society founded in 1905. It said that the members of the Servants of India Society 'frankly accept the British connection as ordained, in the inscrutable dispensation of Providence, for India's good.'[40]

This philosophy of 'Divine Dispensation' never found ready acceptance in all the sections of Maharashtrian intelligentsia. In fact, the unconscious ethos of the old ruling elite had never accepted the transfer of power in 1818 as anything more than a tactical retreat. Much had to be learnt from the British, and the available forces recognised, before the tables could be turned and the lost ground recovered. Consequently, there has always been a militant strand in the development of politico-economic thought in Maharashtra as revealed in the strong anti-British writings of early 1840s. The idea that British rule was not a 'Divine Providence' but the 'most bitter curse' was softened for a while under the influence of a few liberals but not given up. It found a fuller expression in the writings of Vishnushashtri Chiplonkar, and it was not an inconsequential factor in the growth of Extremism in Maharashtra. This line of thought was vigorously propagated by Chiplonkar's friends and disciples like Lokmanya Tilak and Shivram Mahadeo Paranjape who commanded a large following. The royal battle that took place between the Moderates and the Extremists is too well known to be repeated here.

The Extremists severely criticised the whole concept of 'Divine Dispensation' as savouring of slave mentality. They considered the British connection to be a curse, and advocated that 'India quit the Empire as soon as possible by any means'. The reactionary attitude of the diehard British bureaucracy to the Indian problem and the repressive measures taken by the Government to stifle the Indian political aspirations only added to the sharpness of the criticism. Ultimately, under the Extremist pressure, a few years after Gokhale's death, even the Servants of India Society felt obliged to delete the statement 'the British connection was ordained, in the inscrutable dispensation of Providence, for India's good' from the Preamble.[41] And that perhaps, at least theoretically, sounded the death-knell of the theory of 'Divine Providence'.

NOTES

1. J.K. Majumdar (ed.), *Indian Speeches and Documents on British Rule,* Calcutta, 1937, p. 1.
2. Ibid., p. 3.
3. Ibid., pp. 14-6.
4. Ibid., p. 46.
5. Ibid., pp. 77-8.
6. Ibid., p. 89.
7. See the Presidential Address of Dadabhai Naoroji and Phirozeshah Mehta for the years 1888 and 1890 respectively. The idea of British Rule as 'Divine Dispensation' appears in many other Addresses as well.
8. For a perceptive analysis of the Maharashtrian response to the impact of British Rule, see K. Mukerji, 'The Renaissance in Bengal and Maharashtrian Thought from 1850 to 1920', *Artha Vijnan,* Pune, Vol. 4, No. 4, 1962, pp. 331-42.
9. Quoted in T.E. Colebrooke, *Life of Honourable Mountstuart Elphinstone,* Vol. II, p. 199.
10. *The Bombay Durpun,* April 13, 1832.
11. B.G. Tilak, 'Mountstuart Elphinstone Yanchi Karkird', *Kesri,* March 12, 1895, reproduced in *Lokmanya Tilakanche Kesaritil Lekha,* Part I, p. 437.
12. For a detailed analysis of their anti-British writings, see J.V. Naik, 'An Early Appraisal of the British Colonial Policy', *Journal of the University of Bombay,* Bombay, Vols. XLIV & XLV, Nos. 80-1, 1975-6, pp. 243-70.
13. For a detailed account of the writings of Bhau Mahajan, see J.V. Naik, 'Bhau Mahajan and his *Prabhakar, Dhumketu* and *Dunyan Darshan:* A Study of Maharashtrian Response to British Rule', *The Indian Historical Review,* New Delhi, Vol. XIII, Nos. 1 & 2, 1986-7, pp. 135-52.
14. This expression was first used by Bhaskar Pandurang Tarkhadkar (see Letter iv of 'A Hindoo', *Bombay Gazette* (hereafter, *BG*), August 20, 1841, Vol. LIII (N.S.), pp. 174-5. For all the letters of 'A Hindoo', see J.V. Naik, 'An Early Appraisal & C', op. cit.
15. Letter of 'Philanthropy', *BG,* 7 July, 1841, Vol. LIII, pp. 22-3.
16. Naik, 'An Early Appraisal & C', op. cit., p. 268.
17. Ibid., pp. 251-2.
18. Ibid., p. 246, n. 16a.
19. Ibid., p. 247.
20. *Collected Works of Sir R.G. Bhandarkar,* Vol. II, p. 513 (henceforth, *CW*).
21. Cf. B.R. Nanda, *Gokhale: The Indian Moderates and the British Raj,* Delhi, 1977, p. 22.
22. Letter nos. 46, 54, 89 and 94 in *Lokhitwadinchi Shatpatre,* ed. P.G. Sahastrabuddhe, Pune, 3rd edition, 1963, pp. 327, 343 and 347 (hereafter, *Shatpatre*).
23. Ibid., Letter 46, p. 317.
24. Ibid., Letter 54, p. 327.
25. For a detailed discussion on 'Divine Dispensation' and Lokhitwadi's ideas on it, see K.N.

Panikkar's Presidential Address in the *Proceedings of Indian History Congress,* Aligarh, 1975, p. 379.

26. *The Times of India,* September 4, 1877 (quoted in A.R. Joshi, 'Renaissance in Western India: Lokhitwadi (1823-1892)', Ph.D. Thesis (Unpublished), University of Bombay, 1976, p. 210; also see Joshi's chapter on 'A Liberal Patriot').

27. S.G. Mashe and Dhananjay Keer (ed.), *Mahatma Phule: Samagra Vangmaya,* Bombay, 1969, pp. 90, 136.

28. Ibid., p. 315.

29. Ibid., p. 7.

30. Ibid.

31. Dhananjay Keer, *Mahatma Jotirao Phooley: Father of Our Social Revolution,* Bombay, 1964, p. 126.

32. 'Jyotirao Phule, Rebel and Rationalist' in *Rationalists of Maharashtra,* Dehradun, 1962, pp. 22-3.

33. *CW,* Vol. I, pp. 358-9.

34. *CW,* Vol. II, pp. 501-02.

35. N.R. Pathak, *Nayamurti Mahadeo Govind Ranade Yanche Charitra,* 2nd edition, Pune, 1966, p. 393.

36. *Miscellaneous Writings of the Late Hon'ble Mr. Justice M.G. Ranade,* Bombay, 1905, p. 126.

37. See Nanda, op. cit., p. 22.

38. *Miscellaneous Writings & C,* op. cit., p. 226.

39. *Indian Speeches and Documents on British Rule,* op. cit., pp. 185-6.

40. For the original text of the Preamble and the rules of the Servants of India Society, see R.P. Paranjape, *Gopal Krishna Gokhale,* 2nd edition, Poona, 1895, pp. 64-8.

41. P. Kondana Rao, 'Gokhale and Shastri' in *Gopal Krishna Gokhale: A Centenary Tribute,* Maharashtra Information Centre, New Delhi, 1966, p. 131. Despite my best efforts, I have not been able to get the proceedings of the Servants of India Society to ascertain the exact date on, and the circumstances in, which the statement was deleted.

9

The Craft of Bookbinding in Mughal India*

AHSAN JAN QAISAR
RANA FIRDAUS

> 'A book is the only orchard I have seen which can be put in one's sleeve, and the only park which accompanies a man as he goes. The book is the tongue of the dead, and the voice of the living. He is an evening visitor who never sleeps until you sleep, and never utters a word except what pleases you, never reveals a secret or abuses a deposit. He is the most faithful neighbour, just friend, obedient companion, submissive professor, expert and useful comrade with no desire to argue or to be wary of his owners.'
>
> (Anonymous Arabic comment, cited in A. Shalaby, *History of Muslim Education,* Beirut, 1954, p. 76)

Bookbinding has been defined as 'the joining together of a number of leaves (most frequently of paper, parchment or vellum) within covers to form a codex or book as opposed to roll.'[1] But here we will be concerned with the binding of paper-sheets only, to the exclusion of leaves and inner bark of trees traditionally used in India as writing material (viz., *talipot* of *Corypha umbraculifera* and the leaves of palmyra, that is, *Borassus flabellifer*; the common birch called *bhojapattra* or *bhurja* of *Betula utilis*).[2] Paper came to India along with the Muslims among many other technological objects like spinning wheel, stirrup, horseshoes, the Persian wheel, etc.[3] Therefore, the Muslims were the first to introduce bookbinding of paper-manuscripts into India — a craft which was in its evolutionary stage in the Islamic culture-area on the eve of the Muslim advent in the country.

* This article is a revised version of the mimeographed paper presented at the Indian History Congress, Bodh Gaya Session, 1981.

Islamic bookbinding is considered to owe much of its early artistic inspiration and technical skill to Coptic, Sassanian, and Hellenistic traditions when the Muslims ran over and conquered Egypt, Greco-Roman world and the areas of the Near East.[4] Predictably, as in other matters, the Muslims modified and changed their "newly gained Hellenistic, Coptic, and Sassanian heritage" to accommodate it with their 'own taste and fancy'. Timur, the great 'assembler' of artisans from diverse climes, gave this art a shape by bringing Syrian and Egyptian craftsmen to Herat which reached a high level at that place under the patronage of his son Shah Rukh (d. A.D. 1447).[5] In the words of Peterson, this technology in the hands of Muslims eventually reached 'heights of inventiveness, elegance, and sumptuousness which has never been excelled before or after by anything in bookbinding art the world has ever seen.'[6]

Details of bookbinding craft as practised in the Islamic culture-areas have been preserved in at least three books written during the medieval period, two of these by master binders themselves.[7] But we draw blank when we look for such literary sources written in medieval India. Our Persian works often refer to calligraphers and scribes but rarely mention bookbinders. Abul Fazl goes into raptures when he describes calligraphy (*kitābat*) and calligraphers (*kātib*), but there is no word from his pen at that place for bookbinders.[8] A somewhat earlier work mentions one Mulla Fakhr as bookbinder (*mujallid, sahhāfi*) under the service of Humayun, but without shedding any light on the craft itself.[9] Nevertheless, this deficiency is compensated to some extent by Indian paintings. What follows is an attempt to study bookbinding technique as depicted in some paintings collected by us to date. At any rate, this craft during the Mughal rule would not be much different from that current in the Islamic culture-areas at that time.

Our study is primarily based on three separate published paintings with supportive evidence from other ones, mostly of the Mughal school. Of the former, one is preserved (Plate 25) in the Freer Gallery of Art, Washington (henceforth 'Washington folio'),[10] and the other (Plate 26)[11] is lodged in the Keir Collection of Edmond de Unger (henceforth 'Keir folio'). The third (Plate 27) comes from the India Office Library and Records, London, Add. Or. 111 (henceforth 'I.O. folio').[12] The tentative datings of their composition are A.D. 1600-1610, 1585-90 and early eighteenth century respectively.

Before we examine the above paintings, it is appropriate here to point out that 'book-production' involved a number of craftsmen — paper manufacturers (*kāghazī, kāghaz sāz*) including auxiliary artisans (e.g., paper burnisher); scribe (*kātib*); painter (*musavvir*) who did the illustration by adding figural paintings; *muzahhib* or the worker in gold who did the page-illumination, that is, 'embellishment with abstract designs in gold and colours'; bookbinders (*mujallid, sahhāfi*); goldsmith (*zargar*) to prepare gold dust for painters and illuminators, and gold leaf for tooling by binders; carpenters (*darūdgar, najjār*) to make book-rests (*rahl*); and leather-workers to provide leather for board-covers.[13]

Taking up the first painting, the 'Washington folio' exhibits broad margins with a piece of calligraphy, approximately in the centre. Such broad margins remind us of the trend that set in during Jahangir's period.[14] Our main interest, however, lies in the six separate compositions on its margin (along the three sides of the calligraphy piece: top, left side and bottom), intermixed with rocks and foliage depiction. These six compositions display human figures engaged in distinct operations. For convenience, we will henceforth refer to these compositions as 'units'.

Starting anti-clockwise from the top, the first unit shows a man burnishing or smoothening a sheet of paper kept on a flat rectangular board, perhaps wooden, and slightly sloping towards the workman (Plate 28). A pile of such sheets can be noticed near the board, presumably for polishing, or they have already been polished. The craftsman is crouched on his knees, with his sleeves rolled up above his elbows. He is rubbing the sheet with a heavy, round and flat-bottomed tool having a short handle which he holds with both hands. In medieval times, the tool for burnishing paper-sheets in order to impart it a glossy sheen was known as *mohrah,* and the workman who specialised in this work was called *mohrah kash.*[15]

The next operation of 'book-production' was taken over by the scribe. The two paintings referred to in note 15 show the *mohrah kash* at their work while the scribes are engaged in writing on the polished sheets provided by the former. A scribe appears in the Washington folio as the last and the sixth unit, taken anti-clockwise (Plate 29). He is shown squatting cross-legged before a low writing-desk: the writing platform overhangs the supports beneath. The scribe dips the pen, held in his right hand, into the phial-like blue and white ink-pot, while he holds the one-half of the open bound 'volume' with his left. Another bound 'volume' and a pen can be noticed on the writing-desk. But this clearly is not logical if the painter of this entire composition wants us to believe that scribes were called only after the sheets were bound within covers. This surely was never the practice as exemplified in many Mughal paintings. Perhaps the only explanation could be that the scribe is in fact going through the bound manuscript to correct errors, if any.

After the scribes, illuminators and illustrators had completed their respective jobs, bookbinders took the stage. Their first task was to arrange the loose sheets in proper order. This was done with the help of catchwords (*tark*) written on the left bottom margin of the sheets which was a common practice and which, incidentally, points to the close understanding between scribes and binders. The sheets were now grouped into sections or signatures (*juzw*). Section or signature is the 'basic cell' of a book's construction "composed of multiples of four pages".[16] Next, the desired number of such sections or *juzw* were sewn up together, which became a 'volume' or book after having been bound within covers. The latter two basic processes are called *juzw bandī* and *jild sāzī* or *jild bandī* respectively. Our paintings do not reveal the actual operations of making sections and sewing them up. But, for the latter, many sewing and stitching tools could be seen in the second unit (Plate 30) of the Washington folio. Two small tools can be noticed on the craftsman's desk on his right side. One of these, near the edge of the desk, is a tool for boring holes at one end of the sheets for sewing purposes. Bookbinders nowadays call it *bātkin,* a corruption of the English word bodkin (perhaps a nineteenth century linguistic adoption). The other is a tool with wavy turns used for a very special purpose in stitching. Again, three long needles of different shapes for sewing the sections (*shirāzahbandī*) are shown lying on the ground, to the right side of the craftsman. These needles are now called *sutālī.*[16a]

Gluing or application of adhesive to the spine (*pushta*), the third important stage in bookbinding, does not find a place in our paintings. But there are indications for the same. The I.O. folio displays an earthen pot with a stick, half of it thrust inside: this is a gum-pot, still used by binders in India. We may also notice another pot, perhaps containing water. But we do not know the material from which glue (*serīsh*) was made; in Persia, either leather glue, boiled from leather scraps, or fish glue, made by boiling the swimming bladder of the sturgeon, was used.[17]

Now the stage is set for actual binding. The I.O. folio shows in the foreground two cardboards (*moqavvī, patthā*) cut to size and mounted with white cloth. A bound book with brownish leather cover can be seen kept on the left knee and held by the left hand of the binder, while his right hand is giving finishing touches with the aid of a tool which cuts off the unnecessary cardboard projecting out of the leather covering. Related to *jild sāzī,* we must turn, once again, to the second unit (Plate 30) of the 'Washington folio'. It shows a craftsman sitting cross-legged before a low working-desk at the level of his waist. A bound 'volume' lies on the desk, half of which is kept in position by the craftsman's left hand, while his right hand holds a flat-bottomed heavy tool by its handle in the act of thumping the bound 'volume' with it. This tool is certainly the *mushta* (also *thāpī, mugrī*) of bookbinders.[18] The purpose of this tool was to uniformly press down the gummed materials used in the binding. Obviously, this does not indicate stamping as interpreted by Atil.[19]

Some details of leather binding are available in the 'Keir folio' (Plate 26). The composition introduces us to a two-storied building. The upper storey is being used as a workshop with five persons busy at their respective work. A bearded old man sits on the verandah of the house with a low working-desk across his knees. A raw pelt is spread upon the desk. The old man holds a fleshing-knife (*dās, dhās, rānpī*) in his right hand, giving some direction to the man sitting opposite.[20] Below the verandah, on the tiled courtyard, a workman kneels and smoothens out (*saiqal zanī*)[21] the wrinkles of a square piece of red-coloured leather put on a sloping board. This is being done with the aid of a stone burnisher (*saiqal, mohrah*) worked by both hands. Another person sitting opposite him is holding a rectangular object which is probably the pair of cardboards on which the burnished leather piece will be stretched out. A young boy is seen entering the courtyard from the outer door of the courtyard, carrying a bundle of hides on his head.

Often a special type of bookcover with triangular flap (*bainī, jivha*)[22] was also prepared in order to give maximum protection to the book since the flap, projecting out from one of the hard covers, completely 'closed' the book when it was 'mounted' over the hard cover. One such binding is visible in the 'Washington folio' (second unit: near the working-desk, to its right) (Plate 30).

All our 'primary' paintings under study display one tool of the bookbinders, that is, *shikanjah* (press).[23] This was used for more than one purpose. The third unit of the Washington folio depicts a craftsman engaged in trimming the edges of the paper-sheets (and the hard cover) of a bound book in order to keep the sheets uniform (Plate 31). This is being done by securing the book tightly between the two wooden boards of a *shikanjah.* As shown in the painting, this contraption consists of two rectangular wooden boards put parallel to each other, and joined by two metallic 'torniquets' (one at each end) driven through the holes made in the two parallel boards near their edges. These 'torniquets' have screw grooves.[24] The space between the boards could be enlarged or reduced as required according to the thickness of the book. The frame is finally fixed or tightened with the clip, called *chutki* by binders, which are attached to the 'torniquets'. The craftsman in this unit is in a sitting posture, his left leg stretched out and the right one bent inwards while supporting the *shikanjah* on his legs. The main implement for trimming is a long knife, rather like a straight sword, called *saifah,*[25] with a broad blade, which is held at the edge with the left hand, and the handle gripped with the right. The action shows that the knife is being guided gently but firmly along the length of the book. Two books are shown lying on the ground, and one on a low desk by the side of the craftsman. According to the modern binders, this skill of manual trimming as shown in the painting must have been a highly specialized job since this work is now done only with the aid of machine.

Another use of the *shikanjah* was for 'backing', the purpose of which was to impart a roundish shape to the 'back' or *pushta* of the book. This operation is still performed in India with *shikanjah.* Its third use, if we have interpreted it correctly, can be derived from the 'Keir folio' (Plate 26) wherein a youngman, sitting opposite the old person, is shown holding a *shikanjah* in his hands, in the act of tightening it. A book, though not very clear in the black and white reproduction, can be noticed between the two parallel boards of the tool. Could it be that in this operation the leather covers of the bound book are being smoothened and stretched out by the force of the press, a little similar to what was done with the *mushta* as exhibited in the second unit of the 'Washington folio'?

From the utilitarian view, binding was complete at this point. But the craftsmen involved in this art had yet to go one step further to meet the aesthetic demands of their rich patrons and prosperous booklovers. This led to the decoration of bookcovers. One method to do it is called blind tooling, but this is 'unguilt' in contrast to hot tooling or gold tooling (*tilā kobī*). The former in its simplest form consisted in 'pressing lines into the cover material' with a wooden or unheated iron tool. In the second unit of the 'Washington folio' (Plate 30), we may notice two small identical objects, rectangular in shape, lying on the desk. These are geometrical rulers for drawing lines (*khat kashi*) known as *mistar.*[26] Most probably they were used in blind tooling for getting straight lines. However, elaborate blind tooling had developed in the Islamic culture-area by using varied dies or stamps to enliven the tooled designs like roundels, annules, squares, lozenges, stars, rosettes, etc.[27] In Herat, a new technique was evolved when single blocks engraved and carved with elaborate designs were used.[28] Lacquer painting was adopted from China.[29] We may fairly presume that all these techniques must have come to India by the time of the Mughals: albeit, blind tooling has not been shown in our paintings. But for gold tooling, the presence of a goldsmith with all his tools and implements in the fifth unit of the 'Washington folio' is a definite evidence. The depiction of a goldsmith in a composition relating to bookbinding should not surprise us: gold, especially in the form of dust and leaf (*panni*), was used not only by painters and illuminators but by calligraphers, scribes and bookbinders, too.[30] Gold tooling was done with the help of a metallic tool called *charkhī*[31] in India. The *charkhī* carried letters or designs. The technique was to heat up this tool in the fire and then to put it on a gold leaf. The heated tool took the gold onto itself which was then transferred onto the bookcover by pressing the *charkhī* hard upon it. But before this last operation, a thin coat of shellac solution was smeared upon the cover which ensured transfer of the gold leaf from the *charkhī* due to its sticky property. None of our paintings displays *charkhī,* but the I.O. folio (Plate 27) reveals the result of gold tooling, that is, gilded covers although the designs shown are very simple.

As mentioned above, the human figure in the fifth unit of the 'Washington folio' is a goldsmith (Plate 32). He is shown sitting upon his haunches on some cushion, blowing into a mouth-blower (*phunkni*) held in his right hand while heating a small object in the smith's portable hardbaked furnace called *borsi,*[32] the object being caught between a pair of tongs (*chimta*). The other paraphernalia of a goldsmith is scattered on the ground: three hammers, big and small, a pot for water, and a small block (of iron) to be used as an anvil which is kept upon a large slab (of stone?). One narrow rectangular object may be identified as a file. In all probability, the man is preparing a sheet of gold leaf.

The fourth unit of the Washington folio is not directly related to bookbinding *per se*: it exhibits a carpenter (Plate 33), making a wooden support or rest for books known as *rahl*.[33] *Rahl* was used for reading books, especially of religious nature. That these *rahls* were in general use in medieval times is borne out by their depictions in some paintings.[34] The carpenter is shown sitting on a flat stone with his right leg half stretched; the *rahl* is held against the bent knee of the left leg and the right foot as he wields a tool to cut the timber into two flaps of the *rahl*. The tool is a straight hand-saw (*ārī*).[35] Three other implements kept near the craftsman can be easily identified. One is the *basola*[36] with the handle at right angles to the blade, for shaping the wood. The other tool is the carpenter's *barma*[37] (bow-drill) for making round holes. In between them, a third one can be seen which is used for minor chipping operations like a chisel.

To sum up, our study clearly establishes the fact that the craft of 'book-production' involved a distinct division of labour, commissioning the specialised skills of a number of craftsmen at its various stages.

Moreover, the 'Keir folio' points to the manufactory or workshop system (*kārkhānā*). The two-storied house wherein the upper portion was used for residential purposes and the lower as the workshop is a rare evidence of the domestic organization of craft-production. The old man with a white beard is most probably the owner of the house, the person sitting opposite him with the *shikanjah* may be his younger brother or son. Both are well-dressed and sit on the verandah with the air of men in command. The other three persons must be their hired craftsmen. The old man is perhaps a master-craftsman; he is not a merchant-entrepreneur because he is shown working at the desk himself. But, he could be a rich artisan, capable of running a manufactory under one roof with the help of his family members, apprentices and wage-earners. Indeed, his house is itself a witness to the fact that he is a craftsman with reasonable capital.

ADDENDUM

How much did it cost to produce an illustrated manuscript in Mughal India? And how was this amount distributed amongst its producers by way of wages? To my knowledge, there is one such manuscript wherein we get answer to the two queries.

The above manuscript is lodged in the National Museum, New Delhi. Its title is *Khāwarnama,* written and illustrated during the reign of the Mughal Emperor Farrukh Siyar at the Imperial atelier (Persian MS no. 89.1065). The date of its completion given in the manuscript is A.H. 1127, that is, A.D. 1717. (We are grateful to Dr. Naseem Akhtar, Keeper, Oriental Section (Persian), National Museum, New Delhi, for drawing our attention to this manuscript.)

The manuscript has 321 folios, carrying 37 paintings executed quite indifferently. The length of each page is 34.7 cms., and the breadth is 24.7 cms. The length and breadth of the written space (average) on each page are 26 cms. and 16.5 cms. respectively.

The cost of production is given on the title page, preceded by the following inscription:

> *hisāb ānche bar kitāb Khāwarnama siwai inā'm ba*
> *ma'rfat Mansa Ram musharrif ba kharch dar āmdah*
> *do sad wa haftād wa hasht rupaya kamā faslat*
>
> Translation
>
> An account of the amount of what was spent on [the production] of the book *Khāwarnama,* excepting [the expenditure by way of] rewards, through [the hands of] the accountant Mansa Ram, comes to two hundred and seventy-eight *rupaya* as detailed below.

Then follows the break-up:

kātib (scribe)	....	80	*rupaya*
musavvir (painter)	....	92	"
jadwal kash (line-drawer)	....	75	"
mujallid (bookbinder)	....	05	"
shams wa sar lauh (illuminated title page)	....	07	"
ajurah tashih (correction charges)	....	09	"
kāghaz (paper)	....	10	"

The above details are quite revealing. The low price of paper is obvious from the fact that 321 folios of 34.7 x 24.7 cms. cost only ten *rupaya.* It is astonishing that the wage of the bookbinder — five *rupaya* — is the lowest compared to other artisans. The highest wage was given to the painter (ninety-two *rupaya*), closely followed by the scribe and the (ruled) line-drawer. The above table also reveals that the work of the scribe had to be checked and corrected by someone else who received, in this case, nine *rupaya,* for his job. However, we are not told about the remuneration of the *mohrah kash.* Was this included in the wages of the scribe who might have employed a *mohrah kash* himself?

Indeed, it would be quite worthwhile if we could get such details for illustrated manuscripts of the seventeenth century.

NOTES

1. *Encyclopaedia Britannica,* vol. 3, 1768 edition, p. 929.

2. See Jeremiah P. Losty, *The Art of Book in India,* London, 1982, pp. 6-8.

3. Cf. P.K. Gode, 'Migration of paper from China to India, A.D. 105-1500', in *Studies in Indian Cultural History,* vol. iii, Poona, 1969, pp. 1-12. Also Irfan Habib, 'Technological changes and Society: 13th and 14th centuries', Presidential Address, Medieval India Section, *Proceedings of the Indian History Congress,* Varanasi, 1969.

4. See Theodore C. Peterson, 'Early Islamic Bookbinding and their Coptic Relations', *Arts Orientalis,* 1, 1954, p. 43.

5. Basil Gray (ed.), *The Book in Central Asia,* UNESCO, Paris, 1979, p. 59.

6. Peterson, op. cit., p. 64.

7. These are: Ibn Bādis (A.D. 1031-1108), '*Umdat al-kuttāb*; Sufyani, *Sina'at tasfir al-kutūb*; and Al-Qalqashandi, *Subh al-'asha.* (For this information, see Hans E. Wulff, *The Traditional Crafts of Persia,* Massachusetts, 1966, p. 237.)

8. See Abūl Fazl, *Ā'in-i Akbarī,* vol. 1, ed. Blochmann, Calcutta, 1867, pp. 111-15.

9. Bayazid Bayat, *Tazkira-i Humāyun o Akbar,* ed. Hidayat Husain, Calcutta, 1941, pp. 65, 66.

10. This has been published in colour in Esin Atil, *The Brush of the Masters: Drawings from Iran and India,* The Freer Gallery of Art, Washington, D.C., 1978, pl. no. 63.

11. This has been reproduced in black and white in B.W. Robinson, et al, *Islamic Painting and the Arts of the Book,* Faber, 1976, pl. 117 (V. 34).

12. See Albertine Gaur, *Writing Materials of the East,* London, 1979, Add. Or. 111.

13. See Losty, op. cit., p. 16; T.W. Arnold and A. Grohmann, *The Islamic Book,* Paris, 1929, pp. 97, 99; Ahmad Shalaby, *History of Muslim Education,* Beirut, 1954, p. 92; Basil Gray, op. cit., p. 50; Kazi Ahmadmian Akhtar, 'The Art of Waraqat', *Islamic Culture,* vol. ix, no. 1, January 1935, p. 137.

14. Compare reproductions in V.E. Kuhnel and H. Goetz, *Indian Book Painting,* London, 1926. Also see S.P. Verma, 'Margin Painting in Medieval Indian Art', *Proceedings of the Indian History Congress,* Waltair, 1979, pp. 460-66.

15. See Tek Chand 'Bahar', *Bahār-i 'Ajam,* Nawal Kishore edition, Lucknow, 1894, *s.v. mohrah kash.* Compare Maulvi Zafarul Rahman, *Farhang Istalāhāt-i Peshawarān* (henceforth *Farhang*), vol. iv, Delhi, 1941, *s.v. mohrah,* p. 191. By the twentieth century, yet another term came to be used for this tool, that is, *istrī* (see *Farhang,* op. cit., *s.v. istrī,* p. 186). For the technique and the tool, see F. Buchanan, *An Account of the Districts of Bihar and Patna in 1811-12,* vol. ii, Patna, n.d., p. 625; P.K. Gode, 'The Regional History of Indian Paper Industry' in op. cit., vol. iii, p. 27; S.A.K. Ghori and A. Rahman, 'Paper Technology in Medieval India', *Indian Journal of History of Science,* vol. 1, no. 2, 1966, pp. 140, 143.
For other examples of this process, cf. "Mir Abdullah Mushkin Qalam with a Helper" (Colophon of the *Diwān* of Amir Najmuddin Hasan in the Walters Art Gallery, Baltimore, W. 650) and "Abdur Rahim of Herat with a Helper" (Colophon of the *Anwār-i Suhailī* in the Bharat Kala Bhavan, Varanasi, no. 9069). Both these compositions have been published in S.P. Verma, 'Portraits of the Calligraphers Depicted in the Mughal Miniatures: A Historical Study', *Islamic Culture,* vol. LIV, no. 3, July 1980, Pls. II & III.

16. *Mcgraw-Hill Encyclopedia of Science and Technology,* 5th edition, 1982, *s.v.* Bookbinding. Also see *Farhang,* op. cit., *s.v. juzw,* p. 228.

16a. *Farhang,* vol. iv, *s.v. sutali,* p. 229.

17. Wulff, op. cit., p. 238.

18. Cf. *Farhang, s.v. mushta,* p. 230.

19. Atil, op. cit., pl. 63.

20. *Farhang,* vol. ii, *s.v. dās, dhās,* p. 213. It was a tool, shaped like the *rānpī,* with a sharp blade to clean the inner side of the pelt. In fact, modern bookbinders call it *rānpī.*

21. See Wulff, p. 232. In India, it is called *chakkas* or *chaks,* made of wood or stone (cf. *Farhang,* vol. ii, *s.v. chakkas,* p. 213). The operation itself was called *bursai,* for which see *Farhang,* vol. ii, *s.v. bursāi,* p. 211.

22. For *bainī,* see *Farhang,* vol. iv, *s.v. bainī,* p. 227 (see also the sketch on p. 228). For *jivha,* see Losty, p. 13 (*jivha* from *jeebh,* that is, tongue).

23. Cf. *Farhang,* vol. iv, *s.v. shikanjah,* p. 229 (also the sketch). The sketch does not show the clips, called *chutki* by binders.

24. For the Indian method of making screw grooves, see A.J. Qaisar, *The Indian Response to European Technology and Culture, A.D. 1498-1707,* Oxford University Press, Delhi, 1982, p. 144.

25. See *Bahār-i 'Ajam, s.v. saifah.* Also see *Farhang,* vol. iv, *s.v. saifah,* p. 229 (also the sketch). For the use of this tool in Persia, see Wulff, p. 238. (In Persia it was called *kard* or *seftah.*)

26. Cf. *Bahār-i 'Ajam, s.v. mistar.* Also, F. Steingass, Persian-English Dictionary, reprint, Delhi, 1973, *s.v. mistar.* For a sketch of this tool, see *Farhang,* vol. iv, p. 229.

27. Cf. Peterson, p. 47.

28. Basil Gray, op. cit., p. 60.

29. Ibid.

30. See S.P. Verma, *Art and Material Culture in the Paintings of Akbar's Court,* Delhi, 1978, p. 66.

31. Cf. Munshi Wajid 'Ali Khan, *Matla'-ul 'uloom wa majma'-ul funūn,* Urdu translation by Munshi Zainul Abedin Khan, Nawal Kishore edition, Lucknow, 1893, vol. ii, p. 244.

32. *Farhang,* vol. iv, *s.v. borsi,* p. 17.

33. See *Bahār-i 'Ajam, s.v. rahl.*

34. Cf. Robinson, et al, op. cit., pl. 112 (V. 17/119a).

35. *Farhang,* vol. i, *s.v. ārī,* p. 18.

36. Ibid., *s.v. basola,* p. 26.

37. Ibid., *s.v. barma,* p. 24 (also the sketch).

10

The *Chhatri* (Cenotaph)* of Maharaja Sawai Jai Singh II of Jaipur: An Appreciation

NEELIMA VASHISHTHA

The idea of acquiring permanence is the basic dimension of all ancient civilizations which is evidenced in the form of tombs, statues, pyramids, *samadhis, chhatris, maqbras,* etc. This idea is also associated with acts of chivalry, valour and heroic deeds of self-sacrifice. The commemoration of such heroes, distinguished persons, kings, etc. has also resulted in the making of images and image worship.[1] The purpose was to cherish the memory of such persons and their deeds so as to remind their progeny and succeeding generations of their glorious acts. Installation of images in the memory of dead heroes and the worship of such persons is also reflected in literature.[2]

The reverence for the dead heroes was expressed according to the funerary practices and beliefs regarding death. Modern practices and beliefs regarding the disposal and care of the dead person also retain the traces of the past practices. This tradition of commemoration has produced a variety of art in different periods and civilizations. The artistic expression may have adopted different forms but, in spirit and content, these memorials are universal. For instance, the tombs of ancient Egypt included not only statues of the dead kings but also the statues of servants who, it was believed, would attend to their needs.[3] The belief in the continuation of a similar life after death was prevalent in Egypt. This practice also existed in China and Japan. Hence it manifested in the form of graveyards, family shrines and clan temples to preserve the bodies and souls of the ancestors.[4]

However, there is a difference between the tombs of the dead in Egypt and China

* Cenotaph means an empty tomb. It is derived from Greek. These tombs did not contain body but were designed for worship only. In modern times it combines the idea of commemoration.

and the cenotaphs of medieval Rajput rulers. The family graveyards and shrines of China and Japan in the strict sense served as memorials to the dead persons. These exhibited themes to remind their past deeds and glorious achievements to inspire esteem and respect among the people. Contrary to this tradition, the cenotaph of Sawai Jai Singh II (b. 1688; d. 1742) portrays the religious and secular themes of music and dance prevalent in that period, and not his personal achievements. However, like the oriental countries such as China and Egypt, the mausoleums or cenotaphs were built in India from ancient times despite the tradition of cremating the dead body. The *samadhis* were built in India in memory of the heroes who sacrificed their lives on the battlefield. There was a tradition to worship the symbols, relics, foot-prints, trees, serpents, etc. as symbols of the heroes.

The Vedic literature also refers to the erection of *sthuna, vasti, losthachiti,* etc. in India in memory of the person cremated.[5] The *Satapatha Brahmana* refers to circular and quadrangular (*chatuhsrakti*) mounds erected in memory of dead ancestors. It also gives in detail the process of making *shmashana* and *samadhi* of the person, the selection of place for cremation and the proper time for building a memorial.[6] The Buddhist texts, too, refer to the erection of wooden posts and worship of relics of Buddha and other teachers. Similarly, the memorials of Pasupata Saiva teachers have also been referred to in literature and epigraphs.[7]

This tradition of building memorials to the dead was current almost among all castes and faiths. During the medieval period in Rajasthan, there was a tradition of erecting cenotaphs of the Rajput rulers or monuments of those Rajput heroes (*Jujhars*) who had sacrificed their lives on the battlefield or for some noble cause. Moreover, the cenotaphs were considered auspicious places to be visited by the members of the family to seek blessings and pay homage before or after completion of ceremonies such as birth, *jata karma,* marriage of children and proceeding or returning from war. On these occasions, especial gifts of sweets and cash were offered for distribution among the *brahmins* and the poor besides the routine worship. The royal couples used to pay homage whenever they planned to visit their family deity at Jamwa Ramgarh near Jaipur. The *Dastur Komwar* records of Jaipur State reveal such information regarding the visits, offering of gifts in cash or kind and performing worship at the *chhatris* of Bhatiyaniji Sati, and Sawai Madho Singh I at Amber and Sawai Ishwari Singh at Jaipur.[8] Among these, the *chhatri* of Sawai Ishwari Singh was believed to be a place of pilgrimage. The records reveal an account of continuous visits by the members of the royal family from A.D. 1756 to 1767 to this cenotaph.[9] Besides, this was also worshipped by the students of music, and lovers of music paid their homage by holding concerts there.[10]

Memorials of distinguished persons achieved plastic architectural form in *chhatri* during the medieval times. Initially, a memorial took the prevalent architectural forms with some adaptations keeping in view the purpose and financial resources. In Rajasthan, the memorial pavilions of war heroes, Rajput rulers and persons associated with royal families that developed in the 18th and 19th centuries into architectural form are popularly known as *chhatri.* The ruling houses of Jaipur, Jodhpur, Udaipur, Kota and Bikaner built *chhatris* for their ancestors.[11] Among these, the *chhatri* of Sawai Jai Singh II in the royal cemetery of Gaitore is noteworthy for its grandeur. It has been erected according to the Vedic traditions of memorials. It is built of marble which now carries a pale yellow hue with the passage of time.

Sawai Jai Singh II founded the new city of Jaipur in 1727. The city was divided into nine parts. Among these, two divisions of the northern side were meant for royal residence, offices and observatory.[12] On the same side at the outskirts of the city, the cremation ground at Gaitore for the royal family was also planned. Its gate and outer boundary were built in 1741.[13] The place is picturesque because of the valley and a natural waterfall which is flooded during the rainy season. The valley of Gaitore was known to have covered the area of Brahmapuri, Kala Hanuman, the *Yagyasthala* (the place where *Asvamegha* sacrifice was performed by Sawai Jai Singh) and Jalmahal. It was inhabited by Mina tribe before it was occupied by the Kachhwaha rulers of Amber.[14] Owing to its being situated beyond the royal palace on the northern boundary of Jaipur with a slope towards south and a picturesque background, the place must have appeared suitable for royal *shmashana* to Sawai Jai Singh. It seems quite possible that Sawai Jai Singh took into consideration the physical situation and environment of Gaitore for royal cenotaphs in consonance with the Vedic texts. For instance, the *Satapatha Brahmana* gives a detailed account of how to select the site for *shmashana*:[15] it should be *udichina pravana* or in the northern direction of the village, sloping towards south; and it should have picturesque background with a river or other source of water and should not be seen from a distance. Accordingly, the site of Gaitore proved most suitable.

The cenotaphs at Gaitore are surrounded by a boundary wall within which there are three courtyards. The present entrance is from the courtyard which contains the cenotaphs of Sawai Madho Singh II, his two sons and Sawai Man Singh II, the last ruler of Jaipur. The second courtyard contains a number of small *chhatris.* The rear courtyard which is at the extreme end contains the *chhatri* of Sawai Jai Singh (Plate 34). This courtyard is enclosed with a boundary wall, separated from the hills and forest at the back. It also includes five other cenotaphs, viz., the *chhatri* of Sawai Jai Singh II, Sawai Madho Singh I, Sawai Pratap Singh, Sawai Ram Singh II and Sawai Prithvi Singh.

This memorial of Sawai Jai Singh carries some patterns of temple structure, along with the stone canopy resting on twelve pillars over the plain *vedi* — probably the site of cremation. The canopy or the *chhatri* symbolises *chhatra,* a symbol of royalty. The cenotaph has a carved plinth (*pitha*) of *triratha* type plan, and a pillared dome in elevation. Moreover, it shows elaborate structures of four drum-like oblong vaults which are slightly lower in height than the main dome, and are placed on the four sides of the main dome. These are within the common framework surrounded by a pent roof (*chhajja*). The interior of the main cupola is embellished with Pauranic themes in the blind window-arch frames, while the exterior is fluted to suggest gigantic closed inverted lotus flower. A square *vedi* in the centre of a raised platform signifies the exact place where the mortal remains were kept. A small square *chhatri* known as *jot ka bangla* was meant for keeping the burning lamp and for protecting it from rain and wind.

Several scholars have presumed without evidence that the *chhatri* of Sawai Jai Singh II in its present form was built by his successors and sons Ishwari Singh and Madho Singh.[16] On the contrary, the records of Public Works Department of Jaipur State tell us that the *chhatri* of Sawai Jai Singh II was built in 1881[17] by Sawai Madho Singh II who was the great-grandson of Sawai Jai Singh II (Plate 35).

The estimate and plan of the cenotaph of Sawai Jai Singh II was prepared and approved in 1880 by Col. S.S. Jacob in collaboration with Rambilas Usta (*Ustad*). The file of correspondence between Jacob and Royal Council of the State reveals that this plan was approved after examining many designs submitted by the architects of Jaipur. Its construction was entrusted to Jacob (Plates 36-8). The estimated cost was Rs. 72,564, and Jacob was empowered to spend this sum according to requirements.[18] The plan of the cenotaph was included by Jacob in his *Jaipur Portfolio of Architectural Details* (Volume 12).[19] Moreover, there appears much similarity between the printed plan and elevation of the cenotaphs of Sawai Jai Singh II and Sawai Ram Singh II. Sawai Madho Singh II, while thinking of building a cenotaph for his father Sawai Ram Singh II, also felt the need of a grand cenotaph for Sawai Jai Singh II, the builder of the Jaipur city. It was an appropriate tribute from Sawai Madho Singh II to the memory of his ancestor who was himself a great builder. The *Satapatha Brahmana* states that the memorial of a person should be built long after his death when the memory of his deeds starts fading away. In this way, this cenotaph also fulfils the textual directions of the text.

Since the *chhatris* of Sawai Jai Singh II and Sawai Ram Singh II are built on the same quadrangular plinth and are exactly similar in plan, elevation, carvings of sculptural themes and architectural motifs, it confirms that the two cenotaphs were built by the same person. The models of these two cenotaphs were sent by Sawai Madho Singh II to be exhibited in the Crystal Palace, London, in 1853.[20]

The cenotaph of Sawai Jai Singh II attracts the viewer because of its centrality in the courtyard. The plinth is high and is reached by a flight of ten stairs from the front. The quadrangular platform has a plain stone railing and four square canopies at the four corners of the railing which surrounds the two cenotaphs.

The plinth of the main structure is square with four small projected squares on its four sides making it an adaptation of *triratha pitha* type of temples. It has twenty relief panels—five panels on each side of the main square plinth. These panels depict hunting scenes, a pastime in vogue among the Rajput princes of medieval Rajasthan. The reliefs on the interior of the dome are composed in triangular frames and depict religious themes. Besides, the carvings on the pillars include (i) round sculpture on its shaft, and (ii) relief sculptures at its base. The round sculptures on the inner side of the pillars represent standing female figures of musicians, singers and dancers holding musical instruments and performing dance gestures. The reliefs at the base of the pillars are carved in arch-shaped triangles and represent the themes of music and dance.

The sculptural representations may be classified into three categories: (i) the decorative panels on the *pitha* of the cenotaph; (ii) the relief panels in the interior of the dome, and (iii) carvings of the pillars.

(i) Decorative Panels on the *Pitha*

The relief panels on the *pitha* of the cenotaph are rectangular in format and represent themes in decorative style. The panels on the front of each side represent two elephants facing each other (Plates 39-40), each with two riders. One rider is holding a flag which depicts the Jaipur *dhvaja* (flag) of one and one-fourth (*sawai*), the honour bestowed on the rulers of Jaipur by the Mughals. The other rider is driving the elephant. Between the two elephants is carved a decorative lotus plant with buds and full blown flowers and leaves. The elephants are shown plucking lotus buds with their trunks. They are embellished and decorated with small ringlets and bells around their feet. The panel is beautifully carved and repeated ten times with minor changes in the carvings of the lotus flowers and buds.

The second theme depicts tiger hunting from horseback (Plate 41). Here two horse riders are represented attacking a tiger with spears: one of them has struck the tiger which has caught the hoof of the horse of another rider. The tiger is carved in the centre of the panel where one hunter on foot is shown fighting the animal. The scene of hunt has been treated here in purely decorative manner by repeating two horse riders on either side of the tiger. A tree with decorative foliage and five peacocks perched on its top symbolises the forest. The panel carvings reveal arms and tactics used in hunting. Besides the use of swords, spears, arrows, guns also have been shown. This theme is repeated on eight panels of the plinth with slight changes.

The third theme represents elephant and horse fight which was very popular among the Rajput nobles (Plate 42). It was known as *satmari.* This theme is repeated twice. In one of the panels the horse rider is shown bedecked with jewellery and dressed like a prince. Hence some scholars have identified it with prince Ishwari Singh whose favourite sport was *satmari.*[21] But this is not correct. The games of *satmari,* polo and horse riding were popular sports of all the Rajput princes and nobles. Therefore, the panel may represent any prince, most probably one of the sons of Sawai Madho Singh II in whose reign the cenotaph was built.

In the game of *satmari,* an elephant is provoked to attack the horse, and the horse rider while driving the horse away from the elephant attacks the animal with his rod. The elephant tries to entangle the horse but the tail of the latter slips from the grip of elephant's trunk as it is made slippery by smearing it with oil. The panels of elephants in lotus pond is another theme repeated ten times.

(ii) Panels in the Interior of the Dome

The main dome is carved with Pauranic and historical themes. Among these, the themes from the life of Lord Krishna such as flute-playing in the forest of Vrindavana, *chiraharan* by the bank of the Yamuna, *kaliyadaman,* and Krishna and Balrama entering the palace of Kamsa, *samudra manthan,* Siva and Parvati seated at Mt. Kailash, the battle between Rama and Ravana, and Mahisasura fighting with the goddess Durga are also represented (Plates 43-51).

There is one panel which reveals the welcome celebration of a king and his army after returning from war. In this panel, the cavalry is being led by the king seated on an elephant. He is shown returning to his palace where ladies are waiting to receive him with pitchers full of water and other ceremonial objects.

The depiction of the Ramayana scene is full of minor details. Here, Rama and Laksmana are shooting arrows, while Hanumana and other monkeys are attacking the enemies with maces or stones. Ravana is carved with twenty hands and five heads (Plate 43). The panels representing the events of the life of Krishna are beautifully presented with all the details. For instance, Krishna and Balrama entering the palace of Kamsa are shown ascending the stairs of the three-storeyed palace. In its courtyard are shown the mad elephant Kuvalayapida, which was controlled by Krishna; two wrestlers Mustika and Chanuara lying on the ground with their *musalas* and the hunchbacked woman Kubja who met Krishna on his arrival at Mathura.

The representation of trees, river, mountains and other motifs in these panels follows exactly the same pattern as in the 17th and 18th centuries' Rajasthani school (Plates 44-7). Similarly, the theme of churning the ocean depicts the mountain *mandara* in a conventionalised form of a rod standing on the back of a tortoise, and the serpent is represented as a rope. Here, the demons can be identified from their animal-like faces (Plate 51).

The treatment of carving of trees in these reliefs, especially in the panel of *chiraharan*

(Plate 45), is worth mentioning. A tree on which Krishna is shown seated and playing flute is carved in the centre. The tree is decorated with the clothes of *gopis* which are dangling from its branches. It covers the central vertical space of the composition. The treatment of carving in stylized manner reminds the representation of trees in miniature paintings. On either side of this tree are carved two smaller trees with monkeys jumping from one branch to another. In the foreground is the river Yamuna with six *gopis* standing in water and requesting Krishna to return their clothes. The water is depicted in wavy lines. In this way, the whole composition becomes well-balanced and harmoniously unified. The same treatment in the division of space is followed in the panels of *Kaliyadaman,* churning of ocean and Krishna dancing and playing his flute on Mt. Govardhan (Plates 46, 49 and 51).

The panel of *Kaliyadaman* (Plate 49) represents the serpent with seven hoods and Krishna dancing on the central one. The remaining space is filled with the figures of *nagini* along the base. Two stylized trees fill the rest of the composition. These panels are composed keeping in view the requirements of the picture's space. As these reliefs have triangular space, its division with a vertical line in the centre and a horizontal line at the base appears most appropriate and balanced. Thus, the compositions of the above mentioned themes are well placed, giving a sense of harmony and unified action in the centre according to the available space of a triangle. Contrary to this, the compositions representing the fight of Ravana with Rama and Laksmana, and that of Mahisasura with goddess Durga, and the depiction of the return of the king along with his army to the palace (Plates 48 and 50) are composed in horizontal divisions of space. For instance, the vertical figure of Ravana is placed at one corner and Rama and Laksmana at the other end of the triangle. The vertical space of the centre is filled with many small figures of monkeys carved one upon the other which gives the appearance of overcrowding. Similar is the case with the compositions showing Mahisasura and goddess Durga and Krishna and Balrama entering the palace of Kamsa (Plates 47-8).

(iii) Carvings on the Pillars

The pillars of the main dome are decorated with standing female figures of musicians and dancers playing musical instruments such as *veena, tanpura, dholak* and *manjira.* Among these, one figure represents the dancer while the rest are playing music and keeping time with *dholak* and *manjira.* The carving of these figures reveals the fashions of ornaments, coiffure and dresses worn by women, and the musical instruments which were used during the 19th century. Here, *dholak* has replaced *mridanga*; and the dress of the dancer is a transparent *lahanga* and close-fitting *pyjamas* underneath and blouse. As regards the carving of the human body, they appear rigid, static, slightly disproportionate and lifeless. Movement, softness and life-like charm are absent in these sculptures (Plates 52-7).

The relief panels at the base of the square pillars are interesting for the representation of musical melodies, known as *ragamala,* dance and other entertainments of medieval Rajput aristocracy. Among these, some of the panels depict musical themes bearing a direct impact of the *ragamala* paintings and literature which were composed in a large number in the Jaipur State before the construction of the cenotaph of Sawai Jai Singh II. In one of the panels a male figure is carved standing between two creepers bearing flowers. The gesture of the figure indicates singing, while the two female figures on either side are playing *pakhawaj,* keeping time with *manjira.* The whole scene is imbued with the spirit of spring season. This panel clearly shows the influence of the *Raga Vasant* (Plate 60) as painted in the *ragamala* paintings. Similarly, a relief depicts a deer and a female figure holding *veena.* It represents *Kakubha Ragini* (Plate 58). Other reliefs also represent themes of dance, music and other entertainments in the pleasure-gardens of palaces (Plate 59). The depiction of trees and flowers is full of rhythm and the whole composition overflows with the spirit of music and dance.

Another panel represents a dancer accompanied by two musicians — one is playing a flute and the other is holding some instrument (Plate 64). Yet another represents one lady playing *tanpura,* and the other holding a cup of wine and pot, and a motif of tree in the centre of the composition (Plate 61). In one panel is shown a dancer and a musician playing *tanpura.* This panel has also a motif of tree in the centre (Plate 65). Besides these panels exhibiting dance and music, some also represent themes of daily life. For instance, one panel represents three women, two are leading a child by taking its hands; the third, holding another child, is perhaps the maid (Plate 63).

To sum up, the cenotaph of Sawai Jai Singh II provides cultural data of the contemporary social life and religious customs. The figures of male and female dancers, musicians and others shown in the sculptures and relief panels portray the fashion of dresses, ornaments and musical instruments used in the past. Besides, religious themes pertaining to the *Ramayana* and the exploits of Krishna represented in the relief panels indicate the religious ethos of the period. The sculptures of this cenotaph project the spirit and atmosphere of the royal court of Jaipur State which had been a pioneer in providing patronage to painting, music and other fine arts.

NOTES

1. E.B. Tylor, *Anthropology,* Vol. II, London, 1881, p. 91.
2. Valmiki, *Ramayana, Uttarkhanda,* Gorakhpur, V.S. 2042, pp. XCI, 25; K. Krishna Moorthy, 'Commemoration as Reflected in Sanskrit Literature: A Study' in S. Settar and Gunther D. Sontheimer (ed.), *Memorial Stones,* Dharwar, 1982, pp. 4-16; *Mahabharata, Shantiparva,* Chapters 97-8. See also Pierre Filliozat, 'The After-Death Destiny of Hero According to *Mahabharata*' in *Memorial Stones,* op. cit., pp. 3-8.

3. E. Baldwin Smith, *Egyptian Architecture as Cultural Expression,* 1938, pp. 14-5.

4. Francis L.K. Hsu, *Under the Ancestor's Shadow,* London, 1944, pp. 40-3; see also E. Bendann, *Death Customs,* New York, 1930.

5. D.R. Patil, 'The Origin of Memorial Stones' in *Memorial Stones,* op. cit., pp. 50-3.

6. *Satapatha Brahmana,* Chapter XIII, 8.1.4, Delhi, 1970, pp. 1779-83; see also P.V. Kane, *Dharmashastra ka Itihas,* tr. Arjuna Chaube Kashyap, Lucknow, 1975, pp. 1145-49.

7. *Epigraphia Indica,* Archaeological Survey of India, vol. XXI, p. 9.

8. *Dastur Komwar Record,* Register 9, pp. 319, 329, 349 (Jaipur State Records, Rajasthan State Archives, Bikaner).

9. Ibid.

10. Munshi Radha Lal, *Itihas Jaipur* (MS), V.S. 2004, f. 16 (Rajasthan State Archives, Bikaner).

11. H. Goetz, *The Art and Architecture of Bikaner State,* Oxford, p. 64; see also James Tod, *Annals and Antiquities of Rajasthan,* ed. William Crooke, New Delhi, reprint, 1971, pp. 88, 663, 1789.

12. A.K. Roy, *History of the Jaipur City,* New Delhi, 1978, pp. 30-51.

13. For interesting details, see *Toji Records of Imarat Khana,* Rajasthan State Archives, Bikaner.

14. Rawat Saraswat, *Meena Jati ka Itihas,* Jhuntha Lal Nandla, Bassi, V.S. 2025, p. 137.

15. *Satapatha Brahmana,* Chapter XIII, 8.1.

16. Cf. Srikrishna Bhatta Kavikalanidhi, *Ishwarvilas Mahakavyam,* ed. Kavisiromani Bhatta Mathuranatha Shastri, Rajasthan Oriental Research Institute, Jodhpur, 1958 (also see the Introduction by G.N. Bahura).

17. Sanction for the *chhatri* of Sawai Jai Singh, A.D. 1881 in File No. PW 6-8 Archaeology, Rajasthan State Archives, Jaipur.

18. Ibid.

19. S. Jacob, *Jaipur Portfolio of Architectural Details,* Vol. 12, p. 1 (Published by the Maharaja Sawai Madho Singh II, Jaipur, 1898).

20. H.L. Showers, *Notes on Jaipur,* 1916, p. 61.

21. G.N. Bahura in *Ishwarvilas Mahakavyam* (Introduction), Rajasthan Oriental Research Institute, Jodhpur, 1958.

11

Signals from Behind the *Purdah*: Muslim Women During the First Half of the 20th Century

HASSAN IMAM

'Women studies' has been emerging as a distinct discipline in India since a few years; books and articles have come out dealing with the various aspects of this discipline relating to Ancient, Medieval and Modern times. By and large, adequate attention has not been paid to the study of Muslim women. In this paper, we have attempted to project some aspects of Muslim women's views, aspirations, problems, and expectations during the first half of the twentieth century. Our present work is in the nature of a hurried survey of an Urdu journal *Tahzeeb Niswan* which primarily catered to the urban Muslim women in India for decades.

The *Tahzeeb Niswan*, the first journal of its kind, was a weekly published from Lahore since 1898 by Syed Mumtaz Ali, and edited by his wife Mohammadi Begum for the benefit of girls. Its issues were printed at the *Rifah-i Am* Press, Lahore. Its publication continued despite criticism from some quarters: the critics apprehended that the journal would disturb the existing social system. Moreover, printing, paper and other allied problems were somewhat discouraging, but the devoted and hard-working editors overcame these obstacles. After the death of Syed Mumtaz Ali, his sons Syed Imtiaz Ali Taj and Syed Hameed Ali supervised the journal. When their mother Muhammadi Begum, too, passed away in 1908, Wahida Begum became its editor.

Within a short span of time, the journal's popularity grew among Hindu and Muslim women alike. The Hindu ladies praised the editor for her dedication to women's cause.[1] One Hindu lady thought that the journal was meant only for Muslim women, and, therefore, she enquired from the editor whether she could contribute articles like the

Muslim women. The editor gave her consent saying that the journal did not believe in the policy of discrimination. She also informed the Hindu lady that one Hanwanti used to write for the journal in the past, and that she would happily accept the articles of the (unnamed) Hindu lady for publication.[2] In a letter from the widow of Munshi Javed Ali Khan, the *tahsildar* of Bijnor, the editor was informed that she became a widow at the age of fourteen. She narrated the plight of a widow's life and thanked the editor immensely for bringing out a journal which took up the problems of women. According to her, the *Tahzeeb Niswan* had become her lifelong friend and she eagerly waited for its new issues.[3]

The above journal could be a reasonable indicator of the position and the social situation of middle class Muslim women during this period. At the same time, we must point out that males also often contributed to the journal, especially on women's problems and their solutions. Most of the women writers, instead of revealing their names, only used their initials and sometimes requested the editor not to reveal their names. Such writers were mostly concerned with domestic problems. What is significant is that a large number of Muslim women took interest in the journal and got their articles published. The themes and issues discussed and raised reflect Muslim women's views about their social, educational, political and marital problems. Besides, articles concerning political developments of the period such as *Swadeshi* and *Khilafat* movements and the two World Wars were also published. Some female writers also show their awareness of what their counterparts were doing in the Western countries.

Undoubtedly, then, the *Tahzeeb Niswan* steadily became the torch-bearer of women's problems and provided a platform for discussion. By 1930, many Urdu journals came out in its wake. For example: (1) *Auraton ka Akhbar,* a weekly edited by Khwaja Hasan Nizami and Sharif Ahmad; (2) '*Iffat* (monthly) from Delhi under the editorship of Amtul Zohra Begum; (3) *Khatun Mashriq* (monthly) whose editor was Khursheed Iqbal Begum; (4) *Niswani Duniya* from Delhi by Shaukat Ali; (5) *Khatun* from Gwalior whose editor was Mirza Muzaffar Husain and joint editor Noor Jahan Begum; and (6) *Tabligh Niswan* under the editorship of Khwaja Hasan Nizami.

During the first half of the twentieth century, a number of articles were published in the *Tahzeeb Niswan* on the problems of marriage in the Muslim community. It is significant that the question of female education was invariably anchored with that of marriage. In an article by the journal's editor, attention was drawn to a new dimension of the dichotomy experienced by the Muslim society between men and women as a result of the peculiar situation wherein Muslim males had an easy access to Western education as well as exposure to new ideas and values which Muslim women were deprived of.[4] Many males had the opportunity to get higher education in Europe, especially in England, where they interacted with their white colleagues and, on their return, felt frustrated with their semi-literate wives. This gave rise to marital tension, leading to the humiliation of wives at the hands of their Westernized husbands.[5] As an upshot, the editor wrote in another article that some young boys educated in Western institutions started thinking in terms of marrying European ladies (*'mame'*) because the former preferred everything which belonged to Europe. True, the Muslim girls were by and large uneducated, uncultured and ill-mannered, but marriage with European ladies was not the right solution. It cannot be denied that the latter possessed high moral and that they were well-mannered and educated, but these marriages were fraught with social hazards. The European wives would not be able to adjust with their Indian in-laws, and, therefore, the family setup would turn into hell.[6] This might result in the separation of the couple from the extended family. Moreover, the Muslim boys intending to enter into such marriages were asked to consider the consequences that their children would have to face if the European wives did not accept Islam, or followed Islamic tenets casually. Therefore, the (elderly) Muslims must discuss all these issues with the younger generation to dissuade them from acting thoughtlessly in this regard. It is noteworthy that, in the opinion of the author, the real solution for all these problems was to impart proper education to the Muslim girls and adopt measures to uplift their social and cultural outlook so that the young educated boys might be convinced to take a second look at this problem.[7] Someone went to the extreme arguing that if the girls could not be provided with proper education relevant to their marital life, then it was better not to educate the boys, too![8]

The traditional 'cross-marriage'[9] (including cousin cross-marriage) among the Muslims was disapproved for a happy family life. Mutual bickerings between the two families concerned were bound to result in tit-for-tat leading to maltreatment to the wives in such marriages. Women were mainly blamed for this development.[10] The solution offered was that such marriage should take place only after a detailed investigation of the nature, likes and dislikes, etc., of the boy.[11]

For a happy marital life it was advised that the selection of boys and girls should be carried out carefully. Conventionally, emphasis was put more on the girls.[12] For the boys, the only criteria was his education and prospects of employment. No one cared about other qualities such as nature, character, etc.; while for girls, her beauty and fair complexion were the foremost considerations. Only fair complexion and beauty won't do, it was argued, since the girls will keep themselves engaged in fashion, dresses, makeup, and thus they would neglect their duties towards their in-laws.[13] Therefore, it was suggested that the selection of girl should be made on the basis of her deportment and manners; features and fair complexion alone were not sufficient. Further, the ideal Islamic path should be followed by allowing the boys and girls to mutually agree to their marriage. It was necessary that before marriage, the boys and girls should be aware about each other's personality.[14]

Polygamy has been practised in Muslim communities from the beginning of the rise of Islam for which sanction was drawn, rightly or wrongly, from the *Qur'an* and the sayings (*hadis*) of Prophet Muhammad. Muslim women for centuries meekly accepted this institution. It is not surprising, then, that we come across only sporadic and faint observations on polygamy. A woman, whose husband had four wives, narrated her woes to the author of an article. She complained that apart from her five children, she had to look after three children more of her husband from other wives. And, yet, she was not treated well by her husband.[15] The author then explored the situation in other communities and concluded that polygamy was rare in other communities, but it was quite common among Muslims which she did not approve.[16]

Some articles focussed on the problems of divorce. The one reason given for separation was concealment of some details about the girl by her parents which, after marriage, created unhappiness in the family of her in-laws.[17] It was suggested that the proper course was to let the boy and girl know each other for smooth adjustment later. We are not told how this was to be done; at any rate, consent of both the boy and the girl was recommended.[18]

In case of intended divorce, separation often became difficult due to the magnitude of *mehr* generally fixed on the higher side, beyond the boy's earning capacity, which inconvenienced him leading to delay through devious means. Often the husband evaded prompt payment thinking that the ex-wife will exempt him from payment, she being harassed for long.[19]

From the decline of the Muslim power till the emergence of the British rule, it was pointed out, women could not get justice according to the *shari'at* law because men did not fulfil their duties and obligations towards women. To solve this problem amicably, the '*ulama* and the elite classes took steps in this direction. The editor took the initiative to enlighten Muslim women in this respect. He wrote that a proposal was sent to the British Government in this connection by the *Jami'at-ul 'Ulama*. The bill was passed by the government, but a major portion of the original bill was altered. In the original, it was provided that all cases relating to divorce and *khala*', etc. would be decided by the Muslim jurists according to the *shari'at*.[20] This provision of the bill was deleted and in its place it was stipulated that the cases related to divorce would be decided by the civil court, not by the Muslim jurists.[21] The latter had demanded that even in the civil court such cases should be decided by Muslim judges.[22]

Once again, the editor disseminated knowledge about another Act. Before 1939, there was no special law by which the Muslim women could get their *mehr*. To overcome this difficulty, an Act was passed in March 1939 in which provisions were made, based on the *shari'at*, to solve this problem.[23] One of the six provisions of this Act made it easy for the Muslim women to seek their *mehr*. But its implementation became difficult due to *purdah* and illiteracy on the one hand, and complexity in the court procedures and other problems on the other.[24] If the case went in her favour and summons were issued to her ex-husband, the latter would change his address to evade the summons being served. It was, then, difficult for her to trace his new address and get fresh summons issued. Court fees, too, was a deterrent. Sometimes, the woman faced problems to marshall witnesses against her ex-husband. At times, the court issued orders for compromise. Even after compromise, the woman faced similar problems once again. However, this Act made divorce comparatively easier. The editor desired that further measures and facilities be provided to women to solve such problems.[25]

What about the Muslim widows? Not much material is available in the *Tahzeeb Niswan*. In fact, a widow in a letter chastised the editor that while the journal was started for the betterment of women, it hardly gave importance to the plight of the widows.[26] Articles on matters related to better and happy life, personal neatness, affection towards youngsters and elders, conjugal relations, etc. were welcome, but, lamentably, the widow's role in the family was not projected. As an argument, the widow observes that it was embarrassing for her to spruce up herself because the family members would start mocking and passing comments on her. If she showed affectionate attitude, it would give rise to misunderstanding and disparaging remarks. She wished someone from among the Muslim community took up the cause of the widows to eradicate injustice.[27] Another female writer considered the position of the Hindu widow and opined that it was worst. She was not provided with nutritious food; she was asked to fast for the whole month on the occasion of 'Ekadshi'. For her, remarriage was out of the question.[28] She was not allowed to bedeck herself with jewels and wear coloured dresses. Only white *sari* was in her fate. Even perfumes were disallowed, and they were prevented from participating in festivities or marriage ceremony.[29] That's why the Hindu widows preferred to become *sati* rather than die every day in the unjust society which treated them worse than untouchables.[30] The reforms of Raja Rammohun Roy were appreciated, but the position of widows, especially the Hindu ones, had become worse than a *sati* in Bengal.[31] References were made to the Arab society where not much distinction was made between a widow and a married woman. It was concluded that due to the influence of Hindu customs, the position of Muslim women in India had deteriorated.[32]

The *purdah* system was yet another issue which generated discussion in the Muslim community. There was a growing resentment among women who were critical of discriminatory norms. Actually there were two groups of women, the one propagating *purdah* while the other was against this system. These two groups hotly criticised each other. Some thought that *purdah* curtailed women's liberty and that it deprived them of education, knowledge, wealth and personal freedom. Even men published articles in the *Tahzeeb Niswan* on this question. One male wrote criticising *purdah* which was published in the *Awadh Punch*. This was later on reproduced in the *Tahzeeb Niswan*. It was argued that *purdah* was affecting domestic work.[33] But many women supported the custom especially for unmarried girls. However, some tried to prove that *purdah* was not an obstacle to female education and also in the overall development and mental growth.[34] But the critics insisted that *purdah* confined the girls within the four walls of home. Moreover, *purdah* disturbed marital life of those males who wanted to marry a beautiful girl but, due to *purdah*, it was not possible to see her before marriage. This made conjugal life unhappy and miserable.[35]

Shahzad Jahan Begum held moderate views on *purdah*, although she believed in the system itself. But if someone wanted to discard it she welcomed her.[36] The ladies who abandoned *purdah* committed many *faux pas* in social gatherings for which they were ridiculed. This happened because they were not trained how to conduct themselves in a mixed gathering. Therefore, it was suggested that at this initial stage they should be accompanied by male members to rescue them. In her opinion, *purdah* and *niqab* (veil) were two different things.[37]

Sufia Midhat Khanum wrote that in many families where *purdah* was not practised, there were instances when vulgar jokes were exchanged between the brother-in-law (*sālā*) and the sister-in-law (*sālī*).[38]

It was pointed out that the well-educated Muslim girls who courageously abandoned *purdah* and took training in riding, mountaineering, etc., were rebuked by ill-mannered, illiterate and uncivilized women, forcing the former to observe *purdah*. And even those who played with harmonium were not spared by some Muslim women who thought it to be their 'profession' to reprimand such girls.[39]

What is surprising is that some women went to the ridiculous extent of suggesting that young unmarried girls should not show their faces to the women of other families. The argument put forward was that many young unmarried girls born in affluent families lacked manners. They did not learn how to dress themselves properly, nor were they trained how to conduct conversation with others. Therefore, it was not advisable to allow them to expose themselves to women of other families, else the latter might carry tales of their uncultured deportment outside which might degrade the family social status.[40] On the other hand, many educated girls admitted that their perception was unclear over this issue and requested the editor to offer his comments in this regard.[41]

Anywhere differences among the extended family members are bound to arise despite their best efforts. In India, the conflict between the mother-in-law (*sās*) and daughter-in-law (*bahū*) is perennial, which often spills over between the husband's sister (*nanad*) and his wife (*bhābhī/bhāwaj*). From one article we learn how a humble and obedient daughter-in-law was treated heartlessly by her mother-in-law. The latter did not talk affectionately to her and her grandchildren. If a child fell ill for some days, that poor soul was put in a store-room with door closed where he would cry and weep; but the mother could not do anything about it.[42] The daughter-in-law was given shabby dresses to wear which even a poor servant would not accept. One day, her mother -in-law secretly administered opium to her child. She discovered it when she found the child lying listlessly in bed. The mother gave him a medicine which made the child vomit, but it was of no avail. The child ultimately died; but, instead of consoling her, the mother-in-law scolded her severely.[43] In another instance, a daughter-in-law herself described her woeful story. She was married to a Syed boy. Her problem started when her younger sister Abeda Begum came to her in-laws' house. Her mother-in-law did not treat her sister well. She used pejorative words calling her *petu* (a glutton) and reprimanded her for taking airs (*timakna*).[44]

To curtail the frequency and intensity of these conflicts, one Halima Begum suggested that the *nanad* (husband's sister) could play a reasonable role in the *sās-bahū* conflcit syndrome by advising her *bhāwaj* (brother's wife) to adjust herself with the likes and dislikes of the family members to avoid unnecessary confrontation. On the other hand, the *nanad* was expected not to disclose the faults of her *bhāwaj* during the course of her daily family chores to the latter's husband or mother-in-law. Further, the *nanad* was sermonized that Islam did not approve acts that led to dissensions in the family; she was cautioned if she did so she might face similar situation after her own marriage.[45]

Sometimes, the daughter after marriage felt uneasy even in her parents' home. It was observed in an article that earlier it was only the middle class families which were not keen to welcome their married daughters to come and stay with them along with their children fearing disturbance in their set pattern of living. But gradually this disapproval acquired a general phenomenon; even the lower class families adopted this attitude.[46] The author cited her own example — the treatment which she was given at her parents' home, although she was bearing all her expenses except the food. Ultimately, she was told to leave the house.[47] Such cases might not have been numerous; but it must be recognised that this kind of problem did exist.

What about the day-to-day relationship between the husband and wife? What role the husband was expected to play in mitigating family bickerings? Tayyaba Begum thought that generally the wives took care to please their husbands in matters relating to food, clothes and other home affairs, but some were careless in this respect, especially in the selection of the colour and design of their dress. Tiff over such minor incidents created unhappiness in marital life which disturbed the whole family. The wives were advised to avoid such situations by obeying and carrying out their husbands' will. The author gives a few examples: (i) if the husband did not approve that his wife should meet her relatives, she should accept this command; (ii) when he came home after the day's work, she should welcome him, leaving aside all the domestic work; and (iii) in case he fell ill, she should forgo the work schedule and remain by the side of her husband.[48] All these for the obvious reason that without him she did not matter at all. This advice was bolstered up by citing the widespread *hadīs* that if *sijda* (prostration) could be permitted to anyone besides God, it was the husband.[49] But other contributors held different opinion. For example, the editor did not agree with the views of Tayyaba Begum on the position of women. He did not think that wives should be considered their husbands' slaves, with no desire of their own. Nor should they be silenced by husbands. Further, the editor observed that both were equal in society since they complemented each other. Both should respect the likes and dislikes of each other.[50] In one article, it was agreed that every husband desired that his wife would make the home heaven, but it was possible only if he considered it to be his duty to support her to this end. Unhappiness in home was largely due to the failings of the husband, especially when he became careless and did not extend his love and affectionate cooperation to his wife. It was for the husband to guide and make the wife understand about right or wrong rather harbour ill-feelings towards her.[51]

On the other hand, Sufia Saheba Naqvi vigorously attacked men's dealings with women 'on this earth'. She desired that men's social functions should be transferred to women. Till then men had been working and women served them. The time had come when the latter should earn and men serve them. Women would provide them all the facilities that they themselves did not enjoy: the men will not have to observe *purdah,* and they would be given pocket-money and permitted to attend club, watch movies and theatres and visit hotels, etc. After acquiring males' functions, women would not ask them to look after the children, to cook or stitch, etc.[52] They would turn this earth into heaven, if only the women could exercise power. Naqvi concludes that women were not begging for their rights. In fact, they were capable of passing their lives without men, but this was not possible for the latter.[53] This article was an open declaration of gender war; nay, a presentiment of women empowerment. And this should not surprise us: it was published in 1945.

The journal also published articles on other aspects of domestic life such as frugality and the habit of saving, hygiene, recipe, etc. One contributor advised the women of low income groups also to save regularly which one day would accumulate into a large amount and, then, could be used in days of scarcity.[54] Other contributors admitted that women in general had the aptitude for saving which they did out of the money given to them for daily household expenses. They did not receive any pocket-money separately. Therefore, at times, they faced problems while saving. The husbands forced wives off and on to hand over the deposit to them, or they persuaded them to do so under the guile of love by presenting their own problems. Deprived of their deposit, it was not possible for them to buy articles of their own choice.[55] There were instances when wives managed to earn money through manual labour or got some money in gift from their relatives. But it was difficult to keep the money away from husbands' reach once it was known to them. The writer, therefore, sought the advice of the editor where to hide their savings.[56]

Ansa Ibrahim drew the attention of adult women towards personal hygiene. Bad habits like thumb-sucking, nail-biting and putting their hair in their mouth must be shunned because small 'worms' might get into the body system leading to ailments like indigestion, vomiting, loss of appetite, etc.[57]

Begum Nasiruddin Saheba suggested remedial measures for some normal household problems: how to remove spots caused by rain, oil, dust, rust, tea, ink, blood, etc. She also supplied information how to wash a thermos, dining tablecloths, silver pots and shawls.[58]

Often comparisons were made between Indian wives and European ones. A question of a Christian lady prompted a Muslim woman from Chhattisgarh to pose the query: are we better in comparison to European wives? Perhaps the Indian women would answer it in the negative, but the writer did not agree with this impression. For example, it was argued that Indian wives could cook better than the European counterparts. Even the elite and affluent Muslim ladies knew good cooking. On the other hand, cooking in Europe was not done regularly at homes: they preferred to take their meal outside which was easily available in every town at a low rate.[59] Besides, Indian women were more skilled in preparing a variety of designs on clothes which was not possible for European ladies. Zubaida Khanum was sure that such clothes were greatly appreciated by the Europeans even if they were presented a colourful handkerchief. On the other hand, European women enjoyed more liberty. They could attend parties and play games outside their homes. Moreover, on social plane, they did not quarrel like the Indian women.[60]

One set of opinion was that European women were given many rights. They were free to work like men and, yet, they were not allowed to be a 'barrister' in contrast to the American women who were not fettered in this regard. However, in France this restriction was being relaxed. The name of one 'M. Chavin' (sic) was mentioned as 'barrister' who had started practising in the court of Paris in 1901.[61]

It was argued in 1940 that Indian women imitated European ladies' life-style only in connection with fashion. Rafia Khatoon observed that this was not adequate for their emancipation. They must participate in social, political and educational movements like what the European women did. At any rate, it was noted with gratification that Indian women were now coming out of *purdah* and were working not only as teachers, but were taking training in typing and shorthand, etc.[62] An article published in 1945 informed the readers that Mrs. Hijab Imtiaz Ali, the Urdu short story writer, had become a pilot.[63]

It seems that from 1919 onwards, articles pertaining to the position of women in Indian society in general started to be published. Many female contributors took up courage and aired their views uninhibitedly. Qayyum Begum in 1922 did not mince the matter. She observed that women were looked upon as a machine to produce children and do domestic chores only. The whole day they were occupied with cooking, washing and preparing the children to be sent to school, etc. They were deprived of the means of amusement, while the male members of the family could go to clubs and cinema, play games and join social gathering of their friends.[64] The author pleaded with the men to be considerate towards their wives; and the least they should do was to go for the evening walk along with their wives in *purdah* so that the latter's health could be improved.[65]

Even earlier in 1919, an anonymous lady announced that for long women had been tolerating inhuman treatment (*zulm*) in the induced hope that they would be compensated in the other world after death. But now women had become conscious of their rights and duties towards husbands and other family members. The diffusion of this issue demanded that women be educated properly, especially about their correct position enjoined by Islamic laws.[66] Right education would help them in applying their own mind and developing their thinking. She noted that Muslim women had steadily taken to English education at their home and, thus, they had become aware of the English way of life, customs and traditions. The anonymous writer appears to have been well-educated since she refers to the 'freedom movement of women in Europe' started by Henrik Ibsen, the celebrated playwright of Norway. She claimed to have read his plays. Perhaps she was impressed by Ibsen's *A Doll's House.* Further, she revealed that the issue of women's freedom was regularly debated in her home. She declared that she would defy if she was counselled that her likes and dislikes depended on the will of her husband.[67]

Again in 1919, a dialogue between a brother and his sister was published in the *Tahzeeb Niswan* concerning women education. The latter disclosed that her husband did not approve it and he even did not like that educated women should read newspapers. Her brother held that education of women gave rise to dissensions in marital life.[68] God had created women inferior to men; therefore, their only obligation was to bear children. They did not have the right to express their views or ask for their legal rights. But the sister was aware of the rights of Muslim women. She also knew that many social changes were taking place in the Indian society which favoured women emancipation.[69] An anonymous female writer (1922) wailed that men were suppressing their rights even though sanctioned by Islam. At the same time, it was realised that many males were supporting women for equal rights, but the majority was still silent. Zahin Fathpuri from Kanpur requested the editor to clarify women's rights from the Islamic point of view.[70]

Cognizance of preferential treatment given to the son *vis-a-vis* the daughter is also available in the journal. Women felt aggrieved that daughters were neglected with regard to nutritious food while the sons enjoyed everything. Similar was the case with their educational facilities. But the Islamic principle that the daughters would get only one-half of their parents' property was never contested as unjust. The only complaint recorded was that often even this right was not implemented, and when they demanded their legal share it created flurry and tension in the family. Shahzad Jahan Begum, therefore, called upon the fathers to alienate their daughters' share from their property by *wasiyatnama* (will) to avert wranglings after their death.[71]

An important issue was of social consequences of migrant husbands. They went far away from their homes in pursuit of employment. Often they married another girl at the place of their work, neglecting their family. They did not even send money to their wives. This forced the latter to reside in parental home. But it was extremely miserable for those whose parents were not alive. In such cases, it was suggested that the women should be permitted to go in for a second marriage by the *Qazi* (after getting *talāq* or *khala*').[72]

The *Tahzeeb Niswan* also published articles on issues concerning political awareness among Muslim women and their aspirations for higher education. But we postpone these write-ups for some other occasion. However, our present hurried survey establishes one fact that given an opportunity, voiceless suppressed Muslim women could come forward to articulate their problems and demand justice and fairplay. The brave ones did not conceal their names but others, who were comparatively scared, wrote either anonymously or used initials of their names only. Some would just say '*ek dukhiari bahen*' (an anguished sister) or '*mazlum bewa*' (an oppressed widow), etc. But such cases were very few. The female members of reasonably well-educated families were more courageous and outspoken in their views. We can also discern voices of conservatism, or are we mistaken here in assessing them? Perhaps they might have been trying to strike a balance between a variety of strong and mild protestations? Whether radical or mild, it is a fact that no Muslim woman ever asked for reforms in the Muslim Personal Law *per se*; in fact, appeals were made to allow them to get their sanctioned rights within the Islamic parameters.

These appeals were often juxtaposed with the naive belief that Islamic *sharia't* offered equal rights to males and females. Knowledge of European life-style led the Muslim women to civilizational comparisons in terms of values in all these ongoing debates. The editors of the journal must be commended for their forward-looking perceptions. With the passage of time, Muslim women became more exact in their thought-process; they began to see their role in the context of the fast changing social perspectives. The journal had provided them with a platform to rediscover themselves.

NOTES

1. Anonymous, *'Ek Hindu bahen ka khat'*, *Tahzeeb Niswan* (henceforth, *TN*), October 19, 1901, p. 335.
2. Ibid., p. 336.
3. Anonymous, *'Khat'*, *TN*, October 19, 1901, p. 336.
4. Editor, *'Beyāh'*, *TN*, March 16, 1901, p. 83.
5. Ibid., p. 84.
6. Syed Mumtaz Ali, *'European bahuwen'*, *TN*, March 30, 1901, pp. 102-3.
7. Ibid., p. 103.
8. Syed Mumtaz Ali, *'Auraton ki betahzibi ka 'ilāj'*, *TN*, March 23, 1901, pp. 95-96.
9. A form of marriage when one set of brother and sister is married to another set.
10. Editor, *'Beyāh'*, op. cit., p. 83.
11. Ibid., p. 84.
12. Syed Ibn Hasan, *'Ladkiyon ka intekhāb'*, *TN*, March 16, 1940, pp. 253-54.
13. Ibid., p. 254.
14. Ibid., p. 256.
15. Soghra Humayun Mirza (Hyderabad, Deccan), *'Mard ke fra'iz'*, *TN*, October 11, 1930, p. 1017.
16. Ibid., p. 1018.
17. M.A. Samad (Bihar), *'Haqiqat hāl'*, *TN*, January 11, 1930, pp. 44-45.
18. Ibid., p. 45.
19. Ibid., see also Basharat Ahmad, *'Kya khala' men mehr ka sabit hona lazmi hai'*, *TN*, April 5, 1930, pp. 319-21.
20. Maulana Mufti Kifayatullah, *'Qanūn infisākh nikāh'*, *TN*, September 14, 1940, p. 903.
21. Ibid., pp. 903-4.
22. Ibid., p. 905.
23. Abdul Halim Khan (Lahore), *'Muslim tansikh nikah Act'*, *TN*, August 10, 1940, pp. 777-78.
24. Ibid., p. 778.
25. Ibid., pp. 778-79.
26. *Ek Dukhiya Bahen* (An anguished sister), *'Ek bewah bahen ka khat'*, *TN*, August 24, 1901, pp. 268-69.
27. Ibid., p. 269.
28. Rahat Ara Begum, *'Hindu bewāen'*, *TN*, March 15, 1930, pp. 260-62.
29. Ruquiya Begum, *'Bewah'*, *TN*, April 5, 1930, pp. 331-32.
30. Rahat Ara Begum, op. cit., pp. 261-62.
31. Abeda Moin, *'Hamari ghulami ka ek sabab'*, *TN*, April 21, 1945, pp. 243-44.
32. Ibid., p. 245.
33. *Awadh Punch*, *'Main purdah ke khelāf hūn'*, *TN*, March 9, 1901, pp. 78-79.
34. Anonymous, *'Purdah'*, *TN*, May 10, 1919, pp. 289-90.
35. *Bint* (Daughter of) Hafizul Karim Ansari, *'Ladkiyon ka purdah auraton se'*, *TN*, February 2, 1924, pp. 68-70.
36. Shahzad Jahan Begum (Agra), *'Purdah ki nisbat mera khayal'*, *TN*, March 29, 1936, pp. 301-2.
37. Ibid., p. 302.
38. Sufia Midhat Khanum, *'Purdahnashin wa bepurdah khawatin'*, *TN*, September 20, 1930, pp. 934-36.
39. Sufia Midhat Khanum, *'Ladkiyon ka purdah ghair auraton se'*, *TN*, September 27, 1930, pp. 155-56.

40. Ibid., p. 957.

41. Ibid., pp. 958-59.

42. *Bint* Ali Ahmad, *'Mazlum bahu ki faryād', TN,* May 24, 1919, pp. 332-33.

43. Ibid., June 7, 1919, pp. 362-64.

44. Tahera Begum, *'Sas bahu ka jhagra', TN,* August 10, 1901, pp. 252-55.

45. Halima Begum (Patna), *'Meri aziz saheli-sas aur nandon ka saluk', TN,* May 24, 1919, pp. 326-27.

46. Anonymous, *'Suhagin beti maike men', TN,* August 30, 1930, pp. 861-62.

47. Ibid., p. 862.

48. Tayyaba Begum (Hyderabad, Deccan), *'Shauhar ki pasand', TN,* May 17, 1919, p. 307.

49. Ibid., pp. 307-8.

50. Syed Mumtaz Ali, *'Is par hamare kheyalat', TN,* May 17, 1919, p. 303.

51. Anonymous, *'Shauhar bīwī', TN,* April 12, 1919, pp. 227-28.

52. Sufia Saheba Naqvi, *'Mardon ke nam ek khuli chitthi', TN,* December 15, 1945, pp. 801-2.

53. Ibid., p. 803.

54. *Ek kharidar* (a subscriber, Bulandshahr), *'Kefayat Sha'ari', TN,* April 12, 1919, pp. 228-29.

55. Ghain Bano Begum, *'Biwiyan apna rupiya kahan chhupain', TN,* January 18, 1930, pp. 61-62.

56. Ibid., p. 62.

57. B.N. Ansa Ibrahim, *'Bāz buri ādāt', TN,* May 4, 1940, pp. 421-22.

58. Begum Nasiruddin Saheba, *'Kārāmad bāten', TN,* August 18, 1945, pp. 539-41.

59. Sahrai Beyaban (Chhattisgarh), *'Kya ham kisi bat men Europe ki biwiyon se behtar hain', TN,* October 26, 1901, p. 340.

60. Zubaida Khanum, *'European Ladkiyon par hamari fauqiyat', TN,* November 16, 1901, p. 366.

61. Editor, *TN,* March 2, 1901, p. 64.

62. Rafia Khatun, *'Hindustan men niswani taraqqi ka mafhūm', TN,* August 31, 1940, pp. 852-54.

63. Editor, *'Jang aur auraten', TN,* May 19, 1945, p. 328.

64. M. Qaiyyum Begum, *'Auraton ki zindagi', TN,* January 7, 1932, p. 70.

65. Ibid., pp. 7-8.

66. Anonymous, *'Auraten aur Home Rule', TN,* February 22, 1919, pp. 115-16.

67. Ibid., p. 118.

68. Ibid., February 15, 1919, pp. 106-7.

69. Ibid., pp. 108-9.

70. Zahin Fathpuri (Kanpur), *'Tahqīq haq', TN,* March 1, 1924, p. 129.

71. Shahzad Jahan Begum, *'Beti ki haq talafi', TN,* March 15, 1939, pp. 264-65.

72. Zahin Fathpuri (Kanpur), op. cit., p. 129.

12

Classical (Ajanta) Survivals in Medieval Schools of Painting

SOM PRAKASH VERMA

The history of the pictorial art in India before the sixteenth century appears in disconnected pieces — some, like Ajanta, of much grandeur — between which connexions and links are hard to discern. One is not helped by the fact that the surviving examples are often in a deplorable condition and, therefore, any attempt to trace a continuous history by establishing traditions and influences must be treated as tentative.

Ajanta frescoes cover a period of over 500 years of art of classical India, and the earliest group of them is datable about 200 A.D. Varying styles and trends of art evinced in them testify Indian artists' originality and their longing for individuality in expression. Besides, these provide clues to experiments in art-forms and techniques. While the sinuous and living lines of the Ajanta artist defined the contours, tonal modelling is applied in the forms as a reinforcement. It is true that in the early frescoes at Ajanta there is no attempt at defining the contours by modelling, but by the end of the 5th century A.D., there is a clear emphasis on tonal modelling with the gradations of the pigments. Shading applied along the outlines in forms gave an indication of a round solid between the outlines. This may be described as a method of representing mass and volume in classical Indian art. Line and colour work together here for plastic modelling.[1] Even though Ajanta painters did not make use of shadows, as pointed out by Havell, they have attempted roundness in every form with the application of delicate modelling and strength of drawing.[2] No shadows are cast in classical Indian painting as in all Asia painting generally. Rounded plasticity is achieved by modelling the figures, 'by rounding them off with shading in colour, tone and highlights' (Plates 66-7).[3] Methods of shading used in Ajanta conform to the principles seen in early treatises on Indian painting, e.g., *Vishnudharmottara* (*c.* 600 A.D.).[4] Ajanta paintings exhibit the use of dots, and the use of highlight for shading.[5] It would show that the Ajanta painters aimed at achieving relief effect in a two-dimensional plane. Modelling with gradations of pigments resulted in a rounded plasticity, though restrained.

The depth is indicated by an arrangement of figures simultaneously at eye-level and from above, or simultaneously at eye-level and from below, suggesting different planes in one composition. Examples of such composition appear in caves X and XVII.[6] It was an ingenious method of creating a spatial illusion in painting by an arrangement of overlapping planes.[7] This method involved the use of hierarchical perspective in addition to direct view (convergent perspective) and view from above (divergent perspective).[8] Kramrisch defines it as 'multiple perspective'.[9] In the hierarchical perspective the placement of figures and other objects is made in order of their importance in relation to the theme. In such an arrangement, the placement of figures, often in zig-zag order, creates a spatial illusion in painting. In the 'multiple perspective', the bird's-eye view played an important role. Hajek has rightly pointed out that 'it enables us to see what is happening behind the wall or the rock, and in this way an almost physical line is drawn between the nearer and more distant objects.'[10] In fact, the artist has no fixed focal point, nor a vanishing point or a horizon line.[11]

The Ajanta paintings, most of which are narratives of *Jataka* episodes, comprise long panels with space-bands. At Ajanta this effect is achieved through a multiplicity of figures which projected the event forward. Its most outstanding examples are the paintings in cave X, representing 'Shaddanta Jataka'. A rare continuity of this trend can be seen in the Jaina paintings of the 14th century at Tiruparuttikunram, but here we find a lack of appreciation of visual space when compared with the work of the Ajanta artists.[12] An event portrayed at Ajanta in long panels is narrated in a group of units, all complete in themselves. These units while exhibit contacts between the spaces, represent continuity in scene. The relationship between the units is heightened through gestures of hand and facial expression, and the overcrowding of these spaces. Thus the units complete in themselves do not remain isolated in composition. These different units are held by receptacles mostly forming vertical lines comprising architectural columns, hills, trees and the expansion of their foliage, etc.

In the following pages, an attempt is made to trace the continuity of the great tradition of the Ajanta art.

The Ajanta tradition is traceable in cave paintings of 6th-9th century A.D. The important paintings of Badami caves (578 A.D.) are almost ruined, and the remains survive only in one cave. These exhibit a part of a painting, 'Betrothal of Siva and Parvati'. At present there is hardly any trace left of pigments. However, the quality of line imbibing softly curved movements and rounded character, retained in the drawings of a few figures is akin to the Ajanta tradition.[13] Kramrisch finds the thinned modelling in the Badami paintings as an adaptation of the work at Ajanta.[14] The elegant representation of gently poised hands shows its affinity with the Ajanta drawings. The Bagh cave paintings of about 7th century A.D., too, are very close to the last phase of the Ajanta style. In them the figure of Bodhisattva, the method of modelling the figures and gently poised limbs of human body are also very much the same as those at Ajanta (Plate 68).[15]

The Pala school (11th to 13th century) represented by almost exclusively the Buddhist texts (especially the Vajrayana school) retained the Ajanta tradition of plasticity. Miniatures of this school are closely associated with the sculptures of that time, and the linear expression seen in them is closely related to the last phase of the Ajanta painting represented by cave I. There is an emphasis in the Pala miniatures on plasticity and naturalism in drawings the typical examples of which are to be found in the MS *Astasahasrika-Prajnaparamita,* the earliest of which is datable *c.* 1000 or 1080 A.D.[16] It contains 15 miniatures in which the representation of the figures of the Buddha and Bodhisattva and others is imbued with 'wonderfully fluent figure modelling'.[17] Another copy of the same MS is from the 15th regnal year of Rampala (the last quarter of the 11th century).[18] In its miniatures there appears effective use of modelling in forms through sinuous and flowing lines able to suggest volume (Plate 69). Further, the delicate depth and light effect is achieved with the application of colour tones.[19] This method of modelling is characteristic of the Ajanta method, where there is always an effort for achieving relief effect of coloured sculpture. Another copy of the same manuscript, prepared in the 36th regnal year (*c.* 1118) of the same ruler, and illustrated with 18 miniatures, also exhibits the figures of Bodhisattvas modelled after Ajanta style. Losty describes these figures as fully modelled and expressive of volume.[20] He further notices a continuation of this style — marked for sensitive line and modelling — in the illustrations of yet another copy of the above manuscript, dated in the 4th regnal year of Govindpala (1165 A.D.).[21]

Broadly speaking, intrinsic quality is not so high in the Pala miniatures as in Ajanta. Even then, the lines appear imbued with flow and are suggestive of weight and volume and modelled masses in the Ajanta manner.[22] The Pala paintings clearly belonged to the mural tradition as observed by Krishna Chaitanya, with the difference of the dimension reduced to palm-leaf manuscript painting.[23]

Bhattacharya has noticed a MS cover (wooden *patti*) illustrating the Vessantara Jataka of Buddhist palm-leaf manuscript from the Pala school of 11th century A.D., lodged in the National Museum, New Delhi.[24] The images of Avalokitesvara and others exhibit delicate shading carrying the impression of plastic modelling reminding one of Ajanta. In composition also, the method of narration is typically Ajanta. The whole scene is represented in a series of units held by receptacles comprising architectural columns, a wall or a tree.[25]

Another important school of miniature painting was the Western Indian School, which encompassed Gujarat, Rajasthan and Malwa. At first sight there appears little common between this and the Ajanta tradition. However, in the earliest surviving examples of the first half of the 12th century illustrated manuscripts and covers of the latter school show a sort of rudimentary modelling, though it appears finally to surrender to the pure linear means for expression in art. Barrett and Gray say that by the end of the 13th century this major trend governed the art conventions at Western Indian school for another 250 years or so and all attempt on modelling finally disappeared.[26] Thus, the naturalism in the art of classical India, evinced at Ajanta, Badami and Bagh and later in the Pala school, seems to have been totally rejected in the Western Indian school. This trend had already become visible in the Pallava paintings surviving in Jaina caves at Sittanavasal, datable late 8th century A.D. Though these paintings have survived in fragmentary condition, they exhibit figures drawn purely in line without modelling. Also, there appears no attempt at the rendering of rounded effect in forms. Another striking feature of the figures, which drives away its art from the Ajanta tradition, is the depiction of angular projections in the drawings of the body.

The Ellora cave paintings (*c.* 800-900) are close to the Pallava art tradition in exhibiting sharp angular drawings of hips, elbows and other joints of body. In them each joint acts as a halting point. As a result, the action in the figures appears to be jerky, zig-zag, and restricted. The style of projecting angular drawings of the body and purely linear expression in art with no modelling at all are thus two major features of Sittanavasal and Ellora cave paintings which separate them from the main tradition of art at Ajanta.

But at Ajanta itself, towards its last phase, plastic modelling had become restricted. Kramrisch has noticed that in the 'Sibi Jataka' paintings in cave I, the plasticity of modelling has become insipid and the joints of the body become angular.[27] This particular change taking place at Ajanta towards its close becomes partially apparent in the Western Indian sculpture of 800-900 A.D. which show tighter modelling and angular outline; and as we have seen, more noticeably still in the cave paintings at Sittanavasal and Ellora of the same period.[28] This marked change possibly explains a link between the styles of Ajanta and Western Indian school. In the latter, this change is felt in a more emphatic manner but clearly with a variance. There is much truth in Philip Rawson's observation that the last phase of the Ajanta style is closely linked with later styles of palm-leaf manuscripts.[29]

It is yet difficult to trace continuity in the art of painting from the last phase of Ajanta to the known Jaina manuscripts of the Western Indian school datable from 1060 to 1370. There is also no evidence of Hindu manuscripts illustrated in the intervening period, i.e., 600-1100 A.D. The earliest examples of the Pala School (Eastern Indian School) date from *c.* 1000-1080 A.D. Thus we have a gap of almost four hundred years. This makes it difficult to trace the development of the new style based on purely linear means and disposition of angularity in form. Only with the discovery of some new source-material we might be able sometime to fill up this lacuna.

The impact of Ajanta and Ellora mannerism is explicit in the art of the MS covers (wooden *pattis*) of Jaina manuscripts of the 12th century Gujarati school. It is discernible in the representation of human figures, and especially in the treatment of female faces. The Ajanta art traditions are more strongly felt in the floral ornamentation comprising spiral line work with bird and animal figures. The influence of the Ajanta style was thus not entirely lost in the Western Indian school, through which these found their way into the early Rajasthani schools of painting. A good number of painters in these schools belonged originally to the Gujarat (West Indian) tradition.

Coomaraswamy observes that the Rajput [Rajasthani and Hill Schools] paintings though generally small in size are related to the art of wall-painting both in composition and technique. According to him, Rajput miniatures exhibit grandeur when enlarged by photographic projections to many times their original size.[30] These miniatures are really reduced frescoes. He further opines that Rajput painting has no connection with book-illustration:

> Whenever Indian painters desired to illustrate a particular story, as often happened, they prepared a series of portfolio pictures consecutively numbered, and either without any text, or with the appropriate text inscribed behind, or sometimes above or below. Such series are not to be described as illuminated manuscripts, but are like the wall-painting, for example, at Degaldoruwa in Ceylon, if we imagine these transferred to paper and cut up into separate panels.[31]

In technique as well, Rajput painting is precisely akin to fresco technique, notably at Ajanta:

> The same relationship will be made evident if we examine the technique of Rajput painting. We shall find that it is essentially an art of outline, and illustrates, as clearly as the Greek vases or the Minoan frescoes, how drawing and painting can be one and the same thing. The outline, with exception of a few large cartoons apparently in charcoal, is invariably drawn with a brush; this is equally true of the largest and the smallest drawings. The first sketch is freely drawn in red; over this is spread a white priming, through which the red outline shows more or less distinctly. A second outline is then drawn over this with a finer brush, often freely modifying the original sketch. This second outline is highly finished, and contains everything that will appear in the coloured picture. When this outline is complete, the background is coloured, first the sky and buildings, and afterwards the trees. Many extremely interesting drawings are to be met with, that have not been carried beyond this stage. Finally the figures are coloured, and again outlined.[32]

Coomaraswamy observes that the net result of the above methods can be summarized in words used by Herringham to describe the Ajanta frescoes:

> The technique adopted, with perhaps some few exceptions, is a bold, red line-drawing on the white plaster. Sometimes nothing else is left. This drawing gives all the essentials with force or delicacy as may be required. Next comes a thinnish terraverde monochrome showing some of the red through it; then the local colour; then a strengthening of the outlines with blacks and browns giving great precision, but also a certain flatness; last a little shading if necessary.[33]

Coomaraswamy observes that Rajput painting is related to the classic art of Ajanta and is the latest phase of that great tradition which was still developing in the 17th century.[34]

It is relevant to mention that the tenderness, the delicate charm and rhythmic quality and the fervent love expressed in the figures depicted in the Rajput paintings have their sources in the Ajanta art.[35] Consistency of rhythmic lines, soft curves, gently bent postures and rhythmic contours of body are other features which drew Rajput painting close to the Classical Indian art tradition at Ajanta and Bagh (Plate 70). Moreover, in all these schools the depiction is not essentially realistic. In them the quality of realism is subordinated to the ideals of abstract beauty. Rare quality of amazing serenity pervading in the paintings is another common characteristic. Both the art traditions, i.e., Ajanta and Rajput, are religious in character heavily burdened with symbols.

The Mughal school which developed in the 16th-17th century, too, shows traces of Ajanta mannerisms both in technique and composition. Hajek has rightly pointed out that the Mughal method of reproducing volume and mass is similar to that used in the Ajanta paintings (Plate 71).[36] As already pointed out, in this process a thin shading is done along with the outlines leaving the middle region of the form unaffected. It exhibited much definite light and shade modelling. Here the relief effect is heightened with the frequent use of colour contrasts achieved through comparatively darker tones. Hajek indeed argues that Buddhist art at Ajanta played a distinct part in the formation of the Mughal style. He discerns the elements of this great art tradition in the earliest Mughal book-illustrations, i.e., the *Hamzanama,* in the method of the modelling of the eye, and in the softness of the arms.[37] The Ajanta tradition seems to have been carried over through the artists of the Pala tradition (which adapted Ajanta mannerisms), the continuity of which is traced by Goetz in Gwalior.[38] He thinks that the painters from Gwalior region, also employed in the imperial atelier of the Mughals, introduced delicate modelling techniques in the Mughal school. He also feels that the 'lancet' type of eye in the Mughal style is also derived from the Pala art tradition continuing at Gwalior.[39] While the Mughal painters are rarely referred to with their place names in the ascriptions given in their work, Nand Gawalyari is known to have been active at the Mughal atelier.[40]

Hajek also observes the influence of the Ajanta art in the interpretation of space in Mughal miniatures.[41] He notices the so-called 'multiple perspective' in the illustrations of the *Hamzanama.* He holds the view that Ajanta mannerism of interpreting the space appears almost unchanged in the Mughal miniatures even after a gulf of a thousand years.[42] However, the Mughal perspective differs from that seen in Ajanta paintings, as a result of the introduction of new devices of treating the space derived from the European art. Though a direct link between these two schools is difficult to establish, the answer to this problem may be met in the continuity of the Pala art tradition — a carrier of the Ajantan style.

The use of receptacles — a device of breaking up the picture into small units, made by the Mughal painters is reminiscent of the Ajanta style in which groups of figures are held by receptacles. Overcrowding seen in Ajanta paintings employed to establish relationship between the groups or units, is also in the *Hamzanama* paintings. It would not be out of place to mention that in the Persian miniatures plenty of room is allowed in between the groups of figures, but these appear isolated in the absence of the artist's approach to show some kind of relationship between them. The Mughal painters, on the other hand, did succeed in connecting the units through rhythmic movements, gestures and facial expression akin to those employed by the artists of Ajanta. It is true that the Mughal artists showed particular ingenuity in using receptacles with a great success by placing them zig-zag to enhance the receding effect in space.

The superimposition of figures — an Ajantan method of creating the illusion of space in composition — is commonly seen in Mughal pictures. In such compositions the figures are drawn on different planes, one above the other, and thus the figures shown on the higher planes gave an impression of being further away. It suggested vertical perspective in a two-dimensional plane.

An expressive representation of hands and feet seen in the Ajanta art and continuing in the Pala seems to have found its way into the Rajput and Mughal paintings, where its function appears to indicate live action.[43] Moti Chandra has rightly observed that important contributions of the indigenous Indian art to the Mughal school of painting were *mudras* or graceful poses of hands, especially *anjali* (folded hands), *katkamukha* (two fingers extended, the rest closed) and *ardha-chandra* and *patka* (palm with upraised fingers) which are commonly seen in the Mughal pictures portraying human figures.[44]

In the seventeenth century Deccan painting, too, faces are shown in accordance with classical Indian tradition.[45] However, there are also attempts casually made under the influence of European painting to apply darker shade to produce three-dimensional effect. But this attempt largely leaves the consistency of the outline unaffected. In composition as well, Kramrisch finds traces of the Ajanta type of compositions in the Golkunda paintings, where she notices examples comprising long band composition, executed during the mid 17th century.[46] She traces this particular type of composition to the Ajanta cave X, which in turn reminds us of the reliefs on the gate of Sanchi (*c.* 100 B.C.-50 A.D.).[47] Kramrisch further observes that in Deccani examples not only is the narrow band common, the crowded superimposition of figures too occurs.[48]

We may conclude that even if the evidence of the survival of ancient tradition of Indian art in sixteenth and seventeenth century painting is fragmentary, it is not altogether elusive. Certain lines of 'descent' can be identified, though everything is not clear.

NOTES

1. Krishna Chaitanya, *A History of Indian Painting, The Mural Tradition,* New Delhi, 1976, p. 28.
2. E.B. Havell, *Indian Sculpture and Painting,* London, 1980, p. 212.
3. Stella Kramrisch, *A Survey of Painting in the Deccan,* Hyderabad, 1937, p. 19.
4. Stella Kramrisch, *The Visnudharmottaram,* Calcutta, 1928, pp. 8 and 14. Also see Asok K. Bhattacharya, *Technique of Indian Painting,* Calcutta, 1976, pp. 112-5.
5. A. Ghosh, *Ajanta Murals,* New Delhi, 1987, p. 50, 'Plate XLVIII (cave II) demonstrates the use of dots (*bindu*) —a kind of shading achieved by stippling. This technique implies the use of thin brush to prick the surface of painting with innumerable tiny touches. It is a technique similar to that of the pointalists, although the Ajanta artists did not use different colours, as did the impressionists, but only the different shade of the same colour, mostly brown. Stippling was taken recourse to on the edges of a form, with darker colours upon lighter background, to round it off. In terms of the concentration of 'dots', this process of shading gives modelling effects to body-parts by degrees... Except for the very earliest paintings at Ajanta (cf. Plate I), the above mentioned form of shading was abundantly used, though it may not be too visible in the plates due to the finesse of its application.'
   Another technique closely related to the former was the use of highlight (cf. Plates XIII, XXVI and XL).
6. Stella Kramrisch, *A History of Painting in the Deccan,* op. cit., p. 8, pls. II and III; Philip S. Rawson, *Indian Painting,* New York, 1961, pls. on pp. 40-2.
7. Sharman E. Lee, *A History of Far Eastern Art,* London, 1964, p. 114, 'On this shallow stage, space is indicated by movement from below to above, and at the same time by overlapping. The placement of the figures in space is simple, recalling the plain backgrounds of the Gupta sculptures.'
8. Lubor Hajek, *Indian Miniatures of the Mughal School,* London, 1960, p. 28.
9. Stella Kramrisch, *A Survey of Painting in the Deccan,* op. cit., p. 8.
10. Lubor Hajek, op. cit., pp. 28-9.
11. Ghosh, op. cit., pp. 50-1.
12. Rawson, op. cit., p. 78, illustration p. 79.
13. Rawson, op. cit., p. 65.

14. Kramrisch, *A Survey of Painting in the Deccan,* op. cit., p. 69.

15. Vincent A. Smith, *A History of Fine Art in India and Ceylon,* Oxford, 1930, p. 108, 'The vigorous school of art which produced the Ajanta frescoes did not confine its operations to the caves at that place. Several similar excavations near Bagh, a village or decayed small town in the Gwalior State, situated on an ancient road connecting Gujarat with Malwa, exhibit traces of a set of works resembling in general style the Ajanta paintings, and at one time of almost equal importance.' Also see Rawson, op. cit., p. 51, illustration p. 50 ('Dance scene').

16. Jeremiah P. Losty, *The Art of the Book in India,* London, 1982, p. 30, No. 2, illustration p. 25.

17. Ibid., p. 30.

18. Bodleian Library Oxford, MS Sansk. a.7. It is dated (*c.* 1097) 15th regnal year of the Pala King Rampala.

19. Douglas Barrett and Basil Gray, *Painting of India,* Laussane, 1963, p. 53, illustration p. 52. However, Losty (op. cit., p. 32, No. 5) thinks that the covers of this MS were painted later in the 12th century and these represent superb miniatures of Napalese manuscript painting.

20. Losty, op. cit., p. 32, No. 6, 'It is the images of the Bodhisattvas which are the special glory of this manuscript, nine of them in all, drawn with a perfectly controlled line fully expressive of volume, so that even where the paint has flaked on the yellow and white Bodhisattvas the figures still seem fully modelled.'

21. Ibid., p. 33, No. 9, 'It has 15 illustrations...The style is a continuation of the Rampala style and is still at a high level of sensitivity in line and modelling, although exhibiting the standard conventions of the standing and lying Buddha with thronebacks and cushions.'

22. Krishna Chaitanya, *A History of Indian Painting, Manuscript, Moghul and Deccani Traditions,* New Delhi, 1979, pp. 6-7.

23. Ibid., p. 6.

24. Asok K. Bhattacharya, 'An early Pala MS cover with Vessantara Jataka scene', *Roopa-Lekha,* Vol. XXXIV, New Delhi, 1965, p. 19.

25. Chaitanya, *A History of Indian Painting, Manuscript, Moghul and Deccani Traditions,* op. cit., p. 3, pls. 1-2.

26. Barrett and Gray, op. cit., p. 55.

27. Kramrisch, op. cit., p. 66; Krishna Chaitanya, *A History of Indian Painting, The Mural Tradition,* op. cit., p. 28, 'In the last phase, the line loses its suppleness, pointing to the angular and brittle contours of the murals of Ellora.'

28. Barrett and Gray, op. cit., p. 55.

29. Rawson, op. cit., pp. 50-1.

30. Ananda Coomaraswamy, *Rajput Painting,* Vol. I, Delhi, second edition, 1976, p. 3; also in his 'Rajput Painting', *The Burlington Magazine,* No. CVIII, Vol. XX, London, March 1912, p. 16. Also see Raphael Petrucci, 'Rajput Painting', *The Burlington Magazine,* No. CLVII, Vol. XXIX, London, May 1916, p. 76. But see Smith, op. cit., p. 255, where he writes that Rajput painting is identical with Mughal school and is Persian in origin.

31. Coomaraswamy, *Rajput Painting,* op. cit., p. 4.

32. Ibid.

33. Ibid. See Christiana J. Herringham, 'The Frescos of Ajanta', *The Burlington Magazine,* No. LXXXVII, Vol. XVII, London, June 1910, p. 138. Also in Smith, op. cit., p. 98.

34. Coomaraswamy, *Rajput Painting,* op. cit., p. 315.

35. Raphael Petrucci, 'Rajput Painting', *The Burlington Magazine,* No. CLVIII, Vol. XXIX, London, May 1916, p. 79.

36. Hajek, op. cit., p. 30.

37. Ibid., p. 45.

38. Hermann Goetz, 'Die Malschulen des Mittelaters und die Anfange der Moghul-Malerei in Indien', *Ostasiatische Zeitschrift,* Berlin, N.F., III, 1926, pp. 173-87. Cf. Chaitanya, *A History of Indian Painting, Manuscript, Moghul and Deccani Traditions,* op. cit., p. 59.

39. Ibid.

40. Cf. Percy Brown, *Indian Painting under the Mughals, A.D. 1550 to A.D. 1750,* New Delhi, 1981, p. 198.

41. Hajek, op. cit., p. 45.

42. Ibid., p. 29.

43. Coomaraswamy, 'Hands and Feet in Indian Art', *The Burlington Magazine,* No. CXXX, Vol. XXIV, London, January 1914, p. 211, figs. 8, 11-4. Compare S.P. Verma, *Art and Material Culture in the Paintings of Akbar's Court,* New Delhi, 1978, p. 33, pl. XXVI.

44. Moti Chandra, *The Technique of Mughal Painting,* Lucknow, 1946, p. 64. Also see Brown, op. cit., p. 161, 'In all Indian art, the pose and expression of the hands has received special attention; in the Buddhist frescoes this is very noticeable, while with the Hindus the *mudra,* or symbolism of the hands, is a deep study, as revealed in much of their sculpture and painting. The same appreciation of the character underlying these members animated the Mughal miniaturist, and he made good use of it in his portraiture.'

45. Kramrisch, op. cit., p. 149.

46. Ibid., p. 168, pls. XVI-XVII.

47. See 'Visvantara Jataka' (on the north gate), and 'Visit of Asoka to Bodhi tree at Bodh-Gaya' (on the east gate). For their reproductions, see Sir John Marshall and Alfred Foucher, *The Monuments of Sanchi,* Delhi, 1982, Vol. II, pls. 21 (details on pls. 23, 25), 39 (details on pl. 40).

48. Kramrisch, op. cit., p. 149.

13

Women and the Temple in Medieval Andhra: A Note

A. PADMA

The temple is one of the major institutions of organised Hinduism. In medieval Andhra, the temple emerged as a very powerful institution akin to feudal estates. This paper is an attempt to examine the emergence of the temple as a result of the politico-socio-economic factors of medieval Andhra, and the role of women in its development.

The period from the 10th to 13th centuries in medieval Andhra witnessed many changes in political, social and religious sectors. This was a time when there was no strong centralised state. Instead, the region was divided into a number of minor political units. It was only in the later half of the 12th century that the Kakatiyas rose to power and established their control over almost the whole of Andhra.

During this period, the traditional caste system lost its significance. Each caste was further divided into a number of sub-castes. The hereditary professions based on caste became impracticable. Instances of Brahmins entering into administrative services were quite common. However, they commanded respect in the society as owners of *agraharas* or land grants given to them by the kings.

Though the economy was primarily agrarian, the period starting from the 11th century in Andhra was marked by steady growth of craft-production and trade activity. Occupations increased within each caste which got slowly transformed into distinct artisan communities. A hectic corporate activity was also witnessed in this period. We get evidence of the formation of guilds which regulated trade, craft and banking. Prominent among them were the *Pekkandru*, the *Nakaramu*, the *Nanadesi* and the *Telikivevuru*. In addition, certain corporate bodies also existed which were professional as well as communal, such as *Nayakulu, Mahajanulu, Antyajulu, Sanivaru, Srivaishnavulu,* etc.[1] However, most of their activities were related in some way or the other to the temple. Due to this development, the Vaisyas and the Sudras were able to enhance their economic status. The temple economy was also responsible for this change to a large extent.

Thus, there was a gradual transformation in the society. The old traditional order was seen widening and becoming broadbased with the rise of some social groups coming into prominence. They became powerful backed by money power, but, in the traditional hierarchy, their status was not high. Slowly there started a movement which was not favourable to the privileged castes. This is proved by the sudden rise in the status of artisan and merchant communities in terms of wealth, and the rise of Sudras to political power. Political power now was being acquired by the hitherto unprivileged social groups. Their claims of descent from the ancient Kshatriya families show their eagerness to seek higher recognition within the caste framework.

This cultural turmoil gave rise to new beliefs and new cults. Thus we witness sectarian Bhakti movement entering Andhra which was oriented towards Lord Siva and Vishnu. A plethora of temples, music and dance festivals and pilgrimages constituted the core of this movement.[2] The establishment of the temple was the result of the growing desires of the religious orders to reorganise their systems on the basis of new social values and material needs. The theistic sectarian development and propagation further resulted in shaping the temple syndrome into a very complicated pattern. They became the centres of Bhakti cult as represented through Puranic ideology.[3] These received support from all sections of the society. This religious expediency in the society resulted in the introduction of various rituals in the temples. Programmes of music and dance were added to popularise the ritual services. These rituals reflect the socio-cultural life of the period. Further, they extended the demand of numerous commodities for these rituals. Thus, the temples served as markets for internal trade through fairs and *tirunallu.* They provided ample work for the artisans of various communities. Big temples even employed them permanently.

The introduction of different rituals and other services in the temple needed a compact administrative set-up within itself.[4] The temple hierarchy was three-fold: the higher level comprised the priestly order, below which were the non-priestly attendants. The third category was the managerial staff. Their respective functions included performing the daily and special services of worship to the deities, maintenance of temple and providing necessary articles for worship; and lastly, that of the supervision over all the affairs concerning the temple.

The resources for maintenance of the temples mostly came through land grants and monetary donations by all the strata of the society, ranging from the king to the common people. Women, too, played a great role in this movement irrespective of their social and economic limitations. Women belonging to different sections of the society liberally came forward in giving various grants to the temples, such as villages, land, cash, gold ornaments and domestic animals.

Not only as donors, women also played an integral role within the temple administrative set-up as employees. Among the 72 temple *Niyogikas*, some functionaries were women such as the dancers, singers, *chamara*-holders, *Dwadasa seva vilasinis*, instrument players, *devadasis*, etc. They were given their share from the temple property either by way of cash or a part of the *prasada* offered to the deity. Inscriptional evidence suggests that on many occasions lands of fixed measure were also allotted to each of these temple employees.

An inscription from Simhachalam temple dated A.D. 1324 mentions that a lady named Kunasani, the daughter of Marasiha Mukhari, was appointed as *chamara*-holder for which she got a daily share in the *prasada* of 1 *kunchamu*. In the same grant, another woman, named Pratasani, is mentioned to have been appointed to prepare *rangoli* in the temple compound on similar payment.[4] Another inscription from the same temple mentions that a lady Akkama employed a girl Naruvu Nachchapa on a salary of 5 *padmanidhi gandamadas* (gold) and *prasada* of 1 *kunchamu* for performing services like applying sandalwood paste, holding mirror, preparing *rangoli*, etc.[5]

These lady temple employees referred to as *Dwadasa seva vilasinis* were required to perform 12 specific services to the temple deity daily: 1) cleaning the compound; 2) applying cowdung; 3) decorating the surroundings with colourful *rangoli*; 4) tying *torana* to the doors; 5) cleaning vessels required for worship; 6) to bring water; 7) to bring flowers; 8) to make garlands; 9) keeping ready the items of worship; 10) to keep ready the *dhoopa* sticks and *harati* plates; 11) to prepare sandalwood paste and 12) to pour oil in lamps.[6]

An inscription, dated A.D. 1157, at the Kodandarama temple mentions that a lady temple employee (*dwadasa seva vilasini*) should get a share of 24 *khandikas* in the temple's landed property.[7]

The above services in the temple were grouped under the category of *Angabhogamu* to the deity. In addition, there was another service termed as *Rangabhogamu*, that is, entertainment for the divinities, generally performed by a special unit of temple employees, both men and women. In this category were included singers, dancers, instrument players and the *devadasis*. Generally, they were referred to by the term *sani*. This word seems to have originated from the word *swamini*, meaning a respectable lady. In the medieval period, this term was used to denote the household ladies as well as the lady temple professionals, including the *devadasis* and *devaganikas*. Under these circumstances, no clear indication of the class or status of a woman can be made based on this term alone. However, the *devadasis* or *devaganikas* were dedicated to the divinities of the temple.

The *Panditaradhya Charitra*, a contemporary literary work, mentions the story of a woman *Kanakalatha* who was dedicated to Lord Siva as *devaganika* when she was 10 years old. Her job comprised arranging programmes of music and dance within the temple.[8] Occasionally, these girls entertained the devotees and the temple authorities, too. In addition, they were also asked to supervise the music and dance unit of the temple. An inscription from the Mukhalingam temple records the appointment of 2 *devaganikas* by the king Ananthavarma Chodaganga and conferring on them the headship over the singers and dancers of the temple.[9] Generally, these women did not marry; they spent their life in the service of the temple only.

The term *devadasi* also means a female in the service of the temple.[10] Their main function appears to be that of providing entertainment to the divinities. Among them there were instrument players also. They were experts in their arts and existed as one single unit in the temple under the charge of one *mattuvan* (dance master). Not only women but men, too, were admitted into such units. Hence, a combined term *sanulu-manulu* was given to them. We come across this term frequently in the inscriptions of medieval Andhra during the period of our study. Another function of this group was that of supervision over the temple properties and donations made to the temples. Generally, these professionals were permanent residents of the temple and quarters were provided to them in the vicinity of the temple.[11] They were given *vrittis* of land for their survival. Their marital status is not clear. However, some inscriptions record grants made by the family members of the *devadasis* which indicate that they did marry occasionally and had children.[12]

As regards the social strata from which they were drawn, our information is scanty (see *infra*). In the inscriptions of the temples they are mentioned in the backdrop of the temple syndrome, more emphasis being laid on the socio-economic set-up of the temple rather than projecting their social origins. However, they must have enjoyed a respectable position in the society because evidence of grants made by their relatives claiming identity through them is available to us.[13] We also have evidence of the women temple employees themselves making grants of land as well as monetary endowments to the temples.[14]

As for their social origins, we get some evidence from the temples of the coastal Andhra. An inscription from the Simhachalam temple, while referring to an agreement reached among the associations of the temple girls, says that the agreement was obligatory for the whole of the *sudra* caste.[15] The second evidence from Srikurmam refers to the dedication of 30 daughters of *kayastha* families of Kalinga *mandala* by the king.[16] This aspect further gains support from the fact that each of the temple servants was offered a share in the *prasada* daily. This could serve as a means of livelihood for the poorer sections of the society, whereby at least one member (girl) from the family got *bhukti* throughout her life for herself as also for her family.

These girls were closely involved with the temple administration and their services to the temple became more and more important. They soon realized the need for an association which could protect their rights. We come across such associations existing in the temples of early medieval Andhra for which various terms were used: *sani munnuru, sanulu-manulu, sanula samayamu, sampradayamu sanulu,* etc. Apart from their regular chores, these girls through the above associations played an active role in maintaining the temple properties. Their general functions seemed to be the protection of the temple property, leasing out the temple lands, maintaining the title-deeds of each of the employees, headship over the cultural unit of the temple, etc. Individual *vrittis,* however, were allotted by the donors to each of the members of these associations. An epigraph from Kotyadona mentions a grant of a village Jonnapraluru to the temple of Bhimesvara kept under the protection of *sanulu-manulu* so that they could carry out the ritual services to the divinities. The donor was the king, Tribhuvana Malla Choda.[17]

On most occasions, these corporate associations of lady temple professionals were appointed as co-executors of the grants along with the other important functionaries of the temples, such as the *sthanapathi* and the priests. This alone indicates the respect which they commanded in the temple establishment. An undated epigraph from Bhavanarayana temple at Baptala indicates this practice. It also records the names of individual girls to whom the work was assigned and their acceptance.[18]

Generally, each temple had a single association of the temple girls. However, big Vaishnava temples in medieval Andhra maintained more than one such associations. As per the details available through an incomplete record from the Simhachalam temple, it is understood that these associations made an agreement among themselves, stating that if anyone harmed the harmony of the association, such member shall be expelled. This agreement was said to have been made in the presence of the temple priests and Srivaishnava brahmins.[19]

Thus, it is evident that these lady temple professionals by their services in the temple belonging to both *anna* and *rangabhoga* of the deity, either singly or as corporate body, played major role in the administrative set-up of the temple together with the other priestly and managerial staff.

To sum up, under the large cover of the temple, the female employees became important due to the nature of their duties and the significance attached to them. Slowly, they emerged as one dominant group in the affairs of the temple. Moreover, they became experts in the field of arts, music and dance. Their profession was viewed with utmost religious sentiments and great delicacy. Marco Polo who visited Orugallu (Warangal), the capital of the Kakatiya kingdom during the reign of the queen Rudramadevi, described this custom of dedicating girls to the temple service: 'They have certain abbeys in which are gods and goddesses to whom many young girls are consecrated; their fathers and mothers presenting them to that idol for which they entertain the greatest devotion. And when the (monks) of a convent desire to make feast to their god, they send for all those consecrated damsels and make them sing and dance before the idol with great festivity. They also bring meals to feed their idol withal, that is to say, these damsels prepare dishes of meat and other good things and put the food before the idol, and leave it there a good while, and then the damsels all go to their dancing and singing and festivity for about as long as a great Baron might require to eat his dinner. By that time they say the spirit of the idol has consumed the substance of the food, so they remove the viands to be eaten by themselves with great jollity. This is performed by these damsels several times every year until they are married.'[20]

In the later period, their status became degraded and they were completely equated with the *bhogastreelu* whose profession was mere entertainment. For the first time, an epigraph dated A.D. 1291 from the Simhachalam temple mentions the appointment of 4 *lanjalu* (female prostitutes) in addition to two lady singers from *sampradaya sanulu* group by a noble of Eastern Ganga king.[21] This was probably due to the growing influence of the priests, landlords, and other dominating sections of the society widely patronising the temples together with its attendants. Hence, these girls of the temple also had to seek protection and coverage under them. Moreover, the Virasaiva movement which was gaining ground in Andhra just at the time, encouraged free sex among the Saivite *jangamulu.* Thus their traditional respectable status and role in the temples in the long run degenerated to mere *bhogamu* of the temple patrons and priests.

NOTES

1. C.V. Ramachandra Rao, *Administration and Social Life in Medieval Andhra Under the Later Eastern Gangas and Suryavamsa Gajapathis (A.D. 1038-1538)*, Nellore, 1976, p. 295.
2. K. Satyanarayana, *A Study of History and Culture of Andhras,* Vol. II, New Delhi, 1983, p. 341.
3. M.G.S. Narayanan and Veluthat Keshavan, 'Bhakti Movement in South India' in D.N. Jha (ed.), *Feudal Social Formation in Early India,* Delhi, 1987, p. 361.
4. K.V. Subrahmanya Aiyer (ed.), *South Indian Inscriptions* (henceforth *S.I.I.*), Vol. VI, Delhi, 1986, No. 707, pp. 304-05.
5. Ibid., No. 1099, p. 442.
6. Alladi Vaidehi, *Andhrula Sanghika Aardhika Charitra* (*Madhyayugamu*), Hyderabad, 1978, p. 62.
7. *S.I.I.*, Vol. X, No. 74.
8. Palkuriki Somanatha, *Panditharadhya Charitra* (ed.), Chilukuri Narayana Rao, Chennapuri, 1974, pp. 188-200.
9. *S.I.I.*, Vol. V, No. 1010.
10. Usha Naik and Aloka Parasher, 'Temple Girls of Medieval Karnataka', *Indian Economic and Social History Review,* 1986, Vol. XXIII, No. 1, pp. 63-92.
11. *S.I.I.*, Vol. IV, No. 989.
12. For example, Inscription No. 664 in the *S.I.I.*, Vol. X, refers to a grant by the father of the *gudi sani,* and No. 117 in the *S.I.I.*, Vol. V, mentions

the grant by the husband of the temple *sani.* No. 1053 in the *S.I.I.*, Vol. V, mentions the grant made by the daughter of the lady temple employee.

13. Alladi Vaidehi, op. cit., pp. 60-1.

14. For instance, grants recorded in the *S.I.I.*, Vol. bearing nos. 1026, 1049, 1094, 1102, 1264, etc. were made by the lady temple servants themselves.

15. *S.I.I.*, Vol. VI, No. 1202.

16. N. Ramesan and N. Mukunda Rao, *Temple Inscriptions of Andhra Pradesh,* Hyderabad, 1980, No. 264, p. 187.

17. *S.I.I.*, Vol. VI, No. 610.

18. Ibid., No. 200.

19. Ibid., No. 1202.

20. K.A. Nilakantha Sastri, *Foreign Notices in South India from Megasthenes to Ma Huan,* Madras, 1939, p. 171.

21. *S.I.I.*, Vol. VI, No. 904.

14

Colonialism and Ethnic Identities in India (19th to Early 20th Century)

KAMLESH MOHAN

The British imperial formation in India was underpinned by the persistent search for a theory and method for understanding, categorising, and hierarchizing the bewildering complex of Indian civilization and culture in the scale of world civilization. Explaining the pragmatic concerns underlying this ambitious project, which had begun with the wide-eyed curiosity of the early Orientalists and ended with the pursuit of 'scientific and historical goals' by the colonial administrators, B.S. Cohn has remarked:

> This information gathering was needed to create or locate cheap and effective means to assess and collect taxes, maintain law and order and it served as a way to classify groups within the subject society. Elites had to be found within Indian society who could be made to see that they had an interest in the maintenance of British rule. Political strategies and tactics had to be created and codified into diplomacy through which the country powers could be converted into Allied dependencies. The vast social world that was India had to be classified, categorized and bounded before it could be hierarchized.[1]

It is a comprehensive statement of the slowly evolved agenda of the British imperialists for ruling their fast expanding empire in India. It included the development of an administrative system capable of exerting greater social control, later on to be geared for the colonialization of Indian economy.[2] The groundwork for such an ambitious imperialist enterprise was done by a large number of Orientalists, Christian missionaries and British administrators-cum-ethnographers. However, this paper is primarily concerned with the role of the colonial ethnographer whose work started immediately after the Revolt of 1857 and was formalized in the last three decades of the 19th century and the first three decades of the 20th century.

My argument in this paper is that the Indological discourse — whether Orientalist, Missionary or Empiricist-Utilitarian—had played a crucial role in the formation of identity of Indians on the twin basis of religion and caste. It shall entail a brief discussion of the motives and changing goals of the British conquest, penetration and mastery of India. It shall also require an analysis of the process how the imperial rulers manipulated their growing knowledge of the multiple religious traditions, institutions and composition of the Indian society and the existing low key dichotomies for defining and fixing the people in rigid primordial social categories through gazetteers, ethnographies and census reports.

I

In order to understand the changing perception of Indian society in the British writings from mid-eighteenth to early twentieth century, it is essential to keep in mind the relationship between the goals and the extent as well as nature of the British control over the Indian territories.[3] This particular issue had determined the approaches to the study, understanding and projection or representation of the subject society. During the period from 1757 to 1785, the major priority before the officials of the East India Company in Bengal was to frame an administrative system, suited for the twin purposes of maintaining law and order and generating a regular income to support the administrative, military and commercial activities of the Company and to earn profit for its owner. Besides the task of assessment and regular collection of land revenue, the British officials had realized the necessity of acquiring considerable detailed knowledge of the structure of Indian society and of the mode of governing the people. With the extension of the Company control over Madras, Maharashtra and upper India, its officials were obliged to deal with a wide range of states. In order to perform the dual task of conquest, consolidation and control through diplomatic dealings, they had no choice but to broaden their scope of information such as knowledge of Indian political history, the internal political structure of Indian states and revenue structure of rural society.

With the rapid expansion of East India Company's territories in the last decade of the eighteenth century (which reached a decisive stage with the defeat of the Marathas in 1818), the British became increasingly aware of the bewildering variety of people's history, social customs and religious practices, political forms and systems of land tenure in the Indian subcontinent. In these circumstances, it became difficult to sustain the mid and late eighteenth century myth of "an undifferentiated Orient characterized by rectilinear simplicity of its social structure, the immutability of its laws and customs, and the primitive innocence of its people."[4]

The sociological information about the peoples of India lay scattered haphazardly in the revenue reports or historical works of the British officers namely Thomas Munro,

John Malcolm, Colonel Tod and Mountstuart Elphinstone who had acquired first hand information about some aspects of Indian society while handling either land settlements in Salem (Madras), or diplomatic relations with Mysore, Rajasthan and the Marathas.

Broadly speaking, three major perspectives on Indian society had crystallized by the end of the eighteenth century: the Orientalist, the Missionary and the Empiricist-Utilitarian. Each had evolved a characteristic view, tied to the assumptions or bias underlying their respective perceptions of India and also to the roles which foreigners including observers, missionaries, Company officials and administrators played in India. As a detailed discussion of the Orientalist and missionary perspective on Indian society is not relevant for colonial ethnography, brief references would be made to it while analysing the role of official-Empiricist in the construction of religion and caste.

THE OFFICIAL-EMPIRICIST

Like the Orientalists, the advocates of the Empiricist-Utilitarian approach, too, belonged to the official hierarchy and thus had a stake in bolstering the image of the Raj and its perpetuation. Both shared common views regarding the essential principles and institutions of Indian society. In their view, religion as the fundamental principle divided the Indian society into two major segments: Hindus and Muslims. These two religious communities were further subdivided into sects or orders and castes or social ranks. Their major difference lay in their method of reconstructing the social formations. Unlike the Orientalists and Missionaries, who had based their vastly opposite interpretations on studies of scriptures, the civilian-turned-ethnographers had collected and codified information about the actual social situation through empirical research. While the Oriental view had identified *varna* as the basis of social organisation, the surveys, through questionnaires by assistants of administrators, found *jatis* or castes. In the case of long term intensive field work in one place, 'brotherhoods' became the basic categories.[5] Thus, official studies from an empiricist angle focussed their enquiries on the institution of caste, its customs, theories of its origin and nature of Indian society.

The institution of caste, which has been considered unique to India and a distinctive feature of Hindu religion from the time of Rev. Smith and James Mill, was projected as a concrete, fixed and measurable entity by the colonial ethnographers. In their opinion, Indian society was a motley collection of castes and its picture varied in accordance with the given time and space. Each caste could be labelled and pigeonholed with the help of quantification method.[6] In order to simplify the pattern of the complicated caste system, Herbert Risley, the Commissioner of Census of India 1901, who had written its chapter on caste, compressed the data on 2,000 castes into many types: tribal, functional, sectarian castes (formed by crossing), national castes and castes formed through change of customs.[7] Using the double criterion of race and caste, he began his classification with the Dravidians as the inferior racial type and ended with Aryan as the highest type of race, but sometimes confused one with the other. The other ethnographers, too, developed their classification systems but Risley's is the most well-known.

These colonial ethnographers were keenly interested in the origin of castes not from the historical point of view but that of utilitarian-imperialist. Unlike the Orientalists, who lauded the role of caste for providing stability to Hindu society, they had manipulated their knowledge on pet theories to prove that social system of India was primitive. Elaborating this point, L.S.S. O'Malley observed, '...because men were not regarded as individuals but as groups of men related by the reality of fiction or blood. The interests of individuals are subordinate to those of the group.'[8]

In their search for the origin of castes, the ethnographers took note of the *varna* theory based on scriptures but racial, tribal or occupational theories fascinated them more. John C. Nesfield, who had worked on the *Census of India* (1881), developed 'division of labour' theory.[9] However, his colleague and contemporary, Denzil Ibbetson, found the theory of 'tribal origin' more logical.[10] Herbert Risley, whose *Tribes and Castes of Bengal* had pioneered the genre of studies under this title for almost every province of British India, had advocated the racial theory of the origin of caste, i.e., interaction of two racial types — white and black or Aryans and Dravidians.[10a] O'Malley, while endorsing Risley's theory of racial origin of castes, had also speculated about the origin of *Panchamas,* the lowest class of Hindu social system in South India. Thus, he had established the principle of hierarchy which underpinned the organization of Indian society.[11]

W. Crooke, who had initiated the trend for eclectic theories, is notable for rejecting the dominant ethnographic approach, emphasizing the immutability and permanence of caste as an institution. In his view, caste was neither peculiar to Hinduism nor to India. Much more social than religious in its nature, 'this occupational or hereditary system of caste...prevailed and still prevails all the world over.'[12] The preference for eclectic theories of origin of caste took its final form in the hands of J.H. Hutton,[13] the last of the British official ethnographers and census commissioners.

Thus, it can be said that the administrative-empiricist view of caste had not only flowed from the methods used for collection of information but also reflected the anthropological interests and theories of the period 1870-1910. For example, Crooke's *The Tribes and Castes of the North Western Provinces and Oudh* in four volumes (1896) devoted considerable space to 'marriage rules' and subdivisions of castes, which are termed as exogamous groups along with an account of their customs and beliefs.

II

The aphorism 'knowledge is power', which had served as the guiding star for the British Orientalists in their search for and construction of Indian languages, religious literature, law and science, acquired an instrumental value for the imperialist projects in the hands of colonial ethnographers-cum-civilian administrators. The colonial ethnographers had inherited the potent tool of comparative method from the Orientalist scholars particularly James Frazer, J.Z. Hozwell, Alexander Dow, William Jones, N.B. Halhed, Charles Wilkins, John B. Gilchrist and C.P. Brown, who had created a theory and method for hierarchizing India into a model of primitive society — an 'archaic civilization, or a museum of ancient practices, from which earlier stages of universal history could be recovered.'[14] Based on their concept of linear directionality of things, ideas and institutions, it could be used 'to establish regression, decay, decadence, the movement through time, away from some original starting point, a "Golden Age" in the past.' The decline rather than the progress model was to be increasingly applied by European Orientalists and Empiricist-administrators for positive and negative interpretations of Indian civilization. It seems that the image of India as a vulnerable territory, subjugated by successive conquerors, became a major explanation for its decadence and retrogression.

Believing that this process of decline could certainly be reversed with the intervention of their civilizing or modernising mission, the civil administrators-cum-ethnographers focussed their attention on the study and analysis of the vast social world of India before it could be compartmentalized and hierarchized for multiple subjugation of the country. To control Indian society without the use of naked, brutal force, i.e., to arrange its acquiescence or 'hegemony', it was essential to locate it in taxonomic systems. With this long term politico-economic objective of the multiple subjugation of India, the colonial state initiated the cumbersome process of counting through ethnographic surveys, census maps and statistical data for constructing and pigeonholing Indians into primordial identities and racial typologies by manipulating scientific theories and methods.

During the period 1870s to 1920s, the British administrators and policy-makers as interpreters and executors of the colonial state's objectives proposed to harness qualitative and quantitative methods. While establishing rational connection between precise knowledge and social control, they were to give statistical content to the 'imagined communities' in B. Anderson's phrase.[14a]

These officially sponsored surveys, enquiries and reports about the ethnographic composition and cultural milieu of colonial society had grown out of British rulers' urgent concern for the security and stability of the Indian empire, threatened by the political turmoil of 1857. One of the most important causes of the upsurge in the opinion of the British officials was the numerical majority of the Brahmins and Rajputs in the Bengal Army and the soldiers, belonging to these castes, took a leading part in the Mutiny. The Special Commission, headed by Lord Peel to suggest measures for the reorganisation of the army, recommended that the 'Indian army should be composed of different nationalities and castes as a general rule, mixed promiscuously through each regiment.'[15] However, the official proclamation following the transfer of power from the East India Company to the Crown in 1858, instead of reflecting the suspicious mood, promised to pay due regard to the Indian people's ancient rites, usages and customs.

Nevertheless, suspicion of the high castes became the decisive factor in the British administrative and state policies. Thus, perpetuation of division in colonial society along caste lines was perceived as a sure guarantee for the security of the empire. Ghurye has cited the opinion of contemporary British officials, namely, Sir Lepel Griffin and James Kerr, who knew that caste divided the Indian people into small groups and impeded the crystallization of the nationalist sentiment. Towards the closing years of the 19th century, the maxim of 'divide and rule' began to be openly preached[16] by historians and journalists alike.

Motivated by these utilitarian interests and concerns, the new crop of the British rulers began its long term 'Know-India' campaign with the compilation of a gazetteer for Bengal in mid-1850s. It was followed by the publication of the *Gazetteer for the Central Provinces,* one of the most disturbed areas during the 1857 Revolt, under the orders of its Chief Commissioner R.C. Temple.[17] This encouraged the Government to compile gazetteers for other provinces of British India. W.W. Hunter, under the instructions of Lord Mayo, began the task of creating a comprehensive scheme that culminated in the Imperial Gazetteer of India in 1881. The gazetteers as a tool for domination on an alien country were sponsored for fundamentally different objectives than the census reports in Western Europe. As studies on an alien civilization and people, these were 'a comprehensive description of a district or state of British India...including historical, archaeological, political, economic, sociological, commercial and statistical data.'[18] Their broad scope had been defined by the colonial government's anxiety to get an intelligible account of 'a population of at least forty millions of many races and creeds, representing interests so important and so varied.'[19] These remarks of H.L. Dampier, the Additional Secretary to the Government of Bengal, revealed the official motives for sponsoring such systematic and detailed enquiries about various provinces of British India.

Thus, the ethnographic enquiries in 1860s, presumably to aid the anthropological researches in England and India, formed an important stage in the imperial hunt for information. For example, in 1861 the Secretary of State directed the Government of India to procure photographs of 'a few characteristic specimens of the more remarkable

Tribes to be found in India'. The provincial governments were given a list of tribes but they were free to include other specimens of interest. They were instructed to submit photographs of a size that could exhibit both the chief physical peculiarities and the distinctive costume of each 'race'. The collection when completed, as the Government observed, would be of 'much scientific value'.[19a]

The list of 'Tribes' circulated by the British Government for this purpose reveals the working of the mind of the administrator-ethnographer whose researches sought to determine the ethnic composition of the subject society. The 'Tribes' listed for Bengal proper fell into four broad ethnic categories. The first included the immigrant 'Koolin Brahmin', and the second some of the principal 'agricultural races' and 'commercial races'. The third embraced the whole range of tribal population, while the fourth one consisted of the various heterogeneous racial elements among the residents of Calcutta such as Moghuls, Parsees, Armenians and Jews. The Bengal collection was finally completed in July 1862 by Dr. Simpson, then the Civil Surgeon of the 24 Parganas.[20] It is evident that the concept of a multi-ethnic society and its central polarity was acquiring a definite shape in the minds of the imperial policy planners.

Herbert Risley had utilized the ethnographic researches combined with ethnological enquiries to resolve the nagging problem of the real origins of the lower and intermediate castes. Relying upon Alfred Lyall's thesis about the gradual Brahmanisation of the aboriginal non-Aryan, casteless tribes, he had collected their customs and ceremonies which they seemed to have borrowed from the higher castes. As an aid to the solution of this puzzle, he applied Paul Topinard's methods of anthropometric measurement to the leading castes and tribes of Bengal.[21]

Justifying the utility of his ethnographic survey for practical administration, Risley observed: 'The native society is made up of a network of subdivisions governed by rules which affect every department of life.'[22] How that 'society will behave under novel conditions; what use, for example, it will make of any particular form of political representation', were questions, which, he believed, could not be answered without 'a fairly minute knowledge' of the internal organisation of society.[23] In other words, ethnic composition had to be taken into account in order to secure proper representation of different segments of the subject society in the representative bodies, so that no particular group could monopolize power. This consideration was to become increasingly important in the colonial reform policies and electoral politics in the early twentieth century India.

Ethnicity had an economic dimension as well because caste, as Risley speculated, was often an index of wealth. Hence, an ethnographic glossary would not merely ensure an equitable distribution of patronage, but would also facilitate 'the assessment of any direct tax'.[23a] Besides, a detailed knowledge about the religious and social customs of the people of their own districts would enable the officials to deal with the current social problems and the policy-makers to stipulate broad measures to influence the emergent social reform movements in the last 19th and early 20th century.[24] Risley believed that the Bengal model would be applicable to the rest of India.

The British rulers, perhaps not enamoured of Risley's scientific interests, sponsored his scheme of ethnographic survey with two expectations. First, it was searching for a depressed under-class, ignored by the vernacular press and left out by the public bodies, vis-a-vis the more privileged sections, 'the leaders of the native society'. Secondly, it wanted to have 'a more minute knowledge' about Indian society in order to face the sensitive question of social reforms without hurting the sentiments of the masses or the people at large.[25] The supposed polarity in Indian society, with small sections of privileged upper castes at the top and the vast body of depressed lower castes at the bottom, had thus taken shape in the perception of the Raj. And this dichotomy had not merely a social or economic but a racial dimension, too, which Risley was trying to find out in the second part of his enquiry, i.e., through ethnological survey. The real recognition for Risley's formulation came when the colonial government appointed him as the Director of Ethnology for India in order to execute the then devised scheme for a systematic and prolonged ethnographic survey of the country.

III

The task of constructing Indian society through the identification of races, tribes and major castes had been largely accomplished by the colonial ethnographers: Herbert Risley in Bengal, Denzil Ibbetson in Punjab, W. Crooke in North Western Provinces and E. Thurston in South India. In their empiricist studies, the pervasive imperialist vision and racist view of the colonial India dominated. It is not accidental that the Hindus had been defined in terms of their racial characteristics and demarcated as primordial social groups, fixed in status or ranks on the basis of *varna,* purity-impurity criteria and marriage customs. This ethnological description of Hindu society could not be of much use for the formulation of administrative decisions and state policies unless supplemented by knowledge about their numerical position and relative socio-economic conditions. Hence, there was an urgent necessity of rigorous objectification and classification and this was fulfilled by the decennial census. Between 1901-1931, it was perfected as an instrument for constructing identities on the basis of religion and caste, for recasting self-image and world-view of Indian people and manipulating them for managing India politically, sociologically, militarily, ideologically, scientifically and epistemologically.

Unlike Britain, where religion had never appeared in census except in 1853, since 1801 the colonial state used religion as a general rubric for describing, enumerating, analysing and conceptualising Indian people.[26] Despite being based on the same principles, the British and Indian census showed marked differences in content and scope of investigation over the years reflecting the working of colonial official-cum-ethnographic thinking, their new concerns and priorities. Their projection of religion as the governing principle of the Indian society gradually became a vital consideration influencing colonial policies and legislation concerning each aspect of Indian life.

The first North-Western Provinces Census (1853) counted and recorded the number of Hindus and Muslims separately. But the caste and occupation were not added till the next census in 1872. A similar practice was followed in the Punjab Census indicating that religion was a primary concern for the colonial administrators graduating from the role of ethnographers to Census Commissioners. Over the decades, religion was given more space and weightage in the compilation of reports and statistical tables. The second Punjab Census (1868) listed religious groups under seven categories: Christians, Mohammedans, Hindus, Sikhs, Buddhists, Jains and others. Further, the Punjab Census Report (1891) had identified the major sects or orders in each religion and its subdivisions; while in Hinduism, the Census Commissioners analysed the orders of *yogis* and *sannyasis*; in Islam, they computed the percentage of Sunnis, Shias and Wahabis, and the Christians were subdivided into Anglicans, Presbyterians, Baptists, Roman Catholics, etc.

For an insight into the process how religions were defined, stretched into communities, bonded and fixed into ethnographically framed slots, we may turn to the discursive sections of the successive census reports of various provinces. In the case of Punjab, the decennial census had kept a careful record of the history of contemporary socio-religious organisations such as Brahmo Samaj, Arya Samaj, Dev Samaj, Radha Soami, Sat Sangh, the Ahmadiyas, Singh Sabha and others. Religion was used as a basic category for estimating the increase or decrease of population. The census officials carefully studied the changes in the size of all religious groups as well as shifts in their relative strength. The amorphous religious affiliations were defined as 'communities', mapped and enumerated in order to indicate their geographic distribution and areas of either majority or minority status. Any changes that took place in these patterns of distributions were also carefully noted. The Punjab Census Report (1891) provided an example of actual mapping in the case of both the Jain and Sikh communities. The data on each religion included the total number of adherents, its representation in total population, the rate of relative growth or decline in relation to the whole population and in relation to other religious groups; in some cases detailed references to concentration of a given religion in certain districts were also taken note of.

However, this attempt to provide reliable statistical data on religions proved difficult, particularly in regard to Hindus who needed to be defined. The search for a satisfactory definition caused endless problems. In the first Punjab Census, Sikhs were included in the definition of 'Hindu', but in the second Punjab Census (1868), they were placed in a separate category of their own. This was an official recognition of Sikhism, and a corresponding diminution of the number and percentage of Hindus in the province.

The issue of defining Hindus raised another difficulty: whether untouchable castes and tribals should be included within the Hindu community or listed separately. The second Punjab Census left the question unsettled but encouraged categorization of castes: for example, the *chamars* were listed both by district and religious affiliations — Hindu, Sikh or others. The division of castes into religious groups would become a standard element in future census reports. This problem arose in the compilation of Bengal Census (1872) also. Over the years, many definitions were formulated but the issue remained unresolved.

The problem of definition also arose in the case of Sikhism: who was a Sikh, Keshdhari or Sahajdhari? In the Punjab Census (1881), no attempt at the definition of the term 'Sikh' was made. Thus the Sahajdhari Sikhs were also returned as 'Sikhs'. But the Punjab Census Report (1891) coined a definition: "By a true Sikh is meant a member of Khalsa, a follower of the ordinances of Guru Gobind Singh.' By implication, he is a Keshdhari Sikh. The practical test which was to be applied in the enumeration was that 'a Sikh should be one who wears uncut hair and abstains from smoking.'[27] Thus, the Sahajdhari Sikhs were to be returned as Hindus. However, they were permitted to enter their sect as Nanak Panthi — a follower of Guru Nanak or any other *gurus.* The 1901 census also adopted this definition of 'Sikh' without enumerating its sect. By 1911, however, the census definition of Sikh changed. Enumerators were instructed that 'the religion to which a person claimed to belong must be accepted.'[28] Being aware of the fact that the instructions regarding the practical test to be applied for identifying a Sikh had been 'almost universally ignored' coupled with resentment of Sikhs and Jains who wished to be classified as Hindus, the British Government decided to create a new identity, i.e., Jain-Hindus or Sikh-Hindus in 1911. This broader definition of the term Sikh, which included both Sahajdhari and Keshdhari Sikhs, was used in the Punjab Census (1921).[29]

This dominant trend in ethnographic thinking was also reflected in the first All India Census (1871). Placed on a decennial basis and standardised in its content as well as procedure, it had retained religion as a basic category for analysing statistical tables on age, caste, occupation and education of the population. The colonial ethnographer's fixation with religion was illustrated from its description and analysis in the discursive sections and the numerical tables. For example, information on education was subdivided into a series of tables according to geographic distribution, sex and religion.[30] The census officials had also focussed on the religious dimension of caste of the agricultural and non-agricultural population, distribution of females — in fact, all data concerning the Indian people. The only significant area of the census without a religious dimension was the section on infirmities, the deaf, dumb, blind, idiots, insane and lepers.[31]

It may be inferred that collection and the reproduction of sociological and anthropological data in the successive all-India or provincial census reports had been done with a view to accentuating divisions along religious and caste lines. By conceptualising religion as community and judging its strength or weakness by numbers, the census officials had encouraged religious competition. The practice of extensive recording of conversion from one faith to another through tables, statistics and discussions was initially necessitated by the British rulers' desire to map the impact of intensive proselytization campaign by the Christian missionaries on Hinduism, Islam and Sikhism. The census focussed greater attention on the triangular religious competition as it became more broadbased and bitter through conversions and counter-conversions of Christians, Sikhs, Muslims and Hindus.[32] This extensive descriptive and statistical data on conversions and reconversions had been systematically created and circulated by the end of the nineteenth century.

The element of religious competition was also injected in the economic life of the people as the census officials described and enumerated wider occupational patterns in terms of caste and religious community. For example, the Punjab Census (1891) had not only divided all occupations into five groups (Agricultural, Professional, Commercial, Artisans and Performers) but also gave the percentages of each within the Sikh, Hindu, Jain and Muslim communities.[33] In its discursive sections, relationship between the religion and occupations was explicitly mentioned. The educated Punjabis found extensive examination of economic and occupational patterns in the Punjab Census (1911) such as breakdown by religion and caste of the individual serving in the imperial army, armies and government service of the Native state and foreign states, police, municipal and local governments. Owners of factories, mines and other business were also listed in the census reports and holders of non-agricultural wealth in the tax records.[34] By giving direct and indirect information on caste and religion of the individuals, the British rulers had heightened their awareness as a community about their representation in various kinds of economic activities, and thus added a religious dimension to their economic life.

It may be conceded that the civilian-turned-ethnographer-cum-Census Commissioner had dissipated the amorphous character of Indian religions and transformed each one of them into 'enumerated' communities. Kenneth Jones has put this succinctly:

> Religions became communities mapped, counted and above all compared with other religious communities. Furthermore, this was not a static concept; since each decennial census measured changes for good or ill in the state of community and

might even reshape a community through a new definition...Also, the concept underlying a religious community was fundamentally insecure, always open to change which might or might not prove favourable.[35]

IV

Apart from religion, the British ethnographers had used a variety of other criteria to classify Indian population. According to the Commissioner of Census (1891), the major aim in prescribing the classification was 'as much uniformity as the nature of statistics will allow, so that the returns of each province may be dealt with on the same basis.'[36] In the earlier census reports (1865, 1872 and 1881), *varna,* which covered the Hindus[37] throughout India, was used as a principle of classification. In 1891 census, the *varna* principle of classification was replaced by the principle of race classification. Ibbetson's ethnological report on Punjab was used as a model.[38] Nesfield had also formulated a theory of origin of caste to justify his application of occupation criterion.[39] According to Bernard Cohn, Nesfield's theory reflected the influence of Victorian anthropology which had emphasized material evolutionism. It fitted well into the intellectual premises of the colonial discourse justifying British imperialism.

Herbert Risley, the Director of the Indian Census Operations (1901), dubbed the classification of castes in the 1891 Census as a 'patchwork classification, in which occupation predominates, varied here and there by considerations of caste-history, tradition, ethnical affinity and geographical position.'[40] Its major defect, according to Risley, was the violation of rules of identity-ritual status, religious community and race. As a result, he proposed a Brahmin-centred classification, i.e., the Brahmin being the fixed point in traditional ritual hierarchy, while the *Kshatriya, Vaishya* and other castes stood in relation to the Brahmin only.

Risley's scheme of classification[41] was given up in the next census for administrative reasons as it had encouraged fierce caste-competition in the first instance. Secondly, it did not provide a suitable grid or classificatory table which would help the colonial administrators in constructing an all-purpose conception of caste-ranking.[42] Finally, caste became a special target and site of knowledge for the ethnographer in the last three censuses of British India (1911, 1921 and 1931). Their contents reveal that caste, which had been firmly located as the essence of Hindu religion, formed the theme of a special chapter and was related with a variety of data: sex-ratio, age distribution, occupational patterns, vernacular and English literacy by caste. It may be said that the collection and reproduction of anthropological and sociological data about caste and its distribution at district, provincial and all-India levels was done with a view to highlight the essential attributes and vulnerability of the Indian people. This idea was first expressed in census literature in the third All-India Census Survey (1891).

What was the value of this qualified and quantified information about caste as administrative strategy? R. Saumarez Smith has argued that the development of administrative records and survey reports in colonial India was linked to the formulation of a new strategy of political control in the second half of the nineteenth century. In his view, there was a 'correspondence between the gradual construction of an official understanding of Indian society and the gradual extension of the rule of law'.[43] After 1840s, caste in the village records and settlement reports became a reference point for defining customs, rights and duties, particularly revenue obligations, instead of each village negotiating the terms for running its own affairs.[44] Thus, the village society became 'fragmented into countless statuses in knowledge and law'.[45]

Unlike the 'village community', which had the resilience to survive the ruin of empires, caste was a different kind of concept serving different purposes. 'More a unit of knowledge than administration',[46] its importance for the colonial administrator-turned-ethnographer lay in the fact that it embraced the whole of India and all sections of Indian society. Having limited utility as a unit for revenue assessment, it could be more easily manipulated for controlling majorities and minorities through a number of laws and constitutional measures by statutory imperial government. That's why from 1840s onwards, institution of caste was gradually impaled in the settlement reports and other records. But before caste or agricultural and other tribes could be used as foci for the enactment of law, a statistical picture incorporating colonial view of caste had to be officially constructed, published and shared by the members of the ruling classes. Hence, Indian census from 1860s to 1930s was perfected as an instrument for breaking Indian society into a group of individuals, and then piecing it together through quasimathematical methods. Having composed this statistical picture of society, the British Government was no longer obliged to function through the mediation of 'powerful families' or the 'little republics' of village communities.

As the British perceived caste as a site of multipurpose information and statistical tool for generating a synthetic understanding of Indian society, all data about 'castes' was not useful to them. A careful perusal of the various census reports would show that 'numerical' status of a caste was an important consideration for special attention. For example, the first caste census of North-Western Province (NWP) in 1865 contained statistics about the population concentration of the most numerous subcastes of *brahmins, kshatriyas, vaishyas* and *shudras.*[47] The NWP Census of 1872 recorded numerically dominant castes by *pargana.* Out of 304 separate subdivisions of the non-twice-born castes, it was decided that the district-wise tabulation would be drafted only for 50 subcastes which comprised the main body of the persons classed under 'other castes' as differentiated from the 'Great Castes'. In the NWP Census of 1881, the provincial officials were instructed to collect data only for numerically important castes. As a result, it presented a statistical picture of the 'Eleven Large Castes', 'Ten Large Agricultural

Castes' and thirty-seven castes of the non-twice-born castes whose numbers exceeded 1,000,000.[48] However, in the case of Punjab, where caste had more fluidity than elsewhere in India owing to the presence of three interacting religious communities (Hindu, Sikh and Muslim), the multiple criteria of caste, religion and occupation was used to determine the status of individuals. The political importance of each of the three communities in the past, too, was kept in view while composing a picture of the Punjabi society. Here, the concept of 'majority' and 'minority' was defined in terms of religion.[49]

The British were also interested in recording the statistical position of minorities like Aggarwals and Marwaris who had a wide interregional network. Another category of minorities that figured in the population census reports, had a reputation for flouting British law and order. They were grouped under the broad category of 'criminal tribes', thugs, etc. Such minority castes or tribes as were crucial to the maintenance of law and order were also listed in the NWP and Oudh Census of 1919 under the instructions of the Census Commissioner.[50]

With an eye on utility for the *raj* rather than progress of Indian society, the British ethnographers-cum-administrators located large amount of information on caste divisions, caste rituals, etc. which was given in the Army recruitment handbooks on each of the 'martial races'. The Handbook on Garhwalis, for instance, was largely concerned with identifying the particular subdivisions of Rajputs and Brahmins which were amenable to military discipline.[51] Captain A.H. Bingley's study on Sikhs and Captain R.W. Falcon's *Handbook on Sikhs for the use of Regimental Officers,* published in 1890s, were written with the object of maximum utilization of their fighting potential for the defence of the *raj* and territorial wars. The army officers' insistence that Sikh recruits must retain their traditional symbols or obtain them through baptismal ceremony upon joining the army revealed their keenness to intensify religious and caste consciousness.[52]

V

From the preceding discussion, it is clear that the colonial ethnography or, to use a broader term, colonial sociology had been standardized and perfected as an instrument to identify the physical and cultural traits of various communities and to quantify their numerical weightage, socio-economic and educational progress in order to determine their potential value as allies or opponents of the *raj.*

Out of the entire corpus of imperial literature on India, the census turned out to be the most valuable official recorder in the period between 1871 and 1931. Its successive survey reports became a useful source for understanding the impact of ethnographer's constructions of religion as community, caste and primary social relationships. The student of modern Indian history may regard the census as a statement of the colonial policy and perspective. To some extent, it is an important index of the working of the mind of the rulers, tabulators and collators.

Equipped with the multifaceted knowledge about horizontal and vertical divisions on the basis of religion and caste, as well as cultural and ideological differences within various social groups in the Indian society, the British tried to manipulate them to promote colonial goals after 1857. They tried to create an administrative machinery as a constituent of the larger imperial system of control, co-opted the Muslim community as their long-term allies and encouraged them to develop vested interests in the perpetuation of the *raj*. Its chief motive was to neutralize the strength of the majority status of the Hindus at the all-India level and to keep the two major Indian communities in a state of constant friction. But the position of Muslims within this system of control depended on their social and economic importance in different provinces. Outside the United Provinces, the Punjabis appeared to be of great importance to the system of control. In Punjab, the Muslims' fortunes improved under the British rule after the 'Mutiny', in which this community had played a notable part in putting it down. That is why the Punjabi Muslims became a vital element in the imperial military strategy. For this reason, the *raj* bolstered Muslim interests in Punjab, and when irrigation schemes led to the reclamation of a large area of West Punjab in the later part of the nineteenth century, the Muslims of that area were the chief beneficiaries. This development marked the most spectacular accession of landed wealth to the community during the British period. It gave the Punjabi Muslims a landed position to rival that of their co-religionists in the United Provinces.[53]

During the first decade of the twentieth century when the Morley-Minto reforms were introduced into India, the strategy of forming a firm alliance with the landed class and recruitment of their scions in the imperial bureaucracy seemed inadequate. Henceforth, the British rulers found it expedient to link distribution of patronage and political powers with religion and caste. Unlike Britain, the introduction of parliamentary institutions was not 'a concession intended to absorb those on the outside trying to get in but an attempt to extend and improve the existing system of control by a new method'.[54]

The new imperial strategy sought to enlarge the scope of the concept of communal representation or separate electorates which had been introduced as early as 1880s when the British Government had gerrymandered electoral wards in 1884 so that the Muslims would have advantage over half the area. In Amritsar, it was decreed that ten Hindus and eight Muslims receiving the largest number of votes would be declared elected regardless of their comparative ranking.[55] To fill the vacancies, created by death or illness of any Hindu, replacements were to be made by Hindus alone, and in case of Muslim vacancies, only Muslims could be substituted.

The Morley-Minto reforms are the first significant 'electoral monument' in David Page's phrase to extend the strategy of manipulating and institutionalising religious divisions and tensions. It gave the Muslims special representation with communal electorates. The granting of communal electorates appears to have been an attempt by the *raj* 'to shore up a crucial part of its system of control'.[56] Despite no illusions about the loyalty of the traditional Muslim elite, the British rulers endorsed their strategy of preventing the growing body of young educated elite from the Mohammedan Anglo-Oriental College, Aligarh, from going to the Congress fold. This explains the imperial interest and encouragement to the traditional Muslim leaders like Mohsin ul Mulk and others in the foundation of the Muslim League in 1906. The innovation of separate electorates, later extended to the Depressed classes, is a strong evidence of the British manipulation of religion and caste, like the general electorates. The latter was an attempt to extend and broaden the base of the British rule by drawing in the educated elite of all communities who were divided into various categories of 'interest groups in the imperial system of control'.[57] The extent of their representation was based, in part, on the size of the various communities, as the census conceptualised, categorized and quantified them.

The Montagu-Chelmsford Reforms further extended the principle of communal representation. Separate constituencies were formed for various interest groups such as the universities, landlords, industry and commerce in addition to the seats for religious communities including Muslims, Sikhs and Indian Christians with two other racial categories—Europeans and Anglo-Indians.[58] These changes in the imperial system of control further strengthened the tie between the census and political power, thereby highlighting the crucial role of the colonial ethnographer. Religious identity was now seen in terms of a community as defined by the census reports, a community possessing many qualities and staking a particular claim to political power and share in the economy. However, the limitations of the imperial strategy of exploiting religion for manufacturing competing interests and identities are evident from the Muslim leaders' success in forcing the British rulers to concede their demand for dominance in the majority provinces of Punjab and Bengal.[59]

The significance of the Communal Award, published on 16 August 1932, has to be measured in the context of the increasing power of the Muslims as a religious community to dictate their own terms to the imperial patrons for their support to the British control at the centre in future. The Communal Award had made continued imperial control possible; it had also fortified the Punjabi and Bengali Muslims against the possibility of any other kind of centre. Thus, the period of operation of the Montagu-Chelmsford Reforms produced developments of great significance from David Page's angle: 'The political interests were consolidated around communal issues: the League and Congress attitudes were framed both towards the emergence of provincial autonomy and towards the eventual withdrawal of the British imperialism.'[60]

The Government of India Act, 1935, while retaining the communal representation, added a new social category with seats reserved for scheduled castes and depressed castes. These were members labelled in the census reports as 'untouchables', and individuals who were classified as backward tribes. The final construction of their socio-political identity was preceded by a long period of surreptitious enquiry and tabulation about relative demographic and socio-economic position of the caste Hindus and untouchables ever since the issuance of Gait Circular in July 1910.[61] However, the Hindus perceived it as yet another ploy to reduce their numerical superiority through the redefinition of Hinduism and separation of certain untouchable castes from the rest of the Hindu society. E.A. Gait's suggestion to incorporate a separate set of tables in the 1911 census to the list of 'debatable Hindus' implied a change in the relative numerical strength of all religious communities, for as one grew another lost in numbers.

Thus, the controversy surrounding the Gait Circular had provoked Hindu leaders to adopt suitable measures to uplift the untouchables, turn them into pure caste Hindus in order to tie them more securely to the Hindu community. Responding to the imperialist policy of exacerbating religious differences to the level of irreversible hostility and politicising dichotomies of caste hierarchy in Hindu society, the Hindus in particular were galvanized to work for communal solidarity so as to protect the community against numerical decline.[62] Thus, Shuddhi became both a reconversion institution and a method of radical social reform.

It is clear that the colonial ethnographer's labours in constructing and reordering Indian society into a number of static and timeless categories had been utilized for political and cultural enslavement of India and the colonization of its economy. Based on these conceptualisations, the implementation of the principle of guaranteed political power led to two conspicuous results. In the first instance, it created an immensely complex constitutional structure which varied with the religious, social and ethnic composition of each province. A.B. Keith has described the intricate pattern of distribution of seats in various Madras constituencies. It may be pointed out that this administrative arrangement rested on the data supplied by the census as well as the attitudes of various communities. Secondly, it had institutionalised religious divisions and tensions by applying the criteria of reservation to the legislative bodies, educational institutions and various branches of government services — executive, judicial and military.[64]

VI

To sum up, identities in Indian society which had remained amorphous and indeterminate, were conceptualised as religious communities and caste groups, categorised and quantified for political purposes by the British imperialists. The colonial ethnographer, who was called upon to assume new responsibilities in view of the increasing resistance to the British empire from the growing educated middle classes and a few socio-religious organisations, mapped out and fixed the boundaries separating religious communities, caste groups and ethnic elements, along with an exhaustive account of their biological characteristics, social customs and belief systems. The end-product was a coherent, intelligible, though distorted picture, of the colonial society, whose members had to be controlled, enslaved, and conditioned to perceive themselves as communal and religious entities; their languages, science, literature and cultural traditions as gifts from the intellectually superior, materially advanced and culturally dynamic Europe.

Secondly, the settlement surveys, population censuses, ethnologies, ethnographies and reports on economic and cultural practices (compiled during the colonial period) should not be regarded merely as products of the administrative system but as a corollary to the imperial perception of the relationship between the governability of India and knowledge about its social morphology. In order to enable the administrators and policy makers to gear the imperial system of rule for exploiting the human and natural resources of the subject country, a well-calculated administrative strategy was developed over a long period wherein the concept of religion as community and certain castes were deemed crucial and, thus, worthy of study and analysis from the angle of imperial interests. While compiling the census reports, the colonial ethnographer converted them into categories which were defined, elaborated and given statistical substance over decades. These emerged finally as fixed social and cultural divisions incorporated in the constitutional structure of British India as illustrated by Government of India Act, 1935.

Similarly, the numerical majorities in terms of castes became the subject of special official reports because they could be used for managing masses. The minorities such as the *Aggarwals* and *Marwaris,* having intra-regional network, martial, agricultural and commercial 'races' for their strategic and economic function and 'criminal tribes' as threats to law and order also received patronage, reward or punishment in accordance with their utility in the perception of the *raj.*

Within the framework of this strategy, the precise knowledge about horizontal and vertical divisions in Indian society along religious and caste lines as well as the system of checks and balances regulating the daily conduct of a culturally alien people, their social relationships and life-cycle ceremonies was requisite. The imperial power depended upon its bureaucratic efficiency to operate these controls without conceding substantial political and economic rights to the subject society. This strategic linkage between knowledge and long term imperial goal of 'hegemony' required the breaking of castes into subcastes, religious communities into sects, enumeration of the relevant categories with due allowance to religious competition and consequent conversions and their effect on marriage and social customs. The entire data had to be collected, analysed and marked into separate administrative spaces—provinces, districts and *parganas.* As the listing and freezing of caste-identities and religious communities was done without any reference to actual reality, the 'invented' colonial society, though more intelligible to the imperial administrator, had been deprived of its flexible cognitive system that could encompass geographical mobility. Thus, the construction of colonial ethnography did violence to the traditional social system.

NOTES

1. Bernard S. Cohn, 'The Command of Language and the Language of Command' in Ranajit Guha (ed.), *Subaltern Studies,* Vol. IV, New York, 1985, p. 289.
2. For an analytical account of the impact of the British rule on Indian economy, see Irfan Habib, 'Colonialization of Indian Economy, 1757-1900', *Social Scientist,* Vol. 32, pp. 23-53. Also Bipan Chandra, 'British and Indian Ideas on Economic Development 1885-1905' in *Nationalism and Colonialism in Modern India,* New Delhi, 1979, pp. 82-122.
3. For an account of stages in British rule in India, see Bipan Chandra, et al, *Freedom Struggle,* New Delhi, 1983, pp. 3-16.
4. Ranajit Guha, *A Rule of Property: An Essay on the Permanent Settlement,* Paris, 1963, p. 26.
5. B.S. Cohn, 'Notes on the History of the Study of Indian Society and Culture' in Milton Singer and Bernard S. Cohn (ed.), *Structure and Change in Indian Society,* Chicago, 1968, p. 24.
6. *Punjab Census Report (1921),* p. 434.
7. H.H. Risley, *The People of India,* reprint, Delhi, 1969, pp. 69-91. For O'Malley's classification system, see *Census of India: Bengal, Bihar & Orissa,* Bengal Secretariat Press, 1913, p. 440.
8. L.S.S. O'Malley, *India's Social Heritage,* reprint, Delhi, 1976, Preface.
9. Oliver Cromwell Cox, *Caste, Class and Race: A Study in Social Dynamics,* New York, 1948, pp. 86-122.
10. Denzil Ibbetson, *Punjab Castes* (Being a Reprint of the Chapter on 'The Races, Castes and Tribes of the People' in *The Report on the Census of the Punjab, 1881*), reprint, Patiala, 1970, p. 9.

10a. Risley, op. cit., pp. 69-91.

11. O'Malley, op. cit., pp. 38-9.
12. W. Crooke, *The Tribes and Castes of the North Western India,* reprint, Delhi, 1974, pp. ix-xv.
13. J.H. Hutton, *Caste in India: Its Nature, Function and Origins,* Cambridge, 1946, pp. 89-90.
14. Cohn, 'The Command of Language & C', op. cit., p. 325.

14a. Benedict Anderson, *Imagined Communities: Reflections on the Origin and Spread of Nationalism,* London, 1983.

15. *Report of the Peel Commission on the Organisation of the Indian Army,* 1859, p. 14.
16. Cited in G.S. Ghurye, *Caste and Race in India,* reprint, Bombay, 1990.
17. Sekhar Bandyopadhyaya, 'Caste in the Perception of the Raj: A note on the Evolution of Colonial Sociology of Bengal', *Bengal, Past and Present,* Vol. CIV, pts. I-II, nos. 198-99, 1985, p. 59.
18. Henry Scholberg, *The District Gazetteers of British India: A Bibliography,* Switzerland, 1970, p. iv.
19. Bandyopadhyaya, op. cit., p. 76.

19a. Scholberg, op. cit.

20. Bandyopadhyaya, p. 60.

21. Ibid.

22. Risley, *The Tribes and Castes of Bengal*, Vol. I, Calcutta, 1981, p. vii.

23. Cited in Bandyopadhyaya, pp. 8, 30.

23a. Ibid., p. 31.

24. Risley, *The Tribes & C*, p. ix.

25. Bandyopadhyaya, pp. 67-78.

26. For a sample of census table formats for each decennial census from 1871-2 to 1971, see D. Natrajan, *Indian Census Through a Hundred Years*, Vol. 2, Delhi, pp. 17-448.

27. *Punjab Census Report, 1891*, pp. 94-5.

28. *Punjab Census Report, 1921*.

29. Ibid.

30. *Memorandum* of the Census of British India 1871-2, London, George Edward Eyre and William Spottiswoode, 1875, p. 5.

31. *North Western Provinces, Census Report, 1872*, pp. 26-7, 234.

32. Kenneth W. Jones, *Arya Dharma: Hindu Consciousness in the 19th Century Punjab*, New Delhi, 1976, pp. 126-153.

33. *Punjab Census Report, 1891*, p. 232.

34. *Punjab Census Report, 1911*, pp. 524-27.

35. K.W. Jones, 'Religious Identity and Indian Census' in N. Gerald Barrier (ed.), *The Census in British India: New Perspectives*, New Delhi, 1981, p. 84.

36. *Census of India Report, 1891*, p. 188.

37. See *Census of India Report*, 1865, 1872 and 1891 (especially the chapter on 'Religion'). Also, *Punjab Census Report, 1891*.

38. For the table of classification by occupation, see Denzil Ibbetson, *Punjab Castes*, reprint, Delhi, 1981.

39. J.C. Nesfield, *A Brief View of the Caste System of NWP and Oudh*, Allahabad, 1885, pp. 114-5.

40. *Census of India Report, 1901*, p. 538.

41. For Risley's scheme, see *Census of NWP and Oudh, 1901*, Vol. I, p. 216. For his justification of Brahmin-centred scheme, see p. 556.

42. Rashmi Pant, 'The Cognitive Status of Caste in Colonial Ethnography: Review of some Literature on the North West Provinces and Oudh', *Indian Economic and Social History Review*, Vol. 24, No. 2, 1987, p. 159.

43. Richard Saumarez Smith, 'Rule-by-Records and Rule-by-Reports: Complementary aspects of the British Imperial rule of law', *Contributions to Indian Sociology*, Vol. 19, No. 1, p. 163.

44. Ibid., pp. 169-71.

45. Ibid., p. 163.

46. Ibid., 173.

47. The first North-Western Provinces Census (1853) counted and recorded the number of Hindus and Muslims separately. But the caste and occupation were not added until the next census in 1872. A similar practice was followed in the Punjab Census which indicates that religion was the primary concern for the colonial administrators-cum-ethnographers and it was given more space and weightage in the compilation of reports and statistical tables. The second and third Punjab Census in 1868 and 1891 respectively are good examples.

48. *Census of India Report, 1881*, pp. 277, 281-2.

49. Kamlesh Mohan, 'Constructing Religion and Caste and Manipulating Identities (19th to early 20th century)', *Social Sciences Research Journal*, Vol. I, Nos. 1-2, 1992, p. 152.

50. *Census of India Report, 1881*, p. 278. Also Rashmi Pant, op. cit., p. 150.

51. Captain J. Evatt, *Garhwalis,* 1894. This handbook for the Indian Army was revised by Lt. Col. K. Henderson in 1941.

52. Joyce Pettigrew, *Robber Noblemen: A Study of the Political System of the Sikh Jats,* London, 1975, pp. 41-3.

53. David Page, *Prelude to Partition,* Delhi, 1982, p. 9. Also David Gilmartin, *Empire and Islam,* New Delhi, 1989.

54. Page, op. cit., p. 12; Gilmartin, op. cit., pp. 146-88.

55. Cited in N.G. Barrier, 'The Punjab Government and Communal Politics', *Journal of Asian Studies,* Vol. XXVII, No. 3, 1968, p. 537.

56. Page, p. 14.

57. Jones, op. cit., p. 95.

58. A.B. Keith, *Constitutional History of India, 1600-1935,* Allahabad, 1961, pp. 247-50.

59. Page, p. 257.

60. Ibid.

61. For the text of the Gait Circular, see *The Tribune,* 12 Nov. 1910, p. 5.

62. For some interesting observations on the impact of Gait Circular (1910), see Jones, op. cit., pp. 93-5. Also Indu Banga, 'Emergence of Hindu Consciousness in Colonial Punjab' in P.C. Chatterji (ed.), *Self Images, Identity and Nationality,* New Delhi, pp. 201-17.

63. Keith, op. cit., p. 487.

64. For an analytical discussion of the role of the British policies in the institutionalisation of communal tensions, see *Selections From the Punjab Vernacular Press Reports, 1883,* pp. 553-57.

15

In Quest of Indigenous Approach to Women Studies in India

ABDUL MATIN

Women account for more than one-half of humanity and they work for nearly two-thirds of all the work hours; but they receive only some one-tenth of the world income, and own less than bare 1 per cent of world's productive assets.[1]

There is a tendency towards replicating occidental models and paradigms in India in the areas of women studies without adequate critical thinking. Relevance of this dominant trend in India today has been critically examined in this paper.

Women's struggle originating in occidental societies has different historical experiences in the spheres of industrialization, urbanization and cultural ethos compared to the oriental societies like India. In this background, women studies in the former are characterized by being predominantly 'middle class' and 'urban based'. But in the latter, especially in India, 'urbanization' and 'middle class' are not of the same magnitude. Hence, indigenous realities must be taken into consideration for the relevance of these studies in oriental societies in general and India in particular.

Women studies is already well established in foreign universities and research institutions as a distinct area of specialization. In India, it has started emerging recently. These studies have bearing upon Women Development policies and programmes in India. Matin has pointed out its historical background as well as contemporary reasons for interest among academicians, policy makers, politicians and activists.[2] Literature available on women studies in India is diverse and exhaustive. A cursory examination of the literature on women studies, however, clearly reveals the trend of replication of Western scholarship (occidental models and paradigms).[3] Many Indian social scientists approach Indian women's problems (consciously or unconsciously) within the framework of Western models and paradigms concentrating on urban areas. The inherent limitations of this dominant trend will be argued later. Qaisar has observed:

> It has become a fashion among some scholars of humanities, especially in the developing countries, to mould their researches after *models* and paradigms in the West, and then to tack facts onto them or in their immediate vicinity. I have no intention to denigrate or discourage this style which in my opinion may be due to a drive towards universalism; but, then, there are certain hazards inherent in such attempts because models drawn upon the experience of particular regions of specific cultural milieu may not be applicable to other territories at all. Zest for *universal formula* in history is very tempting but not always laudable: at times the end-product is likely to become an instance of 'Love's Labour Lost'. This is more true when model connected with modern social realities is sought to be projected a number of centuries back. This effort is patently erroneous, misleading and unwarranted.[4]

In fact, the process of industrialization and urbanization leading to the rise of middle classes is not of the same magnitude in India as in the developed Western societies.

An examination of Indian male/female population, growth rate of population and Sex Ratio reveals interesting features. Figure 1 highlights an annual (exponential) growth rate in percentage of Indian male and female from 1901 to 1991. The growth rate of female has been less than the male excepting 1951 and 1981. In the latter years, female growth rates were more than male by 0.02% and 0.06% respectively. Figure 2 shows the declining Sex Ratio (females per thousand males) in India since 1901. It is proper here to cite Petrov at length on Sex Ratio in India:

> The sex composition of India's population is the same as that of the rest of Asia, namely, more men than women. The reverse is true of the developed countries, not only the states of Europe and North America, but also in a developed Asian country like Japan there are more women than men.
>
> Certain biological reasons are responsible for the uneven proportions of men and women, as a result of which more boys are born than girls everywhere. Biological factors affect a person throughout his or her lifetime. But ever since society began to take shape and develop, the part played by social factors has drastically increased. Today, social factors are a decisive force, having a greater impact than biological ones.
>
> At the moment, there are slightly more men on Earth than women owing to the extremely numerous populations of the developing countries. The development process is gradually changing this ratio, slowly reversing it. Remarkably, the persisting ratio in favour of men does not obviously mean their better living

> conditions, but the extremely poor living condition of women in the developing countries is so hard that it results in their higher mortality, especially during their youth, and in the smaller total number compared with men. The same is true of India, too. Here, medicine is relatively less successful in diminishing the mortality of women than that of men, and it is powerless in the face of the persisting backwardness of the social conditions in the country which do in the final count determine the result. It is pointless to seek for the reasons for this lack of correspondence in migration of the population, the consequences of wars, the partitioning of the country or the biological nature of women in the developing countries...The continuing decrease in the number of females in the population is having very serious consequences, for all the censuses say that the numbers of women are becoming relatively smaller, and consequently the actual conditions of their everyday life are not getting any better at all. In this respect, the decades of independent development have not brought the desired radical changes.[5]

Female infanticide/foeticide, less preference for girl child, etc. are some of the plausible explanations of the declining trend in Sex Ratio in India. The practice of female infanticide unlike female foeticide is quite old in India. Literature is available on the former problem. But female foeticide (killing of the female foetus in the womb itself) started around the mid-1970s when amniocentesis was first introduced in India to detect genetic defects. Incidentally, the test reveals the sex of child, too. This aspect of Sex Determination (SD) caught the attention of Indian doctors and the business of SD started booming. In addition to SD facilities available in the cosmopolitan/metropolitan cities, they have been spreading very fast to the rural interiors of U.P., Punjab and Gujarat, where even basic facilities like potable water do not exist.[6] The magnitude of female foeticide may be understood by the fact that 78,000 female foetuses were destroyed in the country between 1978 and 1982 using the amniocentesis test.[7] The trends in Sex Ratio in India, plausible explanations for the declining trend and various aspects of Sex Ratio have been examined by Mitra, Rajan and associates, Raju and Premi, and Oldenberg and others.[8] Cultural, economic and underenumeration of female are some of the important explanations provided in these studies. Oldenberg has underscored economic, cultural and other factors affecting the trends in Sex Ratio in India:

> The economic factors include the value of women in agriculture work, the expectations of financial support, not just in old age; and the burden of providing a dowry. The cultural factors include the need for sons to carry on the lineage; the need for children in religious rituals; and the difference in age between brides and grooms (which allow boys to find brides even in a low sex ratio locale). There is also at least one major emotional support that comes from co-residing with children. These do not by any means exhaust the factors that come into play nor does it suggest a ranking in importance, though an emerging consensus may be captured by Monica

Das Gupta's assertion that 'for India as a whole, the evidence suggests that son preference is primarily culturally determined, and scarcity of resources may at most accentuate the effects of sex bias.'[9]

Women's studies in the Western societies, therefore, concentrate on the issues and problems of predominantly 'urban' and 'middle classes'. The majority of the Indian population lives in villages. Consequently, the bulk of the labour force is in agriculture. Table 1 shows that urban population in India in 1901 was 11.0% of the total population. In 1981, the percentage of urban population to the total population was 23.7. In the USA in 1900, 40% of the total population was urban. While in 1940 and 1980, 56% and 73% respectively of the total population was urban.[10]

Needless to say, women, too, in Western societies are concentrated in urban areas in contrast to India.[11]

Studies on the Indian middle classes are inadequate. But B.B. Misra and Ashok Rudra have done some pioneering work in this respect.[12] Regarding the magnitude of the middle classes in India, we do not have any accurate figure. According to one estimate, about 200 to 250 millions in India today constitute middle classes.[13] If so, its proportion is very less than the developed countries like the USA and UK.

There are some studies focussed on the problems of rural women, especially in the agricultural labour force.[14] In a country like India, the base of women struggle is rural not urban. Hence, women studies should concentrate on rural women work force. Only then women studies in India will be relevant and appropriate.

Literacy and education, employment, health care and population control are some of the important considerations for women's development. The Eighth Plan sets the target of achieving 100 per cent literacy among the people of age group 15 to 35 years in all the states. This will involve changing the literacy status of about 110 million people. Students in Colleges and Universities, teachers and other motivated people will have to be mobilised for this mission.[15] Gandhiji's observation may be noted here that the education of a man is the education of an individual, the education of a woman is the education of an entire family.

The 1981 Census of India reported a literacy rate of 36.23 per cent. This was a considerable improvement over literacy rate of 16.7 per cent in 1951; though, this is still a poor showing for 30 years of planning. Census (1991) reports literacy rate for population aged 7 years and above as 52 per cent. The regional disparities are wide and female literacy is still at a very low level. As per 1991 Census, the female literacy was only 39.4 per cent and male literacy 63.9 per cent.[16] Table 2 shows the literacy rate for all ages and for ages 15 and above by sex and rural-urban residence for 1971 and 1981.

Another problem with most of the women studies in India is that of underrating the *cultural ethos*. As a result, application of Western models and paradigms becomes mechanical and unrealistic. The model of 'Motherhood' in oriental societies, especially in South Asia, demands an approach different from the West. Similar is the case with power sharing by women in South Asia. The values attached to 'Family' as an institution in Indian society do not fall in line with that of the USA, UK and other European societies. Women's status cannot be properly comprehended without a comprehensive comparative study of these dimensions. There are some attempts, however, at examining and unravelling the Indian cultural ethos.[17] *It is very important to take this dimension into consideration before there is an attempt in devising and applying models and paradigms for Indian society*. However, my main thrust in this paper is to point out the areas where priorities may be given for women studies in India.

PROPOSAL FOR FUTURE RESEARCH

In the light of the above discussion, action research may be carried on for Women Development in the following areas:

a. Problems of Women of the Weaker Sections (e.g., Backward Castes, Scheduled Castes and Scheduled Tribes): Females from OBC (Other Backward Classes), SC (Scheduled Castes) and ST (Scheduled Tribes) are relatively more deprived. Their concentration is largely in agricultural labour force. This may be the target group for action research.

b. Rural Women: Technology, Agriculture and Vocational Education: Mukherjee concludes in his study on West Bengal that the displacement effect of modern technology seems to have adversely affected the position of women in at least three ways: (1) by curtailing their employment prospects and hence (2) by curtailing their income, and (3) by curtailing their command over a vital resource, i.e., the quantum of foodgrains they received as remuneration for their husking labour.[18] Similar impact upon rural women and its implications in contemporary India may be researched and ways for ramifications may be worked out.

c. Women and Sustainable Development: For afforestation, water management and other sustainable development programmes, women's active involvement may be sought in action research.

d. Problems of Minority Women: Muslim, Christian and women of other minority groups have specific problems. Some of these have been highlighted by social scientists.[19] More studies may be carried out for identifying their problems, and subsequent solutions sought through action research.

e. Women, Literacy & Education and Women Development Indexes: Further systematic analysis may be pursued on women literacy and education and women development indexes. Ahooja-Patel has developed an Index of Women's Advancement (IWA). Similarly, Human Development Index (HDI) by UNDP (United Nations Development Programmes), Under 5 Mortality Rate (U5MR) by UNICEF, and Purchasing Power Parity (PPP) by the United Nations may be computed for India statewise with male/female and rural/urban variations.[20]

f. Data Base on various aspects of women (e.g., Census Farm Management Studies, NSS (National Sample Survey), etc.) in dBase, Foxbase or in RDB (Relational Data Base) Softwares.

g. Theories, Models, Paradigms and Methodologies for Gender Studies: Devi has pointed out that the available educational theories of 'functionalism' and 'reproduction' perspective, even though they try to explain educational inequalities across social groups, fail to explain the emergence and persistence of gender inequalities in education.[21] However, the existing feminist theories offer empirical insights into the phenomenon of gender inequalities.

The 'Liberal Feminist Theory' which is dominated by sex socialisation paradigm considers that the social system is just by nature and that all deviations from desirable conditions including educational inequality are due to incorrect socialisation, lack of information about the problems confronting women and the absence of adequate legislation to deal with them. According to this perspective, the formal educational institutions tend to perpetuate traditional socialisation and gender discrimination practices through the content (gender stereotypes in text books) and teaching practices (high expectation for boys rather than for girls).

The 'Radical Feminist Theory' considers that the main cause of women's subordination originates from power relations based on gender differences (mainly women's ability to conceive and give birth to children). This perspective views the school as another important agent in the transmission of patriarchal ideologies and explains that low level of literacy among women in many countries is due to governmental apathy towards women in not allocating adequate priorities for their educational development.

The 'Socialist Feminist Theory' sees an interconnection between ideological and economic forces with patriarchy and capitalism reinforcing each other. This perspective sees the school as a site for the reproduction of women's oppression as workers and as women. These theories may be freshly examined in configuration with Matin's Power Model for South Asia.[22]

To sum up, women's studies as a systematic discipline has originated and developed in the Western societies since long. These societies are predominantly urban, and a large number of the population is characterized as middle class. The rural population in these societies is insignificant. Women's movements (as well as their studies for various reasons) in these societies therefore stem from and revolve around the complexity of industrial urban middle class structures and settings. Indian society differs in these respects from the West European or North American societies. The former may be characterized as agrarian society where the majority lives in villages.[23] Workforce in India is concentrated in agriculture compared to the industrial and service sectors. The magnitude of urbanization in India is lower than the USA, UK and other Western countries. Hence, indigenous models and paradigms for women studies may be evolved for understanding the realities and historical experiences of Indian society which are different from the occidental, industrial and urban societies.

Acknowledgments: Ideas in this paper stem from my informal discussions with Ms. Teresa Hibert since 1983, who is a known feminist-cum-activist based in Toronto, Canada. My students in the M.Phil. Course on 'Women Studies in India', in the Department of Sociology, Aligarh Muslim University, Aligarh, in my Thursday lectures have been helpful in shaping the present framework. An earlier version of this paper was presented at the RMCEI (Ravi Mathai Center for Educational Innovation, Indian Institute of Management, Ahmedabad) on 23 September, 1993. Comments from several faculty members, especially Prof. Ananta Giri, have been useful in revising this paper. Dr. Shadbano Ahmad and Prof. A.J. Qaisar provided detailed comments on the earlier draft of this paper. I have revised the paper in the light of those comments and discussions. Ms. Soophia Ahmad has done the proof reading and the editing of its earlier version. I am grateful to Prof. Kamal Nayan Kabra who persuaded and encouraged me to write this paper. However, I am entirely responsible for the ideas presented in this paper as well as errors.

NOTES

1. Krishna Ahooja-Patel, 'Gender Distance Among Countries', *Economic and Political Weekly* (henceforth *EPW*), Vol. 28, No. 7, 1993, p. 296.

2. Abdul Matin, 'Women Struggle in the changing Socio-Economic Formation: With specific Reference to India', Keynote address to the members, Management Professionals' Association, Madras, May, 28, 1988.

3. For details, see Uma Chakravarti and Kumkum Roy, 'In search of our Past: A Review of the limitations and possibilities of the Historiography of women in early India', *EPW,* Vol. XXIII, No. 18, 1989; Neera Desai and Vibhuti Patel, *Indian Women: Change & Challenge in the International Decade 1975-85,* Bombay, 1985; Chandrakala A. Hate, *Changing Status of Woman in Post-Independence India,* Bombay, 1969; Devaki Jain, *From Dissociation to Rehabilitation: Report on an Experiment to Promote Self Employment in an Urban Area,* New Delhi, 1975; Promila Kapoor, *Marriage & Working Women in*

India, Delhi, 1972; Maithreyi Krishna Raj (ed.), *Women's Studies in India: Some Perspectives,* Bombay, 1986; Rama Mehta, *The Western Educated Hindu Women,* Bombay, 1970; B.R. Nanda (ed.), *Indian Women: From Purdah to Modernity,* New Delhi, 1976; Sunita Pandhe, 'Women's Studies and Women's Movement', *EPW,* Vol. XXIII, No. 40, 1988; Patricia Uberoi, 'Feminine Identity and National Ethos in Indian Calendar Art', *EPW,* Vol. XXV, No. 17, 1990.

4. A. Jan Qaisar, 'The Exposure-Response Syndrome: The Case of Medieval India', Presidential Address, Indian History Congress, 48th Session, Medieval India (Section II), Goa, 1987.

5. Victor Petrov, *India: Spotlight on Population,* Moscow, 1985.

6. For details, see Puloma Shah, 'Female Foeticide', *Seminar,* Vol. 410, New Delhi, October, 1993, pp. 42-44.

7. Anjali, 'Prejudice Against Girl abuse of Scientific Discovery', *Social Welfare,* Vol. 34, 1987, pp. 10-11, quoted in Puloma Shah, op. cit., p. 43.

8. For details, see Arup Mitra, 'Sex Ratio and Violence: Spurious Results', *EPW,* Vol. 28, Nos. 1 & 2, 1993, p. 67; S.I. Rajan, U.S. Mishra and K. Navaneethan, 'Decline in Sex Ratio: Alternative Explanation Revisited', *EPW,* Vol. 27, No. 46, 1992, pp. 2505-2508; S. Raju and M.K. Premi, 'Decline in Sex Ratio: Alternative Explanation Re-Examined', *EPW,* Vol. 27, No. 17, 1992, pp. 911-912; Philip Oldenberg, 'Sex Ratio, Son Preference and Violence in India: A Research Note', *EPW,* Vol. 27, Nos. 49 & 50, 1992, pp. 2657-2662.

9. Oldenberg, op. cit., p. 2658.

10. See Petrov, op. cit., p. 208.

11. Table 2 shows the sectoral distribution of labour force in India and other South Asian countries. It clearly reveals that bulk of labour force in India is in the agriculture sector whereas in Canada, USA, and UK, labour force is concentrated in industry and services. In India, 71% labour force was in agriculture, 13% in industry, and 16% in services in the year 1981. Whereas in Canada only 5% labour force was in agriculture, and in the USA and UK 2% each for the same period.

12. For details, see B.B. Misra, *The Indian Middle Classes: Their Growth in Modern Times,* London, 1961; Ashok Rudra, 'Emergence of the Intelligentsia as a Ruling Class in India' (*Dharam Narain Memorial Lecture, 1988,* Institute of Economic Growth, mimeographed, Delhi, 1988).

13. According to the World Bank's World Development Report, 1987, the top 20% of India's population (about 150 million) accounted for a per capita income of Rs. 10,000 and a family income of about Rs. 50,000 in the year 1987. For details, see Amit Prakash, 'How Big is the Middle Class', *The Pioneer,* New Delhi, January 16, 1994, p. 7.

14. For details, see Bina Agarwal, 'Neither sustenance nor sustainability: Agricultural strategies, Ecological Degradation & Indian Women in poverty', in Bina Agarwal (ed.), *Structures of Patriarchy, State, Community and Household in Modernising Asia,* New Delhi, 1988; Martha A. Chen, 'Women's work in Indian Agriculture by Agro Ecological Zones: Meeting Needs of Landless and Land-Poor Women', *EPW,* October 28, 1989; Nata Duvvury, 'Women in Agriculture: A Review of the Indian Literature', *EPW,* 1989, p. 28; Sheila Gujral, 'Indian Rural Women' in B.K. Vashishta (ed.), *Encyclopedia of Women in India,* New Delhi, 1976; Gita Sen, 'Women's Work & Women Agricultural Labourers: A Study of the Indian Census', Trivandrum (Centre for Development Studies), 1982; Gita Sen, 'Women Agricultural Labourers: Regional Variations in Incidence & Employment', Trivandrum (Centre for Development Studies), 1983; Amar Jesani, 'Limits of Empowerment: Women in Rural Health Care', *EPW,* Vol. XXV, No. 20, May 19, 1990, pp. 1098-1103; Vanita Viswanath, *NGOs and Women's Development in Rural South India: A Comparative Analy-*

sis, New Delhi, 1993; Kalima Rose, *Where Women are Leaders: The SEWA Movement in India,* New Delhi, 1992; Usha Jumani, *Dealing With Poverty: Self-Employment for Poor Rural Women,* New Delhi, 1991.

15. Planning Commission, *Eighth Five Year Plan,* New Delhi, 1992, p. 11.

16. Ibid., p. 28.

17. For example, see Veena Das, 'Indian Women: Work, Power and Status' in B.R. Nanda (ed.), *Indian Women: From Purdah to Modernity,* New Delhi, 1976; Kathryn Hansen, 'The Virangana in North India history: Myth and Popular Culture', *EPW,* Vol. XXIII, no. 18, 1988; Dorannee Jacobson and Susan S. Wadbey, *Women in India: Two Perspectives,* New Delhi, 1977.

18. Mukul Mukherjee, 'Impact of Modernization on Women's Occupation: A Case Study of the Rice-Husking Industry of Bengal', *Indian Economic and Social History Review,* Vol. 20, No. 1, 1983, pp. 27-45.

19. Mohini Anjum (ed.), *Muslim Women in India,* New Delhi, 1992; Shadbano Ahmad, 'Methodological Problems in the Study of Muslim Women', in Mohini Anjum, op. cit.

20. For details, see Krishna Ahooja-Patel, 'Gender Distance Among Countries', op. cit., pp. 295-305.

21. M.D. Usja Devi, 'Research Perspective for Understanding Women's Education', *EPW,* Vol. 27, Nos. 24 & 25, 1992, p. 1279.

22. Abdul Matin, 'Power Model for South Asia: Emerging Trend of the Conflict Approach (Dahrendorfian Model) in Agrarian Society' (Mimeographed), Toronto, 1983.

23. For the concept of Agrarian Society, see ibid.

Figure 1: Annual Growth Rate of Gender (India)

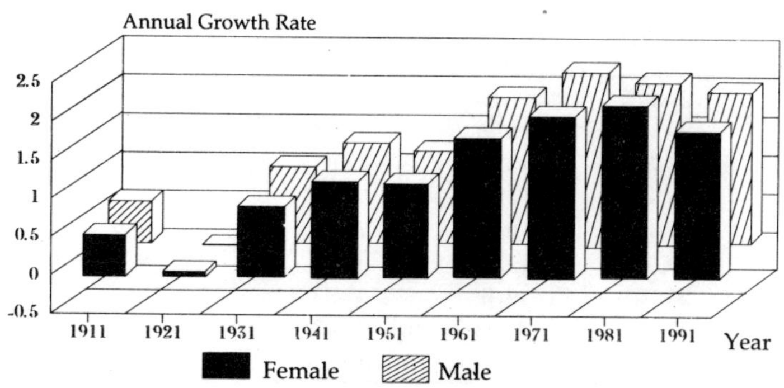

(Source: Based on Table 1, Columns 7&8)

Figure 2: Sex Ratio in India, 1901-91

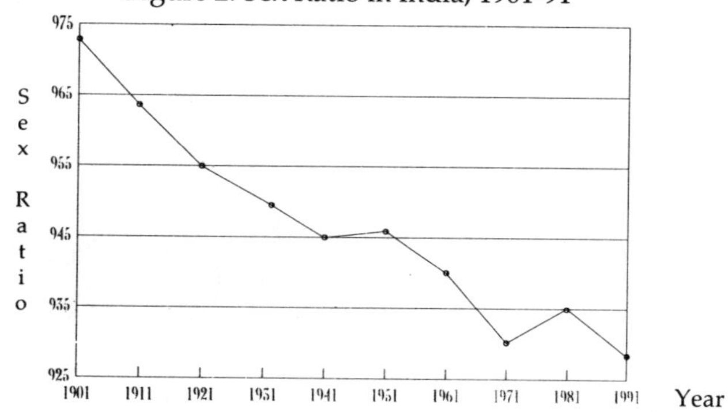

(Source: Based on Table 1, Column 6)

Table 1: Genderwise Population and other Statistics of India

Year	Tot. Pop. (in Million)	Females	% Female Pop.	Males	Sex Ratio	Annual Males	Growth Rate Females	% Urban Pop. to Tot. Pop.	Av. Annual Growth of Urban Pop.
1901	238.39	117.4	49.23	120.8	972	—	—	11.0	—
1911	252.09	123.7	49.07	128.4	964	0.61	0.52	10.4	—
1921	251.32	122.8	48.85	128.5	955	0.01	- 0.07	11.3	0.79
1931	278.97	135.8	48.67	142.9	950	1.07	1.01	12.2	1.77
1941	318.66	154.7	48.54	163.7	945	1.37	1.31	14.1	2.82
1951	361.08	175.6	48.61	185.5	946	1.26	1.28	17.6	3.52
1961	439.23	212.9	48.48	226.3	941	2.01	1.94	18.3	2.34
1971	548.15	264.1	48.18	284.0	930	2.30	2.18	20.2	3.26
1981	685.18	330.5	48.27	353.3	935	2.21	2.27	23.7	3.86
1991	843.39	406.3	48.15	437.6	929	2.16	2.09	—	—

(Source: Computed from the Censuses of India)

Table 2: Literacy Rate for all ages and for ages 15 and above by sex and rural-urban residence, 1971 and 1981

Age Group	Person Male Female	1971			1981		
		Total	Rural	Urban	Total	Rural	Urban
1	2	3	4	5	6	7	8
All ages	Persons	29.49	23.69	52.37	36.23	29.65	57.40
	Males	39.52	33.76	61.24	46.89	40.79	65.83
	Females	18.70	13.08	42.05	24.82	17.96	47.82
15+	Persons	34.04	26.98	60.28	40.76	32.76	65.13
	Males	47.69	40.51	72.42	54.84	47.27	76.36
	Females	19.32	12.88	45.42	25.68	17.57	51.88
35+	Persons	25.16	19.40	49.33	30.18	23.17	54.25
	Males	37.97	31.23	64.47	44.61	37.96	69.42
	Females	10.75	06.47	30.18	14.44	08.62	35.91

(Source: Usha Kunda, 'Employment Position of Educated Women', *Yojana*, Vol. 34, Nos. 1 & 2, 1990, p. 70)

16

The Hindus and the *Dargah* of Ajmer, A.D. 1737-1857

S. LIYAQAT H. MOINI

Elsewhere we published an article 'The Hindus and the *Dargah* of Ajmer, A.D. 1658-1737: An overview'.[1] The present work is an extension of the same theme covering the period 1737-1857.

The previous article was based on a rare collection of documents (Murad Collection) comprising *vikalatnamas* and letters from the devotees of the *dargah,* addressed to Syed Muhammad Murad, the son of Syed Muhammad Jafar *Khadim.* The former, who lived between 1638 and 1737, belonged to the famous *Syedzadagan Khadim* (*Khuddam*) community of Ajmer, who were attached to the shrine of Khwaja Muinuddin Chishti since its inception, in spite of the fluctuating fortunes of Ajmer.

The *khadim* at the *dargah* were invariably accepted as *vakil* by the devotees. The *vakil* used to pray and intercede on behalf of his *muwakkil* (client), invoking the blessings of the great saint for the fulfilment of the client's desires, vows, success, prosperity, health and betterment of the worldly and other-worldly affairs of the devotee/*muwakkil* attached to him. In the absence of devotees, besides praying regularly, the *vakil* had to send *tabarrukat* (sacred articles), especially of the *'urs,* to his client. After receiving offerings *(nazr o niyaz)* from the devotee, his *vakil* performed rituals such as offering of flowers, cloth sheets, *fatihakhwani,* and lamp burning on the former's behalf. If the client came to the *dargah* himself, his *vakil* helped and guided him in the performance of *ziyarat* (religious visit), circumambulation and other rituals. The *vakil* was entitled to get and take away all the *nazr o niyaz,* whether in cash or kind offered by his *muwakkil.*

The *muwakkil/vakil* syndrome was cemented by *vikalatnama,* which was a sort of pledge or 'binding deed' by which a devotee attached or bound himself to a particular *khadim* by accepting him as his/her *vakil* at the *dargah.* The *vikalatnama* was generally written or signed during the pilgrim's visit, but in some cases of nobles, chieftains and high officials these were secured through their trusted persons such as the *diwan,* etc. The present article, like the earlier one, is primarily based on *vikalatnamas* and other supporting documents, such as letters and especially the *dargah* files (1000 in number) preserved in the Rajasthan State Archives, Bikaner, covering a period of more than seventy years (1818-90).

Syed Masud, being the eldest son and successor of Syed Muhammad Murad, received condolence letters from many prominent nobles on the latter's death in 1737.[2] In fact, the name of Syed Masud appeared jointly with Syed Murad in many *vikalatnamas* even when his father was alive.

Syed Murad had once requested Bhola Nath Sahay (an imperial officer at Delhi) to persuade the officers of Ajmer to grant Syed Masud and his brothers daily allowance (*yomia*) from the *dargah waqf*.[3] Syed Masud after his father's death carried on the sacred task of sending *tabarrukat* of the shrine regularly to the previous devotees, and enrolled many new adherents (Plates 72-73) during one of the most crucial periods of Indian history.[4] Due to the constant warfare and disturbances in Rajputana, the Mughals were slowly and gradually losing their grip over and around the city of Ajmer, and with the departure of Salabat Khan, the last Mughal Commander (who was the maternal grandfather of Emperor Ahmad Shah), in 1750, the imperial authority over the city dwindled.[5] Though some *sanads* regarding land grants to *khuddams*, and appointments in the *dargah* and other offices are available till the reign of Akbar Shah II (1837),[6] in fact, the entire administration of the city of Ajmer, including the holy places, was conducted by the Marathas between 1756-1818, except for three years in 1787-90 when the Rathors of Jodhpur captured Ajmer. Finally, it was ceded to the British in 1818. Thus, for nearly sixty years the Marathas, taking full advantage of the weak central authority and internal rivalries amongst the local Rajput chieftains, ravaged the whole area of Rajputana realising as much money as they could. It became a hunting ground for the Sindhias, Holkars, and other *sardars* of the Maratha confederacy.[7]

What was the attitude of these Maratha rulers, officials, etc. towards the *dargah* during this period? It appears from the contemporary records that they all paid the same respect to Khwaja Moinuddin Chishti as did the Mughals and Rajputs, and regularly visited and took keen interest in the affairs of the *dargah* to such an extent that many Hindus even held the highest office of *mutawalli*.[8]

Earlier, Raja Sahu had fixed a sum of Rs. 1000 per annum as *nazr* for Syed Murad and had also granted village Malthan (in his kingdom) for the performance of certain rituals on his behalf at the shrine.[9] His son Fath Singh used to send *nazr* regularly, requesting Syed Masud to pray for the birth of a son to him.[10] Ram Raja of Satara, the successor of Raja Sahu, too, had links with the *dargah* through Syed Masud.[11]

Jogidas Munshi, an official of Raja Sahu, was thrilled on getting sacred *tabarrukat*, and, in response despatched *nazr o niyaz* to Syed Masud.[12] Anand Rao Raghunath, the *vakil* of Raja Sahu, addressed Syed Masud with much veneration and desired to visit the shrine as early as possible to perform the circumambulation.[13]

No direct evidence is available at the moment about the relations of the founder of the Peshwa dynasty, viz., Balaji Vishwanath (1713-20) with the people of the shrine, but from a letter of his wife Radhabai (the mother of Baji Rao I) to Syed Masud, it comes to light that Balaji Vishwanath also held the *dargah* in high esteem. The letter bears the seal of Bapuji Naik Joshi, the famous banker of Raja Sahu, who was once the contender for the office of the Peshwa. In her letter, Radhabai thanked Syed Masud for the holy *tabarrukat* of the shrine and expressed her desire to visit Ajmer on the eve of the Pushkar fair in the month of Kartik, when she intended to offer a horse to the shrine. She also assured Syed Masud to follow all practices which the latter had instructed her verbally through Mallu *qasid* (messenger). It is quite possible that she must have gone to the *dargah* on her famous pilgrimage to North India in 1735 accompanied by Bapuji Naik Joshi.[14]

Her son Peshwa Balaji Rao I (1720-40) issued a *vikalatnama* in the name of Syed Masud in 1736 (Plate 75).[15] Again, the former's son and successor, Balaji Baji Rao (1740-61), the third Peshwa, did the same in 1755 during the reign of Alamgir II.[16] An interesting *vikalatnama* of Shamsher Bahadur, another son of Baji Rao I (from his famous mistress Mastani), completes the list of the Peshwa family's documents in favour of Syed Masud, establishing their devotional links with the *dargah* of Ajmer.[17] Shamsher Bahadur visited Ajmer in 1758 and most probably visited the *dargah.*[18] His son Nawab Ali Bahadur repeatedly requested Syed Masud to pray for his success in getting succession rights (*nāmdari* and *nabīrdari*) of his grandfather, i.e., Peshwa Baji Rao I.[19] However, when Nawab Ali Bahadur came to Ajmer in 1795, Syed Mardan Ali, the grandson of late Syed Masud, was out of city and therefore some other *khadim* led him to the shrine for the performance of *ziarat.* This provided an opportunity for a dispute between the sons of Syed Masud and the said *khadim* who escorted Nawab Ali Bahadur to the *dargah.* The matter came to an end only when the *khadim* assured Syed Mardan Ali and his brother that he had not procured *vikalatnama* from the Nawab in his favour, and will not claim his *vikalat* in future.[20] Later in 1800, Syed Mardan Ali, etc. were able to get a *vikalatnama* in their names from Nawab Ali Bahadur. Further, Nawab Zulfiqar Ali Khan, the son of Nawab Ali Bahadur, also issued a *vikalatnama* in the name of the two sons of Syed Masud in 1821. His brother Shamsher Bahadur II used to visit the *dargah* regularly and offered a valuable tent for the *mehfil* of *urs* and other important ceremonies.[21] Interestingly, Mr. Burn, an Englishman, who had accompanied Nawab Zulfiqar Ali Khan on his Ajmer visit, too, signed a *vikalatnama* and wrote two lines in English (dated 9 May 1821).[22]

Raghunath Rao, a famous Maratha *sardar,* and the brother of Peshwa Balaji Rao, addressed Syed Masud as *haqa'iq o m'arif āgāh* (knower of secrets and facts) and *sajjada nashin* when he sent him a *nazr* of Rs. 200. His adopted son and successor Shrimat Amrit Rao, too, accepted Syed Fazl Ali (the grandson of Syed Masud) as his *vakil* at the shrine, and issued a document to this effect from Benaras in November 1816. Syed Fazl Ali further succeeded in getting a *vikalatnama* from Vinayak Rao, the son of Amrit Rao, in August 1836, from the Chitterkot Cantonment.[23]

Two undated letters, bearing the Marathi seal of Rani Tara Bai (the mother of Shivaji III of Kolahpur), furnish evidence that the opposite group of Raja Sahu also kept contact with the people of the *dargah* and were keen to get sacred *tabarrukat* and to despatch *nazr o niyaz*.[24]

The Holkar chieftains, too, visited the shrine whenever any of them happened to be in Rajputana. The author of the *Tarikh-i Hindi* informs that around 1735 Malhar Rao Holkar appeared in the environs of Ajmer and devastated the territory. But later not only he but all his troops paid a visit to the famous shrine.[25] Malhar Rao Holkar in his two (undated) letters addressed to Syed Masud thanked him for the pain the latter had taken in sending him *tabarrukat*, and also for narrating in detail the prevailing conditions in that area.[26] Ahalaya Bai, the widow of Malhar's son Khande Rao, too, appears to have paid a visit to the shrine.[27]

Tukoji Holkar issued a *vikalatnama* in favour of Syed Masud in August 1791. Again, Maharaja Jaswant Rao Holkar of Indore signed a *vikalatnama* in the name of Syed Muzaffar Ali, most probably during one of his visits to the shrine in April 1804.[28] Many of the successors and officials of the Holkars had accepted Syed Masud and his sons as their *vakil* at the *dargah*.[29] In 1861, the mother of the Maharaja of Indore sent an *ashrafi* and a doll (*guriya*) as *nazr* to the shrine.[30]

Raja Chattar Singhji Bhonsle of Nagpur represented another branch of the Marathas who maintained relations with Syed Muzaffar Ali.[31] No details are available about the attitude of the Gaikwads of Baroda, but late in the nineteenth century references of sending *ghilāf* (costly velvet sheets) suggest that this Maratha family also had established links with the *khadims* of the *dargah*, though not necessarily with Syed Masud and his descendants: they preferred other families of the *khadim*.[32]

The Sindhias, who dominated the affairs in Rajputana and virtually ruled over Ajmer during the second half of eighteenth century, regularly visited the *dargah* of Ajmer. Their role in the Amber (Jaipur) succession and in other disputes among the Rajput chiefs resulted in the murder of their famous leader Jayappa Sindhia by the Rathors in 1756. Nevertheless, Jayappa's courageous and enterprising brother Dattaji Sindhia and his son Jankoji Sindhia carried on their struggle with the Rathors. Finally, a treaty was signed in 1756 between both parties, by which Ajmer was ceded to the Sindhias as prize for *Mundi Katti* (cutting of head) of Jayappa Sindhia. The Sindhia family held it till 1818 when it was ceded to the British.[33]

No details are available about the visits of these early Sindhia chiefs to the *dargah*, but it is reported that Mahadaji Sindhia in April 1791 paid homage to the shrine soon after he recaptured Ajmer from the Rathors.[34] It appears that the early Sindhia chiefs had established links with another *khadim* family rather than traditionally following Syed Masud as their *vakil* with whom the majority of the Marathas kept relations. Syed Muhammad Hayat, Syed Muhammad Umar and other *khadims* were patronized by the Sindhias, and were either appointed *mutawalli*, or deputed as the actual postholders during 1758-85. So close was the relation of the Sindhia rulers with this particular *khadim* family that when in 1787 the Rathors captured Ajmer from the Sindhias, Mir Syed Azimullah, the descendant and successor of the aforesaid *khadims* and *mutawallis*, left the city along with his family and took shelter in Kishangarh state, and returned only in 1790 when Mahadaji Sindhia recovered the city.[35]

However, in October 1797, Syed Mardan Ali, the son of Syed Masud, was successful in procuring a *vikalatnama* from Daulat Rao Sindhia, the adopted son and successor of Madho Sindhia (Plate 75).[36] Daulat Rao Sindhia outclassed the devotion and veneration of all the Marathas by regularly visiting the *dargah*, sending *nazr o niyaz*, and also a cooking *deg* (cauldron). Col. T. Broughton, who had accompanied him in 1810-11, supplies details of all these activities in his letters.[37] Daulat Rao Sindhia also took keen interest in the affairs of the *dargah*, patronized the family of Mir Azimullah *khadim* whom he had reappointed *mutawalli* of the shrine and also granted him Dantra village from the *waqf* of the *dargah* in lieu of his salary (*rozina*). He further recommended his son Mir Aziz Ali to succeed his father as *mutawalli* after his demise. Probably, it was under the influence of Daulat Rao Sindhia and his ancestors, who used to observe the mournings of *Muharram* regularly, that Mir Azimullah, too, reorganized *Muharram* rituals at Ajmer and introduced the practice of the *t'azia* procession, etc. which is still prevalent amongst the *khuddams*. However, in spite of such close links with Mir Azimullah, Daulat Rao Sindhia, on the representation of Syed Fazl Ali (a direct descendant of Syed Masud), ordered and upheld the sitting right on *gaddi/ masnad* of the said Syed under a *khirni* tree just opposite the tomb which was challenged by his cousins.[39]

From a list of the recipients of daily allowance (*rozina*) from the *dargah waqf*, it comes to light that Daulat Rao Sindhia had granted *rozina* to many persons from every walk of life such as *khadim/pirzada*, local *Nawabs*, Hindu chiefs, *Brahmins* and *gaitis* (female singers).[40]

Col. T.D. Broughton was surprised to find that the Maratha *Sardar* was not keen to visit Pushkar after attending ceremonies at the *dargah*, and even the offering that he sent to the chief *purohit* at Pushkar was not so valuable as that given to the *khadims* at the shrine.[41]

Daulat Rao Sindhia's another act is one of the rarest ever done by any contemporary ruler or chieftain of the period. Finding that the famous *Adhai din ka jhonpra* mosque (standing just behind the *dargah*) was so much neglected that the local people had started removing stones from this historic building, he, in 1809, ordered to fix a slab to the left of the main entrance of the mosque, forbidding and appealing the Hindus and Muslims not to remove stones and damage the building. Furthermore, he ordered to repair the central dome of the mosque.[42] Following him, one of his ministers Mulla Madari replaced the two big *degs* of the *dargah* through Seth Abhay Chand Mehta.[43] Bale Rao Ingalia (1803-8) and Gumanji Rao alias Tantia Sindhia (1809-15), the two governors of Ajmer under Daulat Rao Sindhia, also constructed two *verandas* at the shrine of Miran Syed Hussain Khingsawar at Taragarh fort of Ajmer.[44]

Many of the governors and other officials of the Sindhias posted at Ajmer established links with the *dargah* and its people. Prominent amongst them were Gobind Rao, Pandit Shankar Rao, Pandit Bale Rao, Pandit Sadah Shiv, Paras Ram *hakim* of Jalor.[45] Gumanji Rao Sindhia even granted 20 *bighas* of *chahi* land in Jatli village to Syed Kazim Ali *khadim* in 1813-14.[46]

Jankoji Rao Sindhia, the ruler of Gwaliyar, issued a *vikalatnama* in the name of Syed Dilawar Ali, the grandson of Syed Masud in 1835.[47]

Among other prominent Marathas, Rao Nimbalkar, the Mughal *faujdar* of Ahmednagar, used to send Rs. 1000 per annum as *nazr.*[48] Appaji Daccani and Damaji Deccani signed a *vikalatnama* in the name of Syed Masud in 1767, in which the necessity of appointing or accepting a *vakil* to the shrine, his rights and duties, etc. were discussed in detail.[49] Syed Masud also succeeded in getting such document from Gangadhar Savant, the *diwan* of the *sarkar* of Sada Shiv Rao.[50]

A number of *vikalatnamas* were issued at different times by numerous Marathas: Kishan Rao Mahipat, Mahipat Rao Kamanjoo (1814), Balaji Laxamji Kulkarni of Pune (Marathi), Pandurg Vanchagji Ram, the son of Mallaji (Maratha), Ihtramuddaula Kishan Rao Kadam, Muzaffar Jang Bahadur, Bahadur Vithal Rao Shivdeo (1786), and Pillaj Jadav. The documents of all these reflect the veneration of every branch and section of the Marathas to the shrine through Syed Masud and his descendants.[51]

Besides the Marathas, other local chieftains, too, were in regular contact with the *dargah* through the aforesaid *khadim* and his son. Maharaja Abhay Singh of Marwar (Jodhpur) confirmed 125 *bighas* of land in Thanwla village to Syed Masud, earlier granted by the Mughals to his ancestors.[52] His brother Raja Bakht Singh on receiving sacred *tabarrukat* expressed his helplessness in sending *nazr* due to unavoidable circumstances. As the governor of Ajmer in 1752, on the orders of Nawab Javed Khan, he took keen interest in the dispute regarding proper distribution of the *madad-i ma'ash* land of Ghegal and Beonja villages earlier granted to the *khadim* community by Farrukhsiyar.[53]

Kishori Singh and Pirthi Singh were other Rathor *sardars* who addressed Syed Masud as their *vakil,* and considered the *dargah* as *qiblai kaunain* (worship place of the universe) and felt honoured after receiving *tabarrukat.*[54]

The ruler of Mewar (Udaipur), Rana Amar Singh, the son of Rana Jagat Singh, too, had accepted Syed Masud as his *vakil.* Maichi Raj (an official), in a letter on behalf of Maharana Sangram Singh of Mewar, assured Syed Masud about the *vikalat* of his master in the same way as did his ancestors.[55] But from an invitation letter of Maharana Bhim Singh, the ruler of Udaipur (dated 1812), it appears that the Sisodia ruler had changed his *vakil* at the shrine as Syed Inayat Husain *khadim* and Mir Azimullah *mutawalli* were requested to bless the ceremony.[56]

An insurance (*bimah*) of Rs. 11 as *saliyana* was despatched by Kishanjiu, the son of Saligram (an official of Maharaja Zorawar Singh of Bikaner), in response to the sacred *tabarrukat* sent to him by Syed Masud.[57]

Maharaja Ishwari Singh and Maharaja Madho Singh, the sons and successors of Maharaja Sawai Jai Singh of Amber, used to send Rs. 100 yearly, and in response received sacred gifts regularly from Syed Masud. It is interesting to note that the seals of Maharaja Madho Singh fixed on a few early letters addressed to Syed Masud bear the name of Shah Alam, the Mughal Emperor, as his master but later it was replaced with the name of his father Maharaja Jai Singh. This shows the decreasing Mughal influence over the Rajputs.[58] However, in 1840, the ruler of Amber prepared the *deg* of the shrine, and Rs. 500 was also fixed by a chieftain of Jaipur to feed the people during the annual '*urs* of Khwaja Muinuddin Chishti. Maharaja Jai Singh also repaired the silver railings around the shrine, and offered a silver door for the enclosure of the *mazar* (tomb), now called *Jhijhri.*[59]

Due to internal rivalries and conflicts and Maratha intervention, the rulers of Kota and Bundi who earlier had made land grants in their respective *watans,* could not pay proper attention towards the shrine during the period under study. Yet, there is a reference to one Bhawani Singh of Harauti region who used to send *nazr o niyaz* to the descendants of Syed Masud. Maharaja Kota also sent a sum of Rs. 2800 for the cooking *deg,* offering of *ghilaf,* and for other rituals in 1827. It may be pointed out that whenever the populace of Jaipur, Kota and Bundi visited the shrine, they were considered the clients of Syed Masud and his descendants and, therefore, they contacted them for the performance of *ziarat,* thus giving birth to a new system called *basti,* i.e., areas of hereditary influence of the *khadims.*[60]

At present no detailed evidence is available regarding the attitude of the small *zamindars* of Rampura, Deolia, etc.; but a letter in Rajasthani furnishes details about a resident of Rampura village who, in 1748, had granted 20 *bighas* in Bolia village to Syed Masud as *udak* to 'Khwajaji'. Till now it was generally accepted that *udak* land grants were made only to Hindu temples and priests, but this piece of information significantly adds to our knowledge that *udak* was also granted to Muslim sages and divines.[61]

Raja Udai Singh, a noble of Emperor Ahmad Shah, Harnath Singh Taroke (1721), Raja Zorawar Singh, Shri Bijai Partap Singh and Thakur Madho Singh of Navalgarh were other influential local chieftains of Rajputana who had developed devotional links with the *dargah* and the *khadim.*[62]

Raja Man Singh, the son of Raja Raj Singh of Ratlam, and his brother, maintained regular correspondence with Syed Masud whom they considered their *vakil* at the *dargah.*[62] Interesting information is available in some letters written by important Rajas and Mughal nobles. Raja Chattar Singh of Partapgarh wrote that the delay in sending *nazr* was due to the transfer of his *mahals* by the *Nazim* of the province. Raja Jagjiwandas Nagar addressed Syed Masud as his *makhdūm* (master) and that he had great desire to present himself before him at the shrine. He further assured his *vakil* that shortly he was visiting Shahjahanabad for business purpose, from where he will send *mu'tād.*[63] Raja Gobind Das Nagar while thanking Syed Masud for sending him *tabarrukat,* hoped that from some hidden quarters (*pardai 'ghaib*) help will arrive to solve his problem. In another letter (March 1743), he acknowledged the receipt of a rosary of sandalwood, and in response despatched *niyaz.* Maharaja Dhiraj Maharawal Mul Raj Bahadur, besides thanking Syed Masud for the *tabarrukat* and remitting *mu'tad* through *hundi,* requested the Syed to earnestly pray for his success. Rustam Rao, the son of Rao Bahadur (servant of Alamgir II), wrote to Syed Masud that due to paucity of money he failed to send offerings but hoped that as soon as his income increased he will oblige his *vakil*. A *vikalatnama* (August 1754) of Rai Bhawanidas of *qasba* Sodhra (Ibraheemabad) in the name of Syed Masud indicates that the system of enrolling new followers besides the old ones was quite common. Raja Sahab of Pattan (Allahabad) in March 1830 obliged Syed Fazl Ali, the grandson of Syed Masud, who had approached him in person to get a *vikalatnama* of the Raja in his name.[64]

The letters of Dayaram, Maharaja Anup Singh, Himmat Bahadur (August 1781), and Holas Nath Surajdhawaj, tell us that they considered the sacred gifts sent by Syed Masud as great blessings, which made them feel happy and thrilled.[65]

Sabhachand, the *diwan* of Nawab Mubariz Khan, in a letter to Syed Masud in 1736, besides sending *nazr* and expressing his gratitude for the *tabarrukat* he had received, condoled him on the demise of his father Syed Murad. Sanghvi Shanemal, the *diwan* of a local chieftain, also sent a condolence message to Syed Masud on his father's death, and assured the former that the position of *vikalat* had been entrusted to him as usual.[66]

Many non-Muslim *diwans* and other officials of the well known nobles of later Mughals regularly despatched *nazr o niyaz.* Raja Jaswant Singh, an official of Shamsher Ali Bahadur Khan, had once sent a pearl as *mu'tad* to Syed Masud, while Sumal Singh, the *diwan* of Maharaja, assured Syed Masud of his full support to retain a garden which the latter owned.[67]

Two interesting cases must be described here. Once Raja Jugal Kishore sent *nazr* of Rs. 100 to Syed Masud which was taken away by one Muhammad Qutb. When the Raja came to know about it, he sent an urgent letter to Mirza Inayatullah Beg to look into the matter and to realise the money from the person concerned and deliver it to Syed Masud.[68] In another case, one Sadbhoo Ram Sahay, a servant of the *diwan-'ala,* informed Syed Masud that Tela and Ghanem Chand of the Doshi tribe of Ajmer had mortgaged 22 shops situated near Makha gate to him in Rs. 115. The rent of these shops was earmarked for Syed Masud. But now he had come to know that one Hiranand of Bakliwal caste had started collecting the rent of these shops. Syed Mir Masud, therefore, was requested by Sadbhoo Ram Sahay to look into the matter, take control of the shops on his behalf and oblige. This shows the trust of the officials and businessmen in the *khadims* and their *vakils* at the shrine.[69]

Besides these rulers, *zamindars* and local chieftains, there are numerous documents showing the Hindu and Muslim masses jointly accepting Syed Masud as their *vakil* and expecting prayers and *tabarrukat* from him.

The mixed populace of *pargana* Narnol, while accepting the descendants of Syed Masud as their hereditary *vakil* in 1777, considered themselves as servitors of these holy people, and vowed to send *maidani* (annually collected offerings) regularly.[70] Gulab Rai and Muhammad Saleh, the two officials of a noble, had jointly sent a letter and *nazr* through *hundi* in Shahjahanabadi currency.[71] One of the classic examples of this kind is about Gopal Singh Shekhawat, the *zamindar* of *qasba* Udaipur (*sarkar* Narnol in *suba* Shahjahanabad), who in his letter enquired from Syed Masud about the role and attitude of his other brothers with regard to the yearly *maidani* of that region. The *zamindar* further assured the *khadim* that all the people of his area were bound to attach themselves to the direct descendants of Syed Ja'far (the grandfather of Syed Masud), and that they could never think of any change in this respect. He also stated that the *dargah* is venerated equally by both the Turks and Hindus (*Turkawan va Hinduwan*; Plate 76).[72]

Another joint *vikalatnama* (December 1788) not only represented various communities, but also people of different professions, such as *khati* (carpenter) and tailor, etc.[73]

Among the businessmen who had linked themselves with Syed Masud, the *vikalatnama* of Khushal Rai Johri of Shahjahanabad deserves special mention. Though this document is written in Persian, the three lines added to it by Johri are in typical Hindi language based on numerical system frequently used by this class.[74]

Makhan Lal and Munshi Lal, the sons of Sahib Rai Kayastha of Allahabad, not only accepted Syed Masud as their *vakil* but promised to pay rupees one and four *annas* per month till any of them was in service. The letter of Jogia Pandit, etc. (dated 1758) in Rajasthani assured the *khadim* for sending *mu'tad* shortly.[75] Diwan Hazarimal, an official of Muhammad Sultan (a noble of Muhammad Shah), sent a *shamiyana* (canopy) for the shrine.[76]

Devi Rai Muhammad Shahi, the *diwan 'arz,* reported to Syed Masud that due to the attack and ravages of the Deccanis (Marathas), he was unable to despatch *nazr o niyaz.* He requested him to kindly pray for his safety and security.[77]

From an anonymous letter it appears that devotees were regular in sending money for cooking *degs,* velvet *ghilaf, saiban baadla* (tents) and *nazr* through their respective *vakils.*[78]

It is interesting to note that in the company of these Hindu chieftains some Europeans, especially the English, also signed *vikalatnamas* and offered *nazr.* As mentioned earlier, General Burn while accompanying Nawab Zulfiqar Ali Bahadur of Banda, too, had accepted Syed Fazl Ali and Syed Nabi Bakhsh as his *vakils* and wrote two lines in English on the above document (1821).[79] The British residents posted at Udaipur and Kota, Captain Kab and Major Laybee, offered *nazr* (1827) when *deg*-cooking took place on behalf of the Maharaja of Kota. Syed Bahadur Ali and his brother Syed Akbar Ali (the two ancestors of the present writer) shared his *nazr* along with some other *khadims.*[80] One of the *chobdars* (mace-bearer) of Charles Metcalf, too, had signed a *vikalatnama* in 1810 in the name of Syed Fazl Ali.[81] Reference has already been made to Col. Broughton who paid a visit to the shrine in the company of Daulat Rao Sindhia.[82]

Sometimes these *vikalatnamas* became the bone of contention between the family members, as has been found in the case of Syed Muhammad Afzal (son of Syed Lal Muhammad *Khadim*) and his uncle Syed Jan Muhammad in 1799. Both quarrelled over some *vikalatnama.* The matter was put before Krishnaji Bahadur, the *Kotwal* of Ajmer, who ordered them to deposit those documents and, when after some time, both made a compromise, these were returned to them.[83]

What was the attitude of the people of the *dargah* towards the Hindu devotees? No doubt, the *khuddams* carried out the task of regularly praying at the shrine for them, performing rituals on their behalf, and sending *tabarrukat* efficiently. They also invited them to visit the holy place and participate in ceremonies and functions. Hundreds of registers of the *Kachahri* of *dargah* (now called *dargah* files) are preserved in the Rajasthan State Archives at Bikaner, covering a period of about 70 years (1818-90). They supply important details of nearly every aspect of the happenings and occurrences at the *dargah* during the eighteenth and nineteenth centuries.[84] A study of these files combined with other scattered material brings out interesting and valuable facts about the role of the Hindus at the *dargah* and the benefits that accrued to them.

The administrative set-up of the shrine was headed by *mutawalli* (superintendent), assisted by *amins, mushrif, peshkars, vakils* and *mutasaddis* of *diwan, fotadars, qanungos, khazanchis,* etc. On the lower level, the staff included the *jamadar, farrash, chobdars, ghariyalis, naqqarchis, qawwals, maulud khwans, daroghas,* etc. who were called *shagird pesha* (menial staff). Under the Mughals, the office of *mutawalli* of the *dargah* was generally combined with that of the *sadr* of the province; hence, no Hindu could get appointment as *mutawalli.* But during the period under review, slowly and gradually, the office of the *sadr* of the province lost its power and importance, thus providing an opportunity to the people of other communities to serve as *mutawalli.* Gujar Mal Jat, Hukam Chand, Nanak Ram, Hanuvant Rao, Sheyam Rao, Somji, etc. held this important office during the second half of the eighteenth century. In official capacities these Hindus even presided and participated in *mehfils* of *samā*ʻ during the annual ʻ*urs* and on every Thursday night as well as every 6th of the lunar month, and also on the ʻ*urs* of other saints. It was a great and shining example of mutual understanding and liberal attitude.[85]

As far as the office of *amin dargah* is concerned, evidence is available that many non-Muslims held this important office. Rai Bhawani Sahay, Sunder Lal Shiv Sahay (1821), Pandurg Jitti Dev, etc. are found dealing with the affairs of the shrine efficiently during this period.[86] Sakha Ram, *amin dargah* (1820), once enquired about other privileges of the postholder besides the usual salary.[87] Kishan Nath Pandit, the son of Bhawani Sahay, served as *amin* and *tahsildar* of the *dargah.*

In 1829[88] the *amins* generally resided in the house allotted by the *dargah,* most probably in the *Kachahri,* where they were free to construct sheds and verandas.[89] It should be noted that none of these Hindu *amins* ever showed any kind of disrespect to the articles of the shrine or were found corrupt. Therefore, they were never punished. They always got support and good wishes from the *khuddams.* In contrast, Maulvi Abdul Qadir, the *amin* of the *dargah* and *sarishtadar* of Ajmer (who in 1818 had accompanied Mr. Wilder, the first English resident of the city), was dismissed from his post of *amin* on the report of *khadims,* but was later reappointed on their recommendation.[90]

Other important office was that of the *mutasaddi* of the *dargah* which was held by many Hindus. Peyare Lal, *mutasaddi* of the shrine, once submitted a voucher of the expenditure of the '*urs* of *Piran-i Pir* (Khwaja Usmani Harvani), the spiritual mentor of Khwaja Muinuddin Chishti.[91] Ram Nath Mansa Ram held this office in 1809, and received an honorary *dastar* on the occasion of the marriage of his nephew Man Singh. Mansa Ram, too, received financial help for the marriage of his grandsons in 1809 and in 1813. In 1820, Chand Lal, the son of Mansa Ram, was the *mutasaddi* of the shrine which indicates that the office had become hereditary. Chand Lal on his father's death received a *dastar* of condolence and when he himself died in 1823, his successor received a similar *dastar* of condolence (*dastar-i ghami*).[92] Jawahar Lal *mutasaddi* supervised the expenditure on the '*urs* of *Qutub Sahib* (Khwaja Qutbuddin Bakhtiar Kaki) in 1825, while Jawahar Ram acted as *mutasaddi* in 1826-27.[93] Bhuri Lal *mutasaddi* complained in 1824 that he was deprived of a *dastar* during '*urs*; likewise Chogelal *mutasaddi* also complained about it in 1834.[94] Harbilas Rai *mutasaddi* once applied for leave due to illness and later pressed for the appointment of his son Bhawani Prashad in his place. Parbhu Lal, Bilas Rai, Chaman Lal and Ganesh Bakhsh were other *mutasaddis* of the period under review.[95]

Though, generally, Muslims were appointed to the post of *mushrif* which became hereditary under the later Mughals, yet one Ram Nath Kayasth held this office in 1807. He received monetary help on the death of his wife in 1811, and also on the occasion of his daughter's marriage he received a sum of Rs. 20 from the *dargah*.[96]

The offices of *qanungo, fotadar, peshkar, khazanchi,* etc. were generally held by the Hindus as is evident from numerous documents. The *qanungos* enjoyed certain rights during the annual '*urs*.[97]

The sons of Sawroop Lal *qanungo* (1800) namely Rattan Lal, Sambhu Ram *qanungo* and Nand Lal *qanungo* (1817) were all honoured with *dastars* from the *dargah* on their marriage ceremonies. *Dastar-i ghami* were bestowed upon Harnath *qanungo* (1806), Gulab Rattan *qanungo* (1815), Shiv Lal *qanungo* (1820) and Zora *qanungo* on the demise of their relations. The son and wife of Gulab Rai *qanungo* (1813) and Gauruvar *qanungo* received monetary help from the *dargah* on the death of their close relations. Anandi Bakhsh *qanungo's* name is listed for the grant of *dasturi* for *shadi wa ghami* (marriage and death) in the register of the *shagird pesha* staff.[98]

Manak Chand *fotadar* received a salary of Rs. 20 p.m. in 1838. Ram Parshad has been mentioned as *khazanchi* in 1820 and as *fotadar* in 1824. Once in 1828, a Hindu *fotadar* was dismissed on the charge of embezzlement.[99] In 1821, a quarrel arose between the officials of the *dargah* and the *fotadar* with regard to the latter's right of collecting *batta* (commission) from the salaries and *rozina* of the former who wanted it to be abolished (Plates 77-8).[100]

Another official was the *peshkar* of the *dargah.* Harbilas Rai *peshkar* applied for a loan of Rs. 60 in 1838 for his personal work. Anup *peshkar* was sanctioned Rs. 2 and 15 *annas* and 4 paise from the *dargah* treasury. It appears that sometimes more than one person held this office.[101] Nathu Lal *peshkar* applied for leave in 1854; but we find that in 1859 he was working as the *vakil* of the *mutawalli.*[102] As regards other petty officials and menial servants in the *dargah* office, there is an application of one Girdhari Lal for an appointment in the record room (Persian) in 1823.[103] Moreover, it should also be noted that many *vakils, mukhtars* and *mutasaddis* of the *diwan* and *mutawalli* were Hindus, such as Asirdas, Bhim Singh, Lachmi Narain, Pandit Isardas, and Amrit Raj. The salaries of these *vakils* approximately ranged between Rs. 5 and Rs. 20, paid from the *dargah waqf.* They also enjoyed the privilege of *mu'tad* or *dastar* on *shadi wa ghami* of their near ones, and also received monetary help on these two occasions.[104]

It is interesting to note that even Hindu tailors were employed by the *dargah* office for stitching, etc., including the *angarkhas* of the *diwan.* Ram Lal in 1841 applied for his own appointment in place of his deceased brother Jai Kishan. In 1858, one Fath Chand filed a petition against the *diwan* of the *dargah* for the non-payment of Rs. 150 which was the cost of *angarkhas,* etc. purchased by the latter.[105]

For the low cadre servants, there are references to Hindu *khayats, malis, chobdars, ghariyalis, farrash, chiraghchis,* and *daroghas,* etc. serving at the *dargah* and enjoying certain concessions in these capacities and participating in the ceremonies as well.[106]

One interesting aspect is the employment of Hindu *'attār* or *gandi* (perfumers) to supply *'itr* regularly. Fath Ram *gandi* was granted Rs. 4 for supplying perfume in 1838, while Jiwan Ram *'attar* received an honorary *dastar* in 1819.[107] Jawahar Ram was asked to supply rose-flowers for the shrine in place of Shaikh Nathu in 1824 on a salary of rupees three and three *annas* and six *paise* per month.[108] Balram Choudhry of Hyderabad supplied *sandal* powder for smearing the shrine.[109] The regular supply of *'itr*, rose-flowers and *sandal* powder by Hindus has been misinterpreted by Sharda, and following him Currie, that there was a temple of Mahadev in the inner cell of the shrine below the *mazar* and, therefore, the Hindus supplied these articles.[110]

As was common during medieval India, the revenue officials were largely Hindus. Similarly, in the villages given to the *dargah* in *waqf,* large number of Hindus were posted as *choudhris, patels, muqaddams,* etc. These officials served the shrine faithfully and with full devotion, helped and earnestly worked for the realisation of revenue from the attached villages to enable the officials of the *dargah* to run the administration smoothly.

Ram Nath and Daulat Ram have been mentioned as *choudhri* in 1822. We also get reference to those who served the *dargah* as *patwaris* and *patels.*[111] Many *muqaddams,* too, are listed in our sources, and nearly all of them received *dastar* on the marriage ceremony or on the demise of their family members.[112] Even the *zamindars* and *thakurs* of Masuda (1812), Gobindgarh (1813), Korari (1802) and *Bhumias* of Pancholian, Tilora, Kayar, etc. (all *dargah* villages) were the recipients of these honorary *dastars*.[113]

But the most striking and significant aspect was to grant share in the *langar* (free food) and *rozinas* (daily allowances) to its Hindu employees as well as other needy people of the Hindu community besides Muslims to sustain their livelihood. It is not clear whether this practice of granting share in the *langar* and *rozinas* to Hindus was prevalent in the early Mughal period or later. But it is a fact that many grants of *ghalla* (grain) from *langar* and cash as daily allowance to the officials of the *dargah* and even to the *khadims* were initially introduced by the Mughals, later ratified by the Hindu rulers of the region and officials of the city. The Rathors and Marathas not only confirmed these grants but added many new ones. Ataullah *khadim* was granted *yomia* of grain by the *diwan* of Maharaja Ajit Singh of Jodhpur, equivalent to Rs. 12 and 14 *annas* annually. Maharaja Abhay Singh also confirmed the grant of Rs. 57 and 8 *annas* to Munawwar Ali *Pirzadah*. Shanghvi Dhanraj, another Rathor official (1787-90) of Jodhpur, granted Rs. 55 and 8 *annas* per annum to Ashraf Ali Lateef Ali *Pirzadah*. Maharaja Madhaji Sindhia and his successor Daulat Rao Sindhia made a number of grants to numerous Hindus and Muslims from the *dargah waqf*, which included the *khadims*, local *Nawabs*, *zamindars*, *Brahmins* and *gaitis* (lady singers). Even the governors appointed by the Sindhia rulers made some grants from the *dargah* establishment to many Muslims.

The list at our disposal mentions the names of many Hindus who were getting daily allowances till 1821, with the grant seal and orders of the *dargah* officials. Some of these recipients were *Brahmin* mendicants, *bairagis* and *zamindars*. Out of the total 113 stipend holders, 32 were Hindus. However, out of 113 only 45 grants reveal the names of grantors of which 22 were Hindus (Plates 77-8).[114]

Besides this list of 1821 of the *yomiadaran* checked and signed by Ghulam Qadir (*amin* of the *dargah*), there are scattered references which show that some other Hindus were also getting allowance in the form of cash, *langar*, and even grain. One Ramdaji (1821) requested for the grant of daily *langar* which was accepted on the same day.[115] Karna, who was blind, was given a grant of 2 *annas* as daily allowance (*wazifa*) in September 1821.[116] A grant of 12 *annas* per month was sanctioned by the *dargah* for the upkeep of Meena, a widow in 1837.[117] In the same year, the wife of Gopal applied for the grant of grain as allowance.[118] Navin Ram and Maha Ram applied (1837) for the continuation of 4 *annas* as daily allowance which they were withdrawing from the treasury since long.[119] Dhanna *tawaif* (courtesan) pressed her claim for a *yomia* which she had not received since two years.[120] Gobind Ram in 1833 and Lalli in 1820 were granted grain as daily allowance.[121]

The widow of Suraj Mal Kayasth, a native of Ajmer, applied in 1821 for the continuation of Rs. 25 and 10 *annas* as her *rozina*.[122] Harkunwar, the wife of Shiva, demanded her allowance of Re. 1 per month in 1820.[123] Zalim Singh and Nand Lal, too, approached the *dargah* officials in 1821 to regain their allowance.[124] The British, after occupying Ajmer from the Marathas in 1818, started discontinuing *rozinas* of many Hindus which included widows, needy persons and other women. During the eighteenth century, the *dargah* officials and *khuddam* gladly granted and approved *rozina* to the Hindus, but the British officers soon after controlling Ajmer started creating an atmosphere of ill-will between the Hindus and the officials of the *dargah,* perhaps in a bid to give a bad name to this great centre of communal harmony. In some cases, discontinuation of these allowances was justified on account of death or migration of the grantees, but they were very few in number.[125]

Dhanna *tawaif* (courtesan), previously mentioned, was initially granted one *ser* of grain as *rozina* from the *langar* which later Mir Azimullah *mutawalli* converted into 4 *annas* per month as allowance. She was further granted 12 *annas* for her performance on every Thursday *mehfil.* On her death in 1841, according to her will, her niece was appointed in her place.[126] Madaro *tawaif* was getting a *mu'tad* of 14 *annas* on 14th of the lunar month for her performance on the occasion of monthly *fatiha* of Khwaja Qutbuddin Bakhtiyar Kaki, held at the *chilla* of Qutb Sahib on a hillock above the Ana Sagar. It is interesting to note that when this *mu'tad* of Madaro was discontinued, many important *khadims* of the period recommended her application for the renewal of the grant.[127] Manna, a widow, whose daughter was insane, was also granted one rupee monthly to sustain herself.[128]

But the most interesting grant was for Abhay Ram *bairagi* for the maintenance and feeding of the poor at a Hanuman temple situated near the Dudhiya well. The name of Abhay Ram *bairagi,* who was a *pujari* at the temple, appears in the list of the *yomiadaran* dated 1821, prepared by Ghulam Qadir, the *amin* of the *dargah,* who later reported that one of the officials of the *dargah* had granted one *ser* of grain from the *dargah waqf* in 1773 to one Shami Ramdas, and that his *chela* (disciple) Abhay Ram was getting cash grant instead of grain from the time of Bale Rao Ingalia's governorship. Thereafter, instead of grain, one rupee a month was regularly given to him. It was verified by the *mushrif* and *mutawalli,* and also confirmed by the *amin* in his report. Later, in 1832, a dispute arose between Abhay Ram and Shivdas for the grant, but on the findings of the *Panch* (appointed by the *dargah* officials), the right to hold the grant was decided in favour of Abhay Ram. It appears that Abhay Ram was withdrawing a sum of Rs. 18 per annum from the *dargah* as *rozina* which was meant for *bhog,* i.e., for feeding the poor at the temple (Plates 79-81).[129]

Many Hindus were also associated with the *dargah* as contractors and suppliers of various commodities during the *'urs* festival and on other important ceremonies; even on ordinary days as well for the performance of day to day traditional practices. For example, Kiran Mal and Bhure Lal used to supply wax-candles to the shrine in 1837.[130] Mul Chand and Gumaldas had taken a contract of some constructions and repairs at the *dargah* in 1822.[131] During the annual *'urs* of 1843, the contract of the shops within the *dargah* went to Surat Ram.[132] Nandu Ram and Baij Nath *halwai* supplied sweets of Rs. 19 and 8 *annas* for a function in 1837.[133] Generally speaking, specially prepared *dallis* (sweet balls) for the ceremonies at the shrine were supplied by non-Muslim *halwais.*

From a list of the *muqaddamah* (petition/suit) filed by the creditors of the *dargah* in 1820-21, we come to know that Gopal *zunnardar* claimed Rs. 2340 (without interest) for the arrangement of *roshni* (light) and *langar,* etc. till October 1818. Lakhama *teli* (oil-maker) claimed Rs. 37 for supplying *roghan siyah.* Daulat Ram *pansari* (grocer) claimed Rs. 1236 and 7 *annas* for supplying wax-candles during 1807-18. Lacchi Ram Mahajan *Godya* claimed Rs. 130 (without interest) for the various expenses incurred for the *dargah* in 1817. Jiwan Ram *halwai* claimed Rs. 221 for supplying *shirini* (sweets) on every Thursday, and also on the 6th and 14th of every lunar month. Hukam Chand Rup Chando's claim of Rs. 600 and 8 *annas* was against the *mutawalli.* Khwaja Ram Agarwal also filed a petition for the recovery of Rs. 265 and 11 *annas* from the *dargah,* and through another petition jointly with Gopal *zunnardar,* he claimed Rs. 44 and 8 *annas* which was spent for the *dargah.* Jotmal Sahu's claim of Rs. 143 was the balance of Rs. 500 sanctioned for the repairs of the Jhalrah tank. Jai Chand Kasliwal required Rs. 700 and 12 *annas,* including the interest on a loan he had given in 1816. Fath Ram *gandi,* the supplier of perfumes for various ceremonies at the *dargah,* too, had a balance of Rs. 81 to be paid to him. Sahiba and Kewal *Zargar* (goldsmith) claimed Rs. 170 as the labour charges for the repairs of the silver railings around the tomb. Bakhshi Ram Asadh claimed Rs. 152 for occasionally supplying traditional *dastar* to the *diwan* of the *dargah.* Pannalal *sahukar* (moneylender) claimed from the *mutawalli* a sum of Rs. 6051 which he had given him as loan in 1817. Jashraj Ajitmal petitioned for the recovery of Rs. 3484 as the balance of an agreement over a village from the *mutawalli.* Hiral Lal Sahu, too, made similar demand for Rs. 2025 which the *mutawalli* had taken as loan. Jai Chand Kasliwal and Abhayraj Seth also claimed Rs. 227 and 10 *annas* and Rs. 496 and 10 *annas* respectively for some articles they had supplied to the *dargah.* Many Muslim businessmen also claimed their money back which the *dargah* owed them or for the payment for the commodities they had supplied.[134]

It is debatable whether the *dargah* was short of money or the *diwan, mutawalli* and other officials were corrupt, or whether during the last decade of their rule (1808-18) the Marathas, who were hard pressed by political activities in other parts of Hindustan, heavily realised the money from the *waqf* villages. At any rate, these claims show that the Hindus were not linked up with the *dargah* on devotional and emotional levels alone, but commercial and business motives also had their own role whatever devotion the creditors might have nourished towards the holy place. However, indebtedness was not a normal feature. A number of Hindu businessmen supplied various articles to the *dargah* on many ceremonies and received money regularly as has been shown in the documents (*qabzulwusul*) of 1846 and 1863.[135] But it cannot be denied that corruption was prevalent at the *dargah* as we get sufficient information about the extravagant activities of the *diwan* and other officials of the holy place, who were always sued by the *sahukars* for the non-payment of the loans advanced to these high officials of the *dargah.* Partap Mal, the contractor of the Gehlota village, which was enjoyed by the *diwan* and his family as *madad-i ma'ash* in 1860, filed a suit against Qazi Muniruddin, a member of the *diwan* family, to recover a loan. The *bazaz* (cloth merchant), tailors, *palkiwalas,* etc. were always filing suits against the *diwan* and his family members for the recovery of the payment of the material supplied by them or the services rendered. Even the land of these so-called *sajjadanashin*-cum-*diwan* is often found mortgaged on *ijara* to the *sahukars* of the city.[136] In 1818, when the *diwan* Mohtashim Ali Khan passed away, his son and successor *diwan* Mehdi Ali Khan had to mortgage his land on *ijara* to Gulabdas *mahajan* to clear the debt of his late father. It was in this context of Hindu moneylenders and extravagant *diwans* and *mutawallis* that Moulvi Abdul Qadir, the first *amin* of the *dargah* under the British (1818-21), severely censured all these people for destroying the *dargah* by corrupt practices and financial mismanagement.[137] However, it is appropriate here to point out that no *khadim* was ever found indulging in such financial irregularities. The *khadim* community as a whole maintained its separate identity and integrity. They also enjoyed land grants, *rozinas* in cash or kind from the *dargah, mu'tad* of *chaumaha, haftmaha,* and *panjmaha* (on festivals like *Shab-i Barat* etc.), *nazr* of *baridar* (key-keeper) of the day, etc., but they never employed foul means to extract money from the *dargah waqf* to fulfil their lust and extravagant expenditure. In fact, some of them received stipends for religious education, and served as teachers at the *dargah madrasa,* leaving good impress on the people which has been rightly noticed by one of the contemporary writers of the period.[138] The *khadims* not only prayed and sent *tabarrukat* regularly to their respective *muwakkils* but also played an important role in creating an educational atmosphere at and around the shrine. They also performed the task of *rushd o hidayat* (guiding people to the right path) by their character and practical approach. They indeed created a group within the society which was free from regional bias, caste prejudices and communal feelings.

In our previous article in connection with the Hindus and the *dargah* of Ajmer, we have shown how from its very inception down to 1737, the *dargah* furnished a platform for sectarian unity and concord. This role of the holy shrine never dwindled even in the later period. From the second half of the eighteenth century we start getting more facts that reinforce our previous conclusion that the shrine had become one of the most important centres for the diffusion of composite culture that had struck deep roots in the *psyche* of both the Hindus and Muslims.

The Hindu Basant festival was celebrated at the *dargah* by the Muslims also. On the occasion of the *Holi,* the Hindus assembled at the main gate of the *dargah,* reciting verses in praise of Khwaja Sahib, and rubbed *gulāl* (red powder) at the steps of the gate. On the *Diwali* festival, lamps were lighted at the *dargah* by Hindu devotees; and once the *dargah* was illuminated by its officials on this festival. The *dargah* officials took special care to cook such food in the *degs* of the *dargah* and daily *langar* which did not violate the tenets of the Hindus. Supply of rose-flowers and *sandal,* etc. by the Hindus must be taken note of.[139]

It is significant that the city temple of Bhaironji (also called Shadi-Dev), where newly-married couples went for prayer, was looked after by a Muslim *pujari* named Abdullah Shah. This was a surprising fact for Moulvi Abdul Qadir, the *sarishtadar* of Ajmer and *amin* of the *dargah* in 1818.[140] But this was possible because the Hindus knew that the *dargah* had granted daily allowance to a *bairagi* to maintain a temple as mentioned above. And, perhaps, the Hindus had not forgotten that one Sindhia ruler had got a slab fixed on the *Adhai din ka jhonpra* mosque. All said and done, the shaping of a composite culture was the outcome of the liberal and positive thinking and acts of both the Hindus and the Muslims.

NOTES

[The documents of the 'Syed Murad and Syed Masud Collections' are bound in volumes called Registers. Each Register is serially numbered; similarly, each document has been given a number. In the references given below, the first number indicates the Register no. while the second one pertains to that of the document. For example, 7/34 would tell us that 7 represents the Register no. while 34 points to the document.

In the case of nearly 1,000 *Dargah Files,* preserved in the Rajasthan State Archives (Bikaner), covering a period of more than seventy years (1818-90), it should be noted that each file contains both old and new numbers. The first being the old, and the second is new. For example, 838/168 would indicate that 838 is the old number, and 168 the new.]

1. See *Art and Culture* (Felicitation Volume in Honour of Professor S. Nurul Hasan), ed. A.J. Qaisar and S.P. Verma, Jaipur, 1993, pp. 153-63, pls. XLVIII-L.

2. 6/6, 6/42. Syed Murad has been praised by the Rathor chieftain for performing his duties as *vakil* at the *dargah* in the best possible manner.

3. 7/43. Bholanath stated that in fact he did not agree to the practice of signing *vikalatnama,* but out of respect for Syed Murad he did it.

4. 7/375 (Plates 72-3). It is a small list (dated 19 R.Y. of Muhammad Shah) bearing the seal of Syed Masud, the son of Syed Murad, who handed it over to the messenger to supply *tabarrukat* to the officials, family members and rulers of Ratlam, Ujjain, Mandsaur, Chanderi, Amjhera, Jhalawah, Udaipur, Jodhpur, Mohan, Morvi, etc.

5. For details, see S. Liyaqat H. Moini, 'The city of Ajmer during the Eighteenth Century' (unpublished Ph.D. thesis, Aligarh Muslim University, Aligarh), pp. 159-200.

6. Abdul Bari Maani, *Asanid us Sanadid,* Ajmer, 1952, pp. 321-22, 325.

7. Moini, 'The City of Ajmer during the Eighteenth Century', op. cit., pp. 168-266, 339-54.

8. Mirza Abdul Qadir Beg, *Uhda-i tawliyat,* Ajmer, 1994, pp. 53-4.

9. 1/1.

10. 1/3a; 1/9.

11. 1/5.

12. 1/10.

13. 1/4.

14. 7/468. Also see G.S. Sardesai, *New History of the Marathas 1707-72,* Bombay, 1958, pp. 159-60.

15. 1/6 (Plate 74). The seal is in Marathi, while the rest of the document is in Persian.

16. 1/7. The Marathi seal reads 'Balaji Baji Rao, *mukhia paradha*'; and in another letter, he is mentioned '*Rajasv paradha*' on the seal.

17. 1/39.

18. *Selection from Peshwa Daftar,* ed. G.L. Sardesai, Bombay, 1930-35, Vol. II, p. 82.

19. 7/244.8/216. He had addressed Syed Masud as *Syed us Sadat Jamai ul sifar, Kamil ul auqat,* and also thanked him for sending the *tabarrukat* including a *damni* (ladies headcover).

20. 7/245.

21. 8/21a-b.

22. 8/24a.

23. 6/18a, 6/38a, 8/30a-b.

24. 6/22a, 6/366. It seems that she used to send *mutad* yearly.

25. Rustam Ali, *Tarikh-i Hindi,* BM Or. 1628, ff. 528-29, Ghulam Hussain Tabatabai, *Siyar ul Mutakhirin,* Calcutta, 1833, p. 474; Moini, 'The City of Ajmer during the Eighteenth Century', pp. 159, 174.

26. 6/19a, 6/31.

27. G.R. Parihar, *Marwar and the Marathas (1712-1843),* Jodhpur, 1968, p. 104.

28. 1/37, 1/38, 1/40. Also, G.S. Sardesai, *New History of the Marathas,* Vol. III, Bombay, p. 424.

29. 1/41, 1/43.

30. *Dargah Files,* no. 838/168 (1861).

31. 1/17.

32. *Dargah Files,* no. 348/693 (1869).

33. For details, see G.R. Parihar, op. cit., pp. 79-83. *Selection from Peshwa Daftar,* op. cit., Vol. III, p. 48; Vol. XXI, pp. 8204; Vol. XXXVII, pp. 128, 275.

34. *Sindhia as Regent of Delhi,* 1789-91, tr. & ed., P.M. Joshi and J.N. Sarkar, Vol. II, Bombay, 1954, p. 48.

35. *Uhda-i tawliyat,* op. cit., pp. 36-38, 40, 43, 72-4, 88, 93-4.

36. 1/13 (Plate 75).

37. Cf. T.D. Broughton, *Letters from a Mahratta Camp,* Delhi, reprint, 1977, pp. 238-39.

38. *Uhda-i tawliyat,* Document nos. 13, 14, 22; *Dargah Files,* nos. 104/502 (1846), 596/299 (1837), 477/323. *Letters from a Mahratta Camp,* op. cit., pp. 48-51, *Waqai Abdul Qadir Khani,* Habibganj Collection, Maulana Azad Library, Aligarh Muslim University, Persian MS 32/74, f. 225b.

39. Document (Personal Collection).

40. *Dargah Files,* no. 579/281 (1821).

41. *Letters from a Mahratta Camp,* p. 242.

42. H.B. Sharda, *Ajmer: Historical and Descriptive,* Ajmer, 1941, p. 71. *Waqai Abdul Qadir Khani,* op. cit., f.227.

43. Sharda, op. cit., p. 83.

44. S.A.I. Tirmizi, *Ajmer Through the Inscriptions (1530-1852)*, Delhi, 1986, pp. 67-68.

45. 1/11, 1/12, 1/54, 1/55a, 1/152, 1/53b.

46. *Asanid us Sanadid*, op. cit., pp. 331-34.

47. 1/14.

48. 7/467.

49. 1/13, 7/466. It is stated in these *vikalatnamas* that as it is an established practice to have a *vakil* appointed at the shrine on behalf of famous and prominent chieftains, rulers or Sardars, therefore, Appaji Deccani has accepted Syed Masud as his *Vakil*, whose ancestors were the *vakil* of Appaji's forefathers. As a *vakil*, Syed Masud was fully entitled to take all *nazr* whether in cash or kind, or animals, golden and silver articles, land grants and 1/4 of the cooked *deg* or equivalent amount to it.

50. 1/46.

51. 1/41, 1/55, 1/15, 1/19d, 6/34, 6/51.

52. 6/546.

53. 6/6, 6/43, 1/50. *Asanid us Sanadid*, p. 314.

54. 6/86, 7/49, 7/489. G.D. Sharma, *Rajput Polity*, Delhi, 1977, pp. 265-66.

55. 6/7.

56. *Asanid us Sanadid*, p. 334; *Dargah Files*, no. 301/734.

57. 7/434.

58. 7/480-88.

59. *Asanid us Sanadid*, p. 276; *Dargah Files*, no. 301/734; Sharda, op. cit., p. 92; *Waqai Abdul Qadir Khani*, f. 276. During the British period, Mr. Middleton (1825) discontinued the grant of Rs. 500 of the mother of Maharaja Jaipur.

60. 6/63; *Dargah Files*, nos. 437/435, 673/123. In 1819, the ruler of Bundi despatched *niyaz* to Syed Masud Ali and Syed Jafar Ali who were the direct descendants of Syed Masud. For *Basti*, see Moini, Ph.D. thesis, pp. 321-33.

61. 7/149, 7/152a. The village is also referred to as Mobtipur of *pargana* Chattsu, and Pancholi Mansa Ram was the official whose name appears on the grant-deed.

62. 6/13, 6/56, 7/148, 7/151, 7/152a, 7/153a, 7/360, 7/422.

63. 3/50, 6/74, 7/425.

64. 6/17, 72, 79, 53, 3/34, 3/51.

65. 7/383a, 7/453, 6/36a, 6/94.

66. 6/82, 6/96.

67. Sultan Singh and Naubat Rai, the *diwans* of Shamsher Ali Khan (posted at Syleth), Kadumal *diwan* of Fidayar Khan, Fath Chand and Sawab Rai, *diwans* of a Maharaja; Rai Patharmal, the *diwan* of Sarbuland Khan and Lakhpat Rai, the *diwan* of Abdul Samad Khan, were famous non-Muslim officials of the Muslim nobles who were regular in sending *nazr* to the shrine. See 3/6, 5/37, 3/58, 7/433, 7/411, 7/437, 6/75, and 7/410.

68. 6/29. It appears that Mirza Inayatullah Beg was the governor of Ajmer.

69. 6/87.

70. 7/168.

71. 7/428.

72. 7/472 (Plate 76). It also bears seals of the *Qazi* and other Muslim officials of the place.

73. 7/181.

74. 7/150.

75. 7/157, 7/401.

76. 7/190b.

77. 7/435. The two messengers (*qasid*), whom Devi Rai rewarded, were also Hindus, namely, Bhaghwan and Ram Shah.

78. Documents (Personal collection). Actually one Syed Jan Muhammad, the son of Syed Noor Muhammad *Khadim,* received a sum of Rs. 2000 in the capacity of the *Vakil* of a devotee during one of the annual *'urs* of Khwaja Ajmeri. According to the sender, Rs. 1500 was to be spent in preparing a *qabrposh* (cover of grave), *saiban badla* (canopy) and for the *deg.* The remaining 500 rupees were for the said *khadim* as *rusum-i vakil* (a kind of *nazr* or share in the *deg*).

79. 8/22.

80. *Dargah Files,* no. 673/123 (1827).

81. 7/174.

82. *Letters from a Mahratta Camp,* pp. 237-39.

83. Document (Author's Collection).

84. In fact, these are the proceedings of the cases relating to dispute between the *dargah* officials and *khuddam* for their hereditary rights and other benefits during 1818-90. Initially known as *masal,* and then register, earlier these documents remained in the *dargah kachahri* for years, from where they were transferred to the Rajasthan State Archives (Bikaner) and classified as *Dargah Files.* These documents supply valuable information from the time of English occupation of Ajmer (1818 to 1890).

85. Moini, Ph.D. thesis, pp. 347-8, 352; also Appendix C; *Dargah Files* no. 120/517; *Uhda-i tawliyat,* pp. 53-4, 84-5.

86. *Dargah Files,* nos. 50/52 (1821), 665/117 (1824).

87. Ibid., no. 55/29 (1820).

88. Ibid., no. 477/435.

89. Ibid., nos. 642/244, 561/261 (1836-7).

90. *Waqai Abdul Qadir Khani,* ff. 238-9; *Dargah Files,* no. 41/20 (1820).

91. *Dargah Files,* no. 512/316 (1838).

92. Ibid., no 53/36. This file deals with the grant of *dastars* on marriage and mournings between 1805-23.

93. Ibid., nos. 65/40 (1821), 667/119 (1826-27).

94. Ibid., no. 208/607.

95. Ibid., nos. 226/625, 146/545, 148/547.

96. *Asanid us Sanadid,* p. 301; *Dargah Files,* nos. 153/552, 170/559 (1844).

97. *Dargah Files,* no. 530/399.

98. Ibid., nos. 53/36, 226/625.

99. Ibid., nos. 748/197 (1838), 73/25 (1821), 658/110 (1824).

100. Ibid., no. 617/219 (1829). Plates 77-8.

101. Ibid., nos. 536/382 (1838), 828/158.

102. Ibid., nos. 187/586, 257/657, 229/668, 212/611.

103. Ibid., no. 90/84 (1823).

104. Ibid., nos. 103, 129/525, 596/300, 828/156, 834/156, 834/164, 794/123.

105. Ibid., nos. 365/470 (1841), 777/105, 508/354, 226/625.

106. Ibid., nos. 511/359, 533/382, 610/212, 53/56, 226/625, 613/215, 648/250a-b. References are found about Gangadhar *ghariyali* (1832), Khuvesh Ram *Chobdar* (1819), Jaikishan *khayat,* Rudra *chiraghchi,* Bhika and Udai *malis.*

107. Ibid., nos. 509/357, 53/36, 613/215 (1830-4).

108. Ibid., no. 24/29 (1832).

109. Ibid., no. 302/738.

110. Sharda, p. 90. Also see P.M. Currie, *The Shrine and Cult of Muin al din Chisti of Ajmer,* Delhi, 1989, p. 87. It is claimed and generally believed that during the reign of Emperor Shah Jahan a Brahmin was appointed to supply sandal regularly for pasting the shrine (during daily

Khidmat). The Brahmin and his descendants carried the task so devotedly that before performing it, they used to take bath, wore clean clothes and washed the place where the sandal was ground. This liberal appointment has been misrepresented by Sharda and following him Currie, who claim that a Mahadev temple existed there. Both do not mention their source and, therefore, its reliability and authenticity is doubtful. There is no contemporary evidence to support this inference.

111. *Dargah Files*, nos. 83/66, 23/96, 108, 375/470, 533/302.

112. Ibid., nos. 52/36, 226/625 (1841-54).

113. Ibid., nos. 53/56, 761/121 (1827).

114. Ibid., nos. 579/281 (1837), 617/219 (1824). This file actually contains a list of the *yomiadaran* (daily allowance holders) of the *dargah*, at a time when the British had occupied the city in 1818. Out of 113, 61 *rozinas* were continued in its original form, 12 on the orders of English officials while 40 were discontinued which included 12 Hindus. It appears that the English officials did not appreciate or like that Hindus should be benefited from *dargah waqf*, and an atmosphere of goodwill should prevail in the office of the shrine.

115. Ibid., 45/41.

116. Ibid., 79/59.

117. Ibid., 454/301.

118. Ibid., 489/337.

119. Ibid., 495/334.

120. Ibid., 501/349

121. Ibid., 615/217, 76/16.

122. Ibid., 43/35.

123. Ibid., 77/15.

124. Ibid., 48/46.

125. Ibid., 313/746.

126. Ibid., 12/13 (1820), 369/464 (1841).

127. Ibid., 65/40 (1821).

128. Ibid., 35/17.

129. Ibid., 4/4 (1819), 579 281, 738 188. Plates 79-81.

130. Ibid., 469/116.

131. Ibid., 15/81 (1822).

132. Ibid., 389/489.

133. Ibid., 497/345 (1838).

134. Ibid., 57/53 (1820-21). The file deals with the petitions of those who had supplied various articles and commodities to the *dargah*, and even extended loan, etc. to the *mutawalli* and *diwan*.

135. Ibid., no. 322/66 (*Qabzulwusul*, 1876). Parasram supplied barley for daily *langar*, Moluram *halwai* prepared *sharbat* (sweet juice) for *Muharram* and so on.

136. Ibid., nos. 788/117, 791/321, 800/129, 806/136, 518/134, 847/35, 848/66, 831/161.

137. *Waqai Abdul Qadir Khani*, ff. 198, 225b, 247, 228b; *Dargah Files*, no. 771/28 (1843-44).

138. *Asanid us Sanadid*, pp. 264-66, 297-8, 283-84, 301; Abdul Bari Maani, *Jawab Namah*, Aligarh, 1949, pp. 86-91; *Dargah Files*, no. 631/233 (1833-34).

139. *Dargah Files*, no. 743/192; *Waqai Abdul Qadir Khani*, f. 225b; *Rajasthan District Gazetteer* (*Ajmer*), Jaipur, 1966, p. 124.

140. *Waqai Abdul Qadir Khani*, ff. 197-9; Sharda, p. 126.